A JOURNEY
WORTH TAKING

A JOURNEY
WORTH TAKING

An Unpredictable Adventure

REFLECTIONS ON LIVING IN AMERICA
DURING THE YEARS 1933-2011

JOHN F. MERCHANT

To order additional copies of this book, contact:
Xlibris Corporation
1-888-795-4274
www.Xlibris.com
Orders@Xlibris.com
73976

Contents

Photographs

In Memory of

my

Dad—Garrett McKinley Merchant
and
Mom—Essie Louise Merchant

Two wonderful parents without whom I would have lost my way.

They cared with a love that had no boundaries.

and

Barbara Ella Mitchell and Mary Elizabeth Neal

Two beautiful sisters, whom I love and cherish.

Introduction

WRITING THIS AUTOBIOGRAPHY was not my idea, and it has been a chore.

Stephen A. Isaacs, Esq., a Richmond, Virginia, lawyer I met on the golf course at the El Conquistador in Puerto Rico in 1975, was the first to suggest it be done. Subsequently, others encouraged me to do so. He and I have been close friends since we met, a friendship fueled by golf that remains strong in 2011.

Steve is a scratch golfer; I was never that good.

Amused by his suggestion, I chuckled silently and put the thought aside. However, Steve kept urging me to write, and finally, my reluctance eased, and I began trying to put my life and thoughts during it on paper.

Why do folks even consider writing an autobiography? Why should I?

Persons of historical significance, real or imagined, are often inclined to write such. Those who imagine their own significance easily convince themselves that it must be done. Egos often inspire the effort. Public figures, athletes, entertainers, and others may see the writing as a source of income, spurred on by publishing houses in the business of producing a variety of volumes to satisfy a multitude of readers with remarkable appetites for information and insights on various issues.

None of the above inspired me or caused me to write; so be it.

Today, it is clear to me that my journey has been unique, different from most, and, in some ways, historically significant. Yet I do not consider myself "historical" in any true or compelling sense. I did what I did when I did it, simple as that.

I will admit that reflecting upon some of my experiences has been cathartic; I think I enjoyed it. The struggle was to accurately recapture my thoughts during parts of the journey and recite only the truth as best I could. I believe that was done. What has been interesting to me is that I have finally accepted the underlying loneliness that was my constant companion. I realize now that I needed to make peace with the reality of being alone a lot as I was. Deep down inside it bothered me, but not now.

I also came to realize how important it was for me to be a parent, to be a friend, and to have friends like John Lawrence, Harry Van Dyke, John Whitney, Worthy Patterson, Steve Isaacs, and several others. Without them, I'd be empty.

Susan, my daughter, arrived on earth two months early, weighing 3 pounds $5\frac{1}{2}$ ounces and is the best thing that has ever happened to me. She has made me proud over and over again and is an achiever. We are friends, not just father and daughter.

Tabitha Carter, the daughter of my ex-wife's sister, has added enormous value to my life. I am the only father she has known. Her son, Tyler, thus becomes my grandson, and what a joy that has been. He's my buddy.

I am thankful for the opportunities I've had to do some things that hadn't been done until I did them. During the journey, I met and related to good people of all races, creeds, national origins, and backgrounds. In doing so, I gained a perspective not necessarily shared by others, though I wish it were.

Thank you for taking the time to share the journey. Enjoy.

Acknowledgments

I OWE A debt of gratitude to a host of people who encouraged me throughout the process of writing about my journey. The risk in naming some is that I will omit one or more who should be individually listed. I feel compelled to risk offending those omitted and hereby apologize for the omissions.

Some of those omitted will find themselves in the photographs included herein. Or, perhaps, they can forgive the omission because they have been mentioned in the writing. I hope so.

Gigi Van Dyke and Queen Patterson supported the idea during lunch at Jimmie's in West Haven one summer day. Each has known me for more than fifty years.

Frank "Frankie J" Johnson, Bridgeport, Connecticut, read several chapter drafts as they were written and kept pushing me to finish when I was tired and wanted to stop. His comments helped me believe it should be done.

Dr. Maurice Apprey, PhD, FIPA, dean of the Office of African American Affairs at the University of Virginia, offered written critical insight on the effort. I found his comments insightful, meaningful, and helpful.

Roland Lynch read some drafts of chapters and critiqued them, in writing, in words that were constructive, helpful, and adhered to.

John Forbes, Christine Mack, Doc and Lois Lawrence, Betty Hollander, Victor Riccio, Steve Isaacs, Billy Plotkin, and Hildegarde Ayers, among others, also read drafts of one or more chapters and commented objectively and honestly.

Individually and collectively, their input convinced me to keep writing. All felt the effort to be an interesting, readable, and valuable story. I sincerely thank all of them, named and unnamed, for their help.

Blame them; they made me do it!

JOHN F. MERCHANT

Chapter 1

Growing Up In Greenwich, Connecticut

MY LIFE, COVERING more than three quarters of a century, has been a very interesting journey. In some respects, I consider it a remarkable journey during which several meaningful and notable experiences were had. None were preplanned. Rather, they were the result of the times and my being in the right place at that time.

My life included living through a time of wars, notably WWII, Korea, Vietnam, Iraq, and Afghanistan. Racial unrest was a constant. It still exists in America, and around the world, and dominates. Arguably, it has worsened in 2011.

Amazing discoveries were made as the stockpiling of weapons of destruction partnered up with startling economic growth and depressing economic setbacks. Serious population growth throughout the world continues unabated; hunger has reached crisis proportions worldwide, including in America; and new vistas in technology are attained without bringing people closer. Incurring debt, worldwide, became the rule.

Tragically, what I view as the growth and acceptance of greed as a preferred way to live threatens America and the world. It appears to be out of control, or, more to the point, to be in control. Historically, greed has always been a growth business. Today, fully encouraged by debt, it is crippling America and the world.

A constant in my mind is that there was always a time when America was challenged to lead by defining itself on racial and other issues, and be better, but usually, not always, failed to do so.

My journey commenced on February 2, 1933, Groundhog Day, at 10:27 a.m. in Greenwich Hospital, Greenwich, Connecticut. Mom and Dad—natives of Virginia—were both employed by wealthy people residing in the back country of the town. They were part of the *"menial job brigade"* that arrived in the North from the South to provide services to folks who could easily afford to pay the low wages and for whom cooking, cleaning, doing laundry, and raising children were unwanted, or, more likely, desirable, but inconvenient, chores and responsibilities.

My lasting impression is that without the Emancipation Proclamation, too many wealthy Greenwich residents, not all by any means, would have enjoyed being slave owners living on plantations just as much as they enjoyed living on their estates in the back country of Greenwich.

Some of my earliest recollections of Greenwich include the apparent attitudes of those who ran and controlled the town, including folks in the school system. It is important to remember that here I speak about the years 1933-1960 primarily, a different world I believe.

In many respects, their attitudes were praiseworthy. They determined and met their needs themselves by paying for them without governmental assistance (spelled interference), federal or state. The results were generally very positive, including the creation of an environment where residents and their families enjoyed the best municipal facilities and services available anywhere in America, or, at that time, the world, for that matter.

It was a really fine town to grow up in. It could afford the things it deemed necessary and accepted nothing but the best.

I recall my high school history teacher telling the class that Greenwich was the wealthiest town of its size in the world. I believed him.

However, like every town or city, it needed a workforce to provide essential services such as police and firemen, garbage collection, and landscape maintenance. Folks doing those chores needed to reside in close proximity to their workplaces so as to be at work reliably and on time. That was accomplished, and the neighborhood divisions reflected the economic differences.

The town has several sections or divisions, including Byram, Cos Cob, Pemberwick, Glenville, Old Greenwich, Belle Haven, The Fourth Ward, and Chickahominy. Five main post offices served the town, meaning five postmasters appointed through the political process.

Some Greenwich residents were important parts of the Wall Street hierarchy in New York City. Powerful politicians, state and national, resided in Greenwich, such as US Senator Prescott Bush, father of George and grandfather of "Dubya." I delivered mail to Senator Prescott Bush during Christmas breaks from college. I have watched Joe DiMaggio walk into shops on Greenwich Avenue with Marilyn Monroe, his wife, on his arm. I was and am a Yankee, NFL Giants, Rangers, and Knicks fan. Loudly, then, very quietly, early on, I rooted for the Brooklyn Dodgers (Jackie Robinson, et al.) and New York Giants (Willie Mays, et al.).

I grew up in the section known as Chickahominy, an area populated by Italians with a few black families. Racial harmony seemingly existed, although prejudices and racist attitudes resided at or near the surface. Those attitudes were not blatant as they affected me personally. Rather they were subdued, not visible, unspoken, and involved being ignored more than being chastised or victimized.

My childhood friends and playmates were first-generation children whose parents had migrated here from Italy. Clearly, that was the situation on Charles Street, where I lived during most of my growing-up years. Many of my Charles Street friends, and many from Harold Avenue, Alexander Street, Victoria Street, Hamilton Avenue, and other streets, have remained friends down through the years.

In fact, Chickahominy has had an annual neighborhood outing for at least the past fifteen years. Many of us "old-timers" attend and keep in touch that way.

St. Roch's Catholic Church, with its priests and nuns, enjoyed a leadership role in the area, although, as I learned over time, that role lacked adherence to certain basic Christian concepts related to how they viewed the neighborhood's black population. Concepts such as "Do unto others . . . ," "Am I my brother's keeper . . . ," and similar tenets were honored more in their breach than otherwise.

Fortunately, they could not prevent Hamilton Avenue Elementary School from being integrated, and with just one high school, integration existed there. However, they could, and did, work hard at supporting racial division in many areas, especially as concerned social activities. In truth, some of the priests had, and preached, attitudes toward blacks that were similar to, or the same as, those that slave masters had when slavery was permitted by law.

Conversely, no town in the country provided a better school system or better recreational facilities, especially for young people, than did Greenwich.

The predominately Italian neighborhood where I grew up was, for me, a really good place to be a kid. As stated earlier, Greenwich committed to doing everything first class and preferred to do it their way. Governmental help was viewed as something to be avoided because it came with unwanted controls and restrictions. "We'll pay for it and run it our way," was the prevailing philosophy, and leaders of the town were experts in implementing that philosophy.

The problem for lower-income residents, as I see it, was that the town fathers focused their efforts on improving the quality of life more for its wealthy residents than for policemen, firemen, and garbage collectors. People of color were tolerated as needed, but not important beyond the services they performed. The town's black population was small.

Still, all residents could and did enjoy most of the positives of education, recreation, and other available municipal services, especially education. However, even the educational system only tolerated its black students and families. They were not important enough to receive the critical help and support needed to dream the American dream.

In town, the YMCA wouldn't allow blacks to join or even use its facilities. The school system neither assisted nor encouraged black students to prepare to attend college. I never met with a guidance counselor or anyone else in the administration to discuss college or academics generally, despite the fact that I was a twelve-year-old high school freshman who somehow enrolled in the college curriculum and who had spent less than seven years, instead of nine, in elementary school.

As best I can recall, I spent less than a month in kindergarten before they put me in first grade. I skipped seventh grade entirely and entered high school in September 1945 as a 4' 11", 88-pound freshman, at age twelve.

As a result of my birth date, I entered kindergarten in September 1938 at age five plus seven months. I was six years old by insurance standards and graduated from Greenwich High School in June 1949 at the age of sixteen.

My oldest sister, Barbara, was born in June 1931. She started kindergarten in September 1936, two years before me.

Long before anyone ever heard of a head start program, Bobbie served as my head-start teacher. She would go over everything she learned in school each day with me and my younger sister, Elizabeth. Thus, I was ahead of many when I started. I think that was the reason I only lasted a short time in kindergarten; I knew too much.

The short kindergarten stay, and what followed, represented the start of an educational experience highlighted by little interaction with my peers, causing a somewhat stunted social development. Through high school and the first couple of years at college, I struggled looking for my peers and trying to relate to older non-peers I sat with in class. I struggled to figure out where I belonged, but never did. It was a chore; I don't recommend it.

Bobbie and I graduated Greenwich High School in the same year 1949. Her early teachings allowed me to catch up with her.

In my senior year, while sitting in English class, I overheard Howard Guptil telling a classmate that he had been accepted at the University of Connecticut. I asked how he did that and he told me, so I told my parents.

My parents had always talked about the values inherent in being educated and getting a college degree, even though they had no recognizable capacity to afford college for their children.

Yet, we wrote to UCONN, received an application, filled it out, sent it in, and, I was accepted. At school, I asked for help with the process, but no school official helped for reasons I cannot fathom or explain. Years later, I had an occasion to seek a transcript of my high school record. The principal spoke with me and provided the transcript. I cannot forget his comments to the effect that he was surprised that I didn't do even better in high school.

I offered no rebuttal as I thanked him for the transcript. He was the principal when I came through the system and should know the answer regarding my doing better.

Extremely low wages were paid to the "*menial job brigade*," without social security benefits, despite requiring long workdays and six or more days a week for many. Many of the black employees lived in the homes of their employers. There they were required to rise early, prepare and serve breakfast, prepare the children for school, and then finish their day sometime after serving dinner and cleaning up the kitchen and house. They were given a half day off on Thursdays and often, not always, allowed to attend one of the two black churches in town on Sundays.

Employers were condescending, controlling, and opposed any efforts made by the "*brigade*" to educate themselves, or learn, or dream, beyond certain limits. Also, free time, after cleaning up after dinner, could not be spent watching television: there was none. Actually, they needed to rest, not watch TV.

Live-in servants had no children and devoted their full time to catering to the dictates of their employers, offering little or no resistance to the low wages or the oppressive nature of their circumstances. Many were from the South, as were my parents, and low-paying servitude in Greenwich was a big step up from what they might encounter back home. At least they had a job.

Mom and Dad had three children so they could not live in.

Among other bad habits practiced by the back country folk was a way of "*encouraging*" their employees to register and vote . . . as Republicans. My parents complied, or so they told me, but they also exposed me to my first experience with civil disobedience when they named me John Franklin Merchant.

I was named after two Democrats: *Franklin* Delano Roosevelt and his first vice president *John* Nance Garner, both of whom had recently been elected to run the country. The name John was placed first as a way of not disclosing their political preferences to their employers.

John was not only a common name, but it lacked obvious political significance that could have resulted in being terminated. Historically, few care about the name of the vice president, especially after the election. Franklin as a first name might have been a dead giveaway. The last three sentences are not a joke.

If I had been asked, I would have been named Garrett McKinley Merchant II, after my father, but I wasn't asked. Often, as I grew older, I seriously considered legally changing my name to that of my dad but never did. I don't know why my younger sister was named Mary Elizabeth, nor do I know why my older sister was named Barbara Ella. I really like both their names, though I never called them anything but Bobbie and Liz. We were born an average of approximately eighteen months apart: Liz on July 4, 1934, and Bobbie on June 23, 1931.

Bobbie was born in Spring Lake, New Jersey, en route to Connecticut; Liz and I were born in Greenwich Hospital. My parents had come to Greenwich from Lexington, Virginia, to look for work, escape the South and its blatant racism, and to obtain a better education for their children. In truth, when compared with Lexington, Virginia, things were much better in Connecticut.

Neither of my parents went beyond the sixth grade; however, they firmly believed that an education was needed to enjoy anything resembling a good life. With apologies to President Obama, each of my parents had the "*audacity to hope*," dream, and work for a better life for their children.

Both Liz and I graduated from Virginia Union University. Bobbie, who I believe was the smartest of the three of us, never attended college but became one of the best secretaries you ever saw or heard mentioned. She was also a wonderful mother to her four children.

Both of my sisters were cute children and grew into beautiful women. They provided my parents with grandchildren, great grandchildren, and great-great grandchildren. I now enjoy the privilege of having nieces and nephews who are greats, great greats, and great, great, greats.

This entire extended family came together in Virginia in 2006 to attend Bobbie's surprise seventy-fifth birthday. What a delightful mob!

They also came together, almost all of them, when they visited Mom in Greenwich Hospital where she was recovering from a massive heart attack at age eighty-four. Five generations crammed into her hospital room, and she was happy as a pig in slop. She recovered from the massive and lived another two years.

Our extended family includes: college graduates' galore, CPAs, preachers, business people, lawyers, and just plain folks who work every day and support their families. Frankly, I can't keep track of them all, but am in regular touch with many. They live all over the place, including a great niece who lives in Norway. She married a Norwegian, is now a citizen of Norway, has two children, and once held (maybe still holds) the Norwegian national record for women in the four hundred meter run. She ran track at the University of Missouri.

Mom and dad were great parents, and they picked the right town to settle in and raise their children. I don't know what prompted them to choose Greenwich over any other place, but I'm glad they did.

As stated, Greenwich was a great place to be a kid growing up. Despite the attitudes that existed, the advantages Greenwich provided were many, starting with the school system and continuing with the programs and facilities organized and run by the town's recreation department.

Greenwich has three beautiful beaches artfully placed, by nature, in three different sections of the town. Todd's Point served the area closest to Stamford in the East; Byram Shore served the West close to the Port Chester, New York line; and, Island Beach was reached by a thirty-minute boat ride commencing at the foot of Greenwich Avenue, the town's main street.

Incredibly, Greenwich also had a black community center, Crispus Attucks Community Center. It is interesting, to me, how that came about. As told to me, the center's origin arises out of the aforementioned attitude toward blacks.

The Greenwich Boys Club was located across from the railroad station, a long block west of the foot of Greenwich Avenue. It was a very old structure. Its age and condition had made it inadequate for its original purposes.

Accordingly, a new boys' club building was constructed near one end of Chickahominy. It was state of the art, with a swimming pool and other facilities such as a properly sized indoor basketball court. Young black males like me who lived a mile or more away in the Chickahominy section of town, could join and use the boys club, and we did. One feature was movies every Saturday night where Lash LaRue, Hopalong Cassidy, Gene Autry, and their ilk became part of my early days.

The old boys club was abandoned, but not destroyed. It soon became Crispus Attucks Community Center, a haven for the black population, which was small but important. The center happened like this.

Many black domestics were given part of a day off on Thursday and often spent time window shopping on Greenwich Avenue, the main commercial district. When they tired of walking around shopping, they would often rest on the benches at the numerous bus stops on the Avenue. A white man of influence who grew tired of seeing these black women adorning his cherished "*Avenue*," suggested, then lobbied for, converting the old boys club into a center for its black population. It was a place for the domestics to hang out and get out of sight on their day off. Yup, segregated bus stop benches were sought. What?

The "*separate*" facility was by no means "*equal*" but few towns in New England, or Westchester County, New York, had such, thus it was noteworthy and, frankly, a great place for young black children, as well as adult men and women to have available.

The center's leadership, specifically Mr. and Mrs. Alver W. Napper followed by Mr. and Mrs. George E. Twine, was exceptional.

Yes, a black community center sprung up in this enormously wealthy town of Greenwich because of negatives, and the availability of a rundown building that had fundamentally outlived its usefulness. Surely, the Lord works in mysterious ways.

Quickly, the center became a facility that served black populations, young and old, from Norwalk, Stamford, and towns in Westchester (New York), including adults and children, as well as those who sought a comfortable chair on Thursdays. Its proximity to the railroad station located directly across the street from it made it easy to serve that large area.

Black children in Chickahominy and other parts of Greenwich, including my sisters and I, grew up in that center and fully enjoyed the recreational and educational activities it offered, primarily under the leadership of its director Alver W. Napper and his wife Berenice. The white folks used the YMCA as well as the new boys club, whichever suited their convenience. I don't recall any of them ever joining Crispus Attucks, or trying to.

The board of directors was clearly and overwhelmingly white. It's a control thing. Basic funding was provided by the Community Chest.

Looking back, being a black adult in Greenwich must have been very difficult. It would have been very difficult for me. However, being a child, and having the center, made things better for young people and for me.

We lived in three different places before I was four years old, all three in the part of Greenwich called

Chickahominy, the predominately Italian neighborhood. A number of blacks lived in Chickahominy and a few owned their own homes, an amazing fact to me. I have little information about how their home ownership came to be.

The town dump was also located in Chickahominy, down near the state line at Port Chester, New York. The dump provided odors and rats for the menials living far from the landed gentry. The rats were both large and plentiful, often migrating to the house and attic we lived in.

Other blacks lived in the Fourth Ward and the Davis Avenue areas. I don't recall any living in Riverside, Old Greenwich, Glenville, Byram, Cos Cob, Mianus, the "back country," or Pemberwick, all areas of Greenwich as stated.

Most of my growing-up years were spent living in an attic on the third floor at 41 Charles Street, the street directly behind Hamilton Avenue School, the K-8 elementary school we attended. Because we were so close, we were rarely late for school, except me, when I refused to eat my oatmeal. Mom's attitude was that I would sit there until I ate it all. I threw it out when she left for work and left me alone. Then I went to school, late but there.

Cream of Wheat I could handle, but I still don't eat oatmeal; never have and never will. Strangely, I like oatmeal cookies.

Our landlord lived in the house; he owned the house. He was a black man named Peter O. Thompson, called PO by his friends. His first wife and son lived there as well. His son was a dentist who practiced from one of the bedrooms in the house. No one in Greenwich would rent office space to him.

JOHN F. MERCHANT

I believe the son died young, or moved away from Greenwich, because I don't have many memories of him.

Looking back, I wonder just how the son became a dentist. What inspired him? Where did he get his training? How did he find the resources needed?

I believe now that he was a product of a great man I admired, P. O. Thompson, his father and our landlord.

A roomer, Mr. Miller, also lived there, in a small room at the top of the stairs leading to the attic where Mom, my two sisters, and I lived in three small rooms.

Only one bathroom was available for the eight or more who lived in the house. It had a bathtub but no shower and was on the second floor. Somehow, we all managed.

Our attic home consisted of three very small rooms; a kitchen, one bedroom, and a living room. It was clearly an inconvenient situation, but a warm and loving home provided by a wonderful woman, our mother; we called her Mom. My parents separated when I was two years old.

I have early memories of Saturday-night baths in a washtub set in the middle of the kitchen floor. Water was boiled on the oil stove situated between the kitchen table and the icebox. The ice box required regular visits from Mr. Jones, the ice man. Oil for the stove was retrieved in a two-gallon jug from an oil barrel located outside the building. Filling the jug in a timely fashion was one of the chores assigned to me. Bobbie and Liz washed and dried the dishes and, when old enough, did the cooking. They and Mom were good cooks. Mom's fried chicken is still the best I ever had, and Liz and Bobbie could make a mean Spanish rice. Hot dogs and beans were our regular Saturday-night meal. Spaghetti and meat balls once a week were delicious but never reached the level of that provided by the mothers of my neighborhood friends.

Seemingly, every neighbor raised tomatoes and made their own "*gravy*," often called spaghetti sauce by the uninitiated. At one point, I had eaten pasta every day of my life between the ages of twenty-five and seventy-five. I also made my own "*gravy*." It was good but not like what I experienced on Charles Street.

The apartment contained only one small closet in the bedroom for hanging clothes, but it had a cupboard in the kitchen, which was a good thing.

That stove was the only source of heat in our attic, so it made sense for me to keep the oil jug filled. Failure to do so often resulted in Mom telling me to bring back a switch from the hedges out front when you bring back the jug.

Yup, a "whupping" came with the failure to fill the jug in a timely manner, thereby letting the stove die out. I learned that I should not try to be slick and bring back a little switch; something I did only once.

That "whupping" was not child abuse, although today some might consider it as such. I knew it was discipline and learned from it. Incidentally, my sisters and I never had a reason to think that Mom didn't love us, purely and unqualifiedly, despite occasional punishment.

In fact, just how my mother managed remains a mystery to me. No refrigerator, very little space, a full-time job, no washing machine or dryer or other modern conveniences that nowadays we take for granted. Mom refused to even consider going on welfare. Mom did have an iron and ironing board, and we were taught how to use both. I also learned to sew.

Remember, if you will, as you think about that last comment, she had two little girls to dress, comb their hair, and look good every day in school. Homework was done on the kitchen table with Bobbie presiding.

In winter, and sometimes during the fall, we would put our pajamas in the oven to warm them, take them out, put on the warm pajamas, run to our beds, and quickly get under the blankets and go to sleep.

Initially, the three kids used the one bedroom; Mom slept on a couch in the living room. Bobbie and Liz shared the one bed, and I slept in a crib until I outgrew it. Mom then made a deal with the landlord that moved Mr. Miller to a small room on the second floor, and I was given the very small room at the top of the attic stairs.

The joy of having my own room, even one as tiny and cramped as mine, cannot be properly explained. If you have had your own room growing up, then you know. If you have not had your own room growing up, then you don't know, although you can imagine what it might have been like and wished for it.

I loved it and have never forgotten what it means to a child to have his or her own room, his or her own space. I vowed that any children of mine would always have their own room and space, even if I had to work three jobs to provide it.

I now know that we were poor, counted among the working poor, but poor. Most of the neighborhood was in the same shape, so we didn't realize our economic condition.

Most of the Italian families had parents who had come over from the old country. Their children, my neighborhood friends and playmates, were almost all first-generation Americans.

An enviable work ethic dominated the neighborhood. Every father worked; many, maybe most, mothers stayed home and raised the children. Each family had unwritten permission to chastise another family's children if they were misbehaving or doing something silly or stupid. In other words, every family participated in raising the neighborhood children; it was a real neighborhood. A threat to tell your mother what you did or were doing was generally enough to get you to stop. Occasionally, stopping you required a smack on the butt, but not often.

We played in the streets, in the swamp separating the schoolyard from Charles Street, and also in the schoolyard. Parents could look out their windows, or stand on their porches, and see the children playing and call them home for supper.

In the summertime, fast-pitch softball leagues, organized by the recreation department of the Town, played games almost nightly; the entire neighborhood came out to watch the games which were hotly contested. Two all-black teams participated in the leagues; I played for one of them.

Charles Street had several really good athletes. Joe Piro was a solid third baseman; "Chippie" Chiappetta was a talented shortstop who in today's world might be playing in the major leagues; "Nonie" Belmont could play second base with anyone; and, a skinny little black kid wasn't a bad shortstop himself.

Larry Evaristo, Rico Magarone, Nino Sechi, Mike and Donald Biagi, Frankie Putrino, Lou Orlando who played basketball for UCONN and many others were really good athletes. I've left out some names; please forgive me.

As youngsters we built a ball field in the swamp, complete with a dugout. The swampy area for the field was three to four feet lower than the end of the schoolyard. The outfielders played on the school grounds because there was insufficient space in the swamp for an outfield elevated above the rest of the field as it was. It worked. A lot of arguments, but we learned to settle them without violence. We organized our own team, The Charles Street Aces, and would play teams from other neighborhoods, then pass the hat to get money for balls and bats.

Adults did not run our athletics; the kids did. The two best players, we knew who they were, were the captains, and they would select players for each team, then play. If you weren't selected, it was because your peers knew you were not very good. When, if, you became good enough, you were picked. The kids seemed to understand and accept this. Many practiced and practiced, improved, and eventually were selected, a source of pride and status among your peers.

No fathers came down to raise hell with the coach because his kid wasn't playing. We had no adult coach. The kids chose the players and no kid's parents paid a shrink to deal with the boy's trauma over not being picked to play. He knew, we knew, and that settled that. Practice and get better, or, spectate, or, find something else to do.

St. Roch's Catholic Church was an imposing structure situated across the street from the school and visible from

Charles Street. My friends went to mass and confession. We went to the Baptist Church located near Greenwich Hospital, about two miles away from where we lived. We generally walked to church. We also walked about a mile to both the boys club and the Crispus Attucks Community Center. Walking saved the ten cents cost of a bus ride. Truth is, we rarely had the ten cents, so walking was the only option.

The Catholic Church's presence involved an ongoing and effective effort to control the neighborhood people, including on issues related to race. I was told, on unimpeachable authority, that a priest once went so far as to deliver a mass in which he instructed the parishioners not to sell their homes or rent an apartment to black men, women, or families. A tragedy in the neighborhood triggered the mass.

In the late 1940s, the Wiggins family, a black family of seven, including three little girls and two little boys, had a fire. During the fire, Mrs. Wiggins and her three daughters were burned to death. Somehow, Mr. Wiggins and his two sons escaped the fire but were left homeless. The tragedy was so severe that a committee was formed at the Crispus Attucks Center to raise money for funerals and find a place for Mr. Wiggins and his two sons to live.

A white property owner who lived in Chickahominy and worked at the post office came to the committee and offered to sell his three-family house to solve the problem. The priest, who incidentally was a member of the committee, later told the man that if he sold his house to blacks, he'd be excommunicated or something like that, causing the offer to be withdrawn.

Subsequently, on a Sunday morning, the priest delivered his mass to the entire congregation saying, clearly, that no one in the congregation is to sell or rent any property to blacks.

Ultimately, a house was found in Chickahominy for the Wiggins'. Mr. Wiggins was employed at Jenkins Valve in Bridgeport; the sons grew up as friends of mine. Sam became a postman in Greenwich. Richard, who is an extremely talented and skilled musician, eventually worked as a cameraman for the CBS show, "Sixty Minutes," traveling all over the world to gather information that was shared with the American public. I lost contact with Richard and Sam years ago, but I remember them as good friends growing up.

Recently, Richard and I reconnected, and we e-mail each other from time to time. He reminded me that he still owed me a million marbles from long ago when we kept doubling the bet until we stopped at the million number. We had a good laugh. Actually, I was a real good marbles player.

My first exposure to Catholicism came when friends invited me to attend a service. It was then that I learned that religions were practiced differently. Their methods of worshipping differed from those of the Baptist church I attended, although their belief in God was as strong as mine.

Growing up, I sensed very little racism or racist attitudes that prevented real friendships from developing among the kids in our neighborhood.

As an adult, looking back, I wish that the Catholic hierarchy had spoken out against the mass that priest delivered, but I reckon that was too much to expect, or to ask for, in the 1940s. However, it is not too much to ask for in the twenty-first century, so I am asking for it. It would erase any, or many, doubts I harbor about organized religion, including Catholicism, its priests and bishops and the hierarchies of other religions as well.

Since my youth, my personal adult experiences with religion include few negatives. However, I do see a serious lack of effective leadership from the religious sector on many moral issues where you would expect it, including its general tolerance of negative racial attitudes. Maybe this is to be expected when the church, in general, becomes, primarily a business, and secondarily a community asset from which leadership and wisdom are needed.

Ironically, this appears to me to have become a major problem with both the institutions of education and religion. Are we still the most highly educated nation in the history of the world? Are we maintaining that position or losing ground almost daily? Idle thoughts for which I have no answers.

P.O. Thompson had the only black owned house on Charles Street. No other blacks lived on the street. My relationship with the kids who grew up there has continued down through the years and has been fundamentally free of the racial strife that, seemingly, still dominates America and grows.

Joe Strazza, one of seven children who lived directly across the street from us, has been a good and true friend my entire life. He's a few months older than I am. Joe

Ricciardi who lived a few streets away is another friend with whom I have retained a relationship over the years.

Interestingly, for about fifteen years now, a Chickahominy Reunion has been held and is well attended. Many of the families, or their children, still reside there. At the first reunion, or the first one I attended, raffle tickets were sold and a drawing held to pick the winner of the money. I was asked to choose the winning ticket out of a hat and did . . . It was my own ticket and the pot was three or four hundred dollars.

I was shocked and embarrassed and reacted by immediately announcing that the money would be put into a scholarship fund, naming three friends as trustees of the fund. The money was to be used for a neighborhood child attending college who needed a book or a train ticket. That fund was incorporated and has grown over the years, though I do not know its present size. I was told that it had grown to around $50,000 a few years ago.

Greenwich High School was also about a mile from home, and a bunch of us walked there every school day in all kinds of weather. It became a ritual that we looked forward to daily. I'd wait for Walter and Livingston Thomas to get to the corner of Charles Street and Hamilton Avenue and walk with them. They lived down near the dump, another mile or so away from our house.

En route, we'd often run into Harry and Charley Van Dyke, Donald Ward, "Buntsy" and "Teeny" Gordon, Bob Perry, Andrew and "RB" Blackson, Richard and Sam Wiggins, among the boys. My sisters, Bobbie and Liz, did the same with their female classmates.

Weather was no excuse for not walking that mile or so to high school or for being late. The town did not provide buses for the Chickahominy high school students, but did for students from other areas of Greenwich. Why should they? We were the blacks and Italians, low-income, low-class residents who despite being necessary, were not entitled to extras such as a bus.

There were two black churches in Greenwich: Baptist and Methodist, both located near the hospital in what was called the Fourth Ward area.

As a lawyer, I wound up representing the Methodist Church, but the church I grew up in, First Baptist of Greenwich, refused to even hire me to handle the church's mortgage needs. I guess that validates the old adage that it is difficult to be respected in one's hometown.

Of course, there is another explanation for the failure to hire a homegrown professional. Simply stated, back then, too many blacks actually believed that if it was important or if they knew little about it, one must hire a white professional to get it done right. Vestiges of that belief still thrive among many blacks, although the percentage of persons who believe that has diminished considerably during the last fifty years.

Black professionals and tradesmen have overcome that myth by their performance. Education, training, and an opportunity to perform have made the difference over the last half century; that will not change. In fact, the myth can be seen as disappearing on a daily basis as more and more of us become educated, trained, and receive an opportunity to perform.

But we must never forget those who suffered the pain of making the progress real, not just inevitable as many of us were told it was.

I'm told that there was a spirited discussion, and even some animosity involved, in the first and only time the issue as to whether or not to hire me came up. At the time, I was one of the very few college graduates produced by First Baptist Church of Greenwich and the only lawyer. Might still be the only lawyer.

Interestingly, P.O. Thompson's second wife was one of the loudest voices in opposition to my being hired, or so I was told. I never learned why. My experience with her, while never outwardly negative, did not cause her to rank highly in my mind as a true Christian. She seemed to resent my mother, and my mom's three children, for reasons she never shared with me. However, her daughters, Isabel and Dorothy, were nice people to be around and to know.

I believe that she married PO in order to upgrade her living situation and move into a real house; can't fault her for that. However, once there, she took charge, or tried to. PO's health was failing and maybe that gave her the rationale to act as she did.

Or, maybe she simply resented having to share a bathroom with us, who knows?

She didn't realize, I guess that PO had been our landlord and our friend for many years before she arrived and that bond was not to be broken by anyone, including her.

PO was a deacon at First Baptist Church; she belonged and became a big wheel with the Usher Board and other church-related matters. I do wonder if she ever paid for a subscription to The Golden Rule or all of the Ten Commandments. As best I can recall, she didn't live by either the Rule or the Commandments in relating to our family.

PO was special. He spent time talking with me helping me to understand life and Greenwich better. He paid me to cut the grass on the property and do other chores. He understood Mom's situation as a single mother raising three children and all that involved, especially since she worked long hours every day.

I respected and admired that man and really appreciate what he did for me. He was wise, not learned. As a landlord, he was kind and gentle; not harsh and unfeeling. He had worked, bought that property, had an automobile, and a job with the *menial job brigade*. He understood being black in or out of Greenwich in the 1940s, 1950s, and 1960s.

He was the kind of wise and caring black male who helped a child to grow and mature in positive ways. Black history is filled with men and women just like him who were there for the children, their own and those of others as well. His actions spoke much louder than his words, though his words were clearly worth hearing and remembering.

A boy needs a male presence growing up, someone who will take the time to teach him, make him think, and, to be there to answer questions and resolve his dilemmas. When that presence is in addition to his father, the boy's chances to become a man expand significantly. Greenwich's black community provided me with several men who filled that bill.

For example, a group of black men in Greenwich came to me when they learned that I was going to enroll at the

JOHN F. MERCHANT

University of Virginia's law school. They were part of a group that played poker once a week as some do. They gave me a phone number and said that I should call, collect, if ever I needed to. They said that they wished me luck but could not help with room, board and tuition. However, what they did, without me asking them for any kind of help, was agreed to cut their card game each week and set the money aside for my use if I asked for it. Their intent was to ensure that I never went hungry at UVA.

Harvey House, Frankie Mohammed, and Allen Ray led the effort to ensure I didn't go hungry at UVA, and so I didn't.

They meant it. I still get choked up when I think about it. I rarely made the call, but it was there for me if I needed to.

That unsolicited offer to help still impresses me. It gave me a sense of security and extended family that was critically important. Their actions also helped teach me humility and gave me an appreciation for what people think about you when you are doing the right thing.

An important lesson for me is that it made clear the value of giving back and helping others. I've tried to give back ever since.

Others such as Albee Mines, Donald Ward, James and John Gordon, Robert Blackson, Bob Ray, David "Scotty" Brown, and George Twine, to name a few, were all men who knew me almost all of my life. They were men who taught me to play sports, encouraged me in school, and, apparently took pride in watching me grow. They cared and watched over me; I will never forget them and what they did.

Scotty Brown's wife Nancy has been a friend and supporter for as long as I can remember. She has been very active in the town and politically on all levels—an unsung, but necessary person, who is needed if progress is to be made. She saw to making some.

Contrast that with the actions of the Greenwich Bar Association.

Unknown to me, Joseph Kaye, an attorney with Hirschberg, Pettingill and Strong, one of the largest law firms in Greenwich, went to the Greenwich Bar Association; advised them about my admission to UVA's Law School, and asked for financial help from the bar association. He knew that my parents couldn't help nor could I earn enough money in the summer to pay my own way, though I tried.

Without hesitation, but with an air of bewilderment, even anger, as to why Joe was making this request, they flat out turned it down. Attorney Kaye survived that storm. He was a very able lawyer and, in his firm and in the state, was the best at what he did; a moneymaker they kept. In later years, Joe's son Joel worked for a time as an associate in my small office; I liked that.

Years later, I learned that a key member of the bar association was also a senior partner in Joe's law firm and was a graduate of UVA's law school. He wasn't about to help anyone integrate his law school and, I'm told, was a major reason for the turndown. C'est la vie.

Harry Van Dyke is remembered. Harry attended every graduation I ever had and was proud to do so. His mother and mine were very close friends; he and his brother Charles were like brothers to me.

I remember an incident when Harry and I played basketball for a team in Norwalk that had traveled to Poughkeepsie, New York, by bus to play a team there. A good-sized crowd attended. At one point during the game, I beat my man and drove to the basket for a layup. I never made it.

The Poughkeepsie player grabbed me as I went by him and threw me into a concrete wall located just behind the basket. It was a small gym with a concrete wall very close to the baskets at each end.

Down I went, rolled over, assessed sources of pain, looked up, and watched as Harry Van Dyke cold-cocked the guy with a right hand that caused the player to drop on the spot.

A mini riot ensued and continued until the police came and stopped it. They sent our team to the locker room to get our clothes; not to shower and change clothes, to *get* our clothes and *carry* them to the bus waiting outside the building. We walked through a police line carrying our clothes, got on the bus, and left. We were told never to return to Poughkeepsie. We never did.

I have to admit that Harry had a good right hand.

Two other persons were like brothers to me, Worthington Reginald Patterson and Roland Morman Patterson; Worthy and Skip. They lived in the Fourth Ward in a house right next to First Baptist Church. Their mother, Mrs. Mae Patterson, was a seamstress and one of the finest people I ever knew. She treated me like a third son and required me to learn and adhere to everything she taught them. Like many at the time, she stressed the need for an education, even arranging for Skip and Worthy to attend prep school at one of New England's finest boarding schools, Tilton School.

Often, after church on Sundays, Mom would let me have Sunday dinner with the Pattersons and spend the rest of Sunday hanging out with Worthy and Skip. The meals were sumptuous, with wonderful hot rolls baked in the wood-burning stove they cooked on. Auntie Ann, who owned a car; Aunt Les, part of the *menial job brigade*; and Gramps, all of whom lived in the house, were part of the Sunday meal.

Upon looking back, it is clear to me that the wisdom at that table and the conversation that flowed created a learning environment to be envied.

Good manners were taught, learned and required; using the correct silverware for the meal was taught and learned. My view of the world was greatly expanded by the contents of the conversations that invariably took place at that table.

What a great experience for a young mind to have on a regular basis!

Mrs. Patterson had a dream, long before Dr. King spoke in Washington. She was totally committed to not allowing the white world we lived in to dominate, or unduly influence, her family's abilities to use their intelligence and education to create a good life for themselves and their families. She believed, and insisted that we accept, that we could achieve more than a second-class position in the world. We listened, learned, and remembered.

She taught me and the others how to dress properly and exposed us to black achievers and their children who talked about and worked for being something and somebody, despite their blackness.

Being "colored" was not acceptable as an excuse for failure; not at the Pattersons, simple as that. No ifs, ands, or buts . . . and no fear.

She also made it clear that if I didn't like her rules there was no point in complaining to my mother. She knew that my mother would fully agree with her and would simply tell me to do what Mrs. Patterson said to do . . . or else. I quickly got the message, retained it, and complied.

Worthy was a great athlete, not a good athlete but a great one, born before his time. He is one of the best ever to come out of Greenwich High School and the State of Connecticut. He played quarterback on the football team, starred on the basketball court, and found time to letter in baseball and track. He received more than thirty scholarship offers from various colleges for football and basketball. He accepted a basketball scholarship at UCONN because two teammates, close friends, were going there.

One of those friends was Lou Orlando, a Chickahominy guy and a friend and neighbor of mine.

Worthy's tenure under Coach Hugh Greer in the 1950s heralded the beginning of UCONN's emergence as a national power in college basketball, an emergence sustained and validated under Jim Calhoun's guidance over the last several years. Worthy was drafted by the Boston Celtics in 1957 but was the final cut before the season started.

Boston decided to keep Bob Cousy, Bill Sharman, Frank Ramsey, Sam Jones, and K. C. Jones, five pretty good players, to man their backcourt.

Personally, I believe they should have kept Worthy and released Ramsey, a well-known player out of the University of Kentucky. Of course, that would have given Boston's backcourt a truly diverse flavor, something not pushed by the NBA, Boston, Boston's management or, probably, its fans. That would have given Boston's back court three blacks out of five; too many for Boston's fans or the NBA. It turned out well for Boston, so it's difficult to fault their decision to cut Worthy.

Worthy caught on with the St. Louis Hawks for a year or two, then went to work in the record industry.

It was Worthy who taught me the game of basketball. Between him and Lou Orlando, I was taught the fundamentals and learned to play defense as well as offense. Without those lessons and playing experiences, I never would have made the teams at Virginia Union University and COMSERVPAC.

I played against Sam Jones in college at Virginia Union, and I believe he was as good as Cousy, but changed his game in order to fit in with Boston. He became a shooting guard and less of a playmaker. Cousy, an acknowledged legend, was the leader and playmaker and deservedly so. Sam did make the Hall of Fame and was an integral part of the great "Celtics" teams.

Sam and Tex Crawford were the mainstays for a North Carolina College team that was a fierce rival of Virginia Union in the Central Intercollegiate Athletic Association (CIAA), a league comprised of historical black colleges. It was a tough league that accessed the country's best black players because white colleges had not yet focused on diversity and

JOHN F. MERCHANT

did not have (m)any black players on their squads. Most had none; that has changed dramatically.

Worthy married Queen Vaughan from New Haven, Connecticut, right after college. They met at UCONN and now live in California near their son, Worthy Jr. his family, and their grandchildren.

Queen is one of those very bright, energetic people who is a joy to be around—a first class lady, a very intelligent person, and, a savvy and caring human being. She has a great sense of humor, is a realist, and is very tuned in to the world in which she lives. Time spent with and around her has always been memorable and a special privilege. They have been married for more than fifty years, and we remain close friends even though we now live on different coasts.

My daughter and niece refer to them as Uncle Worthy and Aunt Queen, a fact that pleases me immensely and makes me proud.

Skip was not nearly as good an athlete as his brother, but no one was. Skip ran cross-country in high school and was a better-than-average tennis player. He and I were very close growing up and spent considerable time talking about the world, the nation, and a host of heavy subjects that interested us, but not many of our friends. I seem to recall that Skip had an IQ in excess of 150. He was and is enormously smart.

Skip had a fascination with math and was amazingly good at it. In fact, he was so proficient at math that he became one of the first black hires at IBM, long before employment opportunities in major corporations became available to blacks. He spent his entire working career at IBM and now is retired and lives in Poughkeepsie, New York.

Skip, like most of us, has his idiosyncrasies. Many of his revolve around, or can be directly connected to, his true love of mathematics and his ability to think analytically.

He was admitted to Middlebury College in Vermont after Tilton School. He didn't stay at Middlebury because he was disappointed over a requirement that he, like every freshman, attend more than just mathematics classes. He was so absorbed in his math work that he often neglected the other courses, many times failing to attend them. The administration learned of this and invited him to take a rest, off Middlebury's campus, and ponder the sagacity of his choice of how to spend his time.

However, talent can neither be denied nor hidden. Once people discover that you have it and will keep working to improve what are exceptional skills to start with, they will seek you out.

Skip enrolled at another college and then went into the army. After the army, he found IBM, or its Research and Development people found him, and, without any fanfare about diversity, hired him. Everyone benefitted, especially IBM.

What I am trying to say here is that the plantation mentality corrupting many in the majority community in Greenwich was not an impediment to me, or Worthy, or Skip. I, we, have been very fortunate to have had good and solid adult support from the black community, starting with our parents, throughout our growing up years. Our response was very positive, that is clear.

For too many black youngsters, in too many communities in America, that kind of support system does not now exist, but is sorely needed.

In fairness to the majority community, during my growing up years, it, generally, had no compelling reason to change its attitude toward black people. The civil rights issues were years away from raising America's awareness, thus their attitudes were often just "business as usual" as much as anything evil.

I doubt that they spent much time thinking about their maids, servants, chauffeurs, and hired help as people, real people, human beings just like themselves, who were "normal" in every sense of the word. The negro population was simply viewed as being a lower class with the wrong heritage and skin color, inferior and not entitled to any more than they were receiving from wealthy residents, and/or from life in America.

Some who did care, at least somewhat, often provided a depressing level of what I call "*negative nurturing*." Kind of like don't worry, we'll tell you what to do and when.

Here, take these clothes home for your children, along with any leftovers from dinner. Of course, you should vote. Register as a Republican and vote; but don't vote for Roosevelt; he's not a good man for America. I'll teach you how to vote and tell you the best man to vote for.

No, don't ask about social security. It's complicated and doesn't affect you. Just one of Roosevelt's crazy ideas; it should be abolished.

Mom's employers began paying social security taxes when I, as a law student, picked her up at work one day and, during a short conversation with her employer at the kitchen table, asked why Mom was not being covered.

Oh, your children are doing well in school, getting As and Bs, that's nice. But, we don't think they should try to be a teacher, or doctor, or lawyer because that's too hard to do and expensive. We can talk about that later, and I'll help you decide what your children should do and be. No, I'm glad to help, and we'll work it out. Maybe your son or daughters can work with you here for a while this summer. It might help them by giving them a real work experience.

Don't be late for work. Yes, I know that the buses don't come up this way, but sometimes we can pick you up in the morning, or you can call a cab to get to work on time each day. You should be able to afford a cab if you are careful with the money we pay you. Really? They must have been kidding?

Pay no attention to those NAACP people and you should not read *The Amsterdam News* or *Pittsburgh Courier*. Too much of what they write about describes events in the South that can't and won't happen to you here.

This attitude was nauseating, to say the least, yet had to be endured to keep a job. Folks who spoke out against this "*nurturing*" were described as "*uppity*" and were not to be trusted.

Many blacks in Greenwich tolerated this nonsense but did not allow it to corrupt their right to think for themselves and work for freedom and equality.

My Mom and Dad accepted the jobs but quietly rebelled against being treated like children. Dad finally started his own house painting business with minimal success. I often worked for and with him.

The Pattersons, Nappers, Twines, Blacksons, Van Dykes, Browns, Steadwells, Fishers, and Broadnaxes, among others, remained in a mostly, but not fully, quiet rebellion mode as well. Privately, they worked to achieve.

They became my role models (though that term was yet to be discovered) and my sources of strength. They taught survival but stressed freedom from any form of servitude as they focused on education as the key. They also taught us to be responsible, advising that we should never fail to think.

In truth, we had solid adult role models whose wisdom influenced our behavior and kept our minds at work. Yes, there was caring, concern, and support available in the black community in and around Greenwich. I see that clearly now and am very thankful for it.

It would be inaccurate, and inexcusable, for me not to mention that many white folks in Greenwich were also very concerned and very helpful to me. Yes, there were many who went the extra mile because they firmly believed it was the right thing to do.

On that note, one story bears repeating. Upon returning from duty with the US Navy, I returned to Greenwich and was preparing for the bar exam and collecting unemployment while doing do. A woman in Greenwich arranged a job interview for me with the man who ran CBS News, Richard Salant. Apparently, they were friends. It helped a lot because I had to actively look for work in order to receive my unemployment check.

I walked into Mr. Salant's office in New York City at the moment in time when CBS was trying to beat ABC and NBC to the airwaves with the John Glenn story on his trip into outer space. When Salant could relax, he talked with me for some time, starting by asking me what I wanted to do at CBS. My answer was that I would like his job. I had looked around his office while he tried to beat his competitors to the airwaves with the Glenn story. I liked the office. It was first class in every respect.

He asked how I came upon his job as a career choice. I answered by saying that it seemed right since he and I had a lot in common, namely, we both had law degrees but had never practiced, and, if he could work his way up, so could I, given the opportunity. He tried to give me that opportunity by arranging nine separate interviews at his company. The interviews were real, and I was offered several entry level positions but declined them.

Mr. Salant tried to provide me with opportunity in a business that was not actively involved in seeking diversity among its labor force. I said no to it.

Some time after that interview, Carl Stokes, left the office of Mayor of Cleveland, Ohio, and became the first black news commentator on one of the three major networks. Makes me wonder if that could have been me, though I'm glad it wasn't.

Admittedly, I did not fully understand what was being taught daily until now. I was taught to listen and to think about what was being said or explained. The importance of listening, learning, and thinking, especially thinking with an open mind, was stressed.

Listening to and respecting the ideas and opinions of others was well taught and learned, though the teaching was almost subliminal in nature. By that I mean that I was not consciously aware of the fact that those things were being taught and learned. The lessons still live in me.

My Dad set the standard in that he talked *with* me, and solicited, then insisted on discussing, my rationale for any opinions I harbored. He taught me the importance of an informed opinion that resulted from a gathering of all pertinent information and avoiding the inclination to simply react and run off at the mouth about something or anything.

That led to a search for information and knowledge. It also helped me to speak knowledgeably, sensibly, and, coherently without closing my mind on my own thoughts, or failing to be aware of and learn from thoughts of others.

In that regard, it emulated law school where the same process prevailed.

Growing old is not an option, growing up is. Without realizing it, I left Greenwich fully prepared to continue growing up. I now know that I also left with a level of immaturity that needed work. That work was done during my journey.

FAMILY and a few FRIENDS

Barbara Ella & Mary Elizabeth
My sisters, none better! I love them dearly

Garrett McKinley Merchant
My Dad, my rock, my friend, I miss him.

Essie Louise Merchant (nee Nowlin)
My Mom, beautiful woman, a real Mother

Liz, Mom and Bobbie

Liz, author and Bobbie
Probably one Easter before church

Watch out Custer (circa 8 or 9)

Should we take show on the Road!
Bottom (L-R) Harry Van Dyke, Ernestine & Wiggie
Top (L-R): Patricia Bowen, Author, forgot name.

YUP, I could palm it. Not bad, huh?

FOUR GRADUATIONS - U.S. NAVY

Graduation from grammar school (1945)

MERCHANT, JOHN F.
"Merc"   February 3
In his trail he leaves a wake of
laughter.
G.O., Dramatic Association, Science
Club, Per Jih Club, Contemporary
Affairs Club, Solo Club.

Greenwich High School, 1949, Yearbook info.

JOHN F. MERCHANT, B. A.
Greenwich, Connecticut
Major: Sociology
1955
Virginia Union University

MERCHANT, JOHN FRANKLIN —
Virginia Union University, B.A., 1955;
Kappa Alpha Psi; 1445 South Maple
Avenue, Buena Vista, Virginia; Read-
ing Guide; J. B. Moore Society; Bar-
rister, Business Manager.

1958
The Law School
University of Virginia

GREENWICH TIME

ATTENDS SCHOOL — Ensign
John Franklin Merchant, son of
Mrs. Essie L. Merchant of 41
Charles St., is attending the
Navy's Justice School in New-
port, R.I. He was commission-
ed an Ensign in June, 1958, and
is a graduate of the University
of Virginia with a Bachelor of
Laws Degree.

GREW UP LIKE BROTHERS

Best friends growing up, more like brothers then and now
L-R Skip Patterson, Harry Van Dyke, Worthy Patterson.

Harry Van Dyke
He understood the word 'friend' and was always a
real friend. Attended all of my graduations and always
pushed me to achieve. A good man!

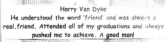

"Skip"
Roland Morman Patterson
Hired by IBM before minority hiring was popular.
Yes, he was that talented, intelligent and smart.

"Worthy"
Worthington Reginald Patterson
One of the greatest athletes ever to
come out of Greenwich, CT

Chapter 2

The University of Connecticut and Virginia Union University

HINDSIGHT MAKES IT clear that I had no business going to college at the University of Connecticut in 1949 when I did. Neither my history nor my age, sixteen, favored doing so. I needed to grow up and mature a bit.

I was smart enough, meaning I could learn and enjoy it, but I was socially inept. My elementary and high school years had been spent without legitimate peers. Classmates were always older than me and were more inclined to ignore a little kid like me during recess and after-school activities. Plus, I worked every day after school, starting in the eighth grade in Stamford, Connecticut.

In addition, I didn't really know why I was going to college. I had no goals, no idea what I wanted to study or become.

Actually, going to school, then to work, were the only things I had ever done, so college was a mere continuation of the only thing I knew. It seemed sensible at the time, and my parents encouraged it. Dad had talked about becoming a lawyer but that seemed like a reach to me. I never really considered it as any kind of realistic ambition at that time.

My age was clearly not an asset. As you know, a one- to three-year age difference is huge during one's early years.

I paid a high price by being younger, though I was not aware of doing so until later in life. I was accustomed to feeling different and somewhat isolated. Lacking peers, I was not part of anything. I was, simply stated, smart and could learn.

My early college years focused on a quest to be included, in some way, somehow, outside of the classroom. Being left out or overlooked was a fact of life for me, a fact I disliked and, intuitively, spent too much time struggling to change. The challenge consumed me though I did not realize it.

The highlight of grammar school for me was the high level of acceptance obtained when the teachers conducted a spelling contest, pitting the boys against the girls in fifth and sixth grades. Ida Barto was usually the girls' finalist; I was always the last boy standing. I beat Ida about 75 percent of the time, or more, and, after school, the happy boys would buy me candy and treat me like a hero for that day. The next day was back to normal. I could hardly wait for next spelling contest.

Continuing efforts to "belong" in college took time away from studying and thinking through what I might want to do if I ever earned a college degree.

On the positive side, I did gain considerable experience at being alone and managed to do okay in the process. My savior was a thirst for information and knowledge. I read voraciously and, because my memory was excellent, I absorbed and remembered most of what I read and learned to apply it in my thinking.

At age eleven, Dad hired me to sweep up the B and S Coat factory on Stillwater Avenue in Stamford where he had a room and was a sort of night watchman. His arrangement included having to sweep up the factory every day, a chore anyone would dislike after working a full day themselves.

Thus, for a year prior to entering high school, and during my four years in high school, I took a bus ride to Stamford every weekday throughout the entire year to sweep up the coat factory and see my dad. No interaction with schoolmates after school ended was possible.

Homework was done at school. In the summer, I would often have to leave my playmates, sometimes leaving my team a man short, and catch a bus to Stamford at 3:15 p.m. Going to the beach and things like that was out of the question. Getting to work on time had priority.

On the bus ride, I read three newspapers and had time on the round trip to read all of each paper. The exposure to world and national news fascinated me, though I didn't understand a lot of it. I enjoyed the opportunity to read the sports news and memorize statistics.

I was, and am, an avid Yankee fan and followed the Brooklyn Dodgers and New York Giants closely. The Knicks, Notre Dame, and Rangers were my teams during their seasons; still are.

Milestone events in sports are remembered. Jackie Robinson, Willie Mays, Roy Campanella, Don Newcombe, Monte Irvin, Larry Doby, and others were heroes for me. Finally, Elston Howard came to the Yankees and that pleased me immensely.

WWII had started in 1941 when I was eight years old and ended in 1945 when I was twelve, the year I entered high school. I was 4' 11" tall and weighed eighty-eight pounds. That's pretty little; no wonder I had no peers.

The end of WWII and the resultant activity, especially the Marshall Plan, dominated the news. It confused me. I couldn't figure out why America was giving money to countries we had just trounced in a war.

Of course, the war occupied my mind throughout its duration. I can recall having a problem trying to understand why some young folks were drafted, fought and died, while other folks got rich. After all, thought I, isn't the entire country at risk and shouldn't sacrifices be made by all? I understand all those things better now.

Then the atom bomb changed the war games many of us played. We could pretend to be tough soldiers armed with .45-caliber pistols and Thompson submachine guns and we could understand the courage displayed by General Doolittle in getting to Hiroshima and dropping the bomb, but we couldn't emulate that event in our games.

Interment camps boggled my mind also. Why were naturalized citizens with nonviolent, nonthreatening histories of living in America as citizens being sent to camps that isolated them from friends and family?

Why was it so difficult for the powers that be to permit black Americans to fight for their country? They let us enlist, then had us loading trucks and driving supplies to places that needed them, and doing other physical labor. I guess that was a step up from picking cotton, but damn, it sure resembled the "menial job brigade" described earlier.

Why did black Americans who joined the military during the war have so much trouble after the war obtaining the benefits provided by the GI Bill? They had fought, when permitted, and died on behalf of America, after which they were immediately returned to a second-class status by the country they fought and died for.

Eventually, that changed a bit. The Tuskegee Airmen proved that we could fly airplanes and do well in knocking enemy aircraft out of the sky. When allowed, we, and a Japanese unit, performed well in battle.

The Navaho Indians gave us a way to transmit and receive messages by using their native language for coding purposes. The Japanese could not break that code, so our military communications were made easier.

The 1940 census reported that the US population was about 131 million with 12.6 million blacks. During WWII, the army had become the nation's largest minority employer; 2.5 million black males registered for the draft through December 31, 1945; more than one million were inducted into the armed forces, except for the Marine Corps which held out for many years.

During WWII, President Roosevelt issued *Executive Order 8802* directing that blacks be accepted into job training programs in defense plants. Thus, discrimination by defense contractors was made illegal. A Fair Employment Practices Commission (FEPC) was established, though enforcing it was a real issue.

Congress terminated the FEPC early in President Truman's time in office.

Translated, that means that Americans fought the Japanese and Germans to prevent America being oppressed from abroad, then worked hard at oppressing its black population at home. What's wrong with that picture?

The internal war was worse than the ones being fought for survival overseas, at least to black Americans.

Think about it! We had registered for the draft, been drafted, and made it clear that we were willing to face death in defense of a country that, apparently, did not even want our help in the manufacturing of weapons and materiel needed to win the survival wars.

Menial work such as loading and unloading trucks was okay, but that was it. It smells like just a small step up from picking cotton.

This was tough stuff for an eight to twelve-year-old, who, while in elementary and high school, read at least three newspapers every day, to comprehend. It also made me wonder about the value of a college education and where it could lead. But there I was at UCONN.

In 1946, and again in 1947, President Truman tried to get Congress to integrate the military by enacting laws requiring it. His efforts caused the Southern senators to threaten a filibuster.

Truman then resorted to his executive powers and, on July 26, 1948, issued *Executive Order 9981* that, among other things, abolished segregation in the armed forces ". . . *without regard to race, color, religion, or national origin* . . ." and ordered full integration of all the armed services.

There was considerable opposition to that Executive Order. If my memory serves me correctly, it took three years *after* the end of WWII in 1945 to desegregate the military. Then, it took until the end of the Korean conflict in 1953 to seriously integrate the armed services.

Dad, Mr. Napper, Mr. Twine, and others helped me understand more than I could by just reading about these things. Through them, I developed the habit of asking questions and receiving answers in return. They also taught me to refer to resource material such as an encyclopedia or dictionary or other resources when in doubt. I still do that. My library at home contains almanacs, encyclopedias, and other reference material that I use regularly and always have.

I recite these things to show that the issues of race, racial attitudes, and race relations have plagued America throughout my life, and still do. As a black male, hardly does a day pass where some information regarding race issues does not confront me. It's the same for many other black Americans.

Small wonder that this writing seems dominated by the issue of race. Race issues have consumed my life, even made it interesting (?)

Anyway, one day in the early autumn of 1949, after graduating from high school, I found myself at the Fort Trumbull Branch of UCONN in New London, Connecticut, an all male facility at the time. My focus was wrong. As stated, too much time was spent on efforts to relate to my peers and not on the course work college required. It worked out okay that first year, although admittedly I did not distinguish myself in the classroom.

Initially, I was assigned to a dormitory room with two veterans who had recently been discharged from military service. They were serious about their studies; I was not. Before long, I moved to another room with folks closer to my age but still older than me.

Intramural sports, especially basketball, became an outlet and, thanks to the things Worthy Patterson had taught me, I was able to handle the basketball competition. I was no star but could play a little, run and jump, play defense, and pass the ball, so I was welcomed to the intramural team from Lightning 3 where I lived.

Some guys from Bridgeport and Fairfield County were teammates. Abe Schacter, Jay Lustig, and Tommy from Byram located next to Chickahominy in Greenwich, were pretty good intramural players also, and, while we didn't become champions, we had fun.

My first-year grades were marginally sufficient to keep me in school and become a sophomore. Fort Trumbull was closed down after that year, and all students were transferred to the Main Campus at Storrs.

Worthy was at Storrs on a basketball scholarship. Through him, I met athletes like "Deacon" Garner from Watertown (Connecticut), an exceptional basketball and track athlete; Phil Tinsley from Waterbury, a running back; "Tillie" DuBois, a gifted running back from Hartford; and Gerard Peterson who played golf but was not on scholarship.

All the above named were black, good athletes and good guys. All mentioned were older than me and more mature, but they tolerated me, and I was an ardent fan of theirs. Some friendships were long lasting, especially the one with Gerard Peterson.

Ultimately, again through Worthy, I joined "Beta Sig," the only fraternity that would accept blacks at that time. I lived in a dormitory but took meals at the fraternity. I enjoyed being around the members.

I don't remember the full Greek name of "Beta Sig," maybe Beta Sigma Gamma, but I do remember feeling at home and making friends there. In many ways, it was a good year. I matured, but not enough.

Soon after the year ended, a letter from UCONN stated that it was best for me not to return as a junior. My grades did not entitle me to become a junior. In fact, they were pretty low all around.

In short, I flunked out. What now? With encouragement from Mom and Dad, I looked for work, finally finding a job at Master Motors in Greenwich, lubricating cars, changing oil, and being a gofer at this foreign car business.

I could walk to work and was there every day, always on time. I was eighteen years old, had a driver's license, and was a good employee. So good that after a time I was allowed to take a car home on weekends for my personal use. Socially, driving a different foreign car most weekends gave me an enjoyable status that others could not match. It was a good time.

Master Motors was owned by a man who, it was rumored, owned a large piece of John Deere, Inc. and lived in Greenwich. True or not, Master Motors was his hobby, and he was a good owner for whom people enjoyed working.

Eventually, I met a guy from Norwalk, and we became friends and started a business. The business was running "numbers" from Norwalk to Westchester, New York, in competition with some folks you don't really want to mess with. They did not appreciate the competition and made that clear after a while. We ceased doing business shortly after being "advised" that we should.

My friend provided the muscle and found the "runners" needed. My job was to plan, keep the books, and generally keep the police off our back. We did well for a while, acquiring increased market share monthly. We made good money, until the powers that be shut us down.

Shortly before being shut down, I was talked into returning to college by Dr. Samuel D. Proctor, vice president of Virginia Union University in Richmond, Virginia. He was in Greenwich to be the guest preacher at First Baptist Church one Sunday.

Without my knowledge, Mom had arranged for him to speak with me about college. It turns out that she was somewhat aware of my "business venture" and feared the worst, since the business was not the kind to sign up with the Better Business Bureau. She feared that I would wind up in jail. Her fears were sensible; it was illegal to do what we were doing. It was also dangerous.

In September 1952, I went down to Richmond with Dr. Proctor and enrolled at Union, hoping and expecting to earn a basketball scholarship and get a degree, in that order.

The experience at Union changed my life and really helped me to take the important steps needed for me to mature.

Union was the first place I'd ever been where I had black classmates. It was also the first experience with an administration and faculty that took the time to really care about all of its students, including me.

It was located on a kind of oasis in Richmond, not a large campus and was one that lacked many of the accoutrements found at many colleges and universities. But it cared about its entire student body and was hell bent on ensuring that each of us received a good education, learned and earned a degree, a caring made evident on a daily basis.

I felt like I belonged and was part of a family. Looking back, I cannot thank my mom enough for making it happen.

Amazing, isn't it, to learn that good parents never stop caring and work nonstop at helping their children to be something and somebody. Mine were good parents.

It's also amazing that once we convince ourselves that we have all the answers, we somehow discover that we don't even know the proper questions, let alone the answers.

Early on at Union, I sensed an advantage when I realized that my high-school education was better than many of Union's students who came from segregated schools in the South, from the "country" so to speak. Some arrived with rope tied around their suitcases and southern drawls.

Case in point was my algebra class. In assessing transfer credits, I was given standing as a sophomore. Bad grades at UCONN caused my third year in college to be viewed as my second year. Still, I was required to take algebra,

However, I had taken algebra, geometry, and trigonometry in high school; many had not. Union required me to take a course in algebra where I soon discovered that I knew as much, or almost as much, as the professor who then developed a habit of calling on me to recite the right solutions to the equations some struggled with. I did that without fail each time, building a reputation as being "heavy" by doing so.

An advantage I did not have was a greater thirst for learning than that owned by almost every student enrolled at Union. They came to learn, wanted to "be somebody," and they applied themselves assiduously to that task.

Good grades gave one status on campus among one's peers. An unspoken, but high level of competition existed between the students. Each sought to learn more and do better than their classmates. Faculty challenged us on a daily basis and the response to that challenge was very, very positive.

Students found outlets for their personal talents as well. Union's choir was as talented a college choir as there has ever been, before or since. Sports, specifically basketball and football, were a source of pride to the athletes, the student body, and the administration.

Required courses for entering freshmen included a course in "Negro History," using Carter G. Woodson's well-written tome as the book of knowledge. I still have the book we used in my library. That book was full of details never ever mentioned by teachers at Greenwich High School. I was impressed enough to make history my minor; sociology was my major.

Soon after arriving on campus, folks learned that I claimed to be a basketball player. That led to members of the team approaching me and inviting me to the "midnight sessions" in the Belgian Building. It was a tradition at Union to have those "sessions," without coaches or spectators present, prior to the official start of practice for the season in October.

Union, like the other historical black colleges, attracted the most talented black athletes from around the country, primarily the South and Northeast in Union's case. White colleges didn't try to attract black athletes in those days.

Union was a member of the Central Intercollegiate Athletic Association (CIAA) and were champions of that conference often, including 1951, the season before I arrived. I learned why at the "midnight sessions."

Those sessions were run by the players and were rugged. No fouls were called unless the offense injured someone, or could have. Conrad Graves, a student from New York, had a job as night watchman that gave him keys to the Belgian Building where our home court was located. The building was situated in such a way that, when lighted and occupied, no one could stand on campus and see the lights or know that the court was being used. Nor could sounds, cussing, or screaming be heard easily.

The team I was trying to earn a place on included a backcourt manned by two guys who were All City out of Boys High in New York City; a center who was All Cleveland in Ohio; a power forward who was All Richmond, and, another Richmond forward who was almost as good, just not as tall.

My confidence level related to making the team dropped sharply. Fortunately, my stubbornness didn't.

One aspirant was All Delaware but, after enduring a couple of the "sessions," he left to go elsewhere. Two football players, both really good athletes, came occasionally but were mostly active on the football field at that time of year. They joined the team after football season.

I had no resume, no known history of playing anywhere, and, thus, was a target of the sessions and severely tested. They wanted to find out if I could play and if I was tough enough to handle playing in the CIAA. Not everyone is, or was.

Worthy had taught me well, and I was a tough little skinny kid who could play a little. That's how much I played during the two seasons on the team . . . a little, very little, except in practice. I played good, tough defense and, in doing so, helped make our backcourt players better. Not long ago I was talking with Howie Jones, our point guard, and he mentioned that he didn't look forward to practice, knowing I would be guarding him during a good part of practice. He also said that he appreciated what I did because it helped him to be better.

I endured the sessions and made the team during regular practice. Shortly thereafter, I was told that no scholarship would be awarded because, under NCAA rules, as a transfer from UCONN, I had to sit out a year before becoming eligible to play. However, I could practice with the team daily.

Union's policy was clear. Unless you were eligible, no scholarship was given. Also, a full scholarship was awarded only to those who played two varsity sports. I believe some exceptions were made for a few.

The difference between a full and a partial scholarship was lunch. Partial entitled you to breakfast and dinner; full added lunch. I obtained full in my second year when I went out for the track team and made it as a sprinter and high jumper.

I had no previous experience at track but was fast and could jump. Union's track team was no real competition for teams in the CIAA, especially Morgan State College and Virginia State College, but we tried. My events were the 100- and 220-yard dashes and high jump. I could barely break eleven seconds in the hundred and once managed to high-jump 6' 3". Neither was ever winning efforts.

Lacking a scholarship in my first year at Union, I turned to Dr. Proctor for help. He arranged jobs for me which included shoveling coal into the furnace at the president's home during the colder months, at around 5:00 a.m. I cleaned the nurse's office daily and also busted trays in the cafeteria three times each day. On weekends, there was work at a car wash in downtown Richmond and, often, as a waiter in the hotels downtown.

I once figured out my schedule at Union, including the hours I had to work at the various jobs, basketball and track practice, and the fifteen hours a week in class. The result showed that I spent 142 out of the 168 hours in a week doing the things set forth above. That includes trying to get four to six hours of sleep per night. Exhaustion dictated a need for at least some sleep.

To save you time, that translates to having twenty-four hours per week for studying and socializing. I managed; don't ask me how. Good study habits were as elusive as finding a gold mine on campus. Paying attention in class, taking good notes, and cramming for exams most of a night were my way of getting good grades. It worked.

I ran into a serious problem busting trays. We were paid $.25 per hour to do that. I thought that should be raised to $.35, so I organized the other guys and scheduled a meeting with Mr. O'Rourke, the manager. I was the spokesperson for "Tray Busters United" (TBU).

All members of TBU attended the meeting. I explained our position. Full support had been promised by my coworkers.

After attentively hearing me present the case, Mr. O'Rourke, in an aggressive and unhappy tone, canvassed each of the men sitting at the table, asking each of them this question: "Is that how you feel, 'Schoolie?'" He called everybody "Schoolie."

Not one of the TBU members supported me. Mr. O'Rourke then looked me in the eye and uttered words to the effect that since I was the only one seeking the increase, "You're fired." Oops! TBU died then.

It was then that self-preservation, as a basic in life, took on real meaning to me. But, not to worry, two years later, Mr. O'Rourke offered me the job as student manager of the cafeteria, and I accepted. That put me in charge of the TBUers who had chosen self-interest over solidarity two years before. I'm pleased to say that I was a good manager, not a vindictive one. No need for that; I had learned a valuable lesson. Besides, the new position paid the increase sought.

As a matter of interest, perhaps, the student manager position was once held by Tee Walker, now the Reverend

Dr. Wyatt T. Walker, who became one of Dr. King's most important and trusted advisors.

Also at Union was a man named Walter E. Fauntroy who became, and still is, a Baptist minister in Washington DC. He also was the first elected congressman from the District of Columbia in its history. The deal to allow that representation provided that he had no vote on issues before the House of Representatives. He could contribute in committee meetings he was assigned to and in the hallways.

Possessor of a tenor voice that was absolutely of the highest quality, he was a member of Union's choir and graduated with honors. I admired and respected that man, along with Tee Walker and others.

Walter owned a high level of intelligence and understood that, even without a vote, his election had given him the power to influence, and he used it wisely.

I have often said that only two kinds of power exist in America: the power to influence and the power to control. The power to control has been rigorously, but unsuccessfully, sought in our democracy, expect that to be a continuing search . . . and a continuing failure.

History suggests that those who somehow acquire the power to control don't usually keep it for long. They become targets, are assassinated, or are run out of town by others who either resent how they use that power or seek it for themselves. In America, they lose elections or leave the airplane with a "golden parachute."

In my view, the power to influence is the only achievable power in a true democracy. Those who seek and work to achieve swift and dramatic change must remember that.

Change takes time and is not necessarily immediately responsive to right or wrong arguments.

If carefully acquired, the influence obtained can have the long life needed to move closer to the ideal we seek. For it to live long, it must be diligently pursued, and protected, and any positives that result should be measured only by the small steps taken by each generation. There is no such thing as immediate gratification, only movement in the right direction as the long, seemingly endless, journey is taken.

Is it any real wonder that huge investments are made by those who can do so in providing financial support to candidates? Or spending huge sums to hire lobbyists? And too many of us don't even bother to vote!

As I look back at the issue of race relations in America, I find that progress made before and after the civil rights movement was engineered by black leadership acquiring and using that power to influence. A high price was paid to acquire that power, but the search for it was steadfast and ongoing, dating back to the arrival of the first slaves. When obtained, it was carefully used and progress resulted.

The price to be paid has lessened in many ways but still exists in the twenty-first century. Yes, the power to influence remains achievable.

The Emancipation Proclamation was probably the first sign of meaningful progress; yet, its promises, express and implied, have not yet produced what we seek nor have the efforts of law makers and others sufficiently closed the gap.

Dr. King clearly acquired the power to influence. He is the only individual I'm aware of in history who was assassinated because his power to influence threatened too many. It was taken away by taking him away. No replacement has ever appeared, nor, in my opinion, will one appear anytime soon, if ever.

Dr. King's assassination slowed down the journey. It did not and cannot stop it, despite efforts of the "far right," Tea Party groups, and those seeking a second chance to reverse the results of the Civil War.

There were other black men and women at Union, and the other HBCs, who added many positives to America and Americans after graduating from Union.

Leroy Vaughn from Baltimore and father of "Mo" Vaughn the baseball player was a classmate with whom I "walked the line" when we both joined Kappa Alpha Psi fraternity. Leroy was a great athlete. He was the quarterback on the football team and an important part of Union's backcourt during the two years that I was a member of the team. We were CIAA champions both years.

One amusing incident regarding Leroy that I recall was the day a few of us stopped to witness an argument between two male students on Union's campus. We stood there as the argument reached the point where a fight could break out. This was prevented when the smaller of the two men reached out, grabbed and ducked behind Leroy, and shouted, "Shazam." This produced bellyaching laughter for all, including the larger of the two men.

What? You remember "Shazam" and Captain Marvel? You must be old.

Leroy married Shirley. They were college sweethearts and now live in Virginia. She has always been Mo's biggest fan, emulated these days by Tiger's Mom being his biggest fan and, probably, the individual most distressed by his fall from the heights in 2009.

Leroy was a walk-on at the training camp of the Baltimore Colts of the National Football League. He received a tryout and was the last player cut, I'm told, despite the fact that his competition at quarterback was a fellow named Johnny Unitas. Bad knees hurt his chances, and I think they tried to make him a defensive back. Leroy went back to school and earned a PhD in Education. He worked in the school system in Norwalk, Connecticut, for many years prior to retiring.

At Union, I also met Kathryn Orientes Elizabeth Smith from Lexington, Kentucky, and dated her. She was my college sweetheart. We parted, reluctantly, at graduation. She returned to Lexington, and I spent the summer contemplating what awaited me at the University of Virginia Law School. I believe that if my plans had been different, or my future clearer, that I would have proposed to her, and she would have accepted. However, under the circumstances that existed, that was not an option.

I did marry after law school, the US Navy, and starting to practice law in Bridgeport, Connecticut.

Mildred Jacob from Barnesville, Georgia, a graduate of Fort Valley State College, was teaching in the Stamford, Connecticut, school system. We met and married in 1964. We divorced in 1970.

A beautiful and intelligent woman; she earned graduate degrees in the area and retired from Stamford's school system as a high-level administrator. She and I are the parents of a wonderful daughter, Susan, who was born two months early. Our first child was stillborn, making Susan very special to us. Actually, Susan has made, and is making, herself special to employers in the corporate workforce as well.

After Union my journey continued; I went to Charlottesville, VA and entered The University of Virginia Law School.

Basketball

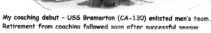

CIAA Champions – Virginia Union Panthers
Howie Jones (far left) and Ronnie Bressant (far right) were both All-City from
Boys High in Brooklyn, NY. Leroy Vaughn (father of Mo Vaughn) on my right.

1954
Union

My coaching debut – USS Bremerton (CA-130) enlisted men's team.
Retirement from coaching followed soon after successful season.

1960
COMSERVPAC

Chapter 3

University of Virginia Law School

FEAR IS A strange thing. It can arrive unexpectedly, though, more often, it is preceded by some period of apprehension, then fear appears, heightens, becomes real, and, too frequently, lingers long.

It is difficult to describe fear to someone who has had little or no experience with it. Also, if one lacks a real understanding of the circumstances giving rise to the fear, it can be easily misunderstood, even passed over as trivial. But, if the experience is personal, it cannot be forgotten. Conceivably, one must "walk a mile in your (my) shoes" to fully appreciate my experience.

Yes, I have known fear, preceded by apprehension, and am not ashamed to admit it. It started fifty-five years ago, in the State of Virginia, and lingered for an extended period of time, three years. I was alone the entire time.

In September 1955, approximately one year after the US Supreme Court decided *Brown V. Board of Education1*[1], I arrived at the University of Virginia (UVA) in Charlottesville to attend its law school, one of the country's best law schools then and now, and the state's sacred cow. I had applied earlier in the year, honestly believing that I would not be accepted. A letter of acceptance was received just prior

---

[1]   347 U.S. 483 (1954). Decision handed down on May 17, 1954

to the release of the *Brown* decision, creating a serious dilemma for me, namely what do I do now?

Looking back, I recall wondering how, and why, I was accepted. Perhaps it helped that on the face of my application I was a Virginian, having used my Dad's address as my own in my application. He lived in Buena Vista, Virginia, a town my application claimed as my residence and, in a sense, it was.

When I applied for admission, I knew that *Brown* was pending and that a decision was expected at any time. I spent little or no time contemplating potential reactions to a plaintiff's decision because, after all, I would not be accepted. My thoughts were focused on graduating from Virginia Union University in Richmond, hoping that NYU or Michigan would admit me to their law schools and worrying about paying for a law school education. If admitted anywhere, paying would be a real challenge. Hell, I still owed for college.

I saw no point in analyzing potential ramifications beyond clinging to a naive belief that if the plaintiff prevailed in *Brown,* it would simply mean that segregation in public education, as practiced by many states, including Virginia, would be deemed unconstitutional and prohibited. We are a law abiding nation, aren't we? Also, it was about time and the right thing to have happen.

My naïveté was inexcusable since Brown was pending *before* I applied. Reactions to a potential plaintiff's decision had begun, and the violence had already started.

Still, as best I can recall, in my mind, I was headed back North and had no conscious concern about something that would not involve me directly.

JOHN F. MERCHANT

No time was spent thinking about the fact that, if the plaintiffs prevailed, the decision could not eliminate the practical issues of discrimination and racism. No thought was given to the Ku Klux Klan's potential for enormous growth in its active membership and activities as a direct response to a decision for the plaintiffs. Yes, I should have known better since the signs were clear, and I was keenly aware of the country's racial issues, especially in Virginia.

Three years at one of the historical black colleges (HBC), Virginia Union University in Richmond, had provided me with a personal exposure to southern attitudes toward persons with an African heritage or any semblance thereof. That knowledge and experience were the major reasons why I was going home, to the North, where things were better, not great but better.

In my mind, there was no *need* to continue an exposure to southern attitudes and actions, by Virginia's government as well as its citizenry. Staying did not enter my mind. My clear choice was to leave my island of safety at Virginia Union and return to a northern refuge where I knew how to cope. Three years of "*Whites only*" signs were enough for me, or so I thought.

The arrival of the acceptance letter changed all that.

I was honor-bound to share that letter with those who had encouraged me to apply in the first place, notably Dr. Samuel D. Proctor, Union's vice president, and Dr. John M. Ellison, Union's president. Reluctantly, I showed them the letter. They were pleased and said so. Two pleased out of three ain't bad, unless you are the third as I was.

Who knew that the decision in *Brown* would trigger some of the darkest hours in our nation's history?

Who knew that, in Virginia, its leadership, political and otherwise, was unalterably opposed to the decision and would take immediate steps to disobey a decision of the US Supreme Court? I didn't.

Unbelievable, when you think about it. Would secession follow?

I soon learned that the darkness of those hours had neither street lights nor paved roads to follow. My fears arose before ever setting foot on Grounds but turned out to be reasonable and justifiable.

After conversations with Dr. Proctor and my parents, I agreed to enroll at UVA's law school. The summer of 1955 then became a time to consider the ramifications deliberately ignored before the acceptance letter arrived. It was impossible to ignore the racial unrest caused by the decision. Acts of violence and hatred kept springing up around the nation. The lion's den loomed and the lions were roaring. Common sense dictated that they should be feared.

Too quickly, September arrived, and I was on my way. Honestly, I literally trembled with fear as I traveled to Charlottesville, alone, captured by thoughts about what might await me, afraid of the known and the unknown.

My arrival marked the beginning of a three-year experience during which I cannot recall being unafraid for any extended period of time. For many different reasons, some level of fear was a constant companion, in and out of the classroom, starting with the confederate flag hoisted

JOHN F. MERCHANT

high (outside someone's dormitory window) on my first day on *Grounds* (a synonym for campus at UVA). This was September 1955.

Now, fast forward to May 1956, approximately nine months after my arrival. At that time a new issue arose, namely, I was hospitalized just before final exams. A fear of failure now merged with other fears I had lived with daily, and it both consumed and motivated me. Then it won the competition with the host of other fears and dominated. I was overwhelmed, depressed, and alone, with no one to talk to or with.

Would I be physically able to take my exams? If I did take them, and if my illness resulted in doing poorly in exams, what then? If I failed to achieve the grades needed to return as a second-year student, then my time would have been wasted. Frankly, given my physical condition, I could easily flunk out. Could the exams be postponed?

By way of background, classes at the law school had ended; only final exams remained. Unbelievably, to me, I had completed almost a full school year at this prestigious southern law school. I had endured, adjusted reasonably well, made some friends, and somehow managed to deal with the many racially inspired negatives that existed, on and off Grounds.

Actually, the law school's student body was not a primary or major source of any problems. That distinction was held by the university's all-male student body and the majority community's leaders and citizens.

Being ignored by many of my "*peers*" was not a problem since it was expected. The required courses and the process of learning were a problem and a real struggle for me. They were the law school's major contributions to my personal difficulties.

On the other hand, it was somewhat reassuring to receive and accept the hands of friendship offered by those classmates who did not ignore me. Although mostly silent, many seemed pleased and supportive of the effort at diversity my presence represented. To the extent practical, they sought to ease the difficulties they knew existed for me in that situation.

But now, in May 1956, the schedule provided two days to prepare for final exams, covering almost all course work during the full school year. Twenty-seven of the year's thirty credits were at risk. Final exam results would determine whether or not a first-year law school student would become a second-year student.

As far as I knew, all first-year students were preparing for finals. Me? I was admitted to the university's segregated hospital. The diagnosis was mononucleosis. If timing is everything, my timing seemed educationally fatal.

Hospitals were unfamiliar to me. I had never spent a night in one except, perhaps, at birth. I had been feeling ill, listless, tired, and unable to eat for several days. Paying attention in class the weeks before had been a real chore; studying for finals was out of the question. The medical help I finally sought led to the hospital admission, an event that exacerbated the real possibility of failing. Failure dominated my thinking, overriding the painful discomfort of the illness.

It had been a long and difficult year, starting with my first day at the law school. Shortly after arriving on Grounds, an eerie feeling of being in a *"foreign country"* appeared and would not go away. Certain facts made it clear to me that I was being watched. By whom, how many, and why, were, to me, serious questions without answers.

The legitimate concerns I had pondered over the summer became real. My active mind raged out of control. I was not acquainted with a single human being in Charlottesville, on or off campus. Advice was not available. A support system didn't exist, and creating one seemed out of the question. I was alone with my blackness, and the dark clouds surrounding me allowed no beacon of light to poke through and point a way.

It was the real beginning of a period of loneliness and fear.

The eerie feeling of being in a *foreign country* rarely left me. Too often, the question I pondered was whether this was the America the history books talked about.

The books and teachers I was exposed to from kindergarten through high school had misled me, unfairly. My three years at Virginia Union taught me that. There, I learned, first hand, that the teachings and teachers in the Greenwich (Connecticut) school system had failed to tell me, and others, the whole truth. Do not fertile minds deserve the whole truth? Of course they do, but it wasn't provided by one of the best public school systems in America.

Virginia Union required, among other things, that all students take a course in Negro History. *Carter G.*

Woodson's history book was the Bible and provided me with an awareness of American history, in stark and scholarly detail, that Greenwich, Connecticut, had overlooked. Truth entered my fertile mind, at last, and was welcomed.

Fortunately, in time, Charlottesville's black community provided the respite needed to maintain a sense of mission, direction, and courage. It gave me time to be and feel normal around friends; wonderful people who went out of their way to ease the burdens. I could not have endured without their help and friendship. Three families named Jackson including: : Punjab, the dentist, and his wife Mae; Edward and Eunice; and, Teresa and her two sons, Bo and Frankie; were, for me, a refuge and a haven to which I could escape and refuel.

Frankie and Bo were special little boys who grew to be good men. They called me "Superman" because they watched me lift a heavy couch for some reason and had seen it done just once . . . on TV, watching cartoons! Young minds are often the soothing balm needed.

In a real sense, Charlottesville's black community provided a refuge and a haven for all of the black pioneers enrolled in the university's engineering, medical, and law schools. The difference, relating to me, was that the engineering and medical schools had other blacks enrolled—three in the medical school, two or three in engineering school, then me alone in law school.

I was told that one year before my arrival, in September 1954, a black student had entered the law school as a full-time first year but had flunked out. No help for me there. In fact, no other black students enrolled in or attended the law school during my entire three years nor did I ever have a roommate. Talking the law makes learning it easier, but I had no one to talk to or with, not in that setting.

Of course, my parents and friends had been supportive during the preceding summer. Their support was welcomed and appreciated but did little to ease my concerns. It was verbal and not strengthened by any personal experiences that remotely resembled what I was about to face.

Sure, my parents knew about the State of Virginia. They were raised in Lexington, Virginia. They left in the 1930s to find work, ending up in Greenwich, Connecticut, where they found work: Mom as a domestic; Dad as a gardener, something he knew little or nothing about.

Almost all blacks in Greenwich had similar employment, working for wealthy white folks. Many lived in the homes of their employers and got very little time off during a normal seven-day period. It mirrored slavery, although they were paid a pittance, along with free room and board, for their sixty- to ninety-hour-work weeks.

Mom and Dad knew about southern attitudes and traditions. They knew about racism; they knew about the need to stay in your place or suffer consequences that could be fatal. However, talking with them did little more than increase my fears. Their support for what I was about to do contained constant references to those negatives and warned about the potential consequences if I failed to conform.

Could I conform? Nonsensical conformance was not a habit I had ever acquired, nor do I have such a habit today.

Meaningful advice or counsel of an encouraging and positive nature didn't exist. I did get a lot of what I called "don't dos." You know, "don't do this, don't go there, don't do that or bad things will happen, keep your chin up" stuff. These warnings foretold nothing but danger and added to my concerns.

My Dad, Garrett McKinley Merchant, despite having only a sixth grade education, was excited and proud. No surprise there, since he is the reason why I ever even considered becoming a lawyer. It's what he wanted to be, but couldn't. So he was bent on living his dream through his son, spending a lot of time discussing such an ambition with me. I had no such dreams, but loved and respected my dad to such an extent that following his dream was a good thing.

He tried to be positive in his talks with me about the South and Virginia and the attitudes and dangers that existed. He talked about the negatives that were increasing and predicted. He believed that the *Brown* decision signaled the start of a more serious conflict between the races in America, especially in the South where too many folks seemed to want a second chance at winning the Civil War. They simply ignored the fact that they had lost, and it was over. Majority community Christians packed the churches for a short time on Sundays, then forgot the teachings the rest of the week, especially as they related to those with an African heritage.

Dad scared me when he made it clear that danger lurked for any blacks involved in making changes that threatened the southern way of life. He advised that I was going into what could be a lion's den, unarmed, except with his conviction that I was doing the right thing. He believed that I had the intellectual capacity to achieve and helped give me the courage to try.

How did I know that he knew these things? He discussed them all at length with me. He convinced me that I must attend and deal with whatever occurred. To him, attending UVA's law school was simply something that had to be done. He apologized for his inability to help financially but promised to do what he could, and did. Between Dad and Dr. Proctor, I had no chance to give in to my fears and go elsewhere.

Dad and I were friends. He was my rock to lean on, a man who loved and parented his children in admirable ways, helping me to grow, understand and expand my outlook and make my mind work objectively.

Growing up, I had the good fortune to spend quality time with him, especially from age eleven to sixteen, despite his being separated from Mom when I was two years old. We talked a lot, or I should say he talked and answered my questions. I listened, asked questions, and learned a lot. He had a good mind and used it.

I still believe he was one of the most intelligent persons I have ever met, unlettered but wise. His focus was on looking ahead, not simply seeking immediate gratification. He believed that in time things could and would change between the races, and he firmly believed that my getting a law degree from UVA would be an important part of the changes that were inevitable. He could not, and would not, even guess at a timetable. He did stress that it would take a long time.

Dad had always wanted to be a lawyer. As stated, he spent many hours talking to me about why being a lawyer was a desirable thing. In that way, his goal became mine. He also talked about being an elected official, a legislator who helped to make the laws rather than just a citizen who had to obey them. I never had any real interest in being a legislator, so I never tried to be one.

He talked about the need to be educated and prepared and the importance of being a real part of one's community, not just a resident. He discussed doing the right thing and doing a job right the first time. He talked about the dire need for justice for all who appeared in the courts, without regard to race, color, or creed. He gave me a strong philosophical basis for existing, one that clearly embraced the teachings of Christianity.

I learned, even as I struggled to understand fully. I accepted and cherished his wisdom, but was still afraid.

There is no substitute for a father who cares and spends time helping a child to grow and develop. I was fortunate. Unfortunately, Dad died before he had a chance to watch me actually practice law. He would have liked that.

I can see him finding excuses to hang around my office, attending any trials I was involved in and critiquing my performance. I litigated a lot, civil and criminal; he would have liked being there for that.

On reflection, I must admit that I did not truly share his dream of being a lawyer. Life's circumstances, my immaturity, and a lack of knowledge and money, made it difficult for me to even dream about being a lawyer. Also, I wasn't really convinced that being a lawyer was what I

JOHN F. MERCHANT

wanted, but, then again, I really didn't know what I wanted to be or what I could be.

I did know that I wanted to be like my father . . . good, strong, wise, smart, caring, courageous.

One might ask why I applied to UVA in the first place. Actually, it was not my idea. It was a request from Dr. Samuel D. Proctor,[2] who also promised to try to help. He said that if I agreed to enroll in the law school, he would try to raise money to help defray the expenses of law school. He kept his word and raised 25 to 30 percent of my expenses in keeping that promise.

Dr. Proctor was a special human being, and I owed him. He took me off the streets and was enormously helpful to me during my time at Virginia Union. I applied to UVA only because he asked me to. Doing so was a way to pay my debt to him, and he insisted on payment without ever voicing that insistence in those terms.

I honestly didn't fully understand Dr. Proctor's all-consuming interest in my attending UVA's law school. *Why me?* Some insight was obtained years later when I read his explanation in a book that he wrote, "*The Substance of Things Hoped For*"[3], a book well worth reading:

---

[2] The Reverend Dr. Samuel D. Proctor, then vice president of Virginia Union University in Richmond, Virginia, talked me into applying to UVA's law school. He wanted the first black graduate to be a Virginia Union man. I agreed believing that I would not be accepted. After acceptance, he helped convince me to attend.

[3] Judson Press, Valley Forge, PA 1995

"... At a conference in Greenwich, Connecticut, a woman came up to me and begged me to take her son off the streets. She was terrified he was going to wind up in jail.

I persuaded him to enroll in our college. John Merchant went down with me, played basketball, waited tables in the hotels, took campus jobs, and made an outstanding record. He had a kind of Yankee audacity about him and a never-give-up tenacity that made him an excellent candidate to break down barriers ..."

Dad firmly believed I could do it and encouraged me to be positive and unafraid. I tried. Dad's advice and counsel, along with Mom's[4] firm, but unsubstantiated belief that it would be okay were major sources of strength. Each was absolutely certain that God would make a way.

I leaned on God, my parents, my two sisters Barbara and Elizabeth, and some friends. Then, I journeyed to Charlottesville, alone, except for the unanswerable questions and persistent fears that travelled with me.

Unknown to me, that "... Yankee audacity ..." also went with me, and apparently, I latched on to that "... never-give-up tenacity ..." Dr. Proctor said I had. Frankly, I never knew that I had those things. All I knew about me was that I didn't know how to quit, but this could be a first.

Somehow, the tuition was gathered and sent, and I was on my way.

---

[4] Essie Louise Merchant, nee Nowlin, a wonderful lady and Mother. My family also included two terrific sisters: Barbara E. Mitchell and Mary Elizabeth Neal, both now in Richmond, Virginia.

First-day experiences connected with moving into the law school dorm to which I had been assigned raised immediate questions. Upon arrival, I carried my meager but adequate belongings into the law school dorms located directly across the street from the law school. The accommodations were comfortably designed for gentlemen: two-room suites containing a bedroom and a combination study and living room, complete with fireplace. The furnishings and furniture were more than adequate, newer and better than those in the attic room I called home. A bathroom was shared with two occupants of an adjoining suite.

While awaiting a roommate's arrival, I met the men in the adjoining suite: two New Yorkers, both second-year students. That was when that confederate flag loomed large.

Why two Northerners, *New Yorkers,* to share a bathroom with a black student at this southern university?

Where was I going to eat dinner tonight? Or lunch? Or breakfast?

In an effort to think positively, it occurred to me that, perhaps, the administration was taking steps to make me comfortable, avoid some issues, and ease the transition. I didn't really believe that; I awaited a roommate.

A roommate never appeared. I did say hello to a student as he was moving into his room directly above me. I learned later that he was from Georgia, and, as best I could surmise, was not at all thrilled to see me.

It didn't take long to realize that I was alone, but not unnoticed. My presence was known, though not heralded.

I believed, and knew, that I was being watched. My hope was that the surveillance was protective in nature, not otherwise, but that could not be confirmed. I prayed; why not?

I also hoped that the Ku Klux Klan (hereinafter Klan) was not watching, a scary thought.

As stated previously, one year before I started law school, in 1954, the US Supreme Court had decided *Brown*, a decision that led to enormous unrest and racial violence throughout America, especially in the South. While at Virginia Union, I was privy to events that led to Brown.

Oliver Hill, a courageous and extraordinary lawyer, was representing a group of black students from the Prince Edward County (Virginia) school system in an effort to eliminate the separate but equal nonsense that was Virginia's educational guidepost for public schools. His efforts were a constant subject of discussion at Union, as were other aspects of the struggle that led to *Brown*. The timing seemed bad, or given my first day experiences, I thought it was bad.

The Klan had been active in Virginia during my three years at Virginia Union University, in Richmond. I had no personal encounters with the Klan at Union but was fully aware of its presence and mission.

Virginia's Governor Battle was soon leading the South in a plan of "*massive resistance*" to *Brown*, designed and fully supported by the Byrd political machine, the media, and Virginia's majority population. Seemingly, Virginia's entire white population bought into Byrd's approach and flaunted their opposition to the Supreme Court's decision in *Brown*.

Civil disobedience demonstrations brought out the worst in people.

Too many seemed to believe that slavery was the only way to deal with people who possessed an African slave heritage. Second-class status, evidenced by the treatment received from the majority community, even seemed too high a classification to bestow upon those who arrived, or rather were brought here, on the wrong boat from the wrong place. That boat did not dock at Ellis Island in New York.

Some behavior required of blacks simply defied belief. Among those are stepping into the gutter so that a white person could use the sidewalk or being dragged away at night and flogged or lynched by the Klan for simply being accused of looking at a white woman, or not being allowed to use a public bathroom when traveling through the South, or buying food when traveling at a window in the back of the restaurant near the garbage cans, or being referred to by your first name only, never Mr. or Mrs. Brown, or being addressed as "nigger" or "boy" with no recourse, or drinking from a water fountain for "Colored," if you could find one, or, facing a bathroom door where a sign said, "Whites Only," knowing the sign meant what it said, or traveling from the country into town to register to vote only to be told by the person at the voting registration window that it was closed, *at 10:15* a.m., and would not reopen that day, or trying to explain to your children why these things occurred and why this is the way it was.

Incredibly, in this, the twenty-first century, many still harbor the belief that the above examples are still the best way to deal with the black population.

Governor Wallace of Alabama soon became a loud voice against both desegregation and integration of the public schools. His negative and provocative behavior deliberately fanned the flames of racial unrest and led to increased violence throughout the South and elsewhere.

Young black children and their parents showed enormous courage as they integrated many public schools in the South, usually accompanied by the National Guard. The fire hose was a weapon of choice in Alabama, and elsewhere, along with clubs and other tools of violence. Local police protection for blacks disappeared as the entire country took sides, often in support of Senator Byrd, Governor Wallace, and their ilk, causing more unrest and incredible violence.

It was not a time for Americans to be proud of their country, their neighbors, and, too often, themselves—their personal thoughts and behavior.

Clearly, the struggle for civil rights had taken on new dimensions. More explosions were inevitable; everyone knew that. For me, a twenty-two-year-old black male, born and raised in the North, in Connecticut, with parents who had fled Lexington, Virginia, it was a scary time. I admit to being scared, even terrified, and that is truth, not an overstatement.

I wondered if I would be involved in any incidents, or even cause one. Either, or both, possibilities existed.

The UVA administration knew I was here; did the Klan? What would be the attitude of the mostly southern student body or the faculty? Would I be alone without friends? How would I, alone, deal with what lay ahead? Where can I eat dinner?

The questions were further complicated by the fact that my personality and general attitude had never been conducive to turning the other cheek. I have always had a basic and fundamental belief in freedom of speech and the need for it. My preference was, and is, for meaningful discussions of issues and differences. Would this become a problem for me? If so, how would I handle it in this *foreign country*, with no known source of help if problems appeared? I was very concerned, and very afraid, to put it mildly.

Still, I forced myself to look into the bathroom mirror where a 5' 11", 158-pound person, totally unprepared for any physical violence that might erupt, looked back at me. I shrugged, unpacked, and sat down.

Fear grumbled in my belly and rose rapidly to my brain. It was frightening. *What am I doing here? How did I allow it to happen?* Yes, I thought seriously about leaving, spelled quitting, and was tempted. *Should I?*

The answers came slowly, but they came. Somehow, I must find a way to change my urge to quit into a commitment to stay and a plan to endure and advance. *Could I?* Not unless you get to work right now, John.

I answered those questions that day, telling myself: ". . . self, you are the reason you are here. You agreed to apply, and you were accepted. You clearly promised your parents and Dr. Proctor that you would matriculate in an attempt to ensure that the first black graduate of this law school was a Virginia Union University man, as Proctor wanted."

"Face it, John," I said to myself, "or start your future as an unreliable failure. If you quit, everyone will know that you quit, an embarrassing thought." I had never quit anything in my life, but it seemed like a good idea at that time. I talked myself into staying, asking God for courage, strength, help, and support.

My thoughts then shifted a bit as I tried to imagine what might lay ahead of me and how I would respond to, and cope with, whatever had to be faced, in and out of class. Would I manage to survive unscarred, physically or mentally? Would I earn the law degree Proctor wanted a Virginia Union man to have? Do I really want to be a lawyer?

Where will I eat dinner tonight?

I made a short list of rules for survival. One self-imposed rule I never failed to obey was that I would not complain about treatment in class or my grades unless they threatened my qualifying for, and receiving, the law degree Proctor sent me there to get. I never violated that rule. I still don't complain about things.

My approach is to try to clearly identify the problem, then, if possible, discuss it with relevant persons, then roll up my sleeves and work to figure out a way to solve it.

It occurred to me that this was just the first day; presumably, three years lay ahead, a seemingly impossible eternity to ponder. A long, long time to be alone in a "*foreign country*" filled with turmoil, racial unrest and violence, and surrounded by a horde of potential perpetrators of those negatives. I told myself, "Take it one day at a time, John, and please don't let the media make you a public person and exacerbate your situation."

The hospital admission triggered thoughts of my only other experience with a southern hospital.

At the age of nine, while visiting grandparents in Lexington, Virginia, I fell out of a tree and dislocated my right wrist. Mom took me to the hospital where I was required to wait three or four hours before the only black doctor in the area arrived to treat me. White hospital staff did nothing except ignore me, totally. They left me alone with my pain and tears until a very competent black doctor finally arrived, treated me, and I was released. My recovery was complete, and I appreciate what he did. I remember it well. Would that treatment be repeated here?

Virginia was not like Greenwich, Connecticut, where I was born and raised. On the other hand Greenwich, in terms of race relations and its attitude toward blacks, was no Garden of Eden.

Its black population consisted primarily of charter members of the "*menial job brigade*," most jobs just one small step above the tasks performed during slavery. Most were domestics who worked for wealthy white folks. Some recollections of growing up there were as bad as I imagined and believed UVA would be. I tried to think positively, but it was a struggle.

In my search for positives, the thought occurred that perhaps after this first year, another black student would enroll and make the task easier by his or her presence. I could certainly hope for that; however, that did not happen.

Would I be alone for three consecutive years? Would I have any friends, later if not sooner? Would the media get involved and how would I handle that if they did? Would

I be able to learn two new languages: the language of the law, and, the languages of specific subjects such as torts, contracts, real property, and others; all first year required subjects?

I was a total stranger to those languages, though many of my classmates were not. The competition had an edge.

Where can I eat dinner tonight? This was not an irrelevant question, especially since wherever food existed I had to walk to get it. In what direction? How far? In the dark? Simple questions, tough to answer.

At that time, and still, the law school was ranked as one of the top ten law schools in the United States, thus it was reasonable to assume that my class would include many who were among the best and the brightest in the country. I expected that most of them would be southerners with southern attitudes and biases. You know, sons of the wealthy and powerful, preparing to carry on southern traditions, most of which were decidedly unfriendly to black citizens. I was wrong about that. The students came from many states, although the South and the State of Virginia were clearly well represented.

Ironically, I did not really fear competing with whites in the classroom. I had learned to do that very well throughout my life in the Greenwich (Connecticut) public school system. Admittedly, I wasn't sure why I was going to school, but I enjoyed learning and was good at both learning and remembering things.

I did realize that I needed to apply myself, develop and maintain good study habits, and learn those skills quickly. Good study habits were a real challenge since I had none. In truth, I have no recollection of ever carrying a book home from high school or of doing homework at home.

I entered high school at age twelve, was 4' 11" tall and weighed eighty-eight pounds.

My entire high school time and my summers involved leaving Greenwich High School at the end of each school day and catching a bus to Stamford, where I swept floors at the B and S Coat Company on Stillwater Avenue. Dad had a room there, and as part of his living arrangement, he was to sweep the floors in the building and around the sewing machines each day, a chore he did not relish after working all day. So, he hired me to do it, and I did, for five consecutive years. He paid me a dollar a day. Bus fare was a dollar a week, school lunch the same, one dollar went to Mom, another dollar was my allowance, and a dollar was put in savings each week. I saw and talked with Dad almost every day.

After cleaning the factory, I caught a bus back to Greenwich, arriving there around 7:00 p.m. For two to three years, I got off the bus on Greenwich Avenue and went to a bowling alley where I set up pins each night until around 9:00 or 10:00 p.m. then walked home to save the ten cents bus fare. This schedule didn't leave much time for studying, so I rarely studied. My homework was done at school during study periods.

At the time, the public school system in Greenwich, Connecticut, was the best or one of the best public school systems in the country. I did well there but would have done better if I had studied or believed that I was preparing for college. I never had a black classmate in high school.

Only one other black that I know of, a female, chose the college curriculum at Greenwich High School. She and I never shared a classroom together. Others opted for the general or business curriculums. The idea of going to college didn't exist. It was neither economically feasible nor seemingly worthwhile for many. The "*menial job brigade*" was assumed to be in our futures. They all understood the dominance of the majority community and did not believe that opportunities would be made available because of a college education. The few college educated blacks in Greenwich, and there were a couple, were simply not allowed to use their college-acquired skills because the majority community denied them employment opportunities.

Alver W. Napper, a graduate of Albany State University in Georgia, finally found somewhat suitable employment when he was hired as the Director of the Crispus Attucks Community Center in Greenwich, the only black community center in the state, if not in all of New England.

Crispus Attucks, 1723-1770, a black man, became the first casualty of the American Revolution when he was shot and killed in what became known as the Boston Massacre.

After earning his degree, Mr. Napper returned to Connecticut. The only work he could find was as a toll collector on the Merritt Parkway, a state job that required a fight to get. Other toll collectors resented his presence and the presence of the very few blacks ultimately hired to perform what can only be described as a simple job, one requiring little educational achievement. Mr. Napper was clearly overqualified.

Mr. Napper had located to Hartford, the state capital, in the early 1940s upon his return. There, he learned about the toll collector opening and successfully lobbied to get it. Of course, he was assigned to the toll booths in Greenwich, a town that borders New York State and is as far away from Hartford as you can get and still be in Connecticut. Getting to work, and getting there on time, was a challenge. Not getting there every day, on time, meant dismissal. He finally found and rented a room in town, after being refused a room at the YMCA because blacks were not allowed to use any of the YMCA facilities then. In truth, blacks were not wanted anywhere in the building or on the property.

I had graduated high school at age sixteen with only white classmates. I had learned early on that they were no more capable of learning than I was. As I recall, not many performed better than I did. Thus, my concern, as stated previously, was learning languages while coping with the pressures, real and imagined, that existed.

Early on, the entire first-year class was convened and told, among other things, that we should "look at the students to our left and right, one of you will not be here three years from now." There is nothing like receiving a morale booster on the first day of the "gathering of the clan."[5] I remember thinking that the professor was slyly talking only to me, a thought that both annoyed and challenged me. The men on my left and right kept staring at me, so I stared back, asking myself which one of them would disappear. False

---

[5]   I believe my class consisted of 167 students and included 86 southerners; 136 graduated in 1958, 80%.

bravado at work, for sure, but often, it's the little things that drive and sustain us.

I wondered where the other students were from. I came from the North, Connecticut. I had graduated from Virginia Union University, one of the historical black colleges. It was there that I first attended a class with other blacks. I was certain that no other person in the building had ever sat in a class with a black student, or not many had.

My tenure at Union was truly an uplifting experience. I watched young men and women enter from southern segregated school systems into a college where they were exposed to a nurturing and an educational experience that I believed, and believe, was phenomenal. They soaked up learning, graduated as well-educated persons, quenching a thirst to learn, and left prepared to face a world of work that fundamentally did not want them. They produced and achieved, many in meaningful and dramatic ways.

Union's student body included others of note, Rev. Wyatt T. Walker, who became Dr. King's right-hand man; the Reverend Walter Fauntroy, a classmate who serves as a minister in Washington DC and who became the first elected congressional representative from the District of Columbia; Leroy Vaughan, a great athlete, hampered by bad knees, who received a tryout with the Baltimore Colts and was one of the last players cut by the Colts that year; and Howie Jones and Ronnie Bressant, two New Yorkers who manned Union's championship backcourt, both All City out of Boys High in New York City, with no chance to play in the NBA because it wasn't scouting or drafting from the historical black colleges then; that happened a little later.

Leroy was a quarterback; the Colts had Johnny Unitas returning. Leroy and Shirley, his wife, are the parents of Mo Vaughan who enjoyed an outstanding baseball career with the Boston Red Sox and New York Mets. Leroy went on to earn a PhD in education.

One Leroy Vaughan incident I recall was the day that two guys were having a heated discussion about something on Union's campus. Leroy and I, among others, stood there watching and listening. When the argument reached a point where it seemed likely to advance beyond mere words, the smallest of the two guys shouted "Shazam" and immediately jumped behind Leroy. You remember "Shazam?" You must be old.

The act of changing into Leroy Vaughan, alias Captain Marvel, caused everyone to laugh loudly and long. It also ended the discussion peacefully.

There were many others who made their mark after leaving Union, a clear tribute to the effectiveness of the historical black colleges and their ability to inspire and produce well-educated productive men and women who positively impacted a culture and a world of work that did not want them. I feel compelled to mention two others, though I leave out too many.

Doug Wilder had graduated Union a year or two before me. You may recall that he became the first African-American elected governor of any state in America. The stories of his elections in Virginia to lieutenant governor in 1985 and governor in 1990 are detailed in two books[6] well worth reading if one wants to know Virginia better and believe that hope is still alive. I have read both.

Sure we are tired, but we've come a long way; America has come a long way. Let's take some deep breaths, rest a bit, and continue the journey. There is a light at the end of the tunnel. To me, Wilder is living proof that Barack Obama can be elected president of the United States.[7]

Henry Marsh graduated Virginia Union in 1956, a year after I did. He earned a law degree from Howard University in 1959 and joined the law firm of Hill, Tucker and Marsh, becoming a partner in 1966. Henry has successfully litigated more than fifty cases against school boards in Virginia and more than twenty employment discrimination cases during a distinguished legal career that is still ongoing.

A brilliant lawyer and a gentleman, his reputation as one of the leading trial and appellate attorneys in Virginia is well deserved. In addition, he became Richmond's first black mayor in 1977 and has served as a senator in the Virginia State Senate since 1991.

Three years at Virginia Union allowed me to be a witness to the racial prejudices and attitudes that prevailed and

---

[6]   "When Hell Froze Over" by Dwayne Yancey. 1988, Taylor Publishing Company, and "Claiming The Dream" by Margaret Edds, 1990, Algonquin Books of Chapel Hill

[7]   "Virginia makes the powerful impression of a country living under a spell, in which time has stood still," Arnold Toynbee, British historian, 1947. This may have been true then, but no longer. Virginia has come a long way, so can we.

JOHN F. MERCHANT

dominated in the South. Now, at UVA, it seemed that I was to be completely surrounded by those prejudices and attitudes and expecting the worse was not unreasonable. The arrival experience did nothing to discourage those negative thoughts.

Then, after enduring those first-year classes and a full year of fear, I found myself in the hospital, still very much alone, awaiting final exams but not physically able to prepare for them. My confidence level was not high. In fact, it was very low, almost nonexistent.

Yes, after about nine months as the only black student at this prestigious law school, in a setting where I was surrounded by Southerners, and taught by a faculty that had never conferred a law degree upon a black student, legitimate concerns abounded. Many of that faculty were UVA law school's graduates themselves, so who could tell what they thought about my being there?

A word about the faculty. Notably, there were those who were sensitive about my situation, supportive of my being there, and helpful in large and small ways. Of course, there were others as well who had different feelings.

Dean F. D. G. Ribble was a gem. He understood and cared.

Hardy C. Dillard, who taught contracts in my first year, is a legend at the law school. I recall that he was the first to call upon me in class to discuss a case and be questioned about it in front of the whole class. That happened to everyone, but I was pretty nervous when my turn came, afraid that I would humiliate myself.

However, Professor Dillard very adroitly and skillfully guided me through the experience in a manner that ensured a solid performance at my first speaking engagement at the law school. I was, and am, grateful for that.

Prof. Charles O. Gregory taught torts and labor law. He was a nationally acclaimed expert in both subjects and taught from books he authored on both subjects. We became friends. He spent his summers in New Hampshire, as did I, and once invited me to dinner at his New Hampshire home.

During that night, I recall that he and I shared the better part of a fifth of bourbon, talked a lot about a variety of subjects, and consumed several loin lamb chops prepared by his wife, a wonderful woman.

There are three different routes one could take to travel to his home from the camps where I worked. I drove back to the camp that night, but to this day, I cannot remember which of the three routes I chose. I do recall that I learned to enjoy bourbon and Charley Gregory, a good man.

I remember thinking that my illness was totally unfair, especially after what I had been through during the past several months. Or I asked myself, "Was this just another challenge laid before me?" I voted for unfair, but accepted the challenge and somehow was not deterred.

Dad had taught me that you are always in charge of your attitude, regardless of the situation or circumstances. "Stay positive and never give less than your best," was his credo. He taught me that failure should be the result of one's inability, not the result of giving less than your best. He believed that you could do almost anything if you applied yourself properly to the task.

JOHN F. MERCHANT

Admittedly, I had serious reservations about Dad's teachings throughout the year, but not enough to convince me that he was wrong. I continued to give my best and was willing to accept whatever result prevailed.

Mononucleosis prevented any studying; it also prevented swallowing food or drinking water without serious pain in my throat. I lost weight and was thoroughly exhausted and weak. I was terrified that I would fail and that my tenure at the law school would end. I struggled with sickness, depression, and loneliness.

I thought back on the school year spent as the only black law student at this prestigious law school, trying to learn and remember new languages, along with the law that applied. Frankly, I was not really confident that I had mastered the languages, let alone the relevant legal concepts that pertained.

Real property? What is a mortgage or a deed? What does it mean to record either one on the land records? Fee simple, fee tail, life estates, tenancies, the Rule in Shelley's Case, bailor, bailee, landlord and tenant rights and responsibilities, the statute of frauds, unenforceable covenants, and a lot more since September. All these were either new words or new concepts to me, none of which I had ever heard mentioned, let alone discussed, prior to entering the law school.

We did not speak about such things in the rat-infested attic on Charles Street in Greenwich, Connecticut, where my mother, two sisters, and I spent most of my growing-up years. In fact, my parents never had a checking account or a share of stock, and we would never have been mistaken for middle-class folks.

My parents separated when I was around two years old. My dad moved to Stamford where he started a house-painting business that was not a smashing success but provided work and some income. As far as I know, he contributed child support to my mom regularly; more when he had more, *without a court order*. He came every Sunday and spent time with his children, always taking us for a ride in his car where we enjoyed singing and harmonizing.

For years, he also gave us a weekly allowance of one dollar; for the three of us, not a dollar apiece. With that money, we joined other young people at the movies at the Pickwick Theatre most Sundays, a veritable ritual for us.

At one point, the movies cost seventeen cents per person. The forty-nine cents remaining was used for candy and popcorn, split three ways. There were weekly discussions over who gets the odd penny, actually more like arguments among siblings. Bobbie usually argued that being the oldest, she should get it. My position was that as the only male in the group I deserved it, a chauvinistic approach soon abolished by a failure to gather the votes. Liz was creative in her arguments but didn't have the votes either, so rarely won the argument, but it was good practice for her.

It just happened that Bobbie sang soprano, Liz was an alto, Dad sang bass, and I was a baritone. The components for harmony were there, and we loved using them. The songs we sang came from three sources: church hymns and gospel, current hit parade numbers, and songs Dad taught us from his youth and memory. Bobbie, Liz, and I sang in the junior choir at First Baptist Church, growing up. We attended church each and every Sunday.

I have two wonderful sisters each of whom I love dearly.

My parents each had an admirable work ethic that they passed onto their children. Receiving welfare was out of the question, but doing well in school was a priority rigidly enforced, as was attending church and staying out of trouble. Ours were really tremendous parents that we were fortunate to have.

Contracts and torts, like real property, were six-credit courses that also contained strange words, combinations of words, and unfamiliar concepts. I believe that most law students will agree that learning the law is made easier when one is able to talk to other students about the law, its applicability, nuances, and twists and turns as you study it. I did not have that opportunity, as did others. I missed the advantage of having a roommate, or other students, to talk with about the law. In truth, learning was a real struggle.

How in the world will I pass these courses, especially with mononucleosis on hand? Visions of disappointing Proctor, my family, my friends, and myself dominated and left me depressed.

The fact that my hospital room was in the "colored" section of the hospital did not help either.

I asked about postponing my exams until I had recovered and was well. The answer was yes; I could postpone them *until next year, May 1957.* Not a very good option to me. Trying to remember after nine months was tough enough.

Waiting twenty-one months impressed me as an excellent recipe for failure.

So there I was, a Connecticut native in the State of Virginia, where my parents were born and raised; the only black student at the University of Virginia Law School, hospitalized in a segregated hospital, concerned about the level of care that could be expected and facing final exams.

A slender, even skinny male who could not eat and maintain weight, now faced a challenge alone, except for my god. I prayed and asked for help; it came.

As I think back, it occurs to me that the hospital administrators probably had their own concerns, though I do not know that they did. If so, they did not share them with me. I thought: a segregated hospital had admitted a black student who was integrating the university's law school, its sacred cow. Would integrating the hospital be his next target? To the hospital, that could mean a lawsuit if the administration and staff failed to provide proper care.

Also, please don't let Merchant die because of inattention or any form of malpractice. The ensuing law suit could possibly do harm to the hospital's budget and bring totally unwanted national attention to a university and its hospital, both striving to achieve, maintain, and elevate their status as one of the South's leading educational institutions, including medicine. If they thought along those lines, they had my total support. I didn't want to die either.

Equally as important, I thought, could be their fear that this law student might later sue to desegregate and integrate the hospital. That would certainly create a problem for a lot

JOHN F. MERCHANT

of people though who knows, or knew, what the result of such a lawsuit would have been?

Little did they know that my thoughts focused only on being able to eat a good meal, gain some weight, feel better, get well, take my exams, pass them, return home to Connecticut for the summer, then, maybe, return to Charlottesville as a second-year student.

The problem was that there was no known cure for mononucleosis. In fact, there was little anyone could do to ease the discomfort though, in fairness, the hospital tried. They tried in many ways to treat me and make me happy and contented. Seemingly, every doctor in the hospital visited me and tried every approach they had ever heard of anywhere to cure me or at least ease my discomfort. In a sense, I felt like an experiment, and probably was, for whatever reason.

In my opinion, there was never any indication of the hospital providing me with less than the best care they could. Their interest and efforts were appreciated, but through no fault of theirs, the immediate medical results left a lot to be desired.

One negative experience stands out in my mind as being totally insensitive, though not directed toward me. I was put in a room set up for two people, but no other patient was allowed in. One wall of my room separated the "white" section from the "colored" section. My first night there, a man who had taken a shotgun blast, close up, on the right side of his head, neck, and body was admitted. He was placed in a bed in the hallway just outside my room, and I listened to him gurgle for two nights. I was told some time later that he died in that hallway, and I have always wondered whether his death could have been prevented.

Was he treated as well as I was? I have no way of knowing. Certainly, he was not placed in any intensive care unit and monitored. Maybe ICUs didn't exist then; I don't know.

The head nutritionist took time to visit me. She told me that I could order any food on the planet and it would be served to me. The condition was that I must eat everything I ordered or that particular food would not again be served. Seizing this unexpected opportunity, I tried steaks and chops but had to quit and go to milk shakes. The pain in swallowing was simply too great to bear. The milk shakes hurt going down but, in sliding down, hurt less and were bearable. I lost weight, but at least did not die.

The exam issue was resolved by my leaving the hospital on the morning of an exam, walking to and taking the exam, then returning to the hospital.

All exams were taken except one. I simply did not have the strength to take the contracts exam. My physical condition was such that I was not upbeat about what results would flow from the exams I had taken. I received permission to delay the contracts exam until May 1957. I took it then and was amazed when I passed with a reasonably good grade.

My grades at law school probably merit some discussion, but I will limit it. It didn't matter to me what my grades were anyway as long as I stayed on the right road leading to a degree. No recruiters were ever going to interview me for a possible position and didn't. I signed up for some without success. Even the federal government was uninterested.

I believe that some professors cheated me on my grades, but no clear evidence of that exists or existed nor did I pursue the issue. Frankly, I honored my rule that I would not contest any grade I received as long as it didn't prevent me from graduating with a law degree.

In my third year, an incident unrelated to grades did trouble me a bit, although I laugh about it now. It involved money.

Shortly before my last semester, I had figured out that I was broke and needed money in order to eat, *at all*, during that last semester. I met with the professor in charge of making loans to students and was initially denied the loan. He told me that existing policy prevented him from lending money to a student receiving financial aid. I told him that the policy could not apply in my case because I was not receiving aid. He insisted, without disclosing any evidence to support his position, that my application for financial help had been approved and that I had received financial aid. No loan could now be made.

I stood up before him and meekly and politely, with hat in hand, convinced him that I had never received any scholarship dollars and, at this late stage, had no interest in fighting about it. Please, just lend me the money so that I can eat. Ultimately, he did.

That loan was needed to cover the cost of one meal a day for a full semester. The meal consisted of elbow macaroni cooked in a pot on a hot plate in my room. To the macaroni was added Cheese Whiz and B&M Baked Beans right out of the can. The beans were warmed by the elbows and eaten out of the pot with a spoon "borrowed" from the cafeteria. I returned the spoon before graduation.

Incidentally, that is a meal I enjoy to this day and eat often. To the elbows and cheese in one bowl, add some broiled chopped sirloin mixed with onions, green peppers, and carefully selected seasonings. Stir until mixed well, then serve with a salad on a separate plate and a glass of Pinot Grigio. Delicious!

One caution: only B&M Baked Beans will make it the culinary delight that it is. Friends have enjoyed this dish over the years; some have even raved about it. They call it "Merchant Goulash." [*Try it, it's really good. Come for dinner tomorrow night and I'll make it.*]

Soon after exams ended, I was released from the hospital, somewhat improved but weak and depressed. I returned home to Connecticut, thence to Winchester, New Hampshire, to work as a camp counselor, as I had done for several summers. The mononucleosis went away, then recurred, but ultimately disappeared totally with the help of Dr. John Houpis in Brattleboro, Vermont, the camp's doctor.

While awaiting results, the fear of failing never left me. More time was spent thinking about how I had happened to attend UVA's law school and why I agreed to go there in the first place. More than one private self-pity party was sponsored by me, for me, *and attended only by me*, until grades arrived. The parties ended when the results arrived and I learned that I had passed all the exams I took and could return in September as a second-year student. But the self-reflection continued and did not ease up.

The wait for exam results gave me time to think seriously about the experience. I found it hard to discuss the UVA experience with anyone. Actually, until exam results arrived, there was little to discuss. I guess you had to be there, sharing the experience, to fully understand my unwillingness to talk about it. Also, not many folks really cared to listen and understand, so be it.

When grades finally arrived with the news that all exams taken were passed with satisfactory grades, I knew I could return in September as a second-year student. Now I could talk about returning. Mom and Dad were pleased; I was amazed and pleased. The challenge had been successfully met and my confidence level related to the education I was receiving was upgraded. The issue for me was whether or not I wanted to return, transfer, or quit. Not an easy question, but answered after several serious discussions with Dad, Mom, George Twine from Greenwich, Dr. Proctor, and a few others.

George Twine, a black man, was the person who hired me to work at the camps in New Hampshire, Rabbit Hollow, and Forest Lake. He was a graduate of Lincoln University, a journalism major, born before his time. Very talented and energetic, he never found employment in his field as should have been the case. Many highly capable black college graduates experienced that problem; some still do but not nearly as many.

The discussions leading to my return were with men who had a vision that exceeded mine. They argued long and hard for returning. When those arguments seemed doomed to fail, they demanded it. They taught me the value of having a vision, the need for courage and fortitude, and the value of patience while working toward an important and desirable goal.

They pointed out that apprehensions about returning had to be significantly less than those concerning attending in the first place. The first year's experience should have eased my fears since I now knew what to expect and how to deal with it.

The real or imagined negatives had been endured without major damage. The university and the City of Charlottesville were now somewhat familiar territory. Supportive friends in the community had been made, thus providing an escape, a respite if you will, from the stress and fears of being alone and lonely. Law students had generally accepted me, or my presence, and were not a source of serious problems.

They argued persuasively that returning should be an easier scenario to contemplate. I knew where to eat and what stores not to enter, even though I refused to step off the sidewalk to make room for white pedestrians, be they students or others.

They recognized that racial conflicts had heightened in Virginia and in the South generally. Thus, they understood that danger still lurked, and given the Byrd inspired legislation championing "*massive resistance,*" conflict could be expected to continue and accelerate. They argued that these things were not and could never be a reason to quit. Easy for them to say!

In response, I pointed out that I was physically, emotionally, and mentally exhausted. Also, I was still afraid and alone. The aloneness and the loneliness were more serious issues for me than I could convey to those with whom I spoke, as was the fear. It was as if no one cared about those critical items except me. They were unimpressed by them.

I was stressed out, and at or near my limits, when I needed to be strong. My reluctance was fueled by a clear belief that there must be a better way or a better person to get the job done. Why me, Lord?

They postulated that there would be a better way, down the road, for others who followed in my footsteps. "You have proven that you can handle the assignment by your first year's performance and can't quit now." "Besides," they argued, "other black students may enroll in September and that would help tremendously. In any event, you have to finish the job. You can and must."

"Also, you now knew where to eat dinner."

They were wrong about additional black enrolment but nothing else. The right decision was made; I returned to Charlottesville.

My second year did see a change in my comfort level, downward.

Unfortunately, during my uncertainty about returning, I failed to send a deposit for a room in the law school dorms, so I was denied one because none was available. Instead, I was assigned to an undergraduate dorm where noise, disrespect, racist attitudes, and continuous conflict characterized my time there. Conflict was never ending, leading to experiences I would rather forget and will not recite, except for one.

It started as a verbal disagreement with three undergraduate students. It escalated to the point where the biggest of the three grabbed me by the neck, backed me up against the wall, and threatened to "whip my negro butt." He could have done so, with or without help from the other two. He balled up his fist and was about to punch my lights out when I looked him in the eye and told him, in effect, that he had better kill me or never walk around another corner without looking first. A failure to look would lead to a meeting with a tire iron that he would not enjoy. He did not punch me.

Later, as I sat in my room shaking, I was surprised by the calm way in which I had delivered my threat. I was even more surprised to realize that I had meant what I threatened and would have carried it out. Apparently, nonviolence, thy name is not John Merchant; a scary realization for a skinny guy alone in this *foreign country*. Not very smart either.

I began to examine the depth of my feelings regarding being at law school and the racial issues that appeared daily in this dormitory.

The examination took place as I left the scene of the incident, then went to my room, then left the room and walked downtown, accompanied by a stout stick and levels of anger and frustration that were unfamiliar to me.

I took that walk in the dark in order to cool off and hopefully find a friend in the community with whom I could vent my rage. I did that and provided an opportunity for a serious common-sense talk with myself, a talk focused on developing better control over these emerging and deeply held feelings. I needed a better attitude, one that enabled

JOHN F. MERCHANT

me to walk away from, not confront, potential or actual conflict, if that was possible. After all, I reminded myself I was in charge of my attitude and could change it.

You know the one: "sticks and stones can break my bones but names can never hurt me" attitude, thus avoiding some violent encounters. But even these sensible thoughts did not eradicate the constant fear that prevailed and consumed me, nor did they help me learn the lessons in the classroom.

The experiences were changing me into someone I didn't know and didn't want to be. And there was no one with whom I could discuss these things as the need arose. I did realize that survival would be impossible without an attitude change. I'm no fighter and would be hopelessly outnumbered even if I were. I threw away my stick and struggled to find new directions.

It is difficult to recall, in honest detail, all that occurred during my three years at the law school, so I will not try. However, a few things are worthy of mention.

Not all the students were southerners, and many, including some of the southerners, became friends over time. My class, as well as the entire student body at the law school, had men from many different parts of the country, including many graduates of the Ivy League schools, Yale, Harvard, Princeton, and others. Three women were part of the class of 1958 as well, including Barbara Coppeto from Waterbury, Connecticut. She later became a Connecticut Superior Court judge where she served with distinction for many years.

No racial incidents involving any of the law school students ever occurred. In fact, many went out of their way to extend a hand of friendship, especially during my second and third years when it became clear that I was there to stay and would do whatever was needed to earn an LLB (Bachelor of Laws) degree.

Years later, I paid $25 to obtain a J.D. (Doctor of Laws) degree. The law school had ceased awarding an LLB some years after I graduated. After doing so, they offered its previous graduates a JD for $25; I accepted. Easiest way I ever heard of to become a doctor and it was done without the need for elbow macaroni.

For whatever its worth, I can be addressed as Dr. Merchant, a moniker that has never seemed correct, whether written or verbal. I have another degree, doctor of laws, but it is honorary, thus not the same. Who knows the difference, or cares?

Most folks who need an attorney or a lawyer do not inquire about his or her grades in law school. They rightfully assume that having an office and a secretary means you are one.

One measure of my experiences at law school involves the social life at the law school. It had its own social agenda a few times each year, off campus at privately owned facilities. In my first year, invitations to the dining and dancing were extended to all students, except me. No big deal and hardly unexpected.

In my second year, a committee of class officers, all third year students, requested a meeting with me at which they apologized for not sending me an invitation to the social events. They explained that the privately owned sites of the dance or other events would not permit me to mingle with other students as a guest. Happily, they didn't say that I could come and be a waiter, dishwasher, or busboy, and I was grateful for that.

The truth is that I was very surprised and pleased by what I viewed as a very positive attitude and an important step for diversity. I could only imagine the discussions that took place and led to the apology. An utterly amazing, but positive, sign to me.

In my third year, members of my class were now the officers with whom I met, at their request. Their agenda was short and had a narrow focus, a focus that humbled me at the time and still does.

Simply stated, they spent considerable time to convince me that I must participate in law school social events, off Grounds, no exceptions, no excuses. In return, if I agreed to participate, they would find a public place that would permit me and a date to be part of any activity scheduled. Hmm, I thought, a date? In Charlottesville? What is that?

In truth, there were few, if any, places in or near Charlottesville that could conveniently accommodate the number of people reasonably expected to attend. Finding such a place would be difficult, probably impossible in the Charlottesville area, but their commitment to the effort was genuine.

The intensity of their commitment to the effort was impressive. Less than four years after *Brown* and despite continuing unrest and multiple law suits pending against school boards and massive resistance legislation, the leadership of this southern law school was adamant about its willingness to help break down existing social barriers, even if it meant incurring the wrath of law school student dissenters who would be inconvenienced by the change of venue.

I declined for many different reasons but still get emotional when I recall the meetings.

My tenure at UVA had not become an issue deserving of major public scrutiny or attention. The only media coverage had been short lived. The timing for any involvement by me in attacking social barriers seemed bad. Let's finish the diversity effort first, then move into other areas. Besides, Dr. King's efforts had a public accommodations focus that was not being generally accepted, although it was slowly making serious inroads, despite taking on casualties.

I didn't believe that I should be at the center of an effort to bring diversity to public accommodations as well as fighting the separate but equal battle. On a more personal basis, I was afraid about the potential fallout if I agreed to participate. Acceptance had the potential to elevate and disclose my presence to a level I did not need, a level that could mean more intense unrest and violence than Virginia was presently experiencing.

It occurred to me that an invitation to me was also an invitation to the Klan and could have undesirable results that I could live without.

Also, I was tired, worn out emotionally, and not mentally prepared for expanding the battlefield. My interests were simple, my goal even simpler. Earn the degree and get out of Tombstone before the Earps and Clantons converged.

JOHN F. MERCHANT

I could get nailed by a wayward gunshot, or even worse, provide the Klan with an additional focus.

On reflection, I am not sure that I made the right decision. My decision had the effect of preventing a leadership group from actively participating in helping Dr. King's dream become a reality and being intimately involved in further pursuit of the promise of *Brown*.

I recall being privately emotional about those meetings and still get that way when I remember and think about them. But I did decline to participate.

Any serious evaluation of my three years at UVA must consider the actions just mentioned. The law school's student leadership totally ignored me in my first year, despite my status as a legitimate paid-up member of the group. In my second year, leadership felt a need to *apologize* for excluding me from participating socially in law school activities. They cited existing values as being immovable barriers, ones that they were unwilling to challenge for many different reasons that were not detailed at our meeting.

Then in my third year, leadership acted to correct an unsupportable community value. They practically begged me to join in their effort knowing that it could not be done without my agreement. I declined but have never been certain that mine was the correct decision. Was it?

It is not totally clear to me what lessons should be drawn from leadership's actions over a three-year period. However, it is absolutely clear to me that my personal evaluation of the time spent at UVA has to be positive partially because of the progression just shared with you, if for no other reason. Other reasons existed, less dramatic perhaps, but clearly, they existed.

In a real way those meetings justify my lifelong search for bridges. They support my commitment to building bridges wherever and whenever circumstances permitted. Happily, circumstances during my journey through life allowed me to exercise my commitment to building bridges.

In many important ways, the UVA experience shaped me as a person and helped construct the foundation needed to direct my life. Many positives occurred to impact my thinking and my attitude. These positives outweigh the negatives by a large amount.

It's not that I don't recall the negatives, because I do. It's just that I see no need to dwell on them, or even mention most of them, considering what I believe the experience really involved and led to, namely, a significant step in the right direction.

Among other things, it confirmed a need to judge people by the "content of their character" and not the "color of their skin" or their heritage. I don't use the term "whitey" when discussing the majority community nor do I use the "N" word. Each is equally abhorrent to me and should be to everyone.

Throughout my life, America has been intimately involved in a never-ending search for fairness, parity, and equality. Frankly, believe it or not, that search is moving forward at a more rapid rate than I might have imagined. It was and is being aided and supported by untold numbers of white Americans without whom progress would not exist.

I firmly believe that continued progress requires finding ways for the different races to actively relate better with each other. Integrating areas of life, where all humans have identical concerns, can provide the arena for better relations among the races. Is there a better way? I don't think so.

Clearly, for me, there is a need to focus on what unites us as human beings, rather than relying on the superficiality of race, color, or creed as the means for judging others.

UVA's law school population came to accept me for a lot of reasons. Among them was the fact that I was doing something, getting an education, helping myself, and not looking for a handout. I was doing something positive, not just complaining about the negatives that confront too many of us on a daily basis and were certainly confronting me in Charlottesville, Virginia.

Additionally, some law school students just didn't care to be involved. Their focus was on their personal lives, concerns, dreams, and issues, a perfectly normal way to act.

Obviously, I spent little time drawing attention to racial issues, and no one ever heard me complain. I did not make fiery speeches that dealt with the race issue that was being discussed rationally and irrationally throughout the country. Not complaining has always been my style. It would be difficult for anyone to recall an instance where they heard me complain about anything. The act of building bridges leaves no room for throwing stones and identifying culprits.

In essence, I believe that if we cannot sensibly discuss issues and resolve them, we can always fight or go to war. But if that happens, people get hurt and even die. Who needs that?

Athletics played an important part in creating positive relationships with other law school students. I had played varsity basketball at Virginia Union and played intramural basketball and softball for law school teams. Sports are often a great outlet. The issue is "Can you play and help us win," not where did your parents come from, although sports can have their rough edges also.

Intramural basketball involved mostly undergraduate teams, many of which had players who apparently were neither appreciative of my being in the league nor happy about the fact that I could play. Consequently, I got beat up pretty good during games, and often. I did become pretty good at giving back.

A law school student learned about the punishment I took and decided he would join the team. I call him Hammurabi. He sat with me and explained that I couldn't afford a physical encounter with a college student and said he would handle things when they got rough. He did just that.

Using the five fouls each player is allotted, he saw to it that any punishments were equal, but separate. When I became a taker of unnecessary physical abuse, he became the giver who equalized things. A serious physical incident involving me was thereby avoided, and I enjoyed having him substitute for me so that I could watch as he gave true meaning to separate but equal.

At last, the concept made some sense to me, but only in this narrow application.

In softball, our law school team, The Barristers, won the university championship in 1957. The win earned us an invitation to participate in an AAU Tournament involving champions from all colleges and universities in Virginia to be played in Richmond. This was a fast-pitch softball tournament involving a lot of good players; an interesting annual event played at Byrd Park in Richmond. I played shortstop and batted at or near the top of the order.

Yup, the park is named after the Byrd family whose son, the US senator, helped to create and champion the cause of *massive resistance* that Virginia was involved with and leading at that time.

A few minutes before our scheduled game at Byrd Park, while we were warming up on the sidelines, we were told that a mistake had been made and our game was to be played at Parker Field, located literally across the tracks in Richmond and not at Byrd Park. We packed up and went there. It was a lesser facility out of sight of the majority community; obviously, separate but not equal. We lost to William and Mary, 2 to 1, in extra innings and returned to UVA.

I thought nothing more about it although we did discuss the relocation on the ride back to Charlottesville. The next week, the May 9, 1957 edition of *The Virginia Law Weekly* was published. This law school newspaper is distributed among students and mailed to alumni who request it. There was a front page story entitled *"Negro's Presence Causes Transfer of Softball Game,"* surprising the hell out of me.

In addition, an editorial was printed criticizing the racial discrimination inherent in the relocation order. Recently, I read the article and had a good laugh when I read the following:

> "Mr. Reynolds (Director of Recreation and Parks) noted also that the lighting at Parker Field was better, in his opinion, and therefore the team was not required to use inferior facilities." [*The game was played entirely in the daylight without the need for, or use of, artificial illumination. (emphasis supplied).*]

I had no idea that the relocation matter would become a media matter. Happily, no other newspapers I know of covered the story, and I had put it out of my mind. We got beat; end of story. Yet I could not help but consider it an act of courage for the staff at the *Weekly* to have taken it up and announced it to their constituency. I often wonder what might have happened if we had gone deeper into the tournament.

The two stories recited here are important memories for me since they describe unexpected and very positive actions by persons who care and are willing to let their feelings be known. The events taught me very valuable lessons that I have retained. The major lesson was that the cause of right has more friends than many in the black community know about, or seek out.

Looking back, they exemplify signs of change that are truly catching on in America whether we approve of the changes or not. The obvious highlight, of course, is

Obama's campaign to be elected president of the United States.[8]

Since receiving my degree, I have chosen not to dwell on most of my negative experiences at UVA, including racist attitudes and behavior, blatant discrimination or scary episodes that involved more than one fistfight. Doing so would have no value and would lead us down the road to nowhere.

It doesn't mean that I have forgotten the episodes, including those on "The Corner," the site of retail establishments and restaurants. A black person could not spend money on "The Corner." Food, clothing, UVA memorabilia, whatever, carried a "whites only" tag, unwritten but very visible. Owners would not allow a black to enter their store or remain there if you did enter. Any effort made to sit in a restaurant and have a burger and fries exposed one to serious bodily harm.

Walking past the stores on "The Corner," especially at night, could be a terrifying experience. Exposure to the negative behavior of students and others who were hanging out there was unavoidable if you wanted to walk downtown to visit friends in the black community, as I did from time to time. Any effort to avoid The Corner's crowd added distance and time to the walk. Eventually, I learned to ignore the comments, keep walking, and not look at the people there. That's not easy to do, and while I was learning how, there were some incidents.

---

[8]   This was written during the summer of 2008, prior to Obama being elected as President.

One major incident occurred because of my unwillingness to do silly things such as stepping off the sidewalk to let others pass. Several times, this resulted in words being exchanged, and more than once, harsh words were uttered and blows were exchanged.

Once it resulted in my damaging a young man's private parts with a well-placed field goal attempt that cured his belligerent actions, but not his attitude. Neither he nor his friends were aware that I ran track at Union, thus they were surprised when I won the race to safety, or vengeance from their perspective. I managed to get a ride back to Grounds later that night and avoided a rematch by doing so. Fortunately, our paths never crossed again, a fact that served me well. I believed that I was destined to lose any rematch.

I am not a fighter, but have fought. My pugilistic record, at and away from UVA, does not distinguish me and, therefore, doesn't merit further comment. Suffice it to say, despite more than one fight, I graduated on time with mental scars, but no physical scars. In truth, upon reflection, even the mental scars are gone.

As stated earlier, the black community in Charlottesville was the critical factor for my being able to endure my three years at law school. They were incredibly warm, friendly, and caring. They provided real southern hospitality at its finest—a meal, conversation, knowledge about Charlottesville and its people, and an important respite from stress. They provided a haven for me as well as for the three medical students and the handful of engineering students enrolled. Interaction with those other black students

JOHN F. MERCHANT

was fundamentally nonexistent and, at best, infrequent. No surprise there since we were separated by different locations, classrooms, and courses of study.

Engineering and medical school blacks had the advantage of others with whom to relate, compare notes, and get sustenance from. As you might imagine, the course work demanded our full attention in that environment. My search for normal outlets, when not in class or studying, did allow us to meet and talk on occasion. Their experiences were similar to mine, but they had each other on a daily basis, something I didn't have, but yearned for. "A consummation devoutly to be wished," to quote "Willy" Shakespeare.

By way of background, all black students mentioned here attended UVA as a result of an abysmal, albeit deliberate, failure on Virginia's part to provide the equal part of "separate but equal" within its own borders.

Virginia State College in Petersburg was the "separate but equal" higher education facility provided by the state for its "colored" population. It had no professional graduate schools, specifically no medical, engineering, or law schools. Instead, the state had a program wherein it would pay the cost for blacks to attend professional and graduate schools in other states if they could get admitted.

Many, driven as much by economics as any other reason, wisely took advantage of this "perk" and became doctors, lawyers, engineers, and teachers, who served, and serve, America well. Master's and PhD degrees were also obtained because of Virginia's largesse (?). Although these "perks" were reluctantly available, they also represented clear evidence that the separate was not equal, nor did the state ever intend it to be.

William and Mary has had a law school since 1866; Washington and Lee since 1779, and, UVA since 1819. None entered into the diversity arena until after it was established at UVA by me.

I could go on with further anecdotes and comments, but I won't. I will end this chapter with the surprise that made my UVA experience forever meaningful and involved what is one of the best days of my life.

My daughters[9] and I took a trip in 1987 to look at colleges and universities. Specifically, we visited Georgetown, the University of North Carolina, Duke, and UVA. Somehow, UVA learned that we were coming to visit and contacted me. A meeting was arranged with John Blackburn, the dean of admissions at UVA. Susan and Tabitha were given a grand tour and were seriously recruited by staff to apply and enroll at UVA.

Tabitha chose to apply and enroll. She earned an undergraduate degree from UVA. Susan, however, had her mind set on the University of Pennsylvania, where she earned a bachelor's of arts degree in 1991.

---

[9] I have one daughter, Susan, and a niece, Tabitha Carter, who has been my delightful "second daughter" since she was about five years old. Her Father is unknown to her; I am well known to her and have been her "father" almost all her life. Her 10-year-old son, Tyler, is considered by me to be my grandson and treated that way. He's my buddy.

After graduating from UPENN, Susan wanted to attend law school, and her choice was UVA. I first learned of her interest from Gerard Peterson, a longtime friend from Hartford, Connecticut, who had known Susan from birth and was one of the many friends with whom Susan discussed her interest in law school.

She and I had never discussed her interest in law. My relationship with Susan did not include telling her what she should be. My only advice along those lines was that she should pursue her interests without any pressure from me and would, when she felt the time was right, speak with me about them. Discussions of many subjects did take place, but none about her interest in the law.

She was accepted at UVA and received her JD degree in 1994.

At some point prior to graduation, a committee of her classmates invited me to deliver the commencement address at her graduation. The invitation was extended without Susan's knowledge and came as a complete surprise to both her and me.

I delivered that address at her graduation where she became the first child of a black graduate to receive a law degree from UVA.[10]

Yes, she created the first black legacy at the law school, a legacy that took thirty-six years to create, but Susan made it happen. That day, I was very proud of her, UVA, and her classmates who invited me to speak. It validated my three years there, erased many negatives from my mind,

---

[10] See entire speech in Appendix.

and set a stage for more to come regarding diversity at UVA. And more has come throughout the university.

That experience ranks with the best day anyone can have. I worked long and hard, preparing that speech. I did not want to embarrass Susan; I did want to make that day meaningful for her, her classmates, and others in attendance. I contacted others, including Governor Mario Cuomo (New York), for some ideas during the preparation. The governor had delivered the commencement address at a daughter's graduation.

I was never more nervous in my life than when it came time to speak. I have given many speeches during my life, but that one stands out for me and is memorable. Susan tells me that some of her classmates still remember, in 2011, some of what I said that memorable day.

Then, to add further significance to the day, a month or so later, I received a package in the mail that contained a videotape of the entire graduation ceremony. Yes, Betty Hollander, a dear friend in Connecticut, with whom I had shared membership on several committees down through the years, had the event professionally videotaped and delivered to me. I cannot watch the tape without shedding tears.

UVA, especially under the leadership of its president— John Casteen—and the commitment to diversity endorsed by John Blackburn—the dean of admissions—has achieved a level of diversity in its student body and faculty that is admirable. The levels achieved rank it at or near the top of America's colleges and universities.

JOHN F. MERCHANT

What really pleases me, in addition to my involvement in the 1950s, is that the effort is ongoing. It's good to know that I have been a part of something significant, worthwhile, and sorely needed, from inception. Admittedly, time and circumstance, not planning, made it possible, but so what?

— classmates all.

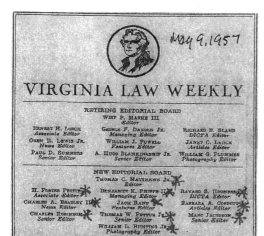
The Law Weekly is available to students on campus and mailed to law alumni across the country, including Virginia and other Southern states

It took courage and commitment to write the below story and editorial in 1957

I knew nothing about it until I read it.

Racial Discrimination . . .

The reasons given by Richmond's Director of Recreation and Parks, Jesse A. Reynolds, for transferring the Law School softball team from Byrd Park to Parker Field seem at first persuasive. Nevertheless we feel the move was unjustified, solely because the underlying cause was racial discrimination.

Two themes thread their way through the reasons advanced by Mr. Reynolds: preservation of the peace and prevention of the discontinuance of future tournaments. That the presence of a negro on an athletic team in Byrd Park could be thought a threat to the public peace is a sad comment on popular feeling. That future contests might be barred because a negro once participated is equally shocking.

If Mr. Reynolds' fears of the consequences that might stem from a negro's playing softball in Byrd Park are unjustified, the city official has made a grave error in a very sensitive area. If his fears are justified, the general public responsible for them is guilty of unreasoned prejudice. In either case the mere existence of this social canker of racism in Virginia today is both frightening and discouraging.

Negro's Presence Causes Transfer Of Softball Game

The Barristers, University softball champions of 1956, were not permitted to play a scheduled game on Byrd Park Field in Richmond Friday night because a negro law student was in the line-up.

At the order of Richmond city recreation officials, the game was transferred to Parker Field, another park owned by the city of Richmond, where the game with an all-star team from William and Mary was played off without incident. The Barristers lost 2 to 1 in extra innings.

Officially representing the University, the Law School softball team was in Richmond to play in

(Continued on Page 3)

Game Transferred . . .

(Continued from Page 1)

the Virginia Amateur Softball Association Tournament. After team members had entered the Byrd Park Field where their initial game was slated to take place, team manager Alan D. Grosecloss was told by tournament director Hank Wolfe that, on orders from an official in the Richmond City Government, the game would have to be played at Parker Field, another city-owned park, and home of the Richmond Virginians, International League team.

Jesse A. Reynolds, Director of Recreation and Parks for the City of Richmond, revealed Monday that he had given the order to remove the team to another park. He stated that the transfer was made as a policy matter and did not involve a city ordinance banning mixed athletic contests,

since Parker Field is also a city-owned diamond.

Mr. Reynolds noted also that the lighting at Parker field was better, in his opinion, and therefore the team was not required to use inferior facilities. The game was played entirely in the daylight without the use of artificial illumination.

Mr. Reynolds explained further that the inhabitants of the area around Byrd Park have been particularly vehement in their opposition to use of the facilities there by negroes. He feared that the presence of a negro on one of the teams participating in the tournament would have occasioned a demonstration by residents of the neighborhood. The city official went so far as to mention the possibility of a violent attempt to remove the negro player from the field by force.

In continuing his explanation, Mr. Reynolds remarked that an incident of this type might have occasioned a permanent ban on out-of-town teams from participating in such tournaments in the City of Richmond. "The tournaments have been highly successful in the past," commented Mr. Reynolds, "and we should like to see them continued."

Chapter 4

The United States Navy

JOINING THE NAVY was never a goal of mine. In fact, as a person who has negative buoyancy, meaning I sink and cannot float, doing so defies logic, but it happened in 1958. Simple economics dictated the decision to enlist.

For many years attending college and law school allowed me to defer being drafted into the army. As an aside, neither the army nor any military service ever made my list of goals. Sadly, the deferment lasted only until I completed law school and received my law degree.

During my third year at law school, as graduation neared, I realized that I would be drafted very soon after graduation. I was neither opposed to the draft nor unpatriotic. The problem related to the draft was that two years in the army, drawing a private's pay, would not allow me to pay off my law-school debts. That concerned me.

The apparent solution to the debt payment issue appeared one day when some of my classmates shared with me their plan to travel to Washington, DC and sign up for the US Navy's Officer Candidate School (OCS). After researching a naval officer's pay compared to that of an army private, I asked if I could go with them, and they said yes.

An officer's pay for three years would allow me to pay my debts in full. The commitment to three years on active duty, after four months at OCS, versus two years as a draftee, did not discourage me. I had no job interviews or offers from any law firm and could not be sure that a legal career awaited me. In truth, the road to finding any kind of employment was not visible.

I took the trip to DC and signed up. My orders were to report to OCS at Newport, Rhode Island, on August 18, 1958.

Now the problem was avoiding the draft board from graduation until August 18. I learned that if the Greenwich (Connecticut) Draft Board discovered that I was in town before August 18, they could draft me immediately and order me into the army for two years. I did not return to Greenwich.

Instead, I skirted Connecticut and went to Winchester, New Hampshire, and a summer job at the camps where I had worked for several summers, hoping no mail came from the draft board and asking Mom not to forward any mail from the draft Board to me. None came.

The camps were my refuge.

In 1952, George Twine of Greenwich hired me to work at the camps as a truck driver ferrying food, people, and other necessaries between the boys' and girls' camps that were located three to five miles apart. I spoke with George and explained that I had to report to Newport in August and could not spend the entire summer of 1958, working. He gave me a job assisting Gramps until I had to leave for Newport.

The job entailed chauffeuring Gramps around and helping him with whatever maintenance chores were needed at Camps Rabbit Hollow and Forest Lake. No compensation, just room and board sounded good to me; I accepted.

Gramps and I had become friends during the previous summers and were buddies. Under his tutelage, my maintenance skills improved, and I became proficient at obeying his orders, carrying his tools, excelling at gofer duties, and at performing various work requirements. I thoroughly enjoyed being in the company of Gramps.

Gramps was a 70-plus-year-old Spanish-American War veteran and a black man. He had supervised the building of both camps from their beginning in the 1940s and spent his summers at maintenance. Gramps knew carpentry, plumbing, electricity, and other skills needed to build the buildings needed at camp. Often, he was referred to as "Gramps the Grump," but not when he could hear you.

My favorite Gramps story that summer involved aiding and abetting him in violating the camp nurse's orders regarding his cigar smoking interests.

"Nursie," that's what we called her, was Gramps' age with a penchant for being obeyed immediately, without any discussion. She and Gramps had a running feud about a lot of things, a constant source of amusement to me and others. She served as Gramps' biggest annoyance, to hear him say it. Their skirmishes provided entertainment for many as she constantly nagged him about something, and he spent a lot of time grumbling as he walked away, hell bent on ignoring her. He rarely argued with her, just went on about his business.

Every Saturday morning, early, Gramps would tell me he had to do some errands in Keene and told me to get the pickup and drive him there, about eight to ten miles away. Upon arrival, we would go to the diner and have breakfast. He insisted on paying. After breakfast, we would head for a bench on Main Street, reputed to be the widest Main Street in the world. Actually, he would head for a bench after giving me some money to go and purchase three cigars; two for him and one for me. He strongly urged me to learn to enjoy cigars.

Then, we'd sit on the bench and smoke cigars. Seemingly, everyone in Keene knew Gramps and stopped by to chat for a moment or just say hello and ask about the camps. We stayed until Gramps had smoked both cigars, then, headed back to Camp Forest Lake.

The first time this happened, Gramps swore me to secrecy about his cigar smoking, saying, "I bought you breakfast, and in return, you must promise not to ever tell Nursie that I smoked these cigars. Never." I agreed, but really had no choice in the matter. I never told Nursie or anyone until now.

The boys camp, Rabbit Hollow, was the original of the two camps. In the 1940s, a man gave five hundred acres in Winchester, New Hampshire to the Church of the Master in New York City. The idea was to build a camp for young black males living in the city, thereby exposing them to a new experience in the country.

The New York newspapers had been covering the growing rise of gangs and gang activity in the city and the gift was an effort to provide an experience outside of the city for gang members and potential members that might expose them to options in life.

JOHN F. MERCHANT

Under Gramps' supervision, a portion of the five hundred acres of forest land was cleared to build cabins, a camp office building, an arts and crafts shop, a mess hall, a kitchen sufficient to accommodate in excess of hundred young people of ages ten to sixteen, and meet total staff needs. Fresh water was piped into the camp from streams. Sewage requirements were met in accordance with existing building codes. A stream on which a dam was built provided a swimming hole, the water in which was "colder than a Landlord's heart."

The camper population changed every two weeks. Counselors were hired from the city as well as from the numerous colleges and universities for which New England is noted. Many college students were unpaid volunteers.

It was an ethnically diverse staff in every respect. It exposed me to young college students and helped teach me how, in America, if we worked together, problems could be confronted, understood, and resolved or at least addressed with the love and caring required to enhance understanding and, hopefully, convince young people that they had options in life.

Those colleges had also provided students who joined the labor pool needed to construct the camp buildings under Gramps' supervision. Most of the college students volunteered their time and did a remarkable job as "construction" volunteers, followed by an even better job as full-time counselors during the summer.

I spent two summers as a truck driver, then, I was told that I could not return unless I did so as a unit leader of one age grouping. I was paid $300 that first summer, a sum that was at the high end of the wage scale. One year as a unit leader led to becoming head counselor for three years, then Gramps' gofer.

On reflection, I am indebted to George Twine for providing me with this opportunity to mature. Working the camps was memorable.

I reported to Newport on time as a part of Class 40 and was assigned to one of the twenty-man units as a seaman recruit. Seventeen weeks, five days, and 12.5 hours later, I left OCS as a newly commissioned ensign.

All new recruits were subjected to a battery of aptitude tests consistent with the courses to be studied for four months. The curriculum roughly paralleled that of the naval academy at Annapolis with one month covering subjects taught at the academy for a year, hence a four-month program.

We were told that if we flunked out of OCS, we would be sent to Great Lakes Naval Training Center and required to serve two years on active duty as seamen with the same pay as an army private. An officer counseled each of us after the results of the aptitude tests were received.

At orientation, we were told that the OCS curriculum included engineering, and I shuddered at the news. The engineering study guide was not helpful. Do you know how many years went into ". . . developing a multi-stage, horizontal, velocity-pressured compound impulse stream turbine?" I don't. What the hell is that anyway? We were expected to learn the answer in six days.

My problem is simple to understand. My counselor had advised me that my score on the engineering aptitude test indicated that I had no aptitude in that area, or very little. I was advised not to try to understand anything taught in the engineering courses. My only chance to avoid flunking out was to simply memorize what I could and put that memory to work on the exams.

I followed that advice and survived, never knowing or understanding why a ship floats and I can't; how a ship's power plant propelled it through the waters; how fresh water was made from sea water; or, anything related to anything mechanical on land or at sea. I also never truly grasped the study guides instructions to "know the interior and exterior fittings of the M, DE, D, A and O type boilers." Say what?

We endured a three-day history of atomic energy that must have Linus Pauling breathless and befuddled as it did me. Admittedly, that three days was easier to take than understanding jubilee clamps that helped one to know the "height of metacenter vs. metacentric height and the angle of maximum righting arm vs. the maximum angle of righting arm." Huh?

Yes, surviving engineering was a close call but my memory and the advice given me by my counselor saved the day.

Other curriculum beauties included navigation (where I learned to run aground in downtown Waikiki), operations (where we were dealt seventy-six cards of flags and pennants to memorize cold), orientation (easier stuff to absorb if one could take time away from navigation and engineering to study it), and seamanship (where the jargon of the sea was handed us to learn.)

We learned that a rope is a line and that the Rules of the Road were important. Lights carried by ships meant something and must be remembered. For example, red over white meant fishing at night. Weapons were studied and words such as, servos, synchros, amplidynes, and breech blocks became part of one's vocabulary, although not always fully understood.

There is more, but suffice to say, I made it. Not everyone did.

My twenty-man section consisted of me, one man from Philadelphia, and eight men from Kentucky and states south of it. The section leader was a first-class bigot and singled me out for more negative treatment than I deserved. Because of that treatment, I promised myself that, after receiving my commission, if I ever ran across that jerk in life, I would nail him with a right hand that he would remember all his life, just as I remember his treatment of me. I never saw him again.

OCS was interesting, tough, intense, and, usually, very military. I do remember one particular unmilitary-like event I had a part in. After lunch, we had a class in operations that was not very exciting to me and so, with a belly full of food, I would frequently nod off in class and not hear everything that was being said.

If the instructor called on you to answer a question, the proper procedure was to stand, say Officer Candidate (your name) Merchant, sir, then answer the question.

One day, I had dozed off but heard my name called, so I stood up and said, Officer Candidate Merchant, sir. However, I had not heard the question, so couldn't provide the answer. Instead, for reasons unknown to me, I started reciting Lincoln's Gettysburg address which amused everyone, including, thankfully, the instructor. He laughed, told me to sit down before I finished with Lincoln, and made some comment about staying alert. I sat down.

This became a ritual any and every time I dozed in his class, which was often. He, seemingly, never failed to notice when I dozed and called on me, at which time I would recite whatever came to mind. After a while, everyone, including the instructor, wondered what I would recite next. Among my selections were: Shakespeare's "To be or not to be"; "Give thy thoughts no tongue," "Casey at the Bat," "Sea Fever" by Masefield, along with many others that came to mind.

Comic relief had come to operations; thanks to an instructor with an admirable sense of humor and a tired recruit who dozed after lunch.

During my four months at OCS, I saw only one other black officer candidate. He was not in my section, and I never got to know him well. There was little or no time to socialize because of the pressures to perform and avoid being sent to Great Lakes Naval Training Center for two years as a seaman.

The pressures affected everyone. Fridays, after supper, when we had free time to go to the gym for a couple of hours, the pressures surfaced. Many of us used that time to play some basketball, during which we took out our frustrations on each other. No fights, because that could get you bounced out of OCS, but there were a lot of "damn nears."

At some point, each officer candidate was asked to list and submit three duty assignments he would like to receive after being commissioned. My first choice was to serve as legal officer on a big ship, with its homeport in California. Surprisingly, my first choice was granted.

To prepare for the assignment, I was ordered to attend Naval Justice School in Newport for two months to study the Uniform Code of Military Justice. Then my orders were to report for duty aboard the USS Bremerton (CA-130), a heavy cruiser home ported in Long Beach, California.

Those orders were the beginning of a real adventure where the recruiting call, "Join the navy and see the world" took on real meaning. I was excited and pleased.

After Justice School, I was sent to Treasure Island, outside of San Francisco, where a plane would fly me to meet my ship. It was at sea somewhere in the Western Pacific on what is called a WestPac cruise.

I owned a car and drove it to California. Another newly commissioned officer with orders to Treasure Island joined me for the trip. We were on per diem and had ten days to travel across country, more than enough time to relax and enjoy the wonders of a large body of land called America, a journey of approximately three thousand miles. We took full advantage of the time we had.

I remember it as a vacation trip across America. We took time to stop and visit many places of interest in America as we drove across the country, mostly on I-80 and I-90, the northern route. The trip took us through sixteen states, including Rhode Island, Massachusetts,

New York, Pennsylvania, Ohio, Indiana, Illinois, Wisconsin, Iowa, Nebraska, Wyoming, Idaho, Colorado, Utah, Nevada, and California. What an experience!

The trip was a much-needed breather after three years in a "foreign country" at the University of Virginia and four months with 90 percent southerners in my twenty-person unit at OCS. Happily the fellow officer traveling with me lacked a bigoted bone in his body. We became friends and made wise use of the per-diem pay we received to relax, live well, and visit places of interest.

We took time to see the Amish country in Pennsylvania, the Midwest and its big cities, Chicago, Cleveland, and Detroit, for example. We took a side trip up to Yellowstone National, then dipped down into Idaho before heading to Salt Lake City, Utah, and the desert there. We tested the gambling palaces located in the then "Divorce Capital of the World," Reno, Nevada, saw Lake Tahoe, and then drove to Treasure Island in California.

The trip gave me a real appreciation for the real estate comprising our country. I recommend it for those who have not taken the time to see this country. Europe is fine and has its attractions; however, America's real estate is a "wonder to behold," especially if one has the time to spend without rushing as we did.

Treasure Island personnel assigned me to a military flight that allowed me to spend four days exploring San Francisco. I eagerly boarded the flight on time. I needed the rest after four days in Frisco.

To get to my ship, I had to endure the following: a weekend in Hawaii, one day on Guam, two days on Okinawa, three days in the Philippine Islands, and thence to Yokosuka, Japan.

The first leg of the trip was to Hawaii on a four-engine, propeller-driven plane, a seven-hour flight as I recall. The plane was crowded with enlisted men and their families; I was the only officer aside from the crew. Our flight was delayed overnight for mechanical reasons, or so we were told. Finally, we were airborne the next morning.

After a couple of hours in the air, while observing the fascinating cloud formations outside my window, I noticed that only one of the two engines on my side of the plane was functioning. I contacted the air force stewardess and asked her to report the engine failure to the captain. She smiled and said that the captain was aware of the failure and urged me not to worry.

Less than an hour later, she returned to my seat and told me that the captain wanted to speak with me in the cockpit. In my entire life, I had never been in the cockpit of a large plane in flight. Additionally, while I had thought about it from time to time, I had never had a flying lesson. Could this be a first for me? I doubted it since the copilot was available.

This fact caused me to wonder about the clear invitation to join the captain in the cockpit, wouldn't you?

Anyway, I followed her there and spoke with the captain. He told me that he needed my help because of engine failure. I recited my earlier conversation with the stewardess about the failure. He then informed me that another engine had failed, on the other side of the plane, and since we had not yet reached the point of no return, he was turning the plane around and returning to California, on two engines! He needed my help, or so he said.

That concerned me. Nervously, I asked what he expected me to do. Both he and the copilot appeared healthy and of sound mind and body, so I sensed he wouldn't ask me to fly the plane. He didn't; I was pleased.

Instead he said that he wanted my help in keeping the passengers calm after he announced the return. I guess he thought an "officer," any officer, could handle that assignment. After agreeing to help, I looked him in the eye and asked one simple question, namely, "Captain, who have you assigned to keep me calm during the return?" He laughed; I didn't see anything funny.

We returned without further incident, and the first thing I did was get out of the plane, go to the tail of the plane, and copy down the numbers written there. Then I went directly to the office that handled naval personnel assigned to a military flight and asked what would happen if a newly commissioned officer refused to board a flight as ordered. He told me he didn't know the answer since that had never happened to him.

I suggested that he look up the rules that pertained, and I would ask again later. I told him that if I was ordered aboard a plane numbered as the one I had written down on a piece of paper I showed him, I would refuse to get aboard it. He laughed after I told him about the overnight delay and two engine failures. I didn't laugh because no jokes had been uttered.

In fact, they rolled out another plane the next day, and we traveled on, as ordered, without further incident.

After a long weekend in Hawaii where, among other things, I experienced the potency of an alcoholic drink called a Mai Tai, delicious and inexpensive at the Officers Club. Also, the plane's captain came in for dinner, and I had a chance to speak with him about our adventure, learning that they would worry only if we got down to a single engine. "Two engines," he said, "are a piece of cake as long as one is patient and accepts the reduced speed that is inevitable." I guess I felt better, though I realized that a similar plane was needed to get to Japan, a long way to go for someone like me who lacked full confidence in the engines powering whatever plane was assigned.

The remainder of the trip involved a few stops in places like Guam and Okinawa, places I had heard about growing up during World War II. That was pretty exciting for me. Goony birds really do exist on Guam. They are all over the place like white on rice.

Upon arrival in Yokosuka, Japan, I was told that I was scheduled on a flight nine days later. I asked the officer what I was supposed to do for nine days and was told that no one cared, just please don't miss the flight. He commented on the amount of paperwork he would need to fill out if I did miss the flight. I laughed this time.

I used the time to spend three days in Tokyo and three days at a wonderful resort not far from Tokyo, events financed primarily by the per-diem pay I was receiving. I caught my flight.

That flight went to Okinawa for a long weekend, then, continued on to Hong Kong to meet my ship. It arrived there the same day I flew in. A small boat took me out to my ship, the USS *Bremerton (CA-130)*, anchored in Hong Kong Harbor. During the boat trip, I seriously practiced the routine required to board the ship. It involved climbing the ship's gangplank, turning toward and saluting the ensign (American flag) mounted on the stern, then facing and saluting the officer of the deck (OOD) as I requested permission to come aboard. I performed those tasks smartly and was allowed aboard.

On the quarter deck, along with the OOD, stood four of the ship's senior officers, including the operations officer, the navigator, the engineering officer, and the gun boss. No, it was not a welcoming committee.

In fact, I noticed that all four seemed to be in a state of shock as we were being introduced and wondered why?

They escorted me down to the wardroom where we sat, drank coffee, and talked for about two hours before they had someone show me to my stateroom. There I met the officers with whom I was to share the stateroom, both nice guys. It turned out that they were two of only three Jewish officers on the ship; the executive officer was the other.

If there were more than three, I don't recall. I learned later that the two-hour social chat I had in the wardroom provided enough time for stateroom assignments to be changed to allow minorities to be together.

Senior officers never spent that much time with lower ranking officers, especially the newest and lowest-ranked officer. Welcome aboard!

I now had a better understanding of the shocked looks on the faces of the four senior officers I had met on the quarter deck. An even fuller understanding came later.

The ship's crew included more than one thousand men and officers. There were seventy-two officers among the crew, all of them senior to me and none of them black. I was "George," a synonym for the lowest ranking officer aboard. I provided the missing diversity to the officer contingent.

Welcome aboard!

The story behind the shocked expressions was that no one had any inkling that a black officer was coming aboard to serve as the ship's legal officer. It seems that the intake officer in Washington DC had been careless and had inserted the term "*Cauc.*" in the block marked "*race*" on the intake records. His mistake was apparently induced by the fact that a light-complexioned black male—me—was signing up with four Caucasians, and he didn't look carefully enough to distinguish us. I served more than a year before learning of the mistake and had it corrected.

Welcome aboard!

The navy was not big on black officers; the marines were worse and the air force deserved few plaudits, though the Tuskegee Airmen became their saving grace; something they bragged about as indicative of their interest in diversity. What a joke!

During my three years on active duty, I saw only four other black naval officers, including one who broke ground repeatedly during his thirty-eight-year career. I refer to Admiral Samuel L. Gravely, who became the navy's first black admiral in 1971.

He became the first black to command a fighting ship in the US Navy when he was named captain of the USS *Falgout (DER-324)*, a destroyer that patrolled the so-called

Pacific Barrier located between the Aleutians and Midway Island for four years under his command. Subsequently, he commanded the USS *Jouett (CG-29)*, a guided missile frigate that cruised the coast of Vietnam. Then in 1971, while commander of the Jouett, he was promoted to rear admiral, becoming the US Navy's first black admiral.

In 1976, he was appointed by President Gerald R. Ford to the rank of vice admiral and was put in charge of the Navy's Third Fleet comprised of one hundred warships and sixty thousand sailors and marines based in Pearl Harbor. He retired in 1980 and died in 1982.

I didn't know the man personally but have felt enormous pride since first becoming aware of him. That pride had two sources: his achievements during his career and the fact he was a product of Virginia Union University in Richmond, Virginia, my alma mater. He, like many others, is clear evidence of the value of the historical black colleges.

I assumed my duties as legal officer and was given an office with a small staff, including Smitty, a superb yeoman who was a big help to me. The EX division that I was part of was under the leadership of a lieutenant whose ego superseded his sense of humanity and who was neither friendly to, nor respectful of, me. A détente was created after the following occurred

My duties included working with the Executive Officer, preparing charges to be handled by the Captain involving minor offenses committed by crew members. My job was to investigate the incidents and draft proper charges under the UCMJ for the accused's appearance at Captain's Mast. There, punishments were handed out by the Captain for minor violations and the more serious charges were recommended for a special court martial or a general court martial, as the charges merited.

My advice was important, welcomed, and accepted 95 percent of the time.

In addition to my legal officer duties, I also stood regular watches in engineering, the combat information center (CIC), and on the bridge. I was not a JAG officer since I had not passed or taken a bar exam. Thus, I was just another junior officer, among many, with watch-standing duties.

Actually, I only stood one engineering watch because it was not hard to discover that I had no business being in charge of anything to do with the ship's power plant or other mechanical devices. I was pleased; it was hot down there.

Early on, Smitty advised me about two issues of significance: the sale of whiskey at sea and the loan shark lending $5 and charging $1 per week for the loan, both serious UCMJ offenses. He privately shared the name of the leader of each with me.

After compiling critical evidence, I met privately with each of the two men involved and told each of them that they were going to jail if: (1) any sailor was caught drinking on watch or was found to be inebriated, and (2) any sailor was abused for late payment of a loan. I told them that I would take no further action if neither of the items noted occurred, although others might.

In return, if there was an incident of any kind involving misconduct under the UCMJ requiring an appearance at

Captain's Mast, they were to provide me with the evidence needed for conviction if and when I requested it. Failure to do what I asked would result in their appearance before a court martial board for selling and lending; no exceptions. They steadfastly honored this agreement, so did I.

The Executive Officer and I met frequently, almost daily, to screen the matters for Captain's Mast. He never could figure out how I was able to continuously provide the evidence needed for convictions and guilty pleas at Captain's Mast or at a special court martial. I never told him about the deal I had made.

However, he learned to rely on me, making his job easier. In time, he began to accept my recommendations for punishment and so did the Captain. Quietly, I became the key to the handling of crime and punishment aboard ship as it related to relatively minor UCMJ violations that did not require a court martial.

More importantly, I was well respected by the Exec and the Captain, a fact that eased the pain inflicted by some shipmate's attitudes and the feeling of "not belonging" that life aboard ship involved. I got along well with many of the officers and not well at all with others, including my division officer and the lieutenant who prepared the watch-duty lists and assignments for the ship.

The latter officer had a bad habit of assigning me to more mid-watches than other junior officers. Watches were scheduled at four-hour intervals starting at 8:00 a.m. through the twenty-four-hour cycle. Hence, a mid watch lasted from midnight until 4:00 a.m., meaning a disruption in sleeping routines and negatively affecting the body's search for regularity in setting its clock. It was unfair and he knew it, but would not listen to reason. Fortunately, that did get straightened out.

After leaving Hong Kong, we sailed to Yokosuka, Japan, where we stayed for twenty-one days. One night, I was in a bar drinking more than I should and needed to use the bathroom. I walked down a hallway and opened a door that I thought was the bathroom door. In the room was the lieutenant in bed with another person. He should have locked the door.

He recognized me; I swiftly apologized for interrupting him, closed the door, and left.

As luck would have it, the lieutenant's wife had filed for divorce back in the United States, and as the Legal Officer, I was made fully aware of that situation, and he knew it. It was not common knowledge aboard ship.

Suffice to say, after that, without further discussion, I received only my fair share of mid-watches.

My division officer was a different story. He and I had a run-in related to Smitty, my yeoman. The Exec needed something involving my office typed up and presented to him for the Captain, and Smitty was doing it. Our office phone rang, and Smitty answered it, hung up, and told me he had to stop what he was doing to go to the division officer's stateroom to take some dictation. He said he would finish typing when he returned. I told him to stay put, then called the lieutenant to explain that the Exec needed what Smitty was working on, and I would send him to his stateroom when it was finished. His reaction was immediate and negative, and the argument started.

During the argument, he used words and phrases that did not seem appropriate to me; in fact, they were insulting as well as inappropriate. I guess he felt that his seniority gave him the right to say whatever he wanted, in whatever tone of voice he chose, using words not admired in polite company. I found it insulting, especially since, when he finished his tirade, he ordered me to release Smitty immediately, then hung up.

Again I told Smitty to stay put, and I went to the lieutenant's stateroom, knocked on his door, and was greeted by my division head dressed in his pajamas and bathrobe. I told him that God hasn't made the man who could talk to me as he had just done nor was I prepared to risk criticism from the Exec for nonperformance of his orders to me. I suggested that, at his option, he could kick my butt right there, or we could meet somewhere away from the ship and settle our differences privately. He had crossed the line.

He declined both options; Smitty finished my work; then, he attended to the lieutenant's presumed needs.

Clearly, I would never have related well to General Patton.

It appeared that a reasonable truce had been reached, and I never had any other issues with the lieutenant, although we never did become buddies.

After leaving Japan, we became part of an exercise at sea that was scheduled to last for two weeks. We were part of a task force in the South China Sea that included an aircraft carrier, four or five screening destroyers, and our heavy cruiser.

One night, when I had the mid-watch on the bridge, we were caught in thirty-foot seas that put the task force at risk. Our 17,500 ton ship was averaging 45-degree rolls; the carrier was averaging 15-degree rolls, and the destroyers were getting close to their righting arm limits, 60- to 65-degree rolls.

Righting arm limits are those where a ship will not recover its stability and can capsize, then vanish into the sea. Thirty-foot seas represent walls of water on each side of the trough the ship is sailing in or about four or more stories high. That's a lot of water in the daytime; this occurred at night! Also, the bridge where I was standing watch was at least eight stories above ground, or sea level, making 45×2, 90-degree rolls—an interesting and exciting, albeit dangerous, experience to endure.

The admiral aboard the carrier was the officer in tactical control (OTC) and would not change course, despite being made aware of the situation. Hell, he was comfortable and tough guys found a way to endure, didn't they?

Personally, I was simply scared and thought he was a first-class jerk. I was concerned enough to wake the Captain who came to the bridge, stayed a few minutes, then returned to his cabin. He appeared nervous as well, an amusing tidbit! But, until the OTC acted, there was nothing he could do except maintain course and speed. So we endured until word was passed that the walls of water had smashed the door to the laundry located on a destroyer's main deck and swept a sailor overboard. The carrier launched a helicopter to look for the sailor. They found and rescued him.

JOHN F. MERCHANT

Miraculously, as he was being swept overboard, a life raft attached to the bulkhead near the laundry door was also dislodged. The sailor was bumped by the life raft, managed to grab onto it, crawled aboard, and was picked up by the helicopter as he was attempting to use the first aid package the life raft contained. He was taken to the hospital on the carrier where, I was told, in excess of one hundred stitches were needed to close up his injuries.

Shortly thereafter, the admiral ordered a course change that was no less stressful, but safer in those seas. I was pleased when my watch ended, but not wild about trying to sleep below decks.

Eventually, at daylight, better weather arrived, and we continued the exercise. It included the carrier practicing aborted landings and takeoffs. I thought it was pretty interesting, even exciting, stuff.

One entire bridge watch, from noon to 4:00 p.m., was spent following the carrier all over the South China Sea as it conducted air operations. My orders were to follow the carrier wherever it went but not to close it less than one knot's distance. The carrier kept changing course to pick up favorable winds, and I had to order the course changes necessary to obey my orders.

That was fun; I can hear myself now, "Left standard rudder, come left to new course 187. Steady as she goes! Reduce speed to twelve knots"; all answered with an, "Aye, aye, sir."

Needless to say, a more experienced officer was looking over my shoulder to ensure that safety concerns came first and that the orders were strictly obeyed. I didn't mind being supervised considering what was at stake. And, in truth, I was not the most experienced or reliable ship handler we had aboard. I felt like a kid with a new toy but was aware of the seriousness of the assignment. I was also pleased and proud that I was trusted to handle the assignment.

It was a thrill just to spend hours ordering course changes for my ship, a 17,500 ton vessel crewed by a thousand men and officers, in a seemingly endless stretch of water, with nothing to do but follow the carrier and watch it practice certain aspects of its war mission, namely launching and recovering its aircraft and practicing aborted landings. It was an impressive performance.

We completed the two-week exercise without further incident and soon returned to our home port at Long Beach, California.

We embarked on another WestPac cruise in October 1959 that lasted four months, returning in February 1960. During this cruise, we revisited places we had been: Japan, Hong Kong, the Philippine Islands, Guam, and Okinawa. We sailed down "The Slot" at Guadalcanal and represented the US Navy at the Coral Sea celebration in Australia.

Students of World War II will recall the Battle of the Coral Sea as an historical sea battle involving Japan against combined forces of the US and Australia, where neither side ever sighted the other and all damage was inflicted by air strikes. Australian folklore has it that the Coral Sea battle prevented Australia from being invaded by the Japanese; hence the battle was celebrated each year by a grateful nation.

JOHN F. MERCHANT

The USS Bremerton (CA-130) was selected to represent the US Navy at the 1959 Coral Sea celebration. Thus, we sailed to Australia and spent time in both Sydney and Brisbane. It was an interesting time.

To get there, we had to sail across the International Date Line (IDL), an event that prompted a ritual involving all hands aboard. Those who had never crossed the IDL were known as "pollywogs"; those who had crossed it had evidence of that fact in their permanent personnel file, the acceptable evidence to avoid the ritual. Those who claimed exemption from the ritual, but lacked personnel file evidence, had messages sent to the Bureau of Naval Personnel in Washington DC, requesting a message back verifying their claim. Woe be unto him who made the claim but got a negative response from BuPers.

The ritual? A week or two preceding the IDL "crossing," sailors sewed together canvas that stretched almost the entire length of the ship, 976 feet, or three football fields. Several canvasses were sewn together forming a series of tunnels with a trough, leaving space on the open deck between them.

Then, rather than dumping wet garbage into the sea, it was saved and dumped in the sewn canvas tunnels, rising to heights of as much as two feet.

Next, the IDL vets spent days and weeks making "shillelaghs" from canvas pieces sewn together and made hard by being soaked in salt water, effectively making a weapon for use as a paddle during the ritual.

On the day of the crossing, pollywogs were gathered in the bow of the ship, facing the canvas full of wet garbage and told to crawl through the canvas and garbage until you reached the ship's stern. Rate or rank did not matter; you either had proven that you were an IDL vet or you lined up on your knees and started the "long crawl." High-ranking officers and enlisted men were treated equally during the "long crawl"; no exceptions. Then, one at a time, the crawl started.

In front of me, men gagged and threw up in the canvas, causing additional issues for those behind them. Men also fell, causing delays and slowdowns that lengthened the "crawl." When approaching areas where the deck was clear, still on one's knees and crawling, it was possible to breathe fresh air for a bit before crawling into the next canvas. A welcome relief and needed respite? Not hardly!

Unfortunately, the open space contained lineups of the IDL vets, on both sides, armed with shillelaghs that were used to whack you on the butt as hard as one wished. Again, men fell, though some crawled faster in an effort to get into the comparative safety of the wet garbage canvas and crawls without an "ass whipping." This continued until the stern was reached by all.

My knees still hurt when I think of the "long crawl."

The experience allowed me to attach a new definition to the word happiness. Simply stated, happiness is reaching the stern alive, breathing fresh air, and knowing that the "ass whippings" were over; I'm a witness.

After getting cleaned up, it was back to business as usual for the ship for all hands, except the dentist, a lieutenant commander, who, rather than face the ordeal, had hidden somewhere on the ship and failed to show.

JOHN F. MERCHANT

To his everlasting regret, attendance had been taken, and no one answered "here" when his name was called.

The Captain ordered all available hands to conduct a search throughout the ship and "Find the lieutenant commander and bring him to me." He was found, thence escorted under guard to the Captain who ordered him to the start of the garbage filled canvas in the bow. He was then ordered to participate alone in the garbage crawl and maneuver his way through the "ass whipping" brigade until he reached the stern. He did that.

As vets, we were allowed to watch his solo act, although we did not have any weapons; a good thing for him. Some were really upset over what he had tried to do, although not many looked forward to having a toothache and giving him a "get even" venue. On to Australia.

Australia, I was told, probably had the worst immigration laws and policies of any nation in the world at that time. People of color were simply not welcome or wanted there. Hearing this, I spoke with the Exec who had the chore of providing an officer at each of the endless social events we were invited to. My plea to him to be exempt from attendance went unheeded.

I told him about my problems aboard ship with a few of the officers. I told him that it was not likely that any women of color would be in attendance at the social events, although females would. I mentioned that in the unlikely event that a female "took a shine" to Mrs. Merchant's only son I did not think I would resist and ignore any apparent interest. That could create even more problems for me on-board.

He looked me in the eye and said, "As long as the gold on your shoulders is the same as the gold on mine, you will follow my orders. And if someone has a problem with that, they will have to deal with me."

I listened and liked his attitude and approach, but being the one who might have to endure the problems until help arrived, I was very unhappy and somewhat depressed by his words.

Admittedly, his commitment brought a level of comfort until I remembered that police help rarely appeared until *after* an incident occurs. Thus any help from the Exec would come after I had endured whatever incident arose, if one did.

It might help you—the reader—to understand better if you keep in mind that this situation was confronting me after three years in UVA's lion's den, four months in an OCS unit surrounded by southerners and their negative attitudes, followed by a change of staterooms that put me together with two other minorities, and the incident with my division officer, where violence was only narrowly prevented.

Yes, I recalled that my dad had taught me that we are always in charge of our attitude. However, en route to Australia, I felt alone and very concerned about what lay ahead. I struggled to be strong and positive.

Upon arrival in Sydney, I had liberty and, still depressed, went ashore and wandered through an area in Sydney with stores, pubs, and people. As I passed one pub, I was hailed by a chief petty officer (CPO) from the ship who was in the pub with some Australians drinking. He invited me in and introduced me to his new buddies. A drink struck me as a good idea, so I ordered one, then another.

Ultimately, one of the Australian drinking buddies invited me and the CPO to his home for dinner, without telling his wife. We accepted and were pleased when his wife welcomed us as she cheerfully threw a couple more potatoes in the pot. The surprise came when we sat down to eat. Their daughter joined us at the table, a good-looking woman, my age, and very personable.

During the meal, the Aussie gave his daughter the keys to one of the family cars and instructed her to be a tour guide for me during my time in Sydney and to be sure that I saw the city of Sydney and enjoyed my time there. I was convinced that he had been drinking . . . too much and too long. I said to myself, "Damn!"

Now, I had a date and a companion and an advantage over all the other young officers that I did not seek. I converted my attitude from one of depression to one of trying to back out, then to *c'est la* "cotton picking" *vie.*

I told them of my social commitments, imposed by the Exec, but they just said, "Take her with you. She cleans up well and will enjoy the party."

I told them that I was the player coach for the ship's basketball team, and we were scheduled to play the Australian Olympic team in front of a lot of people. "Take her with you," was their response, so I did. *C'est* what?

She may have been the only Australian rooting for us in front of a large crowd at the game. The Australians beat our butt something awful, playing international rules with which we were unfamiliar. In any event, we got beat and beat up, although Lieutenant J.G. Harvey Schneider and I each scored nineteen points.

Our reward for bravery was to sit with the Aussies after the game and learn just how much beer and ale they could quaff, more than either me or Harvey or Mary, combined, for sure. We made some friends.

Mary joined me during my social appearances, toured Sydney with me, took me to the beach, and made my stay there very pleasant. Happily, there were no incidents that arose during that stay or afterwards with my shipmates. C'est la vie.

From Sydney, we sailed to Brisbane where we spent seven days, then returned to Long Beach, California, our home port, where we learned that our ship was scheduled to be decommissioned and retired from service. Technology had passed it by, and it was incapable of performing any meaningful military mission.

We had left Long Beach, California, on October 20, 1959, and returned on February 10, 1960, almost four months. Some statistics from that WestPac cruise may provide some insight regarding the size of our defense budget. During that four months' cruise: we sailed 42,082 miles, spent 70.5 days at sea, and consumed 1,877,392 gallons of fuel oil, almost forty-five miles per gallon, not bad for a vessel carrying 1,073 men and displacing 17,500 tons (19,000 tons when loaded for war).

Good thing the government paid less than the $3.00 per gallon for fuel oil that we often pay now as citizen consumers during a summer vacation trip. At $3 per gallon, the fuel oil cost alone would be $5,632,176.00.

Amazing! It can make one wonder about the cost of sending an aircraft carrier to a trouble spot somewhere in the world. We have done that often, as you probably know.

Prior to being decommissioned and taken out of service, the Bremerton made one last cruise, visiting ports on the West Coast including San Francisco, Portland, Oregon, and, Bremerton, Washington, the home of the Puget Sound Naval Yard and the city our ship was named after.

Bremerton's crew included seventy-three commissioned officers. All received orders to new duty stations when our ship was decommissioned. Seventy-two officers received orders to sea duty aboard other ships, or so I was told. One officer, *me*, received new orders to *shore duty* on the staff of the Commander in Chief Pacific Fleet (CINCPACFLT) in Pearl Harbor, Hawaii.

I recall being awakened one morning by the navigator, one of the ship's senior officers. He was shaking my bunk, excitedly shouting, "You're going to Hawaii, you're going to Hawaii . . . ," over and over again. It was the first time since the wardroom discussion that he had ever spoken to me like a real human being and not a subservient.

He was right; that's where my new orders sent me. My new job was as a communications officer doing shift work along with two other officers and several enlisted men. We were located in the basement of a four-story building, maybe only three stories, I don't remember. It lacked an elevator.

Lieutenant John Richardson was the officer in charge of my shift and a five-handicap golfer. He also stood 6' 4" tall and weighed in at two hundred plus pounds. Ensign

Tom L'Esperance was the other officer in our crew; he was a good tennis player, not great but good. Tom was "George."

The absence of an elevator is important only because of the system for identifying the importance and urgency of certain message traffic. Certain messages had to be hand carried from the basement to the top floor as quickly as possible. "George" usually got that assignment, but not always.

One night, an enlisted man told Lieutenant Richardson that a message was coming in with a priority heading that, given the information we had, signified that *war was imminent*. Lieutenant Richardson assigned me the task of personally delivering the message to CINCPAC's officer in charge on the top floor. I was ordered to ". . . run it up there . . ." to the top floor from the basement. A lot of stairs, but I managed and delivered the message.

It turned out that the urgency importance heading had more than one meaning, the second meaning known only to the intelligence people and not to us lowlifes. The second meaning was to the effect that a nuclear weapon had dislodged from a plane into the ocean and marked the exact coordinates where the weapon fell. The message was coded, and we could not read the codes, obviously, so I ran up the stairs and delivered the message, relying on my experience running track at Virginia Union to do so in a speedy fashion. I do remember thinking, "Please, not a war announcement on my watch," and "please don't stumble or twist an ankle getting to the top floor."

JOHN F. MERCHANT

It is true that all's well that ends well. We laughed about it later.

When you worked shifts, you hung out with those who worked with you. I wound up playing a lot of tennis with Tom and could beat him regularly until we reached the finals of the CINCPACFLT Championship when he beat me in a close match, but he beat me.

I was introduced to golf by John, a five handicap out of Burlingame, California. That experience is covered in Chapter 9 entitled "Rebel Yell."

Suffice to say, my lifelong love affair with "The Game" started with playing golf with John at the Navy-Marine course located less than a five-minute drive from my two room suite in the Bachelor Officer Quarters (BOQ) at Pearl Harbor. The tennis courts were about a five-minute walk from that room, and we could walk another three minutes to work.

John and I became good friends. He was intrigued by the fact that he now had a black friend on an island where people of a variety of colors and ethnic roots outnumbered the "*haole*" population by a lot. Not many did, still don't and vice versa. Sad, isn't it? *Haole* is the Hawaiian word for "strangers," usually meaning Caucasians.

John had been stationed at Pearl Harbor for more than two years and had friends he socialized with on a regular basis. Usually, when he was invited to a party, he would ask me to tag along, without letting the hosts know that he usurped their prerogative by doing so. Consequently, eyebrows were raised when we arrived, but we were prepared for that. John always suggested that I bring along my guitar, and he calmed people down by his size and the indication that I would entertain with some folk songs during the night. It worked!

At one of the parties, I met a woman whom I dated during my time there. She lived with Emily who was born on the island of Molokai where her parents still resided. Through them, I was able to see Hawaii from other than the commercialism in and around Waikiki. Every island was visited by me, except for one, the island of Ni'ihau, that did not allow visitors. The highlight was that Emily's dad belonged to a group that entertained each Christmas at the leprosy colony located on Molokai and invited me to join them one year. Quite an experience!

Hawaii's unbelievable great weather allowed walking to and from work every day. An eight-minute stroll was all it took, passing the tennis courts en route.

We also handled message traffic for the commander in chief of all military in the Pacific, army, navy, marines, etc. Admiral Harry D. Felt was CINCPAC, and his office was located on the top floor of the building. A fascinating man! He was short in stature (about 5' 4"), with "a terrifying reputation as an arrogant, caustic, hard-driving perfectionist." Many people were afraid of him ". . . he was pretty rough and mean as hell." One quote attributed to him was, "Trust everyone, but always cut the cards."

I seem to recall, once, that I observed him walking around a two-star army general, who was standing at attention while Admiral Felt chewed him out unmercifully. How it came about that I witnessed that episode is not part of my memory, but the recollection is clear.

The job was not bad, not much to it since the enlisted men did the work while we read the messages and routed them to the proper people. Despite the soft duty, I spent most of my time complaining to everyone who would listen, and some who would rather not hear it, about how dumb the navy was to assign me, a law school graduate, to duty as a communications officer. To me, that was a horrible waste of talent, so I bitched and moaned *ad nauseum*.

Then, it so happened that a sailor stole another sailor's paycheck, converted it, and then committed suicide. A thorough investigation was called for by the Uniform Code of Military Justice (UCMJ). An investigating officer was needed, and I guess the high powered staff of the two commands didn't relish the idea of doing such menial work.

CINCPACFLT's personnel officer, one of the men who heard me bitch and moan about my talents being wasted, apparently recommended me as the person to do the investigation.

I was called in and given the assignment and a car. I was also warned in no uncertain terms that I'd "better do a good job or else." No time table was given, so there I was with an assignment, a car, and on my own.

I completed the investigation in a week or three, and it was well received by the brass. During my work, I met Commander Gene McGuire who, in addition to being the Personnel Officer for the Commander Service Forces in the Pacific (COMSERVPAC), coached COMSERVPAC's basketball team. He invited me to try out for the team. I did and joined the team, after which I received orders to the basketball team as my only duty. I was done with communications, but not done with golf.

In fact, my only duties were to practice and play with the team, leaving lots of free time to play golf at the Navy-Marine Course and Leilehua, the army's course located near Schofield Barracks, out in, or near, the pineapple fields. It cost $13 a month at navy-marine, and $12 a month at Leilehua, $25 a month for unlimited play at two courses. I played every day.

The stars of our basketball team were two: Jack W. Stromberg, who had played three years at Hamline University, and General Lee Davis (yes, that's his real name) who had played one year at Gonzaga University and was a black enlisted man.

"The General" had a great deal, due as much to Coach McGuire's status as personnel officer as to his exceptional basketball talent, talents that McGuire wanted to retain indefinitely, for good reasons.

After the season, "The General" would tell coach where in the Western Pacific he wanted to spend some time, Japan, Hong Kong, etc. To keep him happy, orders would be cut for him to be assigned there, always receiving per-diem pay. When he was tired of one place, he would contact coach and obtain orders to wherever else he wanted to visit, then get orders back to the team when the season began.

Not bad for a black enlisted man who did not own a college degree. It's not clear to me though whether he had a better deal than mine turned out to be, namely a two-year vacation in Hawaii, playing golf, basketball, and fast pitch softball.

In truth, athletes get better treatment everywhere, even me. "The General" was a piece of work and his skills merited special treatment to keep him.

We had an admirable mix of talent on that team. McGuire was a good coach and COMSERVPAC won the All Navy Championship in 1960. I was told that they repeated as champions the next year, but I was gone before that happened, although I served as an assistant coach for part of the season before being discharged in December 1961.

After basketball season, I had time with no duties, so to pass the time, I organized a fast-pitch softball team comprised entirely of enlisted men and one officer, me. I was the team's manager, played shortstop, and batted third. We competed in a military league on Oahu.

That year, the navy's Western Pacific fast-pitch softball Championship was held in Honolulu, and I lobbied for, and received, permission for my team to enter the tournament. We had won the island championship and were eligible to enter the WESTPAC tournament. My buddy, Admiral Felt, made it happen.

We proceeded to win the WESTPAC Championship, thereby earning ourselves a spot in the All Navy tournament scheduled for Patuxent River Naval Air Station in Maryland, USA. We were given orders to Patuxent River and thirteen of us were scheduled to fly military aircraft to California, thence commercial aircraft to Maryland.

Shortly before leaving, one of our players became sick and couldn't make the trip. As the officer in charge, I had been given cash for everyone's per-diem pay and tried to return the amount belonging to our absent player. I was dissuaded from doing that because of the paperwork involved in taking back cash. I was told to retain the cash and speak no further about it. I divided it up equally between the other team members and they were pleased. Nothing for me, but the men were happy. All's well that ends well, I reckon.

We lost in the semifinals, 1 to 0 in overtime, when our opponent hit a home run in the second extra inning. Disappointing, but not bad.

I took some leave and went home to Connecticut for several days, then visited some friends in the Chicago area for a few more days before heading for Treasure Island for my return to Pearl Harbor.

Upon arriving at Treasure Island, I struck up a friendship with the officer in charge of arranging military flights to Hawaii. He asked me if I was really ready to return to Hawaii, and I said something like "not really," so he said he'll mark my orders with something saying that a flight was unavailable. He then told me to contact him personally when I was ready to return.

Then I proceeded to spend eleven wonderful days in San Francisco, visiting some of my old haunts and sampling the cuisine at many fine restaurants. At last, I crawled into my friend's office and begged him to put me on a flight to Pearl Harbor before I died from overexposure. He laughingly complied.

Upon being discharged, I flew to Los Angeles where the band leader from my "Backstreet" days at Waikiki was performing. He introduced me to some people who appeared willing to back my effort to make singing folk songs a career if I was so inclined. I also interviewed at a couple of law firms and was offered a job at one.

I declined a career change, then, at the last minute decided that a law career in sunny Southern California was not for me. So the Merchant of Greenwich came home to Connecticut where I've been ever since.

During my early years of practicing law in Connecticut, I joined the active reserves and was assigned to a ship in New Haven, Connecticut, USS *Coates (DE-685)*. It paid reasonably well and the money was helpful. I believe that the commitment included spending one full weekend per month on the ship and two weeks per year on active duty, usually as part of a unit comprised of three other similar ships from the New York/New Jersey area.

The only negative about reserve service came when we were put on notice that we could be called to full active duty to become part of President Kennedy's embargo of Cuba. Happily, for me, that didn't happen, but I'm told it came close.

One two-week cruise involved sailing the Caribbean with a stop in Curacao, an island of the Netherlands Antilles in the South Caribbean off the coast of Venezuela.

En route I was approached by the ship's Personnel Officer and asked if I was interested in serving as the ship's Shore Patrol Officer while in Curacao. I agreed to do so after learning that such duty involved living ashore during the three days we were to be there, meaning I had no watch-standing duties aboard ship, reporting to the Dutch police and working under their supervision, and best of all, being paid a per-diem for my services.

Each of the four ships in the unit provided a Shore Patrol Officer. I met one of them and we agreed to pool our per diem and take the Penthouse suite in the International Hotel located there. How nice was that?

We reported to the Dutch Police, and they took us on a tour of the island and its "hot spots," where we were introduced to the owners of all the establishments—restaurants, bars, you name it. The Dutch made it clear that they neither needed nor wanted our help in enforcing the laws of Curacao. We were there simply to assist with any interface needed with our ship's Captain if a sailor from the USS *Coates* was involved.

That tour of the "spots" and the introductions led to an unwillingness of the owners to accept any payment from us for food or drinks. We ate and drank free for four days. How good is that?

It turned out that we were required to work only four hours a day and were otherwise free to roam, lie on the beach, sightsee, and act like we were on vacation when off duty. Really now, how good was that? All other officers aboard ship were required to stand watches one day out of the three.

I've been fortunate enough to have spent considerable time in the Caribbean, including The Bahamas, especially Grand Bahama Island, Jamaica, and St. Thomas among other places. The navy provided me with my only experience on the island of Curacao, at no cost to me.

JOHN F. MERCHANT

My naval career ended when I left the reserves to run for statewide office in 1970 since I couldn't campaign and meet reserve obligations. I left with no regrets about the time I spent as a naval officer. It was an incredibly interesting part of my journey.

Chapter 5

Merchant and Melville, Attorneys At Law

I SAT FOR the Connecticut bar exam in July 1962, four years after graduating law school. It was scary, to say the least. I could have taken it in February but declined to do so since it was clear to me that I had neglected to live up to the Boy Scout motto to "Be prepared."

After forty months on active duty in the navy, I was clearly unprepared, and I knew it. In fact, I was very concerned and wondered how in the world I could get prepared . . . ever! Confidence, I did not have.

There was also the need to find a place to live and earn a living. Mom solved the first problem by allowing me to live in the attic with her. I had meager, if any, savings. However, my law-school debts had been paid, thus validating my decision to take forty months in the navy, on an officer's pay, in lieu of being drafted and spending two years earning an enlisted man's pay.

Unemployment benefits answered the income question.

My recollection of the unemployment rules at the time is that one had to actively seek work and report on the search weekly to stay eligible. Obviously, to me, finding work in the field of law would be difficult, unless I took and passed the bar exam. It soon became clear that finding employment as an attorney was probably out of the question based on the interviews I had.

A search for work in my field was undertaken at some Greenwich law firms and found only closed doors. Three firms or the interviewers there did write glowing letters of recommendation after the short interviews, letters from strangers that were fundamentally useless.

I wish I had kept those letters. They would provide a good laugh today. There is little to be said for being highly recommended, in writing, by men who knew me for maybe twenty minutes and would not hire me.

I believe that being black had something to do with that but who knows?

The navy had discharged me. Frankly, I had no interest in a military career and gave no thought to reenlisting.

Fortunately, the people in the unemployment office understood the problem. They agreed that it would not be a good idea to take the February 1962 exam because I needed to study, hard, if I were to pass it. They wanted me to pass as much as I did. I was pleased to have a fan base.

In order to get your check at that time, you had to personally appear at the office, weekly, to report on your job search results. Those appearances over a period of several months gave me time to make friends in the office, and I became like one of them. It was a fun time ending in September when I reported success on passing the exam.

In fact, on a Friday afternoon in September, after I reported having passed the bar exam, they closed the office early, gave me my last check, and had a little party celebrating my success.

Willy Shakespeare was right "Parting is such sweet sorrow."

I met L. Scott Melville while taking the bar exam in 1962. I believe that we were the only two blacks who sat for the bar that July. We talked, became friends, and decided that we should open an office in Bridgeport to practice law if we both were successful in passing the bar.

Scott was staying with relatives in New Haven (Connecticut), and I was living at home in Greenwich. Bridgeport seemed a good place. It was close to midway between our respective homes. Between us, we knew no one in Bridgeport, but being young and eager, we viewed it only as a mountain to climb. It was that . . . and more.

At that time, the results of the bar exam were made public by posting a list on the bulletin board at the state courthouse in New Haven at 9:00 a.m. Scott was there early to get the results. I don't remember the exact date of posting.

I do remember getting a phone call from Scott that morning during which he excitedly and gleefully advised me that he had passed the bar. He rambled on about that for a few minutes until I politely interrupted him and asked if he had looked for my name on the list. "Oh yes," he said, "you also passed."

We agreed to meet in New Haven to celebrate our success; mine being the eighth wonder of the world and clearly something to celebrate. We also needed to plan our future and discuss next steps.

JOHN F. MERCHANT

One of the first items discussed was naming the firm. We agreed that a coin flip would be decisive. I flipped and he called "heads."

Regrettably, for him, the coin bounced off the carpet and trickled under the sofa, leading to an extended discussion as to how best to view the results or whether to flip again. We agreed to flip again. For kicks, by agreement, I carefully eased the coin from under the sofa and saw that it had turned up heads. If it had counted, the firm name would have been Melville and Merchant, a name he absolutely preferred. The winner of the flip could choose the name.

He flipped the second time, away from the sofa, and I called "tails" while the coin was in the air. The coin landed on the carpet and settled down in the middle of the room showing tails. The firm name became Merchant and Melville, and despite his disappointment at not being the "Senior" partner in the firm, we moved on to other pertinent matters.

I believe the name was very important to him. Frankly, being a devotee of Willy Shakespeare, the firm name was of little importance to me. You know, "What's in a name . . . ?" Still, I was pleased to win the flip.

We agreed to start in Bridgeport, looked into where and how to buy furniture and law books, and set a date to search for office space. The search turned out to be a real chore, although interesting.

We spoke with the owner or agent of *every* office building on Main Street in Bridgeport, and there were many at that time. We sought to lease what often was existing empty space that suited our needs. Much of the space was advertised, obviously vacant, but no one would offer us a lease, except David Zimmer who owned a building at 1115 Main Street. We accepted and moved in.

No local bank would offer us a loan to start up our business, despite our having prepared a reasonable business plan outlining our expenses and other necessary components of such a plan.

Welcome to Bridgeport in the land of the free!

David not only leased space to us but was an enormous help to our fledgling firm, immediately, and over the years. The rent was reasonable; he gave us directions to the court house and advised us that we could not represent the buyer in real estate transactions unless we were listed on the approved attorney lists of the bank or other lending institutions providing the financing to the buyers.

As new attorneys who happened to be black, it was not possible to get on any such List. Don't ask me why. It could have been because of our inexperience or maybe being black had something to do with it. I don't know.

David had the solution; he was on every list in existence. He told us that we could use his name with the lenders, provided that the required title search was done by Attorney Victor Riccio, a principal with The Kelsey Company. The Kelsey Company specialized in searching titles to real property, and they were really good at it with a reputation and clientele to prove it.

David's requirement that we use The Kelsey Company led to a friendship between me and Victor, his partner, his family, and his friends that continues to exist despite Victor's untimely death at age fifty-three. That friendship became very special over the years and still flourishes as we enter the year 2011.

In fact, for more than thirty years, we have spent a substantial part of each Christmas Day with the Riccios. Initially, when his children and mine were younger, the day was spent at Victor's home with his wife, Joyce, and six children—Tom, Victor aka "Lil Vic," David, Paul aka "Main Man," Joyce Ann aka "JAR," and Janet.

We enjoy the same visiting tradition with the Lawrence family, making Christmas a very, very special day for us.

"Big Vic" and I had become like brothers over the years. We talked about me joining his firm and being involved in all legal matters except the title search business. That never happened, apparently because his partner wasn't keen on the idea.

It was Victor's suggestion that led to the first Christmas visit. He knew that I spent much of every Christmas Day with Susan and Tabitha and invited us to share the day with his family. "Main Man" was about the same age as Susan and Tabitha, and they had come to know each other as playmates at an early age.

Big Vic's wife, Joyce, passed away within two years of his death. Tom died from a heart attack when he was in his thirties. The others all gather at the home of "Lil Vic" and Susan, his wife, on Christmas with their children and friends. "David and "Main Man" are married and have children. What a joy to have watched the generations grow up and what an enormous amount of pride I feel as we share the day with such real friends. Neither rain nor snow, etc., prevents the sharing.

For many years, when I lived about a mile from Victor, I would stop in around dinner time on my way home from work just as the entire family was sitting down to eat dinner. Rarely did I eat dinner with them because I generally ate later than they did. However, they always made room at the table for me and provided me with a glass of scotch and water from the bottle of scotch they always kept on hand . . . solely for me.

Joyce, Janet, and Joyce Ann served all the males prior to being seated and serving themselves, something I always got a kick out of witnessing. I grew up in an Italian neighborhood where male domination reigned and family was important as a priority. So it was at the Riccio's dining room table then. Not any longer though.

Joyce Ann is a well-respected and successful attorney in Connecticut; Janet has a highly desirable position with a consulting firm, David and "Lil Vic" have their own title searching businesses; and, "Main Man" lives in New York City with Molly, his wife, where he is successfully employed.

I could write an entire book on my time spent as friends of the Riccios but won't. Suffice to say they added enormous value to my life, individually and collectively, and continue to do so as the sun sets for me.

Incidentally, my feelings about the Riccios are shared by Susan and Tabitha, and, I believe, Tabitha's eleven-year-old son, Tyler, although he doesn't talk much about it. He just thoroughly enjoys the visits.

But I have digressed a bit.

Dave Zimmer also made it clear that he did not expect nor would he accept any fee for the use of his name. The lease arrangements were eminently fair and David never hesitated when asked to give us insights on the courts, some judges, other lawyers, and general information that one needs and acquires over time. Fees charged were retained by us when and if received. In truth, I believe that establishing ourselves in Bridgeport without David's help would have been very difficult, if not impossible.

He was our initial bridge toward acceptance in the practice of law in Bridgeport. Others helped enormously as the years crept by. In general, it was a terrific group of lawyers to be involved with and made the practice of law a very enjoyable thing.

Interestingly, many of the men who befriended us and welcomed us to the practice were tenants in David's building. Men like Daniel E. Brennan, Sr. and Leonard Cocco, who later was appointed a Judge of the Superior Court.

Scott and I were the only black lawyers in Bridgeport for years and, I think, in Fairfield County as well. Some years prior to our arrival, a black lawyer with a practice in Hartford tried to branch out and opened an office in Bridgeport. He left after a relatively short stay. I don't know why he left.

Scott and I discussed ways to market ourselves, meaning find clients. We agreed on a strategy that worked, albeit slowly. He opted to get involved in politics to the extent possible; I would seek involvement in the social services arena, hoping to serve on boards as a way of advertising our presence. We both agreed to make our presence known to the black churches and to work with the NAACP to the extent possible.

Obviously, our initial focus was to market ourselves to the black residents of the area. It seemed logical and sensible to us.

That decision to share the load turned out well for us, although my involvement in politics increased over the years, though not by design. Scott's involvement ultimately led to his appointment as a Judge of the Superior Court where he served for many years until retirement.

All indications are that he was a good Judge. I rarely appeared before him because of the obvious conflict of interest issue, thus have no personal experiences that would help me evaluate his performance. Comments from other lawyers regarding his performance gave him mostly high marks, and that came as no surprise to me. I knew him best as a good practitioner.

Scott possessed a good legal mind and an admirable work ethic. He enjoyed practicing law, researching legal issues, and arguing them when appropriate. Those qualities served him well during his tenure as a practitioner and during his time as a Judge.

Personally, I did not have anything resembling his interest in the law. Legal research was not my forte, though I believe that I did a decent job when necessary. I did relish arguing before the state's Appellate Court and Supreme Court where research was important, even critical. For those occasions, I somehow found the enthusiasm to get the needed research done and written up in a legal brief, and, on time for filing with the courts.

Incidentally, I literally dislike writing which may explain why this effort has taken so long to put together. I am also a two-fingered typist requiring time and significant editing. I do enjoy talking and conversing and debating ideas.

A friend once commented that, basically, two kinds of people live in America—those that favor acquiring and discussing *things* and those that favor *ideas* and discussions relating to ideas and their differences. I don't know if that is true, but if so, put me in the ideas column.

Most areas of the law did not capture my attention or interest me. The intricacies of corporate law, trusts and estates, taxes, and other moneymaking areas of the law didn't provide the kind of challenges I relished.

My interest was primarily, maybe solely, in the trial of cases—civil and criminal. In thinking about that, it has occurred to me that the attraction of the court room is that each side is provided with the opportunity to fully discuss their point of view in an effort to be persuasive, unlike normal conversations where folks seem more interested in interrupting when you pause to take a breath. Test that thesis for yourself over the next month.

I loved the challenge of the courtroom and being on trial. I loved the rush it provided and the butterflies that signaled a level of apprehension knowing that someone's rights or freedom or financial health was at risk, and also realizing that opposing counsel was experienced and competent and enjoyed winning, like most human beings do. The competition was the challenge, and I was proud to be a part of helping America work as it promised.

I did not mind the long hours required for preparing a case and actually being on trial, nor did I really get upset over the fact that most of my clients could not afford the cost of an investigator's assistance in preparing their cases. On that score, the State's Attorneys had an edge. They had the local police force to investigate and help them prepare their cases, more than adequate libraries with trained men and women to research issues, even as the individual State's Attorney was before the court on trial.

Then too, someone from their office always sat second seat, an advantage that could be enormously helpful for them, and it often was.

Does that sound like a stacked deck? Well, in my view, it was no more than an advantage provided by taxpayers who were entitled to have justice done in the courts. The prosecutor's oath of office bound them to a search for justice, and I tried to hold them to the dictates of their oath. They also had the burden of proof beyond a reasonable doubt, a burden that lessened their edge.

The States' Attorneys with whom I did business in criminal matters were, with rare exceptions, honorable, competent, ethical, and responsible. Mutual respect flowed, fairness was the standard adhered to in combat at trial, and the Rules of Practice and rules of evidence were known and strictly followed.

The key for me was to work at being fully prepared and to be sure that the state was held to carrying its burden of proof in a manner consistent with the rules of evidence and the applicable law. That was my focus. Each of my clients was entitled to no less than that, and it was an obligation I accepted.

Our efforts to establish and grow our practice by seeking relationships with the clergy and churches provided mixed results. Some of the clergy were very pleased to have two lawyers in the community; others did not really feel good about our presence and didn't really support us. I believe they viewed us as competition for a leadership role in the community, roles they either had or sought.

Rev. A. C. Bass, pastor of Mt. Aerie Baptist Church welcomed us and did everything he could to support us, including referring clients when he could. My first trial was a referral from Rev. Bass, a young man charged with murder. The trial took place during the first several months of starting our firm. Talk about on-the-job training, wow!

Scott and I discussed and then agreed that the young man was my client and that I would be lead counsel in the matter. We collaborated in preparing for trial, claiming self-defense. By agreement, Scott cross-examined a witness or two, helped prepare relevant jury instructions and, properly, left the bulk of the work to me. After several days of trial, the jury returned a "Not Guilty" verdict that annoyed the prosecution but pleased my client.

Obviously, the result pleased me, but was not a complete surprise since I believed in the validity of our self-defense argument. What pleased me as much was the discovery that I truly enjoyed my involvement in trial work. The State's Attorney was an experienced professional who provided a kind of competition that I savored and never lost a taste for. In my opinion, he also underestimated the young, inexperienced black lawyers representing the defendant.

Down through the years, I have tried many criminal cases and relished each one. I don't believe I was ever underestimated again though.

Initially, my trial work was criminal and involved a black defendant. One thing I learned to do pretty well was ferret out racial discrimination during the individual voir dire of each potential juror. It was an important tool for getting a fair trial, especially since the jury pool at that time was drawn from the entire county, thus it usually contained few blacks. It did contain persons from the middle and upper class suburban populations, many of whom had undesirable attitudes about blacks charged with crimes.

In Connecticut, counsel for both sides have a constitutional right to question each potential juror prior to selecting or dismissing them. It's called an individual voir dire. The members of the jury panel are individually questioned by lawyers for both the plaintiff and defendant, and while often a tedious and time consuming event, it is eminently fair in my opinion.

If one could establish cause for dismissal during the voir dire, the juror could be excused and would not count against the limited number of peremptory challenges each side possessed by law. My efforts were geared toward having a juror admit racial bias if my client was black, thus establishing cause. I had more success doing that than one might imagine, but also ran afoul of some Judges' views as to what was proper questioning.

I recall one case in the Judicial District of Fairfield, which included Bridgeport, where a Judge stopped the voir dire and called both lawyers into his chambers. There, he sternly pointed out to me that in his courtroom jury selection was permitted only within the context of a case decided by the Connecticut Supreme Court that he cited. I was aware of that case.

I countered by reading from a federal case I had researched that allowed much more latitude during the voir dire. Stymied by my insistence on proceeding in accordance with the federal case, he proposed a deal.

If he didn't like my question, he would scratch his nose with his right hand. That was the signal advising me that I should modify the question or pursue another line of questioning. I agreed to comply as best I could and it worked out well. He scratched his nose a lot, but so what?

Another time I had a civil case where I was representing seven defendants each of whom was entitled to three peremptory challenges of potential jurors. A total of twenty-one challenges were in my pocket. The Judge, in chambers, made noises about how long this trial would last and what he would and would not countenance during it. I resented his attitude and his arbitrary approach to a trial, so I spoke up regarding his oppressive timetable.

I told him that my real client, an insurance company, had me on the clock, and I was being paid for every hour I worked on this case. With twenty-one peremptory challenges, I anticipated that jury selection could take three weeks or more, followed by a two-week trial. He resented my attitude but set his attitude aside and became much more flexible. After all, there was an individual voir dire and I did have twenty-one challenges, by law.

No longer a dictator who ruled by fiat, he involved himself in a meaningful chambers discussion about how we would proceed. The case was settled before jury selection was completed. A satisfactory ending for all!

My experiences with judges, state attorneys, and other lawyers were primarily positive, although the first few years had me raising questions about some Judges. Yes, I sensed a level of bias that troubled me, but as my experience increased, my relationships with the court and Judges improved.

Judges seemingly became reasonable, friendly, understanding, and professional. In short, they made the practice enjoyable, and in my opinion and experience, they mostly delivered justice in their courtrooms. Many became close personal friends.

On the positive side, my impression is that eventually Judges welcomed me, as both a lawyer and as a black lawyer representing black defendants in criminal matters. The highlight was an appearance before a Judge whom I had previously appeared before, but did not know well. The courtroom was crowded with lawyers and defendants awaiting arraignment. When my case was called, this Judge, with no warning to me at least, spoke to me loudly enough for all assembled to hear, saying, "Attorney Merchant, it's an honor to have you appear in my court."

I was flabbergasted since this was totally unexpected, and I knew of nothing I had done to merit such words. I glanced at my client who appeared very pleased to know that the Judge both knew me and had respect for me. I sensed he was thinking that his case would go well for him and it did, but it merited the result we obtained with or without the comments.

My sense is that many judges welcomed me, a black attorney with black defendants, especially when it came to sentencing in criminal matters. Judges learned that my being part of the black community permitted me to be more knowledgeable regarding the individual, his family, and his potential, thus representations made to the court by me took on a level of reliability that they appreciated, since it helped them make better sentencing decisions. Over the years, comments to that effect were often made to me by Judges I came to know and appeared before often.

I once went thirteen years without having a client of mine sentenced to jail time, most of which resulted from plea bargaining discussions with the State's Attorney and the Judge in chambers.

On the criminal side, the state funded the public defender's (PD) office to represent indigent defendants at no cost to them. I was approached by a Judge, William Tierney, out of my hometown of Greenwich, who was sitting in Bridgeport on criminal matters. He had known me during my growing-up years and wanted to discuss the PD's office. He remarked that an overwhelming number of criminal defendants represented by the PD were black, but that office had no black lawyers at the time. He wanted to correct this and could.

He asked if I or someone from my office had any interest in working as a PD on a part-time basis. I was somewhat interested and thought it was a good idea. I agreed to discuss it with my partners and report back to him.

Merchant and Melville had then become Merchant, Melville, Spear and Seymour with the additions of E. Eugene

Spear, a black attorney and a native of Bridgeport, and Thomas F. Seymour, a very able lawyer and a good man. Tom gave the firm diversity; he was not black.

We had an interest, and I reported this to Judge Tierney.

Shortly thereafter, it was discovered that the state had discontinued the practice of hiring part-time public defenders. It was full time or nothing.

Gene Spear was married at the time, with two young daughters. Gene agreed to leave the firm and take the full-time position. I believe that he was attracted by the advantage of a steady income and benefits, including medical, that the position afforded him and his family. It made sense to me.

Gene turned out to be a great addition to that office. At least four (4) different Judges who sat on criminal jury cases at different times told me that during their terms the best criminal defense lawyer appearing before them was E. Eugene Spear, Esq.

Gene was later appointed Chief Public Defender for the Judicial District of Milford where he continued to excel. After a period of a few years in that position, he was appointed a Judge in the Superior Court where he again served with distinction. He left the Superior Court judgeship when he was appointed to Connecticut's Appellate Court in Hartford by Governor Lowell B. Weicker.

In Connecticut, appeals from the Superior Court, the Court of initial jurisdiction, could be taken to the Appellate Court or to Connecticut's Supreme Court, its highest court. Both Courts sat in Hartford, the state capitol.

My relationships with States' Attorneys, especially in Bridgeport, Stamford, and Norwalk, where I appeared the most, were excellent. Many became good friends without straying from being true professionals in their actions and demeanor. They were motivated by a need to clear dockets and deliver justice in a fair way. They were able to sort the wheat from the chaff in most matters. We both knew when a matter should be resolved by trial before a jury, and we enjoyed the professional competition inherent in a trial.

Two stories remain vivid in my memory on that subject.

For years, I organized a trip to the South in March to greet and prepare for the upcoming golf season. Twenty to twenty-four men made up the group, and Pinehurst, The Homestead, and Innisbrook were among the many courses we played.

During one such trip, Frank Maco, an Assistant State's Attorney, was my playing partner for three days before returning to Connecticut on a Sunday. It was a fun time.

Then on Monday morning, we, Frank and I, started jury selection for a trial involving a major felony matter with the clear intent to seek a fair and just trial and to compete against each other as professionals and beat each other's brains out.

The transition from partners to competitive professionals was made without a hitch, and as I recall, justice was served. The jury found my client guilty of a lesser offense, and he was subsequently sentenced fairly by the Judge. Frank and I remain friends to this day.

On another occasion, Bob Lacobelle, an Assistant State's Attorney, and I were ordered by the court to begin picking a jury in a murder case. Both of us knew that the trial could take more than a month and quickly realized that we each had a previous commitment we wanted to keep on a Friday afternoon in the middle of the trial. We discussed this and finally decided to go to the Judge and let him know about the fact of our commitments, hoping that he would help make it possible for us to keep it.

We spoke to the Judge in chambers and explained the problem. He asked each of us to be more specific about the exact nature of the commitment, but we were reluctant to do that. He told us that unless we told him what he wanted to know we should make other arrangements regarding the commitments.

You see, for several years, at a one-day Member-Guest tournament at my club, Rolling Hills Country Club in Wilton, Connecticut, my guests included John Forbes, Chief Public Defender in Bridgeport, and Bob Lacobelle. This year the tournament had been scheduled on a day during which we would certainly be on trial in this murder case. The one day was an annual event that we treasured.

The Judge looked at us sternly, then appeared flabbergasted, and then, to our surprise, began laughing out loud. When his stomach stopped hurting from the laughter and he had dried the laughter-induced tears from his eyes, the Judge told us that we could keep our "commitments," and he would excuse the jury so they could enjoy a long weekend. We thanked him, profusely.

Thus, approximately two weeks into the trial of a murder case, Bob and I played golf. Then, on Monday, we returned to court and the trial without any further interruptions.

The trial lasted five weeks and, according to the courtroom workers and observers, was conducted in a highly professional manner on both sides. Some even expressed surprise over the jury's verdict to convict my client.

Frank, Bob, and a host of other attorneys remain good friends. I retired from the practice, primarily because I had lost my hearing in both ears, making it difficult to understand what people said, in and out of the courtroom, despite wearing hearing aids. The hearing problem continues, but my days of trying cases have ended. I miss it.

In addition to the several attorneys working in the state's attorneys' office, I learned to respect two men who headed that office during my time. Donald Brown and Jonathan Benedict were both able and responsible civil servants who helped deliver criminal justice without violating their oaths of office. With me, they were gentlemen, albeit tough, and I have tremendous respect for each of them.

In a short time, Scott, Gene, and I, along with Tom Seymour, who joined our office, interacted with members of the bar we enjoyed it thoroughly. I, we, were accepted as professionals and judged only by our skills, attitudes, personalities, and moral turpitude. We joined the Bridgeport Bar Association, worked on its committees, and were an integral part of the whole. We did the same with the Connecticut Bar Association whose members covered the entire state.

Mine was a legal career where almost to a person a lawyer's word was his bond and could be relied upon without qualification. Clients were represented with a level of professionalism in all respects that was, and is, noteworthy.

I'm told that has since changed to the point where one has to be leery about taking the word of many lawyers and relying on it. If true, that's sad.

The practice of law offered me another advantage. It gave me the independence and freedom to do other things as I saw fit and as opportunities arose. So I could serve on different boards, and I did. I could speak up without fear of being muzzled or berated by a boss whose agenda, or business interests, didn't coincide with mine. I could be an activist in the community when necessary and speak on controversial subjects to the right person or audience when appropriate, without fearing a negative reaction from anyone who was involved with my earning a living.

Only my clients were entitled to have me refuse to do or say anything that could be controversial or harmful to them. I represented my clients, not the various institutions and/or people that I believed needed to be informed and educated about their negatives. My quest was not to be a community leader but to be a positive agent for change with the capacity to enforce that quest in the courtroom, if necessary.

Almost from the beginning, I took the position that if a black person was capable of doing a job our office needed done, they would be our preference. We hired secretaries from the black community. Margaret Todd from Bridgeport was our first secretary.

Soon after her arrival, she was told that our office was not where she should plan on making her career. Our interest was in providing her with the knowledge and training that would enable her to seek a similar position in an office where the salary and benefits were higher and more plentiful. Marge spent a few years with us, then, wound up with a secretarial career in General Electric, I think. She was a remarkable lady who needed only an opportunity to convince an employer that hiring her was like finding gold.

Conscientious and a fast learner, she paid attention to detail and had an attractive presence and a polite demeanor. Those outstanding qualities made her a valuable asset in our office. Of course, she could type and take dictation as well. Those were givens. Another outstanding quality was her unquenchable interest in being better at her work tomorrow than she was yesterday or today. We were fortunate to find her early and both sad and very pleased when she moved on to better things.

Every secretary that ever worked with us was a lot like Marge. I would be remiss if I did not mention one other, Kathy McCondichie, who probably was with us longer than any other. She came to us soon after Jerry Rosenblum and I became partners with a primary office in Stamford. In addition, we had space in Bridgeport with Victor Riccio, but Jerry rarely worked from there.

Jerry was a part-time public defender in Stamford when we formed Merchant and Rosenblum. Soft spoken, very competent, and a good friend, Jerry was an excellent criminal defense lawyer who seemingly never let anything trouble him. Very smart, he never raised his voice. He was well worth listening to when he spoke. I admire that man and treasure the seventeen-year partnership we had. It dissolved when Governor Weicker appointed me to the position of Consumer Counsel for Connecticut in his administration.

Originally, I came to Stamford because Bob Levister, a black lawyer, was elevated to the bench and became a judge in the Common Pleas court. He offered to turn his practice over to Scott and me and we accepted.

Scott had absolutely no interest in working out of the Stamford office, so it became my domain. Ultimately, I was there alone after Scott moved on to an Associate City Attorney's position in Bridgeport, thence to his appointment as a Judge of the Superior Court. Gene Spear also accepted an appointment to the bench from his public defender position.

Folks often asked me why I never became a judge but Gene and Scott did. My answer was a Latin phrase that Victor Riccio often used, to wit, "Dues et treis non est malum" (sp), translated, according to Victor, it means two out of three ain't bad.

I never really wanted to be a judge. I considered it too confining and believed it would limit my freedom and prevent me from doing many of the things I wanted to do. I was right about that. Actually, four different governors discussed a judgeship with me, and to each, I expressed no interest.

In fact, Governor Ella Grasso pushed hard by asking me what I wanted from her administration and if I wanted a judgeship.

My response to her was that I would like to see her elevate Bob Levister from Common Pleas court to the Superior Court, making him the first black judge in the

Superior Court. She did that. This is the only time I've ever told anyone of that conversation.

At the time, Connecticut's judicial system had four levels at the initial jurisdiction stage: Circuit Court, Common Pleas court, Superior Court, and Juvenile Court. Each level had specific jurisdictions set forth in the statutes and judicial appointments were made specifically to each category. That has changed. Now every judicial appointment is as a Superior Court Judge with everything incorporated within that framework.

Criminal matters have a part B for misdemeanors and minor felonies; and, a part A for more serious felony matters.

Joel Kaye found Kathy shortly after he joined our office as an associate. She was a college graduate, working for the State Department of Welfare when Joel found her. We hired her on Joel's recommendation, even though at the beginning she could type, maybe, twenty words a minute and owned no secretarial experience. She applied herself immediately and learned fast. Within a short period of time, we learned to rely on Kathy as she grew into a position where she was, in effect, our office manager.

She kept our schedules, handled client inquiries, learned to do things such as real estate closings, and functioned more like a paralegal than a secretary. She was just marvelous and absolutely dependable. We were lucky.

At one point, Jerry and I spoke with her about going to law school. We were willing to pay for her to do so. She was not interested, although she enjoyed working for us and did until the firm dissolved in 1992.

Jerry and I once did a three-year study in an effort to identify the sources of our clients and the issues they brought to us. After three years, the study showed that 70 percent of Jerry's clients were black and 70 percent of mine were not. Jerry's totals were skewed by his public defender work; mine were skewed by the fact that the black communities really did not support black professionals. In truth, if I had to rely on support from my own community to make a living, I would have starved to death. I never really understood that, still don't.

One very disappointing experience that relates involves a black woman who was buying a house and needed a mortgage. I had left ABCD and the State Department of Community Affairs and returned to the practice of law. I was also a director of People's Bank.

One day while walking through the mortgage department of the bank, I saw this woman sitting there with a male companion and was hailed by her, so I stopped and spoke. Our history was that during the staffing phase of ABCD's neighborhood program, I had insisted that she be hired as an assistant coordinator over another woman from the neighborhood who had a college degree. She impressed me as capable and was. She was also a welfare recipient, and it offered an opportunity to have her remove herself from those rolls, earn a living, and provide for her child in a better way.

She asked if I had something to do with the bank and told me she was seeking a mortgage to buy a house. The male seated with her was introduced as her real estate broker. She said that she was still employed by ABCD.

I asked if she had an attorney. She quickly answered that she did and named him. He was someone I knew and was very competent, so I knew she was in good hands legally.

I suggested to her that she should consult with her lawyer and have him help her through the mortgage phase, along with her agent. I declined to speak further telling her that it could be considered unethical for me to speak with another lawyer's client and offer even an iota of what could be construed as legal advice.

I walked away and recall being somewhat upset. Here was a woman to whom I had given opportunity and, to her credit, she had taken full advantage of it. I had ". . . taken her feet out the miry clay . . ." and was pleased about that. On the other hand, although she must have known that I was back in the community, she had not even considered retaining me to represent her, but had chosen a white lawyer and a white real estate agent instead.

Now, obviously, she had a right to choose her own lawyer and agent, and I wouldn't even think about denying her that. But, I thought, given our history, *Why would she act without even considering retaining me or my office to represent her?*

Similar situations are too numerous to recall and set down here. No, I haven't gotten over those experiences and still can't explain to myself the reluctance of blacks to use black professionals that existed, and exist, in the larger black community. Admittedly, and happily, that seems to be changing as more and more black professionals, lawyers, and doctors practice their professions. I hope so.

There was a time when I thought a black law firm covering Fairfield County, and Connecticut generally, was a good idea. With Jerry's concurrence, I contacted several black lawyers, each of whom was a solo practitioner, and we met to discuss the idea. Eventually, all but one agreed to merge and we did for a very short time.

It wasn't long before I realized that the idea would not work. There were several reasons for that. Each cherished the independence afforded by a solo practice. We all had a focus on the black community and that created misunderstandings and some conflicts of interest that often drove clients away, and we struggled with the chief/Indian issue.

It reminded me of an old country western song, the words to which are:

"Nobody wants to play rhythm guitar behind Jesus, everybody wants to be the lead singer in the band."

Among members of the new firm, I had the best opportunity to attract clients in the majority community but, when I did, there was no one willing to do the work the client needed and wanted.

Personally, time was not available to me to do both find clients, a full time job, and do their work in a timely and professional fashion. By way of example, a large insurance company retained me to do defense work and sent me, on average, sixty cases a year, five each month. I found the client through golfing at the country club I belonged to at the time.

JOHN F. MERCHANT

The files required regular work on a daily basis, plus conversations and meetings with the company's adjusters and administrators to keep them advised of progress, possible settlements, and trial schedules. We were compensated for each hour worked at an agreed upon rate, but we had to perform.

No one in the office, or no two of them, were willing to do the work in a timely fashion or in a way that pleased the client. Conservatively, that client could have been worth $60 to $120,000 annually back then, with considerable growth potential. Eventually, the client left us; no surprise there!

There are other similar stories, but suffice to say, our firm dissolved and each went back to their solo practices. Don't get me wrong; they were a good group of guys, good lawyers, but with different ambitions and agendas. So be it.

I still believe that a predominately black law firm in Connecticut could be a very successful venture. Maybe I dream too much, or maybe I'm not the right person to be involved in the effort, who knows? Perhaps one day it will happen, but it's not likely to happen any time soon, despite the number of capable men and women who now practice in Connecticut. More will come, and the numbers will continue to grow throughout the state.

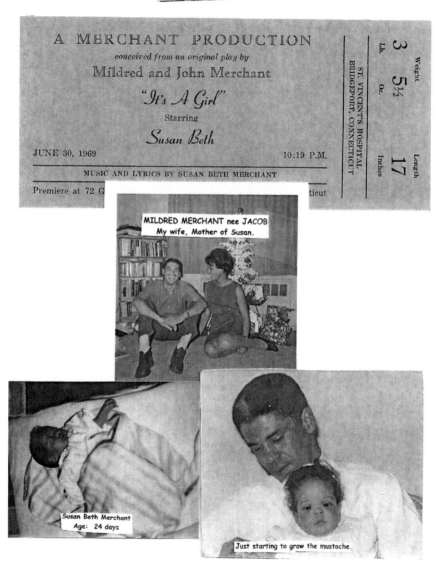

A MERCHANT PRODUCTION

conceived from an original play by

Mildred and John Merchant

"It's A Girl"

Starring

Susan Beth

JUNE 30, 1969   10:19 P.M.

MUSIC AND LYRICS BY SUSAN BETH MERCHANT

Premiere at 72 G   ticut

Weight 3 Lb. 5½ Oz.

Length 17 Inches

ST. VINCENT'S HOSPITAL
BRIDGEPORT, CONNECTICUT

MILDRED MERCHANT nee JACOB
My wife, Mother of Susan.

Susan Beth Merchant
Age: 24 days

Just starting to grow the mustache.

SUSB and OL' TAB – the early days

Mom with me at Parkway just before she took Susan and Tabitha by their necks and held them for a picture. (see next picture)

BE STILL, THIS WON'T HURT

69 Parkway, Fairfield, CT
They spent weekends here with me while growing up. Many happy memories.

Susan and Tabitha in basement at 69 Parkway.

YUP, they are growing .. and special!

Susan and Tabitha
Old enough now to be guests at party; Not just unpaid hostesses and helpers.

Tabitha Carter
I call her daughter but she is really a favorite niece.

SON OF OL' TAB
TYLER CARTER- my man!

Susan in high school a long jumper, sprinter and relays. She was pretty good. Also ran track at the

Bobbie, me, Mom and Liz.
We all get together at Karen's wedding.

UVA Metro Group Julian Bond Event at the Modern
July 24, 2007 024

Karen's wedding in New Jersey
Bobbie, Mother of bride, Tabitha, Susan and Mom.
I gave away the bride. Her Dad wasn't around.

Karen's Wedding

DAWN MITCHELL
Sister, my heart.

KIP MITCHELL
Brother, nephew.

KAREN MITCHELL
Giving away the bride, my niece.
Quite a day for both of us!!

THE LAWRENCE FAMILY

Talented, caring, special people. I've been
lucky to have them as friends for 50 years.

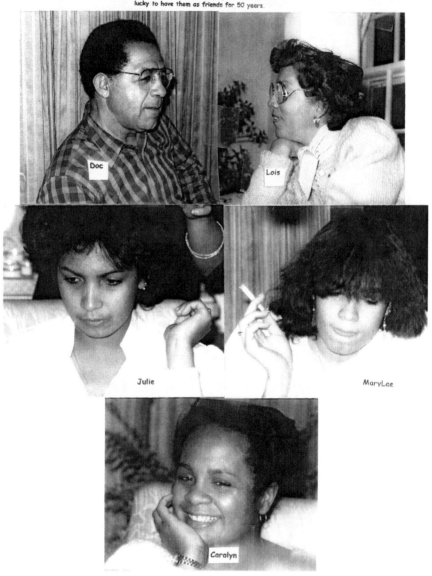

Doc

Lois

Julie

MaryLee

Carolyn

Chapter 6

People's Bank and the 1800 Club

DURING THE SUMMER of 1965, a very unusual and diverse group of men met in Bridgeport, Connecticut, a city suffering all the ills of urban decay and blight including: an unresponsive political system, serious racial disharmony, and an unwillingness, or inability to discuss and deal with community issues of importance to it and the Greater Bridgeport Area.

A strong economic base that thrived during World War II was now eroding at warp speed. A monster headache caused by an unwillingness to address issues raised by the ongoing civil rights movement crippled an already corrupt political system adding fuel to the fire. That headache bordered on being fatal, but little was done by political leadership to address the issues of race relations, bigotry, and discrimination.

Politically, armed with an uncanny ability to constantly employ bad judgment, the system nonetheless found time to seek money from the federal government to suit its own selfish purposes. No one I know trusted Bridgeport's political leadership. Its relationships with surrounding communities were mostly negative, fanned by the flames of distrust. The city of Bridgeport was a mess and, in 2011, still suffers from an inability to stabilize itself and provide for all its residents.

The men who met in 1965 were not part of the political system. They were black men and business a vested interest in the city, an interest that drove them to seek ways to improve that which needed improvement. The list of needs was long.

The first meeting led to meetings being held religiously over a period of twelve to eighteen months at 6:00 p.m. on Mondays. In military parlance, 6:00 p.m. is 1800 hours; hence, the name the group gave itself was "The 1800 Club."

Its impetus for meeting and the group's longevity were not something anyone could have imagined or planned. Never formally organized and without membership requirements, it became a major and very positive factor in a city suffering from a potpourri of urban problems and decay, including race relations, equal opportunity, educational issues, slum landlords, and related matters of critical concern to Bridgeport, and to America.

The Civil Rights Movement, during which the nation was being torn apart by its often violently expressed attitudes and actions about race, laid the foundation needed to bring about the meeting. Looking back, it occurs to me that very little else could have made it happen, since no other compelling rationale existed.

Personal agendas were the enemy of common sense.

The Office of Economic Opportunity (OEO) was the federal agency that administered the government's War on Poverty. It provided funds for programs to communities throughout the nation, primarily through community action agencies (CAA), later identified as CAP agencies.

Bridgeport had a CAP agency named Action for Bridgeport Community Development, Inc. (ABCD), a 501(c)(3) corporation organized by Bridgeport area's men and women, mostly majority community folks who cared.

Initially, ABCD's officers and board were white men and women, community folks, who moved positively and aggressively to join the War and take advantage of an opportunity to help in Bridgeport. No surprise there.

The NAACP and black leaders generally were so busy dealing with the multitude of race-related issues that an awareness of President John F. Kennedy's declaration of war against poverty, and the details of how to get involved, had escaped leadership in the minority community. Help was surely needed, but black leaders were not alert enough, or perhaps did not have or take the time to be first at the door of opportunity. Nor did it have the relationships and networking needed to partner up early with those who did.

On reflection, that was not a bad thing. Those who organized ABCD were good people and the right people. They cared about the Greater Bridgeport area's many issues and were desperate to help in any way feasible. Bill Hart, Parker Lansdale, Sam Hawley, Ed Harrison, Nick Goodspeed, Len Maniero and many others were people of courage, foresight, and understanding. They were almost all friends of mine.

Sam Hawley, CEO of People's Bank, became known as "Mr. Bridgeport" because of his efforts. His commitment to Bridgeport and the surrounding communities was real. He brought much needed vision to the table, along with a willingness to actually work on the issues.

His efforts over the years are real lesson in how corporations can relate well to a community. Unfortunately, local government in Bridgeport had its own agenda, one that prevented their honest and sincere involvement.

Fueled by a strict adherence to the Christian ethic in their daily lives and subscribing to a standard of fairness, the men at the 1965 meeting sought to stop the downward spiral toward oblivion that Bridgeport had fallen heir to since the end of WWII. They joined the War on Poverty, as a way to help and organized it in a way that permitted access to the resources that OEO could make available.

Confronting them was a wide variety of seemingly impossible problems that neither Bridgeport's business community nor its politicians had addressed and didn't, maybe couldn't, resolve. Neither spent quality time trying to solve those problems. No surprise there either, since those two groups were not in tune with each other, except, maybe, in a superficial way.

The truth is that if failure to cooperate between them was a crime, a major felony, those groups would have been indicted, charged, and convicted of that crime. A jury's verdict would have been guilty as charged, beyond a reasonable doubt, or any doubt whatsoever.

Racism was evident in every aspect of life among the citizenry, but neither politicians nor the business community gave more than lip service to the need to address and resolve a host of problems. Improving race relations was simply not a priority for political or business leaders.

Among issues that needed to be addressed as priorities were: the public school system; growing unemployment;

JOHN F. MERCHANT

employers moving out of the area, creating a dying business base; an uncaring, ineffective, and often corrupt, political leadership and system; the negatives inherent in the welfare system; the growing number of welfare recipients; and many other issues related to the general demise of opportunities in cities across the nation and, especially, in the Northeast.

Housing needs were enormous, slum landlords abounded and laws related to landlord and tenant issues favored the slum landlords.

The black community comprised 25 to 30 percent of Bridgeport's population, with a growing number of welfare recipients and children with unmet needs. Yet, not many were concerned with those issues. It was easier to blame the downtrodden for the situation, or worse, ignore them.

Poverty existed and was spreading; public education needed serious assistance; lenders were reluctant to lend to blacks, often refusing to do so; employers hesitated to hire blacks or pay them what should be paid for their skills; trade unions and other employee unions discriminated at will; and inter alia, only a small number of black professional men and women existed in the black community. One CPA, a handful of doctors who fought daily for privileges at hospitals, and two lawyers, my partner L. Scott Melville, and I. Scott is a very capable attorney who cared. The above comprised the entire group of black professionals.

Pastors of several black churches sought leadership roles in the spirit of Dr. Martin L. King's leadership and philosophies. Their group, The Interdenominational Ministerial Alliance, was a force and became very articulate in explicating community problems. That articulation suffered from an absence of workable solutions. It further suffered from an absence of meaningful relationships with either the political or business communities. Thus, even if they had ideas, their ability to implement those ideas didn't exist.

Truthfully, I wondered if they really sought solutions or were content to take the easier path of stating problems and assigning blame in a general way to the majority community.

The pulpit became a major resource for stating the issues, assigning fault to the majority population and bemoaning the political system and politicians who had systematically failed to give priority to resolving the issues made clear during the civil rights movement.

The ministers, individually and collectively, urged parishioners to keep the faith and the Lord would find a way. Overlooked was the biblical thesis that the Lord helps those who help themselves.

Going back to leaders, what troubled me then, and still does, was that, in general, too many of African heritage, including many men of the cloth, appeared comfortable with their self-proclaimed status as "experts" at defining the problems. Apparently they assumed that that ability alone made them leaders. Their leadership status, to them, was validated if and when the media published their words, as it often did.

Of course, few analyzed the media's rationale for publishing their words. My sense is that the rationale or "media motive" was not thought through in a positive way.

Too often the act of publication was simply a way to inform the majority community about the presumed negativity and unreasonableness of the minority community, evidenced by comments from its "leaders."

Personally, I can now recall when, following the *Brown v. Board* decision by the US Supreme Court, Virginia's media supported opposition to that decision on a regular basis. It lauded and applauded Senator Byrd and Governor Battle who promoted anti *Brown* legislation in the Virginia legislature and led the South in "massive resistance" to the decision. Media coverage is not always a productive or good thing.

Recently, in the twenty-first Century, some of Virginia's largest newspapers and its state legislature apologized publicly for its sins of the past, admitting that its coverage, and laws enacted, were designed to prevent implementation of *Brown* and to disobey its mandates and requirements permanently. Problem solving was not on their minds.

Freedom of the press is something I subscribe to fully. But abuse of that freedom for personal reasons, such as flaunting the courts or disobeying the law and inciting the general public to do so, is detestable, un-American and wrong. I cannot condone it when used that way.

Back to our "experts," too many of whom saw themselves as potential heirs to the leadership position made vacant by Dr. King's assassination, while seemingly ignoring the issue of finding workable solutions.

Isn't finding solutions a fundamental responsibility of leadership? Or is it enough to obtain personal ego satisfactions by being a spokesperson, an "expert" if you will, in stating the problem and getting media coverage for doing that?

Is it enough to say that you are fighting for my rights, every day in every way you can, without describing and showing me positive results from your efforts? Telling me that you are fighting for me, while ignoring my observation of the fact that we are still losing, big time, makes no sense and will not cause or allow me to accept your claim to being a leader.

Folks with an African heritage, often the only qualification for describing one's self as an "expert," appeared from every nook and cranny in our neighborhoods everywhere and are still in a growth mode today. The net effect, too often, is to exacerbate unresolved problems and inhibit solutions.

Meaningful dialogue between the majority and minority communities remains a needed resource. However, it was, and still is, fundamentally nonexistent. Why? Does hate run that deep? Or don't we realize that? If not, why not?

Neither seems able to find a way to sit and communicate with the other about solutions. An often blasphemous depiction of the problems by the "experts" is too often counterproductive in that many of those being blamed grow tired of hearing that they, individually and collectively, are at fault when they are not.

A good friend who is a white, southern lawyer and with whom I have collaborated over the years in meaningful ways regarding racial issues, expressed his tiredness to me in 2008. He said that he had grown incredibly tired of being blamed by "spokespersons" from the black community for the racial mess existing in America today. He explained that he had worked hard to change things, within the context of his ability and opportunity to do so, but was still besieged by careless declarations lumping all persons of Caucasian heritage together as the enemy. He was about to give up his efforts to help and retire to a life of raising his family and earning a living. I understood why he felt that way, but am happy to report that he has not quit . . . yet.

The search for meaningful dialogue and positive communication must be made a priority, however laborious it may be. That search opts against immediate gratification and requires patience as well as a commitment to its attainment. Not easy, but it must be sought, obtained, continued, and stressed, starting yesterday. Having a sensible plan would also help.

Regrettably, the absence of meaningful communication between the races still typifies race relations in America today, in the twenty-first Century.

Have we grown so far apart that we can never get together?

The city of Bridgeport was deteriorating rapidly in every important area of service to its citizens. Many believed that organized crime had established an unyielding grasp in the city, including owning the political system and promoting racial strife. Yet we don't talk with each other, why?

A major problem that ABCD encountered, almost immediately, was that its organizational efforts did not include people of color. Thus it became a target for criticism from the NAACP and black leadership. That criticism led to ABCD employing two black men in important positions. Charles B. Tisdale became director of the Neighborhood

Youth Corps (NYC); and, me. I left my law practice to accept a position as Deputy Director, with the job of supervising the Neighborhood Program.

Both hirings put us in policy-making positions, dealing with programs and services flowing directly to the minority community, with some chance to impact policy making in other areas of concern to ABCD. We had some juice and used it.

Charley Tisdale was tailor-made to head the NYC. Educated at one of the historical black colleges and a four-letter athlete at Harding High School in the city, he had an enlightened view of the needs of young people and an incredibly positive relationship with them throughout the city. He and Roy J. Carroll, his assistant who happened to be white, will never get enough credit for the help they gave, the lives they influenced, or the positive and lasting impact that had on individuals and the community.

Unchallengeable is the thesis that they were what was needed at that time and that they produced positive results.

ABCD's Neighborhood Program divided Bridgeport into five neighborhoods with a coordinator and two assistants in each to work with and for residents of those neighborhoods. All involved reported to me as Deputy Director; all were hired by me. It was a neighborhood staff that cared about those in need and produced for them.

When necessary, they confronted existing social service agencies and their policies. Often, their efforts led to important changes in the provision of services. In addition, they were creative in suggesting programs to be funded by OEO to meet needs they discovered and documented.

As examples, two programs are worthy of note. I believe that the very first legal service program funded by OEO in the states was the one we proposed at ABCD. I personally lobbied for and received the support needed from the Bridgeport Bar Association, thanks to Herb Cohen, then President of the Bridgeport Bar Association and a senior partner at Cohen and Wolf.

OEO required that the Bar Association sign off on their approval of the program, and after a somewhat contentious meeting of its governing body where I argued for support, they voted to support the program.

Also, thanks to extensive research done by Jim Tisdale, Charley's brother and a Neighborhood coordinator, OEO funded its first drug prevention and rehab program. Jim's research established that the drug issue extended far beyond the black community. However, his early warnings were scoffed at and dismissed as being untrue, even silly.

Among other things, Jim's research disclosed that some doctors in Fairfield County prescribed drugs regularly for majority community patients, thus supporting habits that were criminal and they should know that.

He also discovered a young man from one of the white communities in Fairfield County whose parents gave him $90 each week specifically to buy illegal drugs from dealers in one of ABCD' five neighborhoods. Apparently, the family disclosed to Jim that they had no other options since rehab programs did not exist.

Today, in the twenty-first century, Jim would not be dismissed. Drugs are a national problem and their purchasers, users, and sales personnel include many who are not black Americans.

Those two programs are only mildly indicative of the quality and creativity of ABCD's Neighborhood staff. There are several others too numerous to detail.

The four other neighborhood coordinators were: Clarence Williams, a chef by profession and feisty by nature; W. O Johnson, pastor of First Baptist Church in Stratford, Connecticut; Ralphola Taylor, a wonderful woman for whom a community center in the East End of Bridgeport has been named; and, Andrew Allen, a man of the cloth who did not have a church in Bridgeport.

The 1800 Club required no funding, from OEO or anyone. It started by chance and remained viable because the diverse group assembled found common cause to give their time, talents, and energy to dealing with problems. It came about in this way.

On a Monday in July, while at work conducting a staff meeting, one of my coordinators reported that a rumor was circulating in his neighborhood to the effect that a riot would occur on Friday in that neighborhood. He said he had checked it out and found no substance to the rumor.

The next day, Tuesday, I received a phone call from Samuel W. Hawley, president and CEO of Peoples Savings Bank. He was a real friend of Bridgeport and fully aware of, and supportive of, ABCD, its organizers, and mission. He asked if I had heard the rumor about a riot coming on Friday. I lied and told him no, but would check it out. I hung up the phone, waited twenty minutes, then, called him back, advising him that he need not be concerned because there was no substance to the rumor. He thanked me and we chatted for a while as people do.

Then I said to him, "Mr. Hawley, before we hang up, there are two things I'd like to say." He asked what they were, so I told him.

"First," I said, "we do not advertise our riots in advance." He chuckled, I think.

"Second," I said, "Mr. Hawley, please don't call me again in the summer, July or August, with questions like that, unless you are talking with me the other ten months of the year."

His unexpected response was immediate and spoken without hesitation. He said, "You are right. What should we do about that?"

His question caught me by surprise. It also imposed upon me a level of responsibility to become part of a solution. Nothing he ever did after that surprised me.

Over time, I learned that Mr. Hawley was one of a kind, a great man whom I became privileged to know as a friend.

That phone call was the beginning of a friendship that lasted over thirty years and ended only when he died in 2002, at the age of ninety. He began working for People's Bank the year I was born, 1933, and gave real meaning to corporate involvement in the life and lives of people in a city and state.

He was real, he cared, he was committed to Bridgeport, and he was totally unafraid to use the bank's resources to help with urban issues, even the tough ones: housing, race relations, city government, slum lords, and just plain people who resided in Bridgeport and the state of Connecticut.

His question found me unprepared with an answer, so I winged it and said the first thing that came to mind, namely, that he was a bank president and I was a black male. I asked, "Why don't you convene Bridgeport's other bank presidents and have them meet with a group of black males that I will select and invite to the meeting with his bankers and we can talk?"

He agreed and went to work. In less than two hours, he called and advised me that six or seven bank presidents had agreed to meet with my group the following Monday at 6:00 p.m. in the board room at People's Savings Bank.

I knew the names of the bank presidents; he did not know or ask for the names of the men I would bring to the meeting.

By way of background, this came at a time when many in the majority community were clearly apprehensive about being in the company of, or even seeing, a group of men of color. The Watts Riots in 1963 had escalated a fear of dark-skinned or brown-skinned black males, especially a group of them; that was both real and contagious.

It had occurred to me that most of the country's white population had never had what I would consider a "normal" conversation with a black person and vice-versa. "Therein lies the rub," said Shakespeare.

I thought, and think, *That has to stop if we are ever to make progress in race relations in America.* But how to achieve that objective was the burning question. Perhaps

JOHN F. MERCHANT

the proposed meeting was a significant step in the right direction, at least on a local level. It must be done.

"Damn," I said to myself, "this man is both amazing and serious." In truth, I was awestruck. The 1800 Club's birthday was the following Monday. That first meeting was successful. Eventually, it led to regular meetings with Bridgeport's seven largest employers on alternate weeks with the bankers.

The discussions, and they were meaningful discussions, covered a broad area of concerns to all. They also created a networking between the majority and minority leadership in an urban area that helped each understand and trust the other. Expanded communication resulted and many problems were resolved before they became major problems.

I seriously doubt that this effort, and result, was present in any other community in America, but I don't actually know that. I only wish that it would happen more than it did or does.

CEOs and black males, an unlikely alliance, sat and discussed issues as normal, concerned people should, if they can find a way to do so. But people have to look for ways, as a priority, or they will never be found.

Solving problems is a leadership responsibility. That responsibility starts by understanding the problem, identifying and relating to available resources, and then creating ways to apply the resources effectively or add to the resource pile. It works best with a team effort, if you can assemble the team.

We, Mr. Hawley and I, assembled the team.

The 1800 Club provided a setting for learning and understanding, something the races don't often get or seek. Free flowing discussion occurred. It included candid discussion of problems such as racial prejudice in bank lending to persons of color and the host of employment issues in the workplace. Education and understanding began to evolve through honest discussion.

Telephone numbers were exchanged and, lo and behold, a handful of black males had immediate telephone access to the movers and shakers, bankers and employers, in the Greater Bridgeport area. That access was enormously helpful in preventing racial unrest situations in the city. It also helped to resolve issues affecting the businesses run by the CEOs and presidents.

No, it did not provide total solutions to the myriad problems that existed. However, it did provide a meaningful base for understanding and attacking the problems. It needed to live long. Regrettably, its life was too short.

Interestingly, I was told, the Superintendent of Police had his own riot prevention plan in Bridgeport. If true, it was a limited plan, to be sure, because it applied only to a portion of the city and evidenced the unwillingness to deal with the underlying issues in any true sense.

The Superintendent's plan focused on the East End of Bridgeport, where a large number of black residents lived. Many were homeowners and operated small businesses. It was reachable only by crossing drawbridges on three sides. The Plan assumed that it was the area where a riot would start if one erupted. You know about assuming anything, don't you?

The plan involved raising the drawbridges to prevent ingress and egress, then cordoning off the fourth side using police units, after the drawbridges were raised. Obviously, the plan sought to contain any riot activity.

Let them burn their own homes and pillage their own stores, maybe even injure or kill each other; who cares? That was the basis of his plan. What a jerk!

Diversity was not on his agenda, and he ran the police force in a way that catered to his apparent racial prejudices in that police officers with an African heritage had trouble becoming officers, or being promoted, or even being treated like the capable human beings they were, performing in ways that good police officers should. Even today, there is an insufficient priority given to diversity in the city's police force, though there have been improvements, including some initiated by the federal courts. Why?

Of serious import regarding the 1800 Club was the undeniable fact that people were talking and honestly communicating, not screaming at and blaming one another for the problems.

Fear did not attend the meetings. Mutual interests created a bonding that produced actions of significance that mattered to residents and the city, most of whom were unaware of the club's existence.

No effort to involve the media was made. In fact, it was firmly discouraged and fully avoided by design and agreement.

But neither politicians nor the masses needed to know that the 1800 Club existed. It was enough that leadership in both communities was collaborating and leading in positive ways. A real and caring community was born and functioned on behalf of the greater community. Many participants from the majority community took real pride in being involved. There was something real and exciting about being involved is such an effort.

Unfortunately, it died before it became old enough to reach out and include a high level of political leadership as well, although I'm not sure that could ever have happened.

Bridgeport's politicians in general were not admired by any 1800 Club participant and were not trusted by either. There are exceptions, of course. I don't mean to label every politician, elected or appointed, as being corrupt or a negative in the system. However, the *political system* was deemed corrupt by many, and in my view, it deserved its reputation.

I shall not enumerate reasons why the 1800 Club faded, then died. I have my opinion, but few facts and little evidence.

No one wanted Bridgeport to suffer riots such as happened in Watts, and those were avoided with the help of the 1800 Club. The black participants spent weekends at work and on alert in their neighborhoods. If, or when, incidents arose that could flare up into something serious, we contacted each other, converged on the place of the incident, and quieted things down before things got out of hand, or the police had to be called.

Among other things, those meetings led to the creation of a successful lending program for welfare recipients being instituted by People's Bank, the only one of its kind in America. Who would have thought that a welfare recipient could ever be a borrower from a bank?

I am still amazed that it happened, but it did, in Bridgeport, Connecticut, and both the bank and the borrowers benefitted.

In one of many discussions with Mr. Hawley, I shared an aspect of the oft encountered plight of welfare mothers that was not fully understood. Too many saw welfare mothers as lazy leeches whose sole *raison d' etre* was to increase the tax burdens government imposed upon folks who worked for a living. Lazy, no work ethic, parasites and useless was a normal evaluation.

My neighborhood coordinators and I saw things in a very different way. We saw single parents suffering from an inability to both work and raise a child, or children, alone. If work was available, minimum wage laws made it difficult to cope, especially when coping included being the victim of a slum lord's negatives or medical issues affecting a child that raised critical concerns or the school questions that abounded or simply putting nutritious food on the table, to say little about the inconvenience of transporting themselves or their children to school, a doctor's office, or a grocery store.

Busses helped, but not if more than one bag of groceries had to be carried. Supermarkets were not located in minority neighborhoods and very few had automobiles.

By way of example, I posed the following scenario to Mr. Hawley. You are a single parent and the rent is due. However, your child needs a pair of shoes in order to attend school. Without them he will be picked on, laughed at and rejected by his peers, in or out of school. Do you pay the rent or buy the shoes? You can't do both unless another $25 to $50 is found quickly.

Mr. Hawley agreed to establish a special program in his bank to help with that kind of problem, as well as with other related problems. He specially trained a group of employees, modified intake documents, and set a limit of $250 that could be borrowed. Repayment terms were crafted to fit the individual. The program was coded as a PL 9 loan and carefully tracked.

It was understood that if one of ABCD's neighborhood staff brought a welfare mother to the bank, seeking a small loan to cover both the rent and the shoes, the loan would be granted, provided that the process of appearing at the bank, filling out forms, speaking with a lending officer, and subjecting one's self to the normal procedures for seeking a loan occurred.

In short, don't change the bank's way of functioning. Instead, teach newcomers to banks how to deal with the lenders and let them learn that some banks can and will help, when and where possible.

The borrower must not be told in advance that the loan was practically guaranteed. The potential borrowers must put their best foot forward and actually seek the loan and convince the lender that they were worthy. Then, of course, they must repay the loan exactly as they contracted to do. Being responsible was key.

Over a three-year period, these loans were carefully tracked. The result showed that the loan loss ratio for PL

JOHN F. MERCHANT

9 loans was slightly better than that of small loans made by the bank's other divisions. Success; it worked!

Mr. Hawley invited me to speak at some savings bank conferences around the country and explain the program and its success, and I did. Regrettably, not one banking institution in America saw fit to follow People's' lead and create a similar program. Too big to fail? No. Too big to care? Maybe, or should I say probably?

But not People's Bank or Sam Hawley. Many called him "Mr. Bridgeport"; I did. They, and he, cared; and they did not fail. Instead they grew.

Undoubtedly, other banks around the country lacked an 1800 Club or a networking ability with its black community leadership that could serve as a foundation for such an effort. A sad commentary, to say the least.

Can't we change that? We still need to figure out ways to communicate better with each other and form a united front on issues of mutual concern. Sadly, America seems to be moving away from that possibility, beset by "thunder from the far right" and lack of trust from the left.

On a different subject related to the viability and growth of the bank, Mr. Hawley considered expanding the bank's information resources by the act of diversifying his Board of Directors, a board that consisted primarily of persons with a sameness that was not representative of the total community.

Politicians, labor, Catholics, women, blacks, Hispanics, ethnic groups with a European heritage, including Irish, Italian, Slavic, and Swedes, were not represented on his board.

Rather than increase the size of his Board, a difficult thing to get the present Board to agree to, he received Board approval to create a Board of Counselors, consisting of three persons from unrepresented groups or disciplines in the bank's catchment area. He argued that it was good business to reach out in that manner. It was a novel concept and a very sensible business decision.

Each person selected would serve a one-year term during which they were paid and enjoyed all the privileges and responsibilities of full Board membership, except where prohibited by statute.

I was asked to serve on the first Board of Counselors and, after my one year of service, was elected to full Board membership. I believe that I became the first black bank Director in the state of Connecticut, a reality that was years ahead of America's corporations electing blacks to their Boards.

Once again, I entered a situation as a novice, entered an unknown situation and lacked a mentor. I am not a banker; never was and never pretended to be. Truthfully, I took notes at meetings and wrote down words and phrases I didn't know the meaning of. Later, at home or at my office, I would study and learn. If that had not been done, I would not have understood what was being said at Board meetings or its significance.

I bought and studied books on the language and operation of financial institutions and that world. I learned how to read and understand an audit, balance sheet, and other financial documents and implements. I

JOHN F. MERCHANT

learned enough so that I could ask questions and make inquiries without embarrassment.

Of course, I was afforded leeway because I was not asked to join the Board as a banker or as a business man. Everyone knew that.

However, although I was never told the purpose of my becoming a Board member, I believe that Mr. Hawley never regretted inviting me to do so, and I believe that I brought something of value to the Board that had been missing, and nothing but good came from it.

My presence did nothing to stunt the bank's growth. Arguably, it helped in ways that can be documented. For example, when People's decided to expand into Stamford, Connecticut, by buying a commercial bank in Stamford, approval by the state's banking department was required to effect the sale and purchase.

A hearing was held, chaired by the Bank Commissioner. I was asked by Mr. Hawley to testify at that hearing and did. My testimony, a copy of which I still have, was, I was told later, persuasive and a significant factor in the move being approved.

Incidentally, that was not a big deal for me. All I had to do was tell the truth, under oath, about Mr. Hawley and the bank's community involvement record. The truth had to be impressive to anyone hearing it.

Over time, membership on the Board of Counselors included the state's top labor leader, the publisher of the local paper, and many others from various areas of the community. Those selected acquired a relationship with

People's Savings Bank that certainly did no harm to the bank's growth in assets, influence, and profitability.

For many years, an annual dinner meeting of the bank's "alumni" was held, thereby retaining the relationship acquired as a member of the Board of Counselors. No longer a savings bank, the Board of Counselors ceased to exist when the bank changed to another form, selling shares of stock to the public.

However, a dinner meeting continues to he held annually for alumni.

Mr. Hawley also exhibited his astuteness and business judgment by using his Board of Counselors as the means for adding a woman as a Director. He was ahead of corporate America in that regard as well.

Sister Theresa, a Catholic nun was selected. She was the person in charge of St, Joseph's Manor, a Catholic nursing home well respected, well run, and a community mainstay in every respect. She agreed to serve on the Board of Counselors and then, after her year there, was invited to join the full Board. She declined, but the stage was set. Imagine that? Think about it for a moment.

How, in good conscience, could an all-white (except for me) male Board vote against her election? She would not compete for prestige or power and was no threat to continued male dominance, having taken, and lived, her vows.

Her professional life was involved with helping people, not competing for a competitor's market share or a manufacturer's raw materials. In addition, her presence sent a clear message to the Catholic community about People's

Bank. By inference, without marketing the asset, she stood as a possible resource who could attract other Catholics to choose to do their banking at People's.

Incidentally, her talents included being able to bring positive comments to the business of banking and to business concepts and policies that were valuable. She was a real asset to the bank and proved it during her term.

Well done, Mr. Hawley, and for all the right reasons.

In another area, housing, Mr. Hawley proved to be more caring than most and an unusual banker, CEO, and human being. During the late 1960s, government funds became available to build low- and moderate-income housing in America. Connecticut enacted a law creating a Department of Community Affairs (DCA). Among its other responsibilities, DCA had a duty to work with Connecticut's 169 municipalities, especially the state's largest cities, and build housing to accommodate the needs of low- and moderate-income residents.

Mr. Hawley assigned his chief mortgage lending officer the task of identifying each and every piece of land within Bridgeport's city limits upon which such housing might be built. This was done and retained in a file.

A savvy lending officer was made available to find, then work with, any actual or potential nonprofit sponsor to determine site feasibility and, where feasible, work with sponsors and government officials to purchase the land and build housing.

Many affordable units were built in that manner, and the quality of life for many city residents was considerably enhanced.

Ironically, although some black churches sought and became sponsors, none hired the law firm of Merchant, Melville, Spear and Seymour to represent them in the process.

I served as Deputy Commissioner of DCA, by appointment of Governor Dempsey, for four years. I had a direct responsibility for operations in all of DCA's work, including housing. I never sought to influence a sponsor in its choice of an attorney, but am still amazed that black clergy in the city never once asked the city's only black law firm or any black lawyer or firm to represent it.

I reckon that an age-old myth still abided in the minds of black leaders, namely, that only someone in the majority community can perform well when professional assistance is needed. That myth has had a long life in America's black communities. It may have been somewhat accurate at one time, but not in the late 1960s. Today, it still lives but is dying.

L. Scott Melville and E. Eugene Spear, law partners of mine, both became Superior Court Judges in Connecticut. Both were excellent professionals and well respected by their peers. Mr. Spear was ultimately elevated to the state's Appellate Court, where he served with distinction for several years until his untimely death at an early age.

Earlier, I made reference to Bridgeport's black clergy, members of the Interdenominational Ministerial Alliance, (IMA) who worked hard at preaching about the racial and social problems, and even perfected the art of assigning blame to the majority community, without naming names or excluding friends who happened to be

JOHN F. MERCHANT

white. Regrettably, too many of them chose not to support their own community's professionals when they could and should have. Why?

I hasten to add that not all black clergy turned their backs on their own black professionals in the city. Frankly, without the support of men like Rev. A. C. Bass at Mount Aery Baptist Church and William Kenney at Shiloh Baptist Church, it would have been very difficult for Scott Melville and me to find clients sufficient to get a fledgling law practice like ours off the ground and help it to grow into a community staple as we did. I owe a debt of gratitude to those men and fully appreciate what they did.

On the other hand, there was discord and disharmony in the ranks of black leadership in Bridgeport.

Historically, the church was our strength and provided leadership in black communities. College-educated, unlike almost everyone else, ministers maintained this status despite not always earning it, primarily because they had little or no competition. In my view, too many men of the cloth believed that they were entitled to that status and entitled to be recognized and respected as owners of it. Dr. King's national leadership, in the minds of many black preachers, solidified that ownership right. Not true.

Dr. King was one of a kind. He lacked the capacity, and probably, the inclination to transfer his leadership role to any, let alone every Baptist minister or non-Baptist minister.

He was and is irreplaceable, although he does serve as a role model to clergy that could and should be a source of inspiration.

A responsibility to their parishioners was their clear priority. A wider community leadership role has to be earned by those who could. Often earning that role escaped them. It required a higher level of cooperating with others and functioning as a team member, not as the team leader. A hard pill to swallow for many who assumed that leadership belonged to them.

Regrettably the ability to be a significant leader was often lacking, but not realized or admitted. Often, it seems, their fiercest competition was with each other in a search for recognition

One problem this created was that the power in the white community recognized this lack of unity and could not be as responsive as many would like to have been. They found it easy to ignore the Black Panthers and SNCC but weren't entirely comfortable with the NAACP after the *Brown* decision and the difficulties arising from it. Then there was the Urban League to consider.

The majority community's leadership faced difficult questions such as to whom does one talk in the minority community? Whom does one follow? What philosophy should be embraced, along with its proposed directions? Where can I find the time to investigate, talk, and work with the different factions? Is it possible for me to choose while I also try to operate and manage a business or cater to those voters who elected me? Who has their finger on the pulse and the support needed to lead? Not easy questions to answer.

Differences among black leaders was not unexpected nor should it be criticized as being a problem that existed, and exists, only in the black community. People—black, white or polka dot—have differences. Also, leadership in any aspect of life is not exempt from experiencing conflict arising out of those differences in philosophy and approaches.

However, the majority community, in my mind, has always expected the black community to have one leader who spoke for all, someone they could approach, maybe befriend, and obtain whatever result or information they sought.

That is not only impossible to attain; it is patently ridiculous to expect it anywhere, and the majority community should know that.

Perhaps the dominant business/CEO mentality opts against learning and applying such an approach. I mean to say that business, seemingly, functions via a philosophy that has dictator like qualities deeply embedded in it. The CEO has spoken; end of discussion. If that approach can incorporate some or any level of benevolence and show profits, growth, and dividends on a regular quarterly and annual basis, it is heralded as the way to go.

Human beings like or dislike other human beings, sometimes with good reason, sometimes not. Similarly, they agree or disagree, and that is normal.

In that vein, not all black clergy applauded the arrival and presence of two young lawyers, Merchant and Melville, into their "territory." Perhaps they saw us as unwelcome competition. Or maybe they simply resented our intrusion, disliked us personally, or had other reasons. I don't know their rationale. I do know that some clergy spent an inordinate amount of time knocking me, privately, for no apparent reason that I was aware of, or told of, by them or anyone.

One story about black clergy should be told. It may show the difference between their way of functioning and mine. It also touches on the need to focus on doing what is right, despite petty reasons not to.

As a bank director, I was privy to detailed information submitted by persons seeking a mortgage loan to buy a home. A long time ago, directors personally reviewed applications for some loans, primarily the more expensive loans involving large amounts of dollars.

In one meeting, an application was presented that led to an extensive discussion because the buyers were close, but didn't truly qualify for the mortgage they were seeking. The Board hemmed and hawed for a while, knowing that the application could, maybe should, be turned down, but no board member was willing to make the arguments to cause that result or make a motion to deny it.

Finally, one Board member spoke up, saying to the CEO, "They're okay, some of us know them." The mortgage was immediately approved.

A year or so later, one of the black clergy applied for a mortgage loan seeking to buy his family's first home in a neighborhood not heavily populated by black homeowners. He was not financially sound, and the mortgage request could easily have been refused under the guidelines. He was close to qualifying, close enough to rival the people described above. However, no Board member wanted to make a motion to deny or approve the application.

JOHN F. MERCHANT

Apparently, my presence caused a level of reluctance on the part of some to speak their minds, so they remained silent or vacillated. I sat there as a silent observer, paying close attention to what few comments were spoken and to the body language of those who spoke and those who did not speak. I listened carefully to all comments, apparently oblivious to the tension that existed in the room, and made no comments.

Finally, I spoke up saying, "They're okay. Some of us know them." Amazingly, to me, the mortgage was approved and quiet sighs of relief were registered and noted. After all, now I was the person who recommended the mortgage and bore some unspoken responsibility if a default occurred at a future date. None ever did.

Also, I believe that I was the only Director who was personally acquainted with the preacher and his family. I believed he was a good risk so I said so.

The specific clergyman never knew the story about how his home purchase was made possible. I wouldn't tell him. Nor will I tell you, the reader, his name. Bank matters are confidential.

Ironically, he also had no use for me, for reasons never made clear to me. He often went out of his way to make negative remarks and told lies about me, many of which were repeated to me by friends who heard the comments and the lies being told. They asked me what I had done to cause such animosity. I could not answer because I had not "done" anything I was aware of, did not know the answer, and still don't.

Strange world we live in, isn't it? But real life is like that, and even men of the cloth are not perfect, or are they?

Knowing him, his personal ambitions, his huge ego, and his desire to be Connecticut's Dr. Martin Luther King, I am certain that he would never have had the grace to do for me what I did for him.

Nor was it possible, given his abilities, for him to bear more than a minor resemblance to Dr. King. He just didn't have it. Some do, most don't; he didn't.

So be it. I'm pleased with what I did, but not dumb enough to name names or bear a grudge for the abuse I received from him over many years, abuse I did nothing to earn and did not deserve.

Interestingly, no black clergy was ever involved with the 1800 Club, and that was not an accident. My choices for the meeting with bank leadership that resulted in the creation of the 1800 Club did not include them. Our good works were not hampered by their absence. They did their work, preaching every Sunday, defining the issues repeatedly, and we went about doing our work, effectively, without their input.

My active involvement with the 1800 Club was severely limited after I accepted Governor Dempsey's appointment as Deputy Commissioner of DCA. Time was simply no longer available for real participation, given my new responsibilities. It saddened me to limit that involvement because I thoroughly enjoyed every minute of it and believed it could seriously herald the dawn of a new era in Bridgeport, a city that needed it.

JOHN F. MERCHANT

I have often tried to figure out what really caused the demise of the 1800 Club, its good work and its potential for more. I couldn't figure it out. I believe that in my absence new black leadership of the effort resulted in a loss of trust by the majority community participants. New leaders and new agendas caused the death of trust and once it dies failure is practically guaranteed. The significance and effectiveness of the effort slowly diminished, then disappeared. What a pity!

I remain proud of what we were able to do for Bridgeport, the State, and people, though I still mourn the passing of the 1800 Club. I shall never forget how Sam Hawley, Ed Harrison, Parker Lansdale, Lenny Manero, and Nick Goodspeed made it happen. I wish for more and more of the same in America, though in 2010 it seems headed in the wrong direction.

Also, I can never forget the lessons I learned through involvement in the 1800 Club's. High on the list of lessons learned is the fact that men and women of goodwill exist in communities. If they can be reached to honestly discuss issues, learn to trust each other and focus on a broader community interest, significant change can occur.

Sadly, I know of no other community in America where an 1800 Club existed or exists. Nor it seems is an effective search for such underway anywhere. A pity!

Sam Hawley and I were brought together by chance. I have been a beneficiary of his wisdom, intellect, courage, common sense, commitment to community, and thinking outside the box ever since. He taught without lecturing; I learned and grew in the process.

Nick Goodspeed, Len Manero, Jim Biggs, Jack McGregor, George Dunbar, Ed Harrison, Betty Hollander, among others, impacted my learning in positive ways, especially Nick Goodspeed who succeeded Sam Hawley as CEO.

Nick became a good friend, and I simply adored Bee Jay, his wife. They never missed my annual January party that had a seventeen year life and involved more than a hundred guests. I have fond recollections of them sitting and tapping their feet to the gospel music provided by Gigi Van Dyke and a few members of her Serendipity Chorale. Yup, the spirit moved them, and they showed it.

Actually, it moved all who heard it. It was fabulous!

Gigi is a special lady, blessed with enormous musical talent and enviable energy. She has a sense of humor and smile that is downright magnetic. She was never the first to arrive at the party, but when she did arrive, the party rose to another higher level.

My daughter, Susan, said that Gigi walked in with an air about her that seemed to say, "Okay, folks, it's time to party," and that's what was done.

The party's guests included Susan and Tabitha, who spent almost every weekend with me as little girls. Early on, each was given an assignment. Susan, as hostess, greeted the guests and stored their coats. Tabitha, the bartender's assistant, worked from the basement, getting water, orange juice, club soda, etc., as needed. They seemed to enjoy their jobs.

Over the years, they came to know bank presidents; judges, state and federal; attorneys; my Greenwich friends; neighborhood people; and you name it. Equally important, all those folks came to know them during their growing-up years.

The party usually ended in the wee hours: Susan and Tabitha were sent to bed around ten or eleven. I wasn't ever going to cancel my weekend with them just because a party was going on. They were included, simple as that.

That party included live jazz delivered by friends from Greenwich and lawyer friends on bass and the piano. Scotty Brown on drums, Donald Ward on bass, a chore he shared with Attorney Fritz Ober. Attorneys Doug Schwartz and Alan Neigher played the piano. The music they delivered was superb and fully appreciated. They were good, really good, and performed every year for the seventeen years I gave the party at my home at 69 Parkway.

The Easton Banjo Group also entertained, and somewhere in the mix, when the others needed to catch their breath, I was allowed to do some folk songs on my guitar. It was, in a sense, a musical extravaganza.

A moment more with Nick Goodspeed, an amazing man in my view; he had the ability to focus on whomever he was speaking with in a way that made it seem that nothing in the world was more important than what was being said and discussed at that time. He remembered what was said and kept his word once he gave it. He was a kind man, generous and an able banker who continued to lead the bank in ways that complemented what Mr. Hawley had put in place. Hawley cared, really cared, so did Nick.

Bridgeport, the Greater Bridgeport area and the state of Connecticut were the direct beneficiaries of the talents of these men. Extraordinary men who ran an extraordinary bank. For me, an unparalleled learning experience.

Chapter 7

A Cowboy's Life and More . . . ,
Arizona and Idaho

LIKE MANY, I have had a love affair with the American West and cowboys that began as a young child. I was fascinated and thoroughly entertained by the "shoot 'em ups" gun fights, saving the pretty damsels from harm, and how tough and courageous the cowboys were. The good guys always won. Of course, the good guys were always white men, a portrayal I thought little about growing up.

I did notice that the Indians almost always lost and, according to the scripts Hollywood served up, deserved to lose. I also recall being really excited by what still remains as one of my favorite western movies, *Custer's Last Stand*, although it took me a while to understand why. Simply stated, the Indians finally won one, although not because they were smart, capable, and tough. It was because the unbelievably egotistical Custer made some serious mistakes. Really? You mean he wasn't outsmarted in some respect as well?

I didn't care about *why or how* they won, still don't. My satisfaction came from the fact that they did win one. My biases are two: both Blackfoot and Cherokee Indian blood are part of my heritage, and, historical truth is fundamentally important to me. The West was settled *after* we destroyed the Indians way of life, by force, to accommodate our own self-proclaimed needs. That's the truth.

Another noticeable fact was that Hollywood's Indians were rarely real Indians, just Caucasians made up to look like Indians and, so Hollywood would have us believe, to act like Indians; unbelievably wrong and misleading!

I wondered why they didn't hire real Indian actors, didn't you?

Except for Tonto, that didn't happen. But it seemed that all he ever said was "Kemo sabe" something. But being young and immature, I spent little time pondering his speaking part; my focus was on cowboy heroics.

Many childhood hours were spent playing as a cowboy, strapping on a toy gun, tying the holster around my thigh, and climbing aboard anything I could imagine as being a horse. Predictably, I always won the shootout before Mom called me for dinner.

Initially, Hopalong Cassidy, Lash LaRue, The Lone Ranger, Gene Autry, Roy Rogers, Johnny Mack Brown, The Durango Kid, and their ilk, were my heroes, along with the singing cowboys who kissed their horses. Hmmm!

Then, adult westerns came along, and that was better in that the characters seemed more realistic and the bad guys were not always Indians.

Hollywood made it clear that greedy cattle barons had an insatiable appetite for more land on which to graze their cattle and provide water for them. They took advantage of small ranchers, deplored the existence of any land needs of farmers, detested sheepherders, and ruthlessly sought to obtain all the land and water in sight until some good guys came along and put an end to it.

Notorious outlaws, killers, stagecoach robbers, gamblers, and other criminal types were ultimately done away with by the good guys.

Law and order slowly came to the West in a way that, seemingly, was designed to restore one's faith in the belief that the bad guys would never survive and the good guys would not only prevail in the end, but also get the girl. Riding off into the sunset became memorable and frequent.

The country has remained actively involved with trying to sustain that myth, with limited success, in the twenty-first century. The issue now may be to correctly identify and deal with the bad guys.

Regrettably, we still have "bad guys," many wearing suits and ties, who win a lot. They don't all carry guns, rather many "*new bad guys*" deal with economic matters less than nobly. Who is winning? Is the middle class the new "Indian?" Where is Bin Laden?

Interestingly, to me, it is the failure of Hollywood to portray few of the bad guys as blacks, let alone any of the good guys. That failure carried over to its treatment of women. Until Belle Starr showed up, Hollywood tried to convince us that women had no significant role, good or bad, in the settlement of the American West. That is a bunch of garbage that Hollywood sought to have us buy into, and for the most part, we did.

Occasionally, an escaped slave was part of an outlaw band or rode with the good guys. Perhaps that was a good thing, although historically inaccurate.

JOHN F. MERCHANT

No surprise there because Hollywood is more often historically inaccurate than not in much of what it has done and does. It still promotes myths about cops and spies as it features them in lieu of cowboys, Indians, and ranchers. And we still buy into it.

Over time, High Noon, Shane, Gunfight at the O.K. Corral, The Magnificent Seven, and other movies became my new favorite westerns. The singing cowboys, Autry and Rogers, and the unrealistic others, disappeared, along with kissing one's horse.

Real men were portrayed on the screen as the men who helped tame the West and brought the law and order needed to make it livable for settlers and families. John Wayne, Randolph Scott, Jimmy Stewart, Alan Ladd, Glenn Ford, Steve McQueen, Clint Eastwood, and others brought realism to westerns, although Hollywood hasn't yet gotten around to telling the whole truth. Guess it doesn't sell. Or maybe they are unaware of the facts; I am not unaware of the facts.

The truth is that all the major players in the settling of the West were not disgruntled Confederate soldiers and their families, neighbors, friends, and relatives. Certainly, many fit that definition; however, more than thirty years of researching the history of black involvement in the settling of the West has provided me with a much different picture and many surprises not contained in my public school books or Hollywood's propaganda.

The legendary director, John Ford, broke the mold in 1960 when he gave the title role in the film *Sergeant Rutledge* to Woody Strode, a black man with an admirable history as an athlete at UCLA, where he played in the same backfield with Jackie Robinson of baseball fame and with the Los Angeles Rams of the National Football League.

Despite some opposition, Ford cast Strode in the title role as a member of the famed Ninth Cavalry falsely accused of rape and murder. That film is a favorite of mine and comes closer to reality than anything I have seen from Hollywood regarding life as a "Buffalo Soldier" in the West. Hmmm, maybe the truth does, or could, sell.

I am thankful for a series of unplanned circumstances that permitted me to spend time in the West, mostly Arizona and Idaho. There, I experienced a real taste of what a cowboy's life was really like. It was not an easy life by any measurement.

Meadowlark Lemon, the Clown Prince of Basketball, when he played for the Harlem Globetrotters, resided with his family for a time in Fairfield, Connecticut, where we met and became friends. He once asked me to represent him in contract discussions with the Globetrotters many years ago, and I did. Subsequently, he left the Globetrotters and started his own team in competition with them. It failed after a short time. His friends called him Lark; so did I.

Prior to leaving the "Trotters," Lark purchased a working ranch near Bisbee, Arizona. Escondido, his ranch, was twenty-five square miles in size. Bridgeport (Connecticut) has seventeen square miles of land and in excess of one hundred thousand people living there; Escondido has twenty-five square miles of land, two trailers, two permanent residents, Mike and Joan, and approximately three hundred mother head of cows, plus a few bulls.

JOHN F. MERCHANT

Lark too had a love affair with the West and was both pleased and proud to be a rancher. During one meeting we had at his home in Bel Air, California, to discuss his new team, he spoke to me about the ranch. He then asked if I had time to accompany him there when he drove a recreational vehicle to Bisbee to leave at the ranch, and I did.

The drive from Bel Air, California, to Bisbee, Arizona, was long, and I recall being pleased when he announced that we had arrived, in the dark, near midnight. A sign said "Escondido Ranch," so we turned off the paved highway onto a rocky and somewhat rutted dirt road, 2.5 miles long, up an incline, to two trailers located on the ranch.

It was dark, no street lights, and bumpy. No electricity either, nor was there any food in the trailer.

After checking our beds to be sure no snakes, lizards, or insects had staked claims to the beds, we spent the night in one of the trailers, rising early when the sun came up in the east, which was at our backs. I was in awe as we looked over Arizona awakening. No neighbors could be seen, since none existed; just land and scenery from an elevated view.

We were surrounded by the Huachuca Mountains in the west, the Prederosa and Swisshelm Mountains to the east, the Dragoon Mountains to the north, and south was Mexico, six miles away as the crow flies. The Chocolate Mountains were in the mix somewhere, but I cannot recall their exact location.

Twelve miles northwest of the ranch was the town of Tombstone, the site of the *Gunfight at the O.K. Corral.* That fight featured Wyatt Earp and his brothers, joined by Doc Holliday, against the Clantons and some of their men.

The Clantons were outlaws who, among other crimes they committed, crossed the border regularly and rustled cattle in Mexico. The cattle were driven to the Clanton ranch near Tombstone, then, sold to miners and other residents of the town. I once enjoyed a picnic on what used to be the Clanton ranch.

Tombstone was once a thriving town because silver was discovered and mined there. It is said that large amounts of silver still remain but cannot be reached because of water that can't be redirected in a way that would allow mining to take place.

South of the ranch is the town of Bisbee located about twenty miles south of Tombstone in the Mule Mountains. Bisbee was once a thriving community in a district that produced eight billion pounds of copper during approximately one hundred years from about 1877 to the 1970s. It is now a sleepy little town located two or three miles from the Mexican border and favored by visitors, artists, and retired people.

It was once home for one of the world's largest copper mines, the Copper Queen Mine.

The mine shut down in 1943, but in its heyday was a major producer of copper and many semiprecious stones including turquoise, malachite, azurite, and others. I believe that Phelps-Dodge, Inc. owned and operated the mine.

Tours of the mine are still conducted, taking one far enough into the bowels of the mountain to provide a realistic view of what a miner's life must have been like. Bring a sweater or better yet a jacket and a sweater, even gloves, to deal with the under fifty degree temperature, down

JOHN F. MERCHANT

from one hundred plus degrees outside the mine, during the ninety minute tour.

If you are ever in the area, you really should take time out to put on a hard hat, lamp, and yellow slicker provided by the tour guide and take a ride underground, deep underground, on a miner's tram. The tour will expose you to the history, drilling tools, blasting methods, loading of ore and moving it out of the mine, and other mining features. I am still amazed over the fact that men worked under such conditions, mining ore for "*pennies*" and other uses of copper. Scary stuff, especially way back when.

One of the largest manmade holes in the ground I have ever seen is The Lavender Open Pit that exists about one mile south of Bisbee and can be viewed from a parking area off US 80. I'm told that more than 350 million tons of ore was scooped out of the ground to make this particular hole.

Mike had worked in the mines in his youth, but only as long as he had to, quickly pursuing a cowboy career when that opportunity arose.

The view from Lark's trailer was breathtaking. One could see the mountains 20 to 40 miles away and lots of desert that looked flat but wasn't. I had never seen anything like it.

For many, the word desert conjures up visions of sand and camels and an occasional oasis, where water can be found. The desert I viewed and spent twenty-seven years riding over and across was not like that. Mine was a scattered and unimpressive assortment of vegetation—cacti, rocky ground, mountains, rattlesnakes, and arid conditions.

No buildings in sight except the two trailers. No people walking or scurrying around, no autos contaminating the air. Only the sounds of nature awakening interrupted the peace and quiet of the desert as we sat a while before heading up to the second trailer, located nearby, where Mike and Joan lived. They managed the ranch for Lark.

Mike and Joan had married while in their teens and had children, two boys and a girl. They had also acquired a small ranch in Bisbee, an investment that took Mike out of the mines. He ran cows on it before being hired on by Lark to run his spread. One son ultimately took over running the Bisbee place when Mike acquired Lark's place some years later.

Below the mountains seen from the trailer, to the west, lies the town of Sierra Vista, the home of Fort Huachuca. I was told that, through the efforts of Senator Barry Goldwater, Fort Huachuca was handed the military mission of testing electronic and communication gear held by Fort Monmouth in New Jersey. Acceptance of that mission became the foundation for enormous economic growth in the area, growth it sorely needed. New Jersey was left to its own devices and ingenuity to replace its economic loss.

Years ago, in the nineteenth century, Fort Huachuca was a home for the Ninth and Tenth Cavalry who fought and captured Geronimo, then went into Mexico, illegally, and captured other Apache leaders, bringing them back to face their fate.

Yes, this was Apache country, and though it was the West, no buffalo roamed here, only Buffalo Soldiers, under white officers, fighting the Apache.

JOHN F. MERCHANT

The Fort was started as a temporary camp, ordered by the army to deal with Apache raids that threatened settlers and travelers in the San Pedro Valley. In 1886, Fort Huachuca became the advance headquarters for the campaign against Geronimo, who surrendered in August 1886, and thence was retained to deal with outlaws and renegade Indians near the Mexican border.

One of those officers, Lt. John Bigelow, Jr. kept a journal . . . "which chronicled the day-by-day experiences of the Negro Tenth Cavalry's wearisome and dangerous campaign against the Apaches under the ubiquitous Geronimo . . ."

Bigelow's journal was published in serial form in *Outing* magazine in 1866, then became a book by Lieutenant Bigelow entitled "On The Bloody Trail Of Geronimo," with illustrations by Frederick Remington and other artists. It was published by Westernlore Press in 1986, Tucson, AZ 85740.

Inside the front cover it states that the book

"... constitutes one of the truest and most candid pictures ever portrayed of Army life during the long-drawn-out Apache rebellion."

Remington was an easterner, a Yale graduate, who accepted an assignment from a friend, a New York magazine editor, to go West and write about and paint scenes from the West for publication. He traveled with the Tenth Cavalry, and his artwork stands as a historically accurate depiction of military life for those stationed at Fort Huachuca, with a focus on the men of the Tenth Cavalry, the "Buffalo Soldier."

For many years, a museum in New Britain, Connecticut, was the primary location for many, maybe most, of Remington's original artwork, but no longer.

For those who don't know, the Ninth and Tenth Cavalry, along with the 25th Infantry Division, were military units created by Congress after the Civil War. All three were black outfits, with white officers. All three played major roles in the settling of the West, though their efforts were rarely reported or studied east of the Mississippi.

I learned nothing about them in Greenwich, Connecticut, and its outstanding (?) public school system.

Some publicity has been given to the "Buffalo Soldiers" during the past forty or fifty years, though it has not come close to telling the complete story of the roles of blacks in the settling of the American West. William H. Leckie's book, *The Buffalo Soldiers*, published by the University of Oklahoma Press in 1967 is worth reading.

It is said that the Indians gave the "Buffalo Soldiers" their name, referring to the kinky hair of the black cavalrymen and its resemblance to a buffalo's hide, or so the story goes.

Lark and I went up to Mike's trailer for breakfast prior to spending the day with Mike as he went about his ranch duties. The day included saddling up and riding out to one of several pastures to check on cows, fences, and the windmills that provided water for the animals.

It was my first experience on horseback, and damn near my last. At the end of the day, I ached in places I didn't know my body possessed. During the day, there were times when I had to dismount and walk a bit because I was stiff and sore from the bouncing around riding a horse entails, especially for a tenderfoot who is new to the experience and had never ridden a horse.

Walking in cowboy boots, on uneven and rocky ground, proved not to be a bargain either, just a different form of torture. After stumbling, almost turning an ankle often, and experiencing bone-wearying walking, I needed to be carried again. So I would climb back into the saddle and endure until it was again time to walk. And we were out there all day, from around 8:00 a.m. until close to 6:00 p.m., nothing nine-five about a cowboy's day.

In fact, the usual day began when the sun rose in the East and ended when that day's work was accomplished, however long that took. The workweek was seven days long and no overtime was recorded or paid. Actually, none of the small ranches, like Escondido, had employees who might ask for overtime pay. Mike was the sole cowboy; Joan worked in town and helped out when needed, as did their children. Other than that Mike was it.

Weather didn't change the need to tend to the cattle, make sure they had water, brand calves, or move the cows to another pasture when nature's food was exhausted in the pasture the cattle were in. In addition, one had to keep his gear in shape: repair saddles, reins, and other tack; call the vet to care for sick cattle; and brand, gather, and transport calves for sale. Clothes needed laundering, and time must be reserved for little things such as eating, sleeping, and shopping for groceries and other items needed for normal living.

Mike set the schedule at Escondido and was in charge all day every day. Saying that he worked hard is an understatement.

The good news is that phone calls were never a distraction nor was one's schedule changed by faxes or e-mail. There were no unnecessary discussions or senseless negotiations since you did what Mike said do, period.

Mail was picked up from time to time in Bisbee after a seventeen-mile round trip to its post office. There was no mail delivery to the ranch, thus no daily mail to interfere with your daily routine.

Benefits abound, such as fresh air, a healthy appetite, sound sleeping at night, and being around animals that could be ornery but never cursed you or talked back. Thus, the life has a lot to like. The entire experience was ideal for me, so I commuted often to revive myself and obtain relief from the pressures of the courtroom and practicing law.

Yes, it was my way to escape, be revitalized, and live a childhood dream.

Damn, I was tired when we finally returned to the trailer. I wanted to sit down, or lie down, somewhere soft and comfortable. However, that was not to be, at least not immediately.

Mike made it clear that before resting and relaxing, we had to first take care of the horses. I had to unsaddle my horse, rub her down, turn her out in the corral, store the saddle in the barn and watch out for snakes while doing so, and get hay from the barn and put it in the corral, along with some grain, for the horse to eat.

The horses were grained only if they "worked" that day; otherwise they were turned out on the ranch to live off the land, just as the cows did. That kept costs down, a necessary practice.

Taking care of one's horse was an inviolable priority. No matter the time of day or how tired one might be, you always took care of your horse first.

After caring for our horses, we washed up and ate dinner prepared by Joan. It didn't matter what she had prepared because I was always hungry enough to go bear-hunting with a switch, fully prepared to eat any food available. All I sought was *plenty* and we had that. After dinner, I was ready for bed, but it was not to be. Chores around the house needed attention, especially if some daylight remained. There is always something needing attention, or so I came to learn.

Finally, after chores, we could sit down and relax a bit while watching a beautiful sunset in the West.

Mike and Lark discussed issues relating to the ranch, and I soaked up information about the trials and tribulations of running a small ranch and the economic realities of doing so. The business of the ranch was raising, then selling, four-five-hundred-pound calves to a middleman who fattened them up for sale to slaughterhouses as part of the process of making beef available in butcher shops and supermarkets in America.

Three hundred mother head (cows) ideally produced two hundred plus calves annually. Nature and weather conditions dictated the size of the calf crop. All animals lived off the land until the calves grew. Then the calves were separated from Mom and Dad and either were delivered to a buyer who had contracted for them or were taken to auction in Wilcox, Arizona, approximately forty miles away. Selling calves produced the income needed to run and sustain the ranch.

As you might surmise, in order for cows to live well-off the land, nature had to provide the food. Their food requires rain to grow. Arizona is not famous for large amounts of rainfall annually, so the business risks were plentiful.

The bulls must remain healthy and the cows healthy and productive. Occasionally, an animal would be slaughtered for food by Mexicans crossing the border illegally. Similarly, a mountain lion could enjoy calves' liver, and other parts of a calf, as a sumptuous meal, and there could be occasional death of a cow caused by rattlesnakes and disease.

If a mountain lion was determined to be around killing calves, priority was given to hunting it down and killing it. One year, when I was there, a lion killed a four-hundred-pound calf, apparently dragged it a couple of hundred yards to shade, then, dined at its leisure. Vultures ate up any scraps or leftovers.

Upon finding evidence of that lion activity, Mike contacted an old-timer who made a living hunting mountain lions for ranchers. He was an elderly man, around sixty-eight; he had hunting dogs and an eighteen-year-old horse; both were experienced at hunting lion. This particular lion hunter had been told by his doctors that his cancer was incurable. He then made a decision to hunt lion until death came. I was at the ranch when the hunt started and was invited to join the effort—toughest hunt I was ever involved in.

The dogs picked up the scent and started after the lion, barking all the way while taking a route that was both rugged and difficult for a horse to follow but not bad for either the smaller and more agile lion or the dogs. For me, it was a scary ride, one that found me lagging behind often, then catching up after a while. No one waited for me to catch up.

The dogs found the lion and chased it up a tree, where it sat, snarling and making noises that, quite frankly, scared me. I feared that it might leap out of the tree at me, so I kept my distance and watched as the hunter calmly drew his pistol and shot the lion, killing it. It fell to the ground.

His shots were well placed and ensured that the lion posed no threat to us. The ease with which the lion was destroyed was a bit disappointing after such a rigorous hunt. Hell, aside from its snarling, the lion just sat there and ate the bullets for dessert. No big deal!

This lion that had dragged the four-hundred-pound calf a couple of hundred yards weighed in at about 168 pounds, same as me, although I did not possess the strength to drag that many pounds of calf anywhere near that distance. I vowed never to mess with a mountain lion.

If the going price for calves on the hoof was one dollar per pound, you could cover your overhead, scrape out a living, and net, I'm guessing, between $20,000 and $30,000 dollars in a year. If the price dropped to ninety cents or eighty-five cents per pound, it was time to consider selling some cows, meaning that at some later time, you would have to buy replacement animals.

That lion had cost Mike and Lark $400 with more losses to come if it was not destroyed, hence the priority it was given. Coyotes were treated the same way; kill them, each and every one you find. They are scavengers and pests and unwelcome. I think they also enjoy calves' liver, thus must go.

As dusk settled in, a gas-fired generator was started to provide light inside the trailers. It served both trailers and was located next to Lark's trailer, about fifty yards from the trailer where Mike and Joan lived. We kept it running so that Lark and I had lights, but when darkness truly arrived, so did the urge, spelled *need*, to sleep. However, no sleep could be had until someone walked out in the dark, hoping not to run into snakes or lizards, and turned off the generator, then walked back into the trailer and went to bed.

A flashlight would help; we had none on my first visit.

Sleep came immediately; so did morning!

Incidentally, utility bills were not a regular headache. Electricity needs were met by the gas-fired generator. It was adequate, although *expensive,* even more expensive than what we now pay in Connecticut. Thus, the general rule was to turn off the generator as early as possible and go to bed when darkness arrived, always rising early just as the sun came up—not a bad way to live unless one craves the night life and the city; I don't.

In addition to generating one's own electricity and digging a well for water, no phones existed on the ranch at that time. The nearest phone was in Bisbee, eight or nine miles away. Water was provided to both trailers by a well with a windmill.

I was told that the power company would run a line to provide electricity at a cost approximating $100,000, followed by a monthly bill of $300 to $400. Cell phones loomed on the horizon but had not yet appeared in the area where the ranch was located. When one did appear, Mike and Joan signed up.

Their phone allowed about five minutes of conversation at a time, then one heard: ticktock, ticktock, ticktock, and the phone shut down, no questions asked. Better than nothing, I guess. I don't know the phone's monthly cost.

As we saddled up the next morning, it occurred to me that I needed a minor miracle to survive another day with Mike, checking cows and windmills on horseback. Only the macho instinct (disease?), prevalent in many males, forbid my taking the day to rest. I survived the second day but just barely, then on the third day, Lark and I went back to California.

That evening, feeling a long-dormant and surprisingly magnetic attraction to the experience, I asked Lark and Mike if I could visit some time when they rounded up cows and branded calves. Lark gave me permission to use his trailer any time I wanted and Mike agreed to tolerate my presence despite my clear status as a tenderfoot. I was excited. Mike also agreed to let me know in advance when the next roundup and branding of calves would take place and, if convenient, I could fly out and go to work for a couple of days.

Also, we agreed that during hunting season, I could hunt mule deer on horseback with Mike, provided I obtained a permit and tag from State authorities. Now I was really excited; I had never hunted deer, or anything living, in my life.

Thus began an adventure that lasted twenty-seven years and involved flying to Tucson as many as nine times a year, over a weekend or a long weekend. I learned to round up and trail cows for eight to ten miles to the corral near the trailers, where the calves were branded and then trailed back to a pasture.

The process involved as many as four to nine of us and often included Mike, Joan, two sons, grandchildren, and me; a family affair to be sure. I was welcomed as an extra hand. At times, I helped during roundups at other small ranches in the area. No hired hands were on the payroll of these small ranches either; they couldn't afford to hire. Family and neighbors helped each other, without compensation. I was a welcome addition, especially as I acquired some level of skill.

One talent I had from the beginning was to follow orders. I did what I was told to do to the best of my ability, offering an opinion only if asked for one. There was no reason for me to try to fool anyone into thinking that I knew what I was doing. My tenderfoot status came with being an easterner and made me, at best, a student who posed no danger in becoming a top hand or a trail boss. I accepted that status and tried to learn and improve my skills so that I would be welcomed back.

It was strictly on-the-job training one learned or suffered. Mike would tell you something just once, then, he assumed you knew.

JOHN F. MERCHANT

Over time, I became sufficiently skilled and experienced as a cowboy to the point where if you were driving cattle from Texas to Abilene or Dodge City, you would hire me to help on the drive. However, you would not make the mistake of putting me in charge of the drive; I never reached that skill level. I was good enough to be hired for the drive, although I probably would be the last one hired.

A roundup for the purpose of branding calves involved heading out to a pasture, six to seven miles away, finding and rounding up the cows and calves, keeping them together at a gathering spot, and then moving them up to the corral near the trailers.

Finding the cows was not a simple matter. Riding through rugged country with cactus and brush everywhere, chasing cows, and then moving them to the gathering place for the drive was real cowboy work, as was the branding of the calves. After the branding and the tally, we still had to drive the cows back to pasture before returning to the trailers.

It was a hard day's work for all, including the horses, which, as in the old days, were invaluable assets.

My law practice was such that I could not take normal vacations of one to two weeks as many can and do. My relief from the pressures of courtrooms and trials, criminal and civil, was found in Arizona, working as a cowboy. I loved it.

Eventually, I became reasonably adept at picking up and throwing a three- to five-hundred-pound calf to the ground and holding it there, without being injured by being kicked, while a red-hot branding iron burned a permanent brand onto its side and its ears were cut, a process the calves never enjoyed but had no choice except to endure. At times, I wielded the branding iron, a chore that requires more skill to do correctly than one might imagine.

My proudest moment rounding up cows also turned into an embarrassing situation for me. It happened in about my eighth year on the ranch when I was no longer restricted to riding just Gato I had been allowed to ride younger, more spirited horses in my third or fourth year, a sign of progressing from a tenderfoot toward an experienced cowboy status. I was pleased with the apparent promotion.

Mike and I were paired up in ninety-degree weather. While searching for cows, we spotted about a dozen animals up on a steep hill near a mountaintop. Mike told me to go up and bring down the cows and calves, then hold them together while he circled the mountain looking for more.

"Damn," I said to myself, "he trusts me to do that . . . all alone?" Then off he went, and up the mountain I went. I think my horse knew what to do, so I let her. Me and Baja, mostly Baja, got the animals down and held them together until Mike arrived. No other cows had been spotted by him. He then nonchalantly pointed in a general direction and said something like "drive the cows to that *windmill*" where a herd was being gathered and held. Mike then rode off in another direction to find more animals without further explanation.

After he left, I looked toward where I thought he had pointed and could not see a windmill. I did recall that we had passed a *tank* on our way out and decided he meant for me to take the animals there.

A *tank* is an indentation in the ground made by nature that fills with water when it rains and serves to quench the animals' thirst. Some hold quite a bit of water for a lengthy period of time. So I headed the thirteen cows and calves in that direction, a drive, as it turned out, of two to three miles.

En route to the *tank*, I picked up additional animals and, using Baja's quarter horse speed and savvy, persuaded the newcomers to join my herd until I had a group of fifty-four animals, totally under my sole supervision and control. If one or more strayed from the direction, we needed to go, as many did; Baja and I simply chased them and turned them back into the group.

"Damn," I remember thinking, "this should be on camera." I was feeling like a real cowboy and was very proud of myself.

As we neared the *tank*, my herd smelled water and headed directly for it, allowing me to relax a bit. But, lo and behold, as my herd converged on the water source, their abrupt and noisy arrival inadvertently chased away about a dozen cows that were there drinking. I decided to go after those cows while mine quenched their thirst and add them to my herd.

It took a lot of time to look for the "dirty dozen," only four were found. I returned to the tank with the four and was astonished to learn that my fifty-four had left and wandered off, not to be found anywhere. It was then that I noticed, off to the Northeast, Mike and the others moving a sizeable herd in my direction. There was nothing for me to do but wait for them.

Mike asked me about the cows he had left in my care. Sheepishly, I told him the truth, "They got away." He was not pleased but did not berate or curse me. Silently, I rode drag while we herded the cows to the double corral where the calves were separated from their mothers, then loaded onto a truck to be taken to auction.

The original thirteen included three calves ranging in size, I'm guessing, of about four hundred to five hundred pounds each. Prices for calves at the time were $1 a pound on the hoof, so I cost Mike about $1,300 plus that day. I never told him about the fifty-four that probably included as many as fifteen to twenty calves. He might have cursed had I told him that, even though we picked up several from my herd on the drive to the double corrals where cows and calves were separated.

At the corrals, everyone was given a job separating the cows and calves. My job was to close the gate when the calf was pushed into the second corral and the mother was shooed away, a pretty simple job and the lowest on the degree of difficulty scale. My job didn't last long, maybe ten minutes. I lost my job when Mike told me to let his nine-year-old grandson handle the gate. I was relegated to sitting on the corral fence watching, having been fired.

My thoughts were not happy thoughts. Here I was, a young, healthy, strong, well-educated man owning a law degree, having just driven a sizeable number of animals a few miles alone and who had just been fired from a gate closing job and replaced by a nine-year-old boy. It was a low point, for sure.

JOHN F. MERCHANT

Upon my return to Connecticut after the initial visit with Lark, I shopped for a rifle and looked into buying a saddle and tack for use on the ranch. I bought a .270 caliber rifle, recommended by Mike, from Remington Arms in Connecticut. It was a flat shooting rifle, the same caliber used by Mike, and worked well when hunting on horseback where the closest shot one could get was between 150 to 300 yards. It had a kick to it that took getting used to. Mike filled his tag every year using his.

I did not enjoy its "kick," so in later years, it was changed to a .243 caliber rifle. It was flat shooting also, lighter than the .270 but with less range, less kick when fired but less power. One would not use a .243 to hunt elk, a much larger animal, but it worked for me and got me a deer every year, except three out of twenty-seven years.

Subsequently, I bought my own saddle and gear from a place in Woodbury, Connecticut, owned and managed by a man who learned saddle making from his father in the "old country," Italy.

Before shopping for a saddle, I bought a book on saddle making and read it. This gave me a foundation for engaging in fascinating discussions with Dan, the owner of the Woodbury store. We became well acquainted, enjoyed our discussions immensely, and I became a regular customer. Dan gave me a hell of a deal on a used Western saddle as one benefit from the discussions. I used that saddle for more than twenty-two years, finally selling it in 2009.

Over time, I bought two more saddles, reins, breast plates, chaps, and other items, mostly from Dan. At first, I shipped my gear back and forth through UPS; thence simply left it at the ranch where I and others could use it. Others used it all right. In fact, it was often abused when parts would be taken from it to replace or repair their own.

My first visit to the ranch, without Lark, was interesting. I flew into Tucson, arriving around 10:00 p.m., rented a car, and drove about two hours to the ranch. Using the flashlight that I never failed to have with me, I settled into Lark's trailer and slept until the sun rose in the East.

Joan always prepared the trailer in advance, clean sheets, etc., and I usually stopped at a supermarket en route for necessary food items, flashlight batteries, and a twelve pack of Pepsi-Cola—Joan's beverage of choice.

Mike had gone out and rounded up a horse for me to use while there for three days. The horse was an older mare, Gato, gentle, essentially lazy but eminently capable of tolerating an inept newcomer. She was around fifteen years old and an excellent mountain horse. She had a mind of her own until I learned how to make my wishes hers. That took a while.

Mike saddled Gato for me that first day while I watched. Nothing exciting was scheduled for the day, just cowboy drudgery caring for the animals and their needs, a necessary daily activity. Mike knew the number of animals in each pasture. He kept a tally on the birth of calves and their size, assessed, and then acted on the need for a session to brand the unbranded and to change pastures.

The health and status of the bulls, as well as the mother cows and calves, was a never-ending inquiry. The business of the ranch was raising calves to be sold to a middleman by contract or at auction. I learned to understand that the animals were valuable assets to be cared for and tended to regularly. Without the income from sales, the ranch was nothing.

The ranch was divided into several different pastures, each fully fenced in, and cows were moved from pasture to pasture to ensure that living off the land, as they did, was possible. Vegetation was often sparse, since, as stated, rain that allowed plants, called food, to grow was not plentiful. The result was that these twenty-five square miles of arid country could accommodate only up to three hundred mother head but not more than ten to fifteen bulls were needed. Ah, the life of a bull!

The terrain was rugged and rocky, mountainous with narrow trails up, over, and down the mountains, and also far from flat. Dry washes and ravines existed. They were deep enough for someone on horseback, or cattle and deer, to be invisible when in them. The air was fresh, the heat dry but stifling, and several kinds of snakes called the desert home, including large rattlesnakes.

Cactus grew on the land and could be a problem, especially since one's horse would often brush up close to the cactus where its sharp, needle-like growths could injure you. Mesquite and cottonwood trees were sparsely located and provided some shade during the heat of the day. Mike knew every inch of the twenty-five-square-mile spread, thus knew where springs and shade were located. Talk about good-tasting water; nothing like it. A canteen hung from my saddle and was useful between spring visits.

Leather chaparreras (chaps) were worn covering my legs and prevented a lot of damage from cactus. After a few years, I also bought some tapaderos (taps) to protect my boots. Despite the heat, long sleeve shirts were worn 100 percent of the time. Cowboy hats, wide brimmed cowboy hats, were a valuable necessity.

Incidentally, a tapadero is a piece of heavy leather covering the stirrup on all sides, except in back. They are a great protection against brush, cactus, and thorns and saved wear and tear on one's boots.

Tapaderos are a Spanish innovation developed about the same time as chaps, also a Spanish find. I had to buy my own; there were no spares on the ranch.

On a drive from California to Connecticut in 1976, I bought a pair of Justin boots in Cheyenne that were my working boots. Sturdy, durable, and made of fine leather, I still own and wear those boots in 2011. Also, I found a place in South Tucson, Stewart's, which made boots, producing no more than forty pair of handmade boots a day, using fine leather. I bought two pair there over time, black and brown, and I still wear them often.

Most pastures had a windmill that provided water and, periodically, Mike hauled salt and molasses blocks out to each pasture for the animals to lick, and thereby absorb needed vitamins and minerals. Other than that, the animals lived off the land and were checked regularly for sickness, pregnancies, and general condition. Evidence of mountain lion kills and coyote activity was also searched for and too often found.

We spent the day checking cows in a pasture, and I watched Mike change the worn *leathers* on a windmill so that it could pump water. We then *rode fence* looking for damage and making repairs as needed. Mike made note of the number of calves, their size, and apparent health, avoiding any encounter with the many bulls who didn't appreciate our intruding among their harems.

We usually started out around 6:00 a.m., complete with sandwiches in our saddlebags for lunch. Around ten or eleven o'clock, Mike would find a spring and some cottonwoods for shade, where we stopped, unsaddled the horses, and ate lunch, then Mike took a nap . . . for a couple of hours.

I don't recall Mike uttering as many as one hundred words in any single day. If he answered a question once, he would ignore it when asked a second time, even if the second-asking was several weeks after the first time.

Mike was clearly not a talker, never using three words when, in his opinion, two would suffice, but he slept well and did not snore. Mike generally told or showed you something once, then expected you to remember what he said or showed you.

Case in point: my very first visit to the ranch, Mike saddled my horse and off we went. The next morning, I asked him to saddle Gato. He looked at me and said, "You know how . . . ," so I tried. What I hadn't learned from watching the morning before is that horses will often extend their stomachs as you tighten the cinch, then after you turn your back, relax their stomach and ease the pressure of the cinch. That happened.

Later that morning as we were heading up a mountain on a narrow trail, my saddle slipped and instead of being astride Gato, I was perpendicular to her left side and found myself staring at a long drop off the mountain that could have been a nasty fall if I let go. I held on . . . for dear life . . . and she proceeded slowly as I eased off her and very carefully dismounted and rose to my feet. I walked Gato to a safe area and readjusted the saddle.

Mike then told me to tighten the cinch again just prior to mounting Gato, so I did. That's how I learned to saddle a horse properly.

In life, I had rarely slept during daylight hours, but I learned. After five to six hours on horseback, I was beat and welcomed the rest, and the nap I learned to take.

Taking a rest and a nap eased the stress from the extreme heat of the day, for the horses as well for Mike and me. It was part of Mike's daily routine and welcomed by me.

The heat in Arizona can be brutal despite claims that it's a "dry" heat and that the lack of humidity makes it tolerable. Don't believe it, especially when, all day long, you are wearing denim jeans, leather chaps, long-sleeved shirt, taps, and leather boots. Saddlebags and their contents add weight. I rarely wore spurs since kicking the horse with spurs too often can give the horse an attitude you won't like.

It also helps to remember that your horse is carrying you wearing all that stuff, along with a heavy saddle set on a blanket, with saddlebags and, during hunting season, a rifle, and being directed by you to perform as you deem necessary. Excessive pulling hard and often on the reins can result in a sore mouth for the horse leading to an ornery disposition. Don't gallop your horse in the heat unless you

JOHN F. MERCHANT

must to round up cows, and then only as necessary to turn the cows and guide them to the correct location.

A quarter horse is bred and trained to use his short-distance speed to help manage cattle and is the most important tool on a cattle ranch. Their agility, balance, and quickness are critical assets in the cattle-working business. A good quarter horse may not have the best bloodlines and may not look sleek and beautiful like a thoroughbred with papers, but that doesn't matter. Many possess what ranchers call *cow savvy*, an uncanny ability to know what a cow is going to do before the cow does it. They are uniquely qualified, serviceable, and dependable in the rough and rugged work of rounding up and driving cattle yet can also be unpredictable and display rare moments of rage as well as observable pleasure.

One learns to appreciate an experienced quarter horse that has learned its job. That appreciation increases as one's cowboy skills improve and you learn to ride and make the horse a member of your team, something it wants and is trained to be. It's best if the horse joins your team, not vice versa.

Also, remember as you sweat and breathe hard during the day, so does the horse. Horses get tired and need a break and may communicate that need by their unpredictable actions, such as bucking you off their back without warning and running off, probably straight back to the corral that could be a few miles away. Plan against that event at all costs because it's a long and difficult walk back to the trailer, in cowboy boots, if that happens. I'm a witness.

Take time to be thankful that your horse lives a good part of its life in the mountains, dry washes, and gullies of this desert and can navigate the rocky terrain effectively while doing what you ask of it. It's not a task for any but a mountain horse that is trained.

In truth, being, or becoming, an able cowboy takes time and is not a job for those who shun physical exertion or for the fainthearted. It is hard work and involves respecting the horse without fail.

Mike trains his horses himself and at one point had a string of seventeen horses, alternating their use to keep them fit. Working a horse with some regularity keeps it sharp, focused, well-conditioned, and reliable.

I've never been bucked off, but while out hunting one day, I shot a deer, while off my horse, and the noise made it run away back to the corral, where I found it waiting for me after walking quite a distance. I mounted my horse and returned to the deer, put a rope around the deer's head and antlers, and dragged it back to the corral where I hung it to cool, then next day butchered it and packed the meat for delivery to Connecticut.

Yes, I have been surprised many times, but I learned.

Thoughts that involve caring for and about your horse make it easier to tend to it as a priority before you wash up for dinner after a day of work.

A good mountain horse is a blessing when working on Escondido. Incidentally, the horse knows you better than you think and will go the extra mile if it likes you and trusts you. It knows if you are an experienced or inexperienced rider the moment you first climb aboard. Often he will test

JOHN F. MERCHANT

you to decide who will be in charge and is more cooperative when it learns that you know what you're doing. The process is uncanny but real.

It bears repeating to say that 105 to 110 degrees is very hot; dry, or wet. If you don't believe its impact, try walking out of Tucson's air-conditioned airport into that temperature. It's like walking into a wall when one leaves an air-conditioned building and walks out into 110-degree heat. I've done it too often, and am amazed each time.

Hunting mule deer on horseback is another great experience. Mike hunted for meat not trophies; I did too. The hunting was safe in that no one could hunt on Escondido without Mike's permission and generally didn't. Mike knew the areas they were hunting in and the risk of being shot because you were mistaken for a deer was relatively nonexistent.

As stated, Mike has a .270 caliber rifle that he's owned for many, many years. With it, he downed a deer every year he ever hunted. He was an excellent shot, frequently using only one bullet, aiming it as you would point a finger and downing the deer each time. I never saw him miss. I sometimes missed, but I did get a deer almost every time out, sooner or later.

As hunters know, the real chore is finding the deer, followed by getting close enough for a shot. Real hunters also know that simply wounding an animal requires trailing it until you find it, then ending its suffering, no exceptions.

That can take a while but must be done. One has to learn to spot them from a distance, then maneuver close enough for a good shot that does the job. I never had a shot closer than hundred yards, except once. That once ended up with a long walk back to the corral. This is what happened.

Mike was hunting low around the mountain, and I was up high, hoping to flush a deer. I spotted a deer on the ridge, and headed toward it as it went over the ridge. I dismounted and quietly walked to the spot where it had gone over the ridge. My horse was left standing with a lasso tied to my pommel that I strung out on the ground in an effort to make it easier to catch my horse of it bolted at the sound of the shot, an eminently sensible plan.

I was downwind of the deer, reached the ridge, and spotted it slowly moving below. It had not seen or smelled my presence, so I settled in for a relaxed shot, calmly fired, and saw it fall. I marked the spot, then, turned to retrieve my horse.

Regrettably, my horse had bolted at the sound of the shot and was last seen by me heading for the corral, galloping faster than I knew she could run.

Mike heard the shot and started moving up the mountain to help if needed. He saw me, I hailed him and told him that I had downed the deer, but my horse had run off. Mike found the deer lying among the rocks, dead from my shot. He roped it and started to drag it off the mountain to a spot where I could gut it and hang it to cool overnight. No tree was found.

Without much discussion, it became clear that I had a long walk ahead of me, no riding double behind Mike, and I also had a deer to gut and cool.

Mike had not filled his tag yet so his priority was to keep hunting. I had to assess and assign my priorities. I chose to

JOHN F. MERCHANT

gut the deer on the theory that an animal gutted and hung for cooling within an hour after being downed eliminated the gamy taste of venison often talked about. I believe that the theory is accurate. My deer has never had a "gamy" taste.

Mike stayed and watched for a few minutes, then went hunting. I finished gutting and walked back to the corral, the most uncomfortable walk I have ever experienced. Cowboy boots, even when well broken in and comfortable, were not made for walking across rocky terrain or any terrain.

Gato, my horse, was standing at the corral waiting to be fed. I wanted to clobber her with a stick, or something, but she was bigger than me, and I remembered that I may have to ride her again the next day. So I patted her and apologized for scaring her, then mounted, returned, retrieved the deer, and hung it from a tree to cool. I then returned to the corral, tired but pleased to have filled my tag.

Sometime later, Mike appeared. He had filled his tag and left his deer hanging to be retrieved the next morning. Mine was retrieved the next morning as well and the evening was spent butchering both and getting mine ready to be shipped to Connecticut for consumption; Mike's went into his freezer for meat in the winter, leaving space for the calf he would later butcher and use for winter meat.

There are several other hunting experiences that are easy to recall and difficult to forget. One of my favorites occurred during my second or third hunt that included Mike, his two sons, and me—four tags to be filled.

We started out at first light in a direction with which I was totally unfamiliar. No deer were spotted during the morning and at around 1:00 p.m., we came to the top of a steep mountain where Mike split us up. He rode down to the bottom saying he would circle around the base of the mountain. He assigned his sons the task of going halfway down the mountain and circling around. I was instructed to stay put in the event a deer was flushed out in my direction by any of them.

In other words, I was left alone with no specific chore except to sit and wait for them to finish circling. I did that assuming they would circle around and eventually we'd all meet back where I was doing sentry duty. In truth, I was happy to have that break from bouncing up and down on Gato. The chance to rest my weary bones was welcomed.

Next thing I knew, I looked at my watch as the sun was setting in the West. It was 3:18 p.m. Thoughts of abandonment arose, overpowered by the realization that I didn't know my way back to the corral and trailers. That's right, on the way out to this spot, I had failed to look backward for any landmarks that would show me the way to go home. I was lost and concerned.

Then I remembered a salt lick set out for the cows that we had passed and believed I could find my way back to it. If I did that, I thought, I could recognize the direction to be taken to get back to the corral, even as darkness appeared and dominated. I mounted Gato and headed her out to find the salt lick. It took some time but was almost wildly successful.

JOHN F. MERCHANT

The salt lick was found, except that I viewed it from the top of a very tall and very steep mountain. Next question: how to get off the mountaintop down to the salt lick to look for the trail I believed was there? Hope the rattlesnakes are sleeping and we don't wake them. It was getting darker by the minute. No streetlights were in sight.

The decision was made to ease off the mountain using a Z pattern that I thought would be easier on the horse and safer all around. I started Gato on the Z, and she got ornery, slipping and sliding during the rough descent, then stopped and refused to keep going. So I dismounted and, holding the reins, I looked her right in the eye, explained what I wanted, and then whacked her in the head once with the palm of my hand.

I remounted and again started the Z. This time, Gato responded and the Z plan eventually allowed us to reach the salt lick. I breathed a sigh of relief, then searched for the trail I had imagined existed.

Darkness had arrived, but happily, it brought with it a full moon and starry skies that provided some light. It took some time, but I searched for and found the trail and we were off in the direction of the trailer, ultimately arriving there around 7:30 p.m. Gato seemed happy to be on relatively flat ground and kept a good pace. We made it.

A western night with moon and stars is awesome.

After caring for my horse, rubbing her down, and feeding her, I went up to Mike's trailer where he, his sons, and his wife, Joan, were sitting around the table talking, having finished dinner and cleaned up the kitchen. Joan was kind enough to put together some food for me to eat. They seemed glad to see me; I was happy to be there.

I asked Mike what would have happened had I not found my way back. His reply was to the effect that since they didn't know exactly where I was, and because of the darkness, they would have waited until morning and then went looking for me. *Oh,* I thought, *that makes sense, but damn.*

Then, after I described, as best I could, how I had ended up on the mountaintop high above the salt lick with a disobedient horse. Mike, who knew the location, explained two things: (1) the horse wants to return to the corral more than you do and *knows how to get back,* if you only would trust her to do so; and (2) if you had continued along the ridge for a bit, you would have come to a gently sloping trail leading off the mountain and reached the salt lick.

Apparently, Gato did know about the trail, so she balked during the route I had chosen. I now know the right trail and will remember it forever.

Everyone, including me, had a good laugh about the "tenderfoot" they almost lost. I was asked to turn off the generator when I went to my trailer and told we'd go at it again early in the morning.

From that time on, whenever I was at Escondido, I always ignored the wisdom, and sage advice, given by that great philosopher "Satchel Paige," who once was quoted as saying, "Don't look back, someone may be gaining on you."

Satch, my man, I apologize for disregarding your advice, but I need you to understand that there are exceptions to many rules, including yours. Forgive me, but here an exception must be made. He agreed, I think.

Thereafter, I always looked back for landmarks. Further, I learned to trust my horse, especially after a long day and around dinner time.

You know, it may sound weird, but it is not easy for a new rider to be put to work immediately, without a lot of instruction, and learn the basics of being a cowhand. No part of my life included riding a horse until I visited Escondido with Lark. Despite the time spent in Arizona, and Idaho, around and with horses, I never became a skilled rider. I could do what was necessary and do it well enough to please Mike, most of the time, while enjoying the opportunity to learn.

Being a cowboy is tough work, but I loved it, though I never came close to being a "top hand" as stated. I learned just enough to be hired on a drive from Texas to Abilene, but probably would have been assigned to ride drag throughout the drive. Makes me wonder about how we ever really settled the West. Cowboys had to be some tough hombres, and I gained a lot of respect for them.

In order to improve my riding skills, I did take some lessons from a man in Southbury, Connecticut, who was in that business. John Forbes, a lawyer who headed the Public Defender's Office in Bridgeport, is a good friend. He and I spent a few sessions in Southbury taking riding lessons.

John wanted to experience a real working ranch and hunt mule deer in Arizona. I arranged for that to happen. John was not an experienced rider either but believed in being prepared, hence the riding lessons. We had a great trip but did not get a deer.

John is a fascinating guy. He owns an active curiosity about the world in which he lives and has an insatiable interest in experiencing as much as of it as possible. His mind functions at a high-level 100 percent of the time and he possesses a thirst for learning that is unquenchable. Seemingly always cheerful with a great sense of humor, he makes time spent around and with him a joy and worthwhile.

He is a capable photographer and brought his camera to Arizona. I still have some photos taken by him that I had enlarged and framed. They hang in my home today.

Mike assigned a gentle mountain horse named "Joe" for John to ride during the hunt and that worked out well for man and horse.

During our time in the area, we went up to Tombstone where, among other things, we visited the original courthouse that still stands and now houses offices related to law enforcement. A well-maintained courtroom with counsel tables, the judge's bench, seating for observers, and a jury box with twelve chairs was located on the second floor of the building. Everything in the courtroom was original and stood polished and gleaming. I don't recall asking if the courtroom was still used, but it may be.

To a sitting judge's left was a window and a door. We looked out the window and saw the original gallows still standing, also still in good condition, though no longer used.

Assumedly, a defendant would be given his trial and, if the jury found him guilty, and the crime he was found guilty of called for it, it was a simple matter for the sentence to be imposed immediately, and the defendant marched straight to the gallows where he was hanged. A cooperative visitor took our picture standing in front of the judge's bench.

Of course we also visited the OK Corral where the Earps and Clantons clashed and we had a drink at the Crystal Palace where Doc Holliday gambled for a living and had an off and on involvement with "Big Nose" Kate, an independent entrepreneur who catered to the whims of men who could pay but made it clear to everyone that she had a "thing" for Doc, and he for her.

Tombstone now exists as a tourist spot, with regular reenactments of the OK Corral shootout, shops, bars, and restaurants that give off both an aura of the days when silver was mined, and extreme commercialism. Sales of jewelry made with semi-precious stones taken from the mines along with copper ore abound. Some good stuff can be found, although most had a touristy flavor that was not impressive to me. Despite knowing little or nothing about jewelry, and precious stones, I had found a mentor in Bisbee and became a regular buyer. His creations and stones were top grade.

Youngblood, the only name I ever knew him by, was an entrepreneur in Bisbee. He made and sold jewelry using turquoise, malachite, azurite, and other stones. He was a native of the area, born and raised, and knew semi-precious stones like the back of his hand. He was an expert regarding the varieties and quality of stones from the copper mines and could create, design, and make jewelry with the best of them. He was also a terrific storyteller, mostly made up, always embellished, and was as lazy a man as I have ever seen.

Youngblood loved to fish. In fact that is all he ever focused on as a priority. He would spend a couple of weeks making jewelry, then disappear, leaving a woman in charge of his small shop located in a section of Bisbee where you could get hurt after dark if you weren't careful. Seemingly, each time I went to his shop, he had a different woman running the place who could only tell you that "he went fishing" and will be back . . . one day, maybe soon.

Fortunately, Youngblood left standing orders that Mr. Merchant was to receive a 40 percent discount on any item he bought. Over the years, I made a point of buying something for my daughters and the wives and daughters of friends.

Youngblood finally relocated his shop out of the dangerous (at dark) area of Bisbee to a spot near the ranch property on Highway 80. One year, he bought a generator from China to meet his needs for electricity, a mistake he wouldn't admit even though the generator only worked for about a week before it died. Repairs were not possible, he could not get parts. He spent almost two years trying to make the generator work without success. I don't think he ever again bought anything saying "Made in China" and lobbied others to do the same when he wasn't fishing, or maybe while he was fishing.

I can't properly explain the laughs his dilemma provided me for the two years, lasting until he changed the subject to dowsing for water on the 180 acres I had bought adjacent to, and just above, the ranch property to the East. Youngblood did have a good sense of humor. It went well with his active imagination and tendency to make up stories.

Youngblood swore that he could locate a prime spot where a well could be dug to provide water on my 180 acres, using a two pointed stick that would quiver when he located the best spot. He promised to give me a good price for his work; I declined his services. Ultimately, I sold the land and never built on it.

During my trips, I spent time in Tombstone, Tucson, and at Fort Huachuca. I became a member of the Arizona-Sonora Desert Museum in Tucson and visited it frequently. It was spread out over a wide area and had some of everything to be found in Arizona, including animals, insects, snakes, vegetation, cacti, and you name it; fascinating stuff to me.

In Tombstone, I became a friend of the man who owned and operated a shop where he made and sold saddles, reins, chaps, breast straps, and anything you needed to be a cowboy. We became close enough for him to discuss his interest in running for Mayor of Tombstone even asking me to be his campaign manager. I couldn't, since my law practice required my presence, but it would have been an interesting experience.

In Sierra Vista, my attraction to Fort Huachuca was heightened after a visit to its museum where a major part of one floor was devoted to the "Buffalo Soldiers." I was intrigued and developed an interest in exploring the role of blacks in Arizona, and in the American West, a subject that continues to amaze and attract me.

My research over more than thirty years led me to create a college course as an introduction to the subject.

I taught it at Virginia Union as an elective for history majors and other students with an interest. It was well received, but short-lived due to budgets. They didn't pay me to teach. It was also a long commute to work from Connecticut.

In my view, my research of the subject validated me, and blacks in America everywhere, as full-blooded Americans. It establishes that, in addition to our "cotton picking" days as slaves contributing to economic growth, blacks were involved in every aspect of developing this great country. And, despite Hollywood's efforts to mislead by omitting the role of blacks in the West, we were a critical and necessary part of the whole.

I, we, belong here, seeking only a way to be all that an American can and should be. We have no plans to leave and no one can force us to go. America is a good place to be, especially on a comparative basis. Now, if we can just find a way to *crown that good with brotherhood,* we'd all be better off. Hopefully, that is not "mission impossible," though I wonder.

An effort was made to teach the course in Connecticut, specifically at Wesleyan, Yale, and UCONN. Not one of the three showed any interest for reasons that escape me. They are three of America's finest universities, each with some focus on African American studies that they brag about. Yet, the people running that area, often Blacks protecting their turf, apparently shy away from exposing young minds to an aspect of American history that in the 21st Century should, in my opinion, be made an integral part of an honest recitation of America's history.

JOHN F. MERCHANT

It seems that that aspect of black history is not seen as important, certainly not in the way that I do. So be it.

An effort was also made to teach the course at the University of Virginia. That effort was effectively thwarted by the black gentleman running the Carter G. Woodson Institute.

I had met with the Chairman of UVA's History Department who favored adding the course as an elective. He advised, however, that it could not happen unless the Woodson Institute guy approved and signed off on it. That guy turned it down and was less than polite in doing so.

In my view, he was protecting his UVA niche and wanted no competition with his agenda. Thus, he said no to my request. Damn, it was not my intention to compete with anyone, just to expose students who elected to take the course to an opportunity to learn about an aspect of American history that filled a void. It doesn't exist there as an elective.

Look, without the Louisiana Purchase and the development of the West, there is no America of significance. America, and Americans, especially those east of the Mississippi, give priority to slavery, the Civil War and, by and among blacks, the greatness of Africa historically.

I understand that priority and recognize its need and value, but, can't these great schools give students an option to learn that the settlement of the West involved contributions from Black Americans, both before and after the Civil War? I think they should.

How important is the history of blacks in the settlement of the American West? I reckon that is a matter of opinion and can vary.

Still, in elementary school, I was required to learn that Marconi, an Italian, invented the radio, and that fact has been of little value to my economic well being. Perhaps, black involvement in the settlement of the West has the same significance and value, but it is a part of America's history and should be offered to active minds interested in a complete and honest history of America.

My research has identified forty to sixty-five books that either featured, or mentioned, facts relating to that history. Those books are in my library. The majority were published by schools in the West with one outstanding exception.

I came to learn that an outstanding authority on the subject, maybe *the* outstanding authority was and is William Loren Katz, a noted historian and professor of history at Columbia University in New York City. He wrote several books about blacks in the American West including *The Black West*, published by Doubleday & Company, Inc. in 1971; *Black People Who Made the Old West*, published by First Africa World Press, Inc. in 1992; *Black Women Of The Old West*, published by Ethrac Publications Inc. in 1995, among several others.

In 1998, Quintard Taylor, PhD, a black man, who was the Chairman of the Department of History at the University of Oregon, wrote and had published a well-researched book entitled *In Search of the Racial Frontier*, published by W.W. Norton & Co. in 1998, covering African Americans in the American West, 1528-1990. This book challenges the view that the American West is a part of America that has no black history . . . and soundly defeats it.

JOHN F. MERCHANT

Dr. Taylor received his BA degree from St. Augustine's College, one of the historical black colleges, and his PhD from the University of Minnesota. He has more than thirty years of teaching experience, especially on the subject of African Americans in the American West and has authored several books on the subject.

Also of interest is *Black, Red and Deadly* by Arthur R. Burton, published by Eakin Press in 1991. It recalls black and Indian gunfighters 1870-1907. There are others.

For those who possess an inquiring mind that seeks both truth and understanding, I highly recommend all the books mentioned, although you may have to special order them from Amazon or Barnes and Noble, among others. It has interesting stuff. All are books that never made the *New York Times Best Seller* list! In fact, they have never made it to most libraries in our inner city schools or Historical Black Colleges or anywhere. Why is that?

Don't look for them in Eastern or Southern libraries; they are not there. I wonder if they are in libraries such as those at Yale, Harvard, or Stanford? Can they be found in libraries in cities such as Chicago, Boston, Richmond, Virginia; Charleston, South Carolina; or Atlanta, among others? I fear not, though I don't know the answer to the question.

Fortunately, when I attended Virginia Union University all the students were required to take a course in "Negro History." The textbook *The Negro In Our History* authored by Carter G. Woodson (1875-1950) was first published in 1922. My textbook was his fifth edition, published in 1928. It is remarkably researched and very well written. The course was an eye-opener and gave me information that was not made available in the Greenwich, Connecticut, school system.

However, nowhere in its 575 pages does Woodson mention the Ninth and Tenth Cavalry, the Buffalo Soldiers, the 25th Infantry Division, Fort Huachuca, or other aspects of a black presence in the American West. I graduated Union with a minor in history, thus I fervently soaked up Woodson's enlightening writing and approached my research on the West with the same fervor.

One day while in Arizona, browsing in bookstores, I found *History of Arizona,* authored by Robert Woznicki, PhD, that discussed, in Chapter 21, The Black Man in Arizona. Therein he wrote

> "Arizona had many Black cowboys. Between 1870 and 1900, Black cowboys made a big impact on our history but few history books record this information. Black ranch hands constituted nearly one fourth of the work force of the West.
>
> John Swain died in Tombstone, Arizona, in 1945, at the age of ninety-nine. He was a famous black cowboy. Employed by John Slaughter for many years, Swain gained a reputation as the right hand man for Slaughter as he built his cattle empires in New Mexico and Texas. He is buried in Tombstone in the famous Boot Hill Cemetery."

Most of the books and information about Blacks in the West came from browsing bookstores in Arizona, Colorado, and Idaho, yes Idaho. But before some comments on Idaho,

I must briefly relate information about being with my children, Susan and Tabitha, at Escondido, the ranch in Arizona.

As both reached their teen years, it occurred to me that it would be a good idea to invest special time in each of them, individually, as a way to further the parent-child relationship that, inevitably, would change as adulthood neared for them. The result was that each was invited to spend a week with me vacationing at a place of their choosing.

Susan chose a week at the ranch in Arizona. Tabitha, whose love of lobsters is unmatched worldwide, chose a week in Ogunquit, Maine, where each night she selected a lobster for dinner that had slept in the ocean the night before.

Susan and I flew to Tucson, had dinner at a plush country club arranged by Harold and Lila Belmuth, friends from Rolling Hills CC whose daughter worked at the club, then drove to the ranch. There, among other things, we took part in a cattle drive, visited Tombstone, Nogales, Mexico, Bisbee, and Fort Huachuca.

One night, maybe our first night, as Susan was about to go to bed, I heard her scream and call for me. Rushing into her room, she pointed out a lizard that had staked a claim to her bed as a resting place. Upon my arrival, it dropped behind the bed, and I was unable to capture it to remove it. We finally went up to the other trailer and reported the existence of the lizard.

Joan took a large-mouthed plastic jar and returned with us to the trailer. It took her less than a minute to capture the lizard in the jar and dump it outside. We thanked her profusely, and she left. I cleaned the egg off my face. Susan got in bed. I went to my room, and the rest of our visit was lizardless.

A day or so later, we were witnesses to an event that, for me, depicted life in the West dramatically and realistically.

Mike had brought a young cow that was pregnant up to the ranch and placed it in the corral where he could keep his eye on her. He believed that she was too young to bear a calf and would have trouble doing so. He was right.

One morning, as Mike, Susan, and I saddled up to ride the range that day, Mike saw the cow in the beginning stages of labor. Immediately he put plans for the day on hold, notified Joan of the coming birth, and the two of them stopped everything to assist in the birth.

The young cow was struggling with a breech birth wherein the calf was not positioned properly to emerge from the womb. Mike tried to reach in and turn the calf unsuccessfully. He soon realized that the cow, whose insides were being severely damaged, would not survive. He went back to the trailer for his pistol, returned, then shot the cow and attempted a caesarean birth to save the calf, assisted by Joan. The calf was stillborn.

Mike then brought his pickup truck to the corral, attached a rope to the cow, and placed the calf in the bed of the truck. Then he drove out onto the ranch property, dragging the cow and carrying the calf as indicated. There he dumped them for the vultures, or other creatures to dispose of, returned and parked the truck, and told Susan and me to saddle up, and we did. Then without further ado or comment, we embarked on Mike's original plans for the day and completed our work as if the cow-calf episode had never occurred.

All in a day's work, I guess, though I still am in awe over witnessing a total humanitarian effort, albeit with an economic flavor, to save the lives of animals followed by, seemingly, a totally impersonal act of dumping what was left for nature and the elements.

Sure, it was an effort to retain assets, but you had to be there to watch the concern for the animals inherent in the effort. Then reverse the coin and watch the total acceptance of this tragedy, without comment, as we went back to work. Welcome to the West.

The following summer, Susan, Tabitha, and I returned to Arizona, where, despite lacking lobsters, Tabitha had an enjoyable introduction to the West as Susan served as our tour guide.

Idaho

My attraction to Idaho started with an opportunity to hunt elk there. Hildegarde Mauzerall, a remarkable woman whom I met through The Casey E. Family organization for whom she worked in the West. Casey was a client of mine in the East.

She put me in touch with Rex Lanham, an Idahoan who ran cattle outside of Boise and owned a cabin on property located in Idaho's *Primitive* Country on the Middle Fork of the Salmon River. The property was reachable only on horseback or by flying in on a small plane.

I hired Rex to guide an elk hunt that included Mike Power, my Arizona guy, and Charlie Judge from Connecticut. Charlie, along with John and Ron of J&R, has been my auto mechanic forever. I sponsored the hunt for Mike and Charlie as a way to say thank you for all they had done for me over the years.

Charlie and I flew to Boise together where we met up with Mike, then drove to Rex's place, saddled up, and rode to the cabin, in the dark, to begin the hunt the next day. Rex's son and his friend, a young man from the area, joined us. At the cabin, waiting for us was an old-timer, a westerner, who would serve as cook.

I don't remember the names of the son, the young man, or the cook. We were not hunting trophies; our quest was for meat. The young man from the area told me that he really needed to get an elk or there would be no meat at his house in the coming winter. That reality opened my eyes. Happily, we had an agreement that any meat we downed during the hunt would be split four ways and that is what was done.

The cook was a great storyteller and had a sourdough mix that had first been put together in the 1930s, some forty years earlier. He was a whiz and made pancakes, pies, and bread from the mix that hit the spot.

The cabin location and condition confirmed that we were *roughing it* in the true sense of those words. It was cold but plenty of blankets ensured warmth while sleeping.

We split up each morning, with Rex taking Mike with him, and his son taking me, the young man, and Charlie out looking

JOHN F. MERCHANT

for elk. On the second or third morning, the son pointed to an elk in the far distance and told me, "There's your elk, go get it."

I was then told to climb down the mountain, on foot through thick brush, while the others circled around the ridge we were on and continued searching. He said he would lead my horse and pointed to a spot where we should meet.

I got scratched up and fell once or twice coming down the mountain, but eventually reached the flat and walked in the direction I believed he had pointed out. En route, I ran across some bear droppings that scared me a bit but did not deter me. My .270 caliber rifle could handle a bear with a well-placed shot. The fear was that any shot of mine would not be well placed; I'm no Daniel Boone. Happily no bear showed up.

Finally, I reached a steep hill that I climbed for a better view to see if my elk could be sighted. It was more like a mountain than a hill, and the trip up was exhausting. Just as I neared the top, I heard a shot, hurried up the hill, and saw a guy with a rifle walking toward a huge elk he had just downed.

We spoke. I told him I had been tracking that elk for more than a couple of hours. He explained that he was hunting with a friend who was circling around the mountain below while he climbed to the top, an exhausting climb that had induced him to sit down and rest with his back against a tree.

While resting, he saw this elk approach and stand perfectly still for a few moments, long enough to invite this guy to aim and fire at a standing target less than fifty yards away. He accepted the invitation and downed the animal with one well-placed shot. He was as amazed as I was upset, but it was what it was, clearly his elk.

We had a good laugh and I moved on, saying to myself, "Self, that's a big damned animal."

I rejoined my group and we continued to hunt. Later in the day, as darkness approached, we headed toward where we thought Rex and Mike might be and witnessed Mike down an elk, again with one shot. After gutting the animal, there arose a problem, namely, how to get it off the mountaintop, back to the cabin, and ultimately to the local butcher who would "wrap" things up for us.

Rex sent his son back to the cabin to get another horse that we could pack the elk out on. Rex then took the saw that he carried and cut the elk in half, then cut one half again, making it easier to secure on the pack horse or one of our horses. I again thought, *Damn, that's a big animal.*

Darkness was now approaching fast. The pack horse arrived before darkness overwhelmed us and the pack horse was loaded up, secured, and we began the trek down the mountain, single file, with elk aboard. The less than full moon and stars provided some light but not much. Horses can see quite well in the dark and that helped enormously. Besides, I remembered that the horses wanted to get back to the cabin and relax almost as much as we did. Trust your horse. Also, Rex knew where he was going and how to get there.

My horse, apparently annoyed by the long workday, kept walking me into low-hanging tree limbs, so I hollered for us to stop for a moment. Rex suggested to me that he would lead my horse while I grabbed my horse's tail and came (slid) down the mountain, in boots.

Talk about having fun! My horse didn't kick me and that was a good thing. Another good thing was that the fear of being injured by low-hanging branches disappeared.

We made it, but I can tell you I would not want to take that trip again. Clearly I had no future ascending or descending mountains in the dark, wearing boots and holding onto a horse's tail. Nor did I want a "do-over."

We hunted for the few days left in the season without success; then headed back to the ranch with one elk. It should have been three, but I flat-out missed a pretty long shot at one when nerves got me, and Charlie blew a shot at one.

The next year things went better for me, including being able to write off the cost of a (hunting) trip to Idaho annually. That happened like this.

Rex suggested that instead of paying him for the guided hunt, I should purchase a bull he wanted for his herd. It was a registered bull that I bought, complete with papers setting forth its lineage, then leased the bull back to Rex. I was advised that under IRS rules, the basic costs of a yearly trip to Idaho to check on my "investment" could be written off, tax wise. Hunting season seemed the best time to check; I chose it.

Incidentally, my 25 percent share of the meat from that first elk was 129 pounds of edible, good-tasting elk meat. My friends and I enjoyed elk chili, elk burgers, elk roasts, and elk chops for as long as elk remained in the new freezer I bought to store the meat.

In addition, the night after Mike downed the elk, our cook took the liver and created a sumptuous meal for all hands; delicious! I like liver, many don't. Combined with home-fried potatoes and freshly baked sourdough bread, this was the best liver I've ever tasted, before or since. A great meal!

I've stayed in touch with my Idaho friends through the years, last visiting them in the fall of 2009.

Years before, on a trip there, Rex, who flew his own airplane, suggested that we fly up to the "Primitive Country" renamed in 1980 *The Frank Church-River of No Return Wilderness Area*—located in middle of Idaho containing 2,366,757 acres and managed by the Bureau of Land Management and the Forest Service.

Rex had inherited one of a dozen cabins located on the middle fork of the Salmon River from relatives. The cabins were "grandfathered in" when the property was acquired by the federal government. As stated, only two ways to access Rex's cabin existed: fly in through the mountains to a grass-landing strip, where at the end of the strip was a hill that ensured the plane would stop after landing; or by a nineteen-hour ride on horseback, where one could fish en route. The ride took two to three days, each way, depending on how often one stopped to fish the lakes encountered along the way.

That first flight in was exciting (?) as Rex wended his way between the mountains, coping with the wind, and landed perfectly on the strip. The hill worked. I have to admit though that I did wonder about getting out of there when the time came.

The cabin was well kept and in good shape. A man and his wife were year-round caretakers, and, since few owners ever visited their cabins in the winter, the couple spent their winters alone, caring for the properties and the horses stabled there.

Rex and I took time to ride out into the Wilderness Area in which resided 370 species of wildlife, including eight big game animals such as bear and elk. No human feet has trod on most of the area, except for miners seeking gold in the eighteenth and early nineteenth centuries, and, perhaps, Nez Perce Indians. Gold claims were marked by nailing empty tobacco packages, turned upside down, on trees.

We found one such package, severely weathered but still attached to the tree. We had no idea how long it had been there.

The beauty of nature was overwhelming. Whitewater rapids wended their way below great forests of Douglas fir and lodge pole pine, with spruce and fir higher up and ponderosa pine at lower altitudes; the forests were broken by grassy meadows and sun-washed treeless slopes. Fresh air held a crispness and taste rarely experienced. It was a sight to behold for sure—awesome!

Our exploring took us to an area overlooking the Salmon River, where Jimmy Carter, during his presidency, did some whitewater rafting. I tried to swim once near the cabin and found the coldest water one could ever imagine, although I should not have been surprised.

It was not a swim; I was in and out immediately—happy to have not suffered a heart attack or other negative reaction to the trauma. Further, any thoughts of whitewater rafting disappeared, except for watching it on television and wondering why and how anyone would do that.

The area is primarily a dry area, with as little as ten inches of rain in a year. However, as much as fifty inches of rain and snow falls annually on the mountaintops. The snow melts and feeds the river, hence the water temperature.

For me, the entire Idaho experience was a humbling one. It, my time spent in Arizona and two cross-country trips driving across America, provided valuable insights into the landmass called the United States of America. It probably explains why visiting Europe has never been a priority of mine since America has so much to see and marvel over.

When I think back and view these experiences in conjunction with the places I've been in the Western Pacific, including Australia, it is clear to me that I have been very fortunate and, perhaps, can be considered very well traveled. I have spent time in every state, except Alaska. Lucky me, huh?

One result of my travels is that they have given me a perspective not shared by many of the friends I've made over the years, especially those in the black community whose experiences include the negatives of northern city living and the drawbacks of country living in the South. In each of those situations, one finds that negative racial attitudes toward them dominate, leaving little or no time for them to explore, let alone enjoy, the positives America offers or promised in one way or another.

These travels also left me with a level of confusion that still exists. I encountered good people and made good friends everywhere I went, black, white, Asian, you name it. Still, everywhere I went, I found racial animosity, sometimes overt and sometimes quiet and silent but clearly in existence.

Conversely, good friends were found everywhere, even lifelong friends, but it was often difficult to relax and be oneself because negatives were, too often, just the next person away.

America, you must find a way to dramatically increase racial harmony here or who knows what we will become. It's a daunting challenge, I know, but it must be faced and met. Much of my life has been spent trying to do my part.

ARIZONA GLIMPSES

Thanks Meadowlark for making it possible for me
to sample the rugged life of a cowboy.

Mike Powers and I. Meadowlark took photo.
My first day ever on horseback.

Aching bones and joints that first day
called for some relief, so I walked a bit.

Mike's deer.
I think he just asked me, "Where's yours?"

Yes, that's me branding a calf!!

Arizona- Mike's grandson practicing ... on me?

ARIZONA - Gato's been cared for and fed. Time to
store saddle, wash up, find soft chair, sit and eat.

IDAHO and BISBEE, AZ

The biggest man made hole in the ground I ever saw made by Phelps Dodge mining for copper at the Queer mine in Bisbee, AZ.

Three hunters, one elk!

Charlie Judge and Mike Power in Idaho. Charlie is an auto mechanic par excellence!

Rex Lanham, our guide, and Mike Power. Mike ⊛ downed the elk just before dark on the mountaintop.

IDAHO: Rex Lanham checking out the "Primitive Country" (really) near the Middle Fork of the Salmon River. We had recently flown in on his plane and he was showing me around. Interesting, even exciting! Incidentally, the Salmon River water is cold! I know, I jumped in to swim. Lasted about 8 seconds, tops.

Chapter 8

Teaching Career

THERE ARE TIMES when things just happen, things you may have thought about at one time or another but never really thought would happen and involve you. Teaching happened like that for me.

In 1969 or 1970, at around 5:00 a.m., I received a phone call from Father McInnes, President of Fairfield University. He asked if I could come over to the university to help in a situation where several black students, and some nonstudents, had taken over a building at the entrance to the university and barricaded themselves inside.

Fairfield University is located in Fairfield, Connecticut, the town I lived in at the time. My involvement with the university was as a member of its advisory committee. Billy Taylor, the very talented jazz pianist, was also a committee member. Father McInnes said that he had also contacted Billy Taylor, but he lived in New York City, I believe. He had been called but was not expected for a while. I lived five minutes away, so I dressed and drove over immediately.

Upon arrival, I met with Father McInnes and several others who were trying to figure out a course of action to resolve this very serious situation. Policemen were there in abundance as well.

At some point, with prodding from me, it was determined that perhaps I should try to speak with the leader or spokesman for those who occupied the building. I stood outside a window where the leader of the group, who knew me, or of me, invited me to come inside and talk. I accepted the invitation without giving it much thought.

Arrangements were made for me to climb through a window and join the group. It was a fairly large group numbering more than twenty. They appeared pleased to see me and glad that I was getting involved.

Once inside, it quickly became clear to me that not all present were students at the university. The leader and spokesman was a student. I further noted a couple of men sitting and nodding as if they were on something. Maybe they were just sleepy, but my silent reaction was one of concern. It was then that the first indication of fear started moving through me, and, for the first time, I silently questioned my decision to accept the invitation to join the group. Hell, I didn't need this, but here I was—too late to turn back now.

After some discussion, slowly but surely my fear turned toward a deep concern that the ending to this takeover could be a violent one. To the best of my knowledge, Fairfield police had no training in race relations issues and the town was not one that championed diversity involving people of color in any way.

The American experience for several years prior had been one of violent confrontations between police and blacks as a means of quelling unwanted activities by blacks. I did not doubt that this could happen here and now.

The prevailing theme on the part of officialdom seemed to be one of *who the hell do they think they are, let's put them in their place and teach them a lesson.* True or not, my thoughts focused there, and I was concerned.

Once inside, I was given a tour wherein the barricades at the doors were pointed out, lookouts had been posted, and a food supply had been brought in suggesting an intent to hold out for a considerable period of time. I wasn't impressed by the proposed menu, or the amount of food available, but I was impressed with the barricades and agreed with the comment made by the leader to the effect that "They can't get in here, Mr. Merchant." He was right. It would not have been easy for that to happen, without tear gas and a bulldozer; at least that was my thought.

A good hour or two was spent discussing in detail how and why they had quietly taken over the building after midnight, erected the barricades, and brought in food. The event had been planned for some time and the planning was thorough. I listened carefully and eventually learned about their purpose for taking over the building.

They commented on the negative racial attitudes on campus exhibited by students as well as some faculty. They accused the administration of not caring, or at least not doing anything about those things. The absence of black professors was mentioned and many recited a litany of individual, negative experiences they deemed racist and that occurred regularly.

Their frustrations at being black and a student at this white, Catholic University were clearly apparent. They had vented these frustrations by taking over the building and voiced a commitment to accepting any consequences that flowed from their fundamentally illegal actions. A list of demands had been prepared and stated an urgent insistence that those demands be met.

I listened, heard, and understood their frustration, revisiting my past.

It seemed that we talked all morning and slowly, ever so slowly, the tenor of the conversations became more like a discussion than a declaration of war. It pleased me when, after venting their frustrations, loudly and defiantly, they began to think and discuss, rather than vent and accuse.

Conceivably, the tenor changed when they took the time to deal with two questions I asked, namely (1) clearly it would be a chore for anyone to get into the building, but how the hell are we going to get out of the building in one piece and avoid being arrested and going to jail, and (2) how, when, where, and to whom will your list of demands be presented? No cell phones existed, although there was a working phone available in the building.

Obviously, we needed to communicate with those outside. In doing so, I advised, we must encourage a positive discussion that could lead to getting the right answers to my two questions and, hopefully, doing so in a way that avoided arrest or jail as part of the resolution.

With some minor opposition, they agreed and we opened up a line of communication with Father McInnes and school officials. Finally, it was becoming clear that for all their talk, they did not want violence, arrests, or jail to be part of any result. Not an easy result to achieve, but we talked it out at length and, eventually, developed a plan.

I (we) had no interest in talking with any policemen, local, state, or federal and didn't. Nor, at my urging, did we want to talk with any media who were also gathered around outside the building.

We did want, and insisted on, a commitment from law enforcement folks that they would not interfere with the operation of any plan worked out between the students and the administration's officials once entry was allowed into the building. It was given, though we were not sure that we could believe it or rely on it.

Law enforcement's concerns seemed to be the safety of any who entered the building, especially school officials. I understood that and, fortunately, with help from Father McInnes, the police cooperated fully.

We proposed a plan, whereby twelve black leaders from the Bridgeport Area community would enter the building to sit as witnesses to any discussions that took place. The discussions required to formulate and obtain agreement to the plan took all day. Darkness had arrived long before acceptance and implementation of the plan could begin.

The twelve leaders were identified and contacted. It took a while for all to appear. When all had arrived, they were allowed into the building, assembled, and seated. Then, they were told in no uncertain terms that they were to remain silent during the entire process.

No speeches, no comments, no participation, except as a silent listening audience. The student leader made it clear that the only black, aside from students, allowed to speak without permission from him was Attorney Merchant, no exceptions. I was pleased by that expression of trust.

Then, Father McInnes and Dean Schimpf entered the building. They were directed to sit in two chairs set up facing the students who sat as an audience for them. The black leaders were given seats to the left of the students and sat, essentially as a jury of witnesses.

Once settled, the student leader instructed Father McInnes and Dean Schimpf that they were to answer each and every question posed to them, no exceptions.

I then witnessed what I deem an extraordinary act of courage from Father McInnes. He quietly took his seat, leaned back as if he were sitting in his living room in his home, and calmly, without indicating as if he were under duress, stated that he understood the instructions and was pleased to have the opportunity to discuss any issues raised by the group with the group.

His demeanor, words, and body language clearly were all devoid of any sign of fear or concern for his safety. He gave a clear impression that he wanted to talk about and work on some the demands raised by the group. What a man!

His willingness to do that had a calming effect on all and set a tone for the proceeding that was welcomed, at least by me.

Later, after the event concluded, I learned that two of the black leaders had entered the building with weapons hidden in their clothing. One brought a switchblade knife and the other a screwdriver. They expected violence, I guess, and their attitudes and apprehensions going in were in stark contrast to that displayed by Father McInnes.

The questions started; Father answered each and every one and the Dean contributed as required. Calmly, and without acting as if he was under duress, Father agreed to begin work on some of the demands, noted that actions had already been started on others, and firmly said no to some demands and explained why his answer was no.

Father McInnes's participation changed the event from a confrontation to a discussion between the president of the university and some students who needed to air their concerns and understand what, if anything, would or could be done about them.

Father McInnes gave them all that they sought, flavoring it with explanations designed to promote understanding and some level of harmony.

Among other issues, the students raised concerns about the absence of black professors at Fairfield. Father agreed to accelerate the search for qualified black professors but explained that the larger universities, especially those with large endowments, were in the process of doing the same thing in many parts of the country, especially the Northeast. Given that competition, Fairfield University could not compete as well as they would like to, but they would do their best.

The issues, according to Father, were economics and the existence and availability of men and women who would choose to teach at Fairfield University, nothing else. The competition could afford to buy diversity in its professorial ranks that its competition could not. Fairfield did not have the endowment resources that would allow it to be a real competitor.

Besides that, he explained, the pool of blacks interested in being college professors was not large. This had to be considered along with the fact that very qualified people had a choice to teach at Yale or Harvard versus Fairfield.

Much of the pool chose the Ivy League schools and the pay rates offered there. That put Fairfield at an obvious disadvantage.

The event ended around 11:00 p.m. after agreement was reached on an exit plan. No damage of any significance had been done to the building, and, in Father McInnes's view, no reason existed for further involvement by law enforcement folks related to arrest and/or prosecution. His position was that the students should be in class the following day, on time, and prepared to continue their quest for a college degree from Fairfield University. *Wow!*

The barricades were removed, materials were put where they belonged, and arrangements were made for trash removal and those inside left the building to return to their normal lives. The students and I were the last to leave, together with Father and the Dean. The students returned to their dormitories and Father McInnes and Dean Schimpf returned to their residences.

Me, I went home and consumed two good-sized drinks made from my favorite bourbon, then, I slept. It had been a long day. Tomorrow's activities would include explaining to judges, clients, and my office why I was absent all day and didn't call. I felt fine when I realized that all's well that ends well. However I also realized that resolution begins the hard part of compliance.

Later on, I spoke with Father and volunteered to teach a course in race relations at Fairfield as a way to honor his commitment to seek and find black professors. He accepted my offer, and my teaching career began as an adjunct professor, unpaid by my choice.

I taught that course for five years as a seminar, one evening per week. I loved it and derived some unexpected benefits over the years from doing so. Two men who attended my class stand out in my memory.

One was James Ruane, Esq., who went to law school after graduation from Fairfield and practiced in Bridgeport where he excelled as a lawyer, especially representing criminal defendants. I believe he served as a public defender for a time, then, opened his own office. Jim is a very capable gentleman and an excellent attorney. I consider him a friend, and am pleased to do so.

The other was Jim Van Volkenburgh, who later became a probation officer in Connecticut, operating out of Bridgeport where I practiced.

He became the chief probation officer for the area and has now retired. Jim Van is a man whose love for the game of golf and all it involves is unexcelled. He is hard to forget because he frequently came to my 4:00-p.m. seminar late, carrying his golf bag and often still wearing his golf shoes. He also was a good student.

Over the years, Jim and I have played a lot of golf together, including being a part of the groups I organized to go South in March to start the season each year. Jim was a good player. During his college years, he was a member of Fairfield's golf team—a competitor with a great personality and an enormous love for the game. He remains a friend today, forty plus years after being a student of mine. He has provided me with many good memories, and I'm pleased about that.

In truth, there were many memorable moments during my five years of teaching at Fairfield. I am totally incapable of reciting them all at this point, but I can tell you that as an old man, retired, with time on his hands to reflect, it is a joy to look back and recall the experience. I am not sure now that I would again crawl through the window and join the takeover group, but I'm glad that I did. My respect for Father McInnes and Dean Schimpf grew daily and still grows.

Media coverage of the experience, mostly local, did not do justice to what actually occurred inside that building for close to twenty-four hours. No media ever talked to, or with, me. I wonder why?

My next experience at teaching was at Norwalk Community College. I taught business law there for a few years at the request of a lawyer friend. Hopefully, students received something of value from my lectures. There is no way to determine if they did or not. The experience further taught me that I enjoyed teaching, although there was no joy for me in correcting papers and assigning grades. What did impress and please me was the involvement with young and active minds that sought to learn. The challenge was, and is, to teach them and do it well. It's a real challenge that, for me, is a joy to undertake.

My last experience at teaching was at Virginia Union University, my alma mater, in Richmond, Virginia, which I referred to in Chapter 7.

Quite frankly, I had hoped to retire and spend my time teaching a course entitled *The History of Blacks in the*

American West at three prestigious universities located in Connecticut, namely Yale, Wesleyan, and the University of Connecticut. My idea was to teach this elective one day per week at each place, ideally on Tuesday, Wednesday, and Thursday, leaving long weekends for golf and other activities.

Regrettably, this never happened because none of the three exhibited any interest when approached.

My intent was to teach the course in order to expose young minds to a part of America's history that is fundamentally ignored. Tenure and an intimate involvement in the politics of being a faculty member were not on my list of things to seek.

In my view, this course would provide added information, which young Americans could choose to absorb or not. It would be an elective and my status could be that of a visiting professor or adjunct professor or whatever they wanted to call me. I was amazed by the total lack of interest I encountered, especially from black professors who had found a home on those three campuses.

My distinct impression was that in each case, they were protecting their "turf" and using any veto power they had to eliminate competition. No one I encountered agreed with my view that black study programs are tragically incomplete without such a course. No one I spoke with knew much about the subject either.

My view is easy to state. After all, we are Americans, born, raised, and living in America. Finally, we can be aware of and a part of those who benefit from Jefferson's foresight in negotiating the Louisiana Purchase. We were, and are, an

JOHN F. MERCHANT

undeniable part of developing the West, although not enough Americans know that. Doesn't it make sense to find a way to tell them just as we require our educational systems at all levels to teach other aspects of American history?

I believed that many students would have chosen to enroll in the course as an elective. I still believe they would—be they white, black, or polka dot. I guess I was dreaming, and, looking back, am not surprised that I was turned down at every step of the way.

Maybe the problem is a diminishing of interest in the West and westerns. These days, the focus seems to be on cops and robbers, spy capers, international intrigue, and science fiction. Still, TV offers new series every year and eliminates many of the abovementioned annually. Rarely are they replaced by comedies, although some have been offered and endured. Few have had the success of *All In The Family* or *The Cosby Show*.

I further believe that for Americans and others, this information is important and should be made known along with the obvious emphasis on slavery, Africa, and the ancient empires that involved blacks' way back when. But what do I know? I only know it's a fascinating part of America's history.

Efforts have been made by me to interest some folks in devoting Black History Month, at least part of one, to an emphasis on the subject. The result was that hardly a sliver of interest was noted, and on occasion, my suggestion was met with laughter. Again, was I dreaming? The responses received by people at the three universities mentioned say I was.

Actually, there was one spark of interest in the subject. The *Connecticut Post*, the local, Bridgeport area daily newspaper, asked me to write a short essay on the subject, and I did. It was published on the front page during Black History Month and focused on my time in Arizona working as a cowboy as a hobby. I wrote it intending to introduce folks to the subject of the history of Blacks in the American West.

The effort was abandoned, but the subject still gets my attention. Be the good Lord willing, and the "creek don't rise," I will try to write a book designed to introduce folks to the subject. That is if I ever finish this one.

Chapter 9

Rebel Yell

THE IMPORTANCE OF unplanned events that impact one's life in significant ways is often impossible to view as important when the events occur.

Seemingly, my life has been a series of such events. One such occurred in 1975 at the El Conquistador in Puerto Rico on the golf course. It resulted in a friendship with two southern white males: one a lawyer and the other in business. The friendships, still strong after thirty-four years, continue to add positive dimensions to my being.

In 1975, a good friend, Richard Jacobson, told me that he and his wife Carol were going to Puerto Rico to spend a week at the El Conquistador. He suggested that I take a couple of days off and join them. He knew I had been working very hard for a long while. He opined that we could play some golf, enjoy good food, get some sun, and relax. In his opinion a break from work would be good for me. He was right; I agreed to go.

Richard, a fascinating personality and a brilliant lawyer, worked in the state's attorney's office in Bridgeport, Connecticut. He was responsible for representing the state of Connecticut in criminal appeals arising out of trials that his office was involved in. At that time, his office had criminal jurisdiction over most of Fairfield County, Connecticut, including the major cities of Stamford, Bridgeport, and Norwalk.

Richard's work was impressive and effective. He performed in a highly professional manner that earned him plaudits and respect from his peers, in and out of his office.

In my opinion, Richard was the single best resource in Connecticut in the field of criminal law. I often told him so and added that his expertise was such that he should be teaching criminal law at Yale Law School, twenty-five miles away from Bridgeport and consulting in both Connecticut and the Northeast. He is a graduate of Yale University and the University of Virginia Law School, although he was not at Virginia while I was there.

My law practice included substantial criminal work, including major felony trials within the jurisdiction of his office. Over time, we became very good friends, and I have many happy memories of time spent with him and Carol, along with other friends, golfing, cooking, eating, and simply being friends. Richard tended to side with Republicans, while I generally advocated the Democrats' positions. There was much to discuss, some of it quite lively. Carol, an excellent cook, performed miracles cooking, especially pot roast. I dislike all pot roast except hers. She also does a mean job with crab meat, Richard's favorite food.

I recall a time when a friend provided me with a ten-pound package of frozen crab meat that "fell off" a truck driving through the neighborhood. I immediately gave the crab meat to Carol. She proceeded to prepare

JOHN F. MERCHANT

a dinner for a few friends comprised almost entirely of different crab dishes. Richard was in his glory and, as I recall, couldn't stop smiling even when chewing. It was a notable "crab fest" for sure.

I joined Richard and Carol in Puerto Rico. On our first morning there, he and I went to the golf course to play; Carol went to the beach. The starter suggested that we join a twosome about to start their round at the first tee, so we did. We introduced ourselves, as golfers do, and were welcomed by two young men, Mike Kelly and Steve Isaacs, both from Richmond, Virginia. Their accents clearly established that both were southerners, a fact that I found disappointing.

My first thought upon hearing them speak was, *Damn, all the way to Puerto Rico to play golf with two southerners?* I had come here to relax and enjoy myself; hopefully, I would. I wasn't optimistic.

I was tired of the South and southerners after three years in Richmond at Virginia Union University, three more years in law school at the University of Virginia in Charlottesville, followed by four months at the U.S. Navy's Officer Candidate School and three years on active duty in the United States Navy, which, generally, did not seek diversity in its officer ranks.

Yes, I had had my fill of the South, southerners, and southern attitudes. Still, it was dumb to think as I did. I was not pleased with this foursome, but as golfers almost always do, I stayed and played. At the time, my handicap was seven or eight; Richard hovered around twelve to fourteen.

Steve and Mike teed off first in a way that can best be described as both admirable and enviable. Each found the fairway with booming drives of impressive distances. Then, somewhat shaken and intimidated, Richard and I teed off. I believe we were both in the fairway; however, those first swings made clear that if this were the Civil War, the South would win.

The distance between our drives and theirs was highly noticeable, as was the difference in comparative golfing skills displayed throughout the round.

We learned later that Steve and Mike had recently competed for their Club Championship at Willow Oaks Country Club in Richmond, Virginia, with Steve winning. Apparently, Steve had also won a trip to Puerto Rico by making a hole in one in an unrelated golf event, so he and Mike came to play golf for a week. Both were scratch golfers, or close to it, and they became my friends.

Richard and I were not scratch golfers. My single digit handicap could be considered respectable, but my game could not rival that of Mike's or Steve's, and at the end of the game, our scores highlighted the differences.

In truth, I do not remember the exact scores. I do remember that Mike and Steve scored in the low 70s without apparent difficulty. I believe that my score was respectable, 78 or 79, but not even close to the Southern contingent.

It's a good thing that we didn't challenge them to a match involving money. We would have lost, big time, even if they had given us strokes based on handicap differences.

Despite the talent differences, we enjoyed the round and each other's company, something that often happens on the golf course where personalities inevitably emerge and, thankfully, often blend. Almost always you can accurately assess character during a round of golf and friendships can result. That is what happened with the four of us.

It is always a treat to play with talented golfers. Generally, golfers respect superior talent and enjoy the shot-making ability of good players. Usually, a better player will provide helpful hints that improve your game.

Golf is like that!

The critical benefit derived from that round of golf was that it clearly laid a foundation for becoming friends. A socialization piece is usually, but not always, an inherent part of a round of golf and, at the conclusion of the round, we were no longer strangers. We were individuals, likeable human beings, who could converse, laugh, applaud, feel sorrow over any bad breaks, commiserate with one another about the game's undeniable control over good and bad luck, and feel as though the time spent together was both enjoyable and added something of value to our lives.

Golf is like that.

After the round, or maybe during it, Richard invited them to join us for dinner, along with Carol. They agreed and countered by inviting us to their room for a drink before dinner. We agreed, subject to confirming with Carol.

As stated, we enjoyed each other's company, something we learned to do during the round. We found enough interest in the pleasure of each other's company to want more time together, off the golf course. We took advantage of an opportunity to become more than mere acquaintances and share a meal and more conversation.

Golf is like that.

Yes, golf often provides that opportunity and indulging the opportunity is rarely, if ever, less than a plus. For me, as it relates to Steve and Mike, it was the beginning of a thirty-five-plus-year adventure, especially as concerns Steve and me. The time we have spent together during the past thirty-five years and the things we have accomplished during those years are both important and of serious value to others besides ourselves. We are proud of that and would not change it if we could.

Despite having an overzealous day in the sun, Carol agreed to the dinner arrangement and came with Richard to Steve's room for a drink to be followed by dinner. I had arrived there a few minutes earlier.

Two things stood out that night and still remain in my memory. Carol, who is an enormously attractive woman with a personality to match, stood out because of the color of her skin. It was an unattractive and painful looking shade of fiery red, caused by exposure to the sun. It was a totally different color from her normal skin color and caused her considerable discomfort. Yes, she had been burned by the sun, and she suffered.

Then came the "piece de resistance." Steve offered us a drink of bourbon whiskey that he had brought from Virginia. No, not "Virginia Gentleman," a bourbon Richard and I were somewhat familiar with having both received law degrees from the University of Virginia in Charlottesville, Virginia.

A degree from the university automatically bestows upon one the title of "Gentleman"[11]; hence the bourbon's name, for marketing purposes I assume. Neither Steve nor Mike attended UVA. They were gentlemen but, I thought, perhaps lacked the background to choose a desirable bourbon whiskey.

Yet, that evening, the bourbon offered and imbibed earned a special place in my mind and memory. A bottle of Steve's selection, not the same one, nor one that is always full or uncapped, has been in my home since then, in the event that Steve or Mike decided to visit. The name of the bourbon offered was *Rebel Yell.*"

To myself, I again said, "Damn," and lowered the southerners' character rating two full points, 9 to 7 on a scale of 10.

I accepted a drink, actually more than one. It was a good but not great bourbon, not harsh or biting, and I enjoyed it enough to restore the character rating. The camaraderie that followed was a continuation of what took place on the golf course, expanding over time to cover a wide variety of subjects and experiences.

Teasing Carol was a highlight.

Steve and Mike have been my good friends since that day. Over the years, we have enjoyed many good times, on

---

[11]   As I understood it, the honorary and unofficial title of "Gentleman" was part of a tradition that started when Thomas Jefferson founded, designed, and opened the University of Virginia. The university enrolled students, males only, from the "best" Virginia families who were dubbed "Gentlemen" upon graduation.

and off the golf course. Of even more importance are the things we were able to do relating to golf, diversity in golf, and helping to build bridges between the races in ways that we could.

On the face of it, there was no reason, except golf, that Steve and I became the kind of good friends that we are. We have discussed this unlikely friendship often, trying to understand its existence, without success. For me, it supports the thesis that the Lord does work in mysterious ways.

A black lawyer from Connecticut and a white, southern bred lawyer from Virginia found real meaning in the word friendship because of a chance meeting on a golf course in Puerto Rico. Who could have imagined such a scenario or result? Clearly Steve's rating is a ten. I've never had a better friend, and I have benefitted mightily from the relationship.

Golf is like that!

There is an age difference also. I am fifteen years older than Steve and Mike. Richard, Steve, and I have the law in common and that was a plus. Each of us has an inquiring mind that encounters frustration when we ponder the state of the world, the country and the States we live in. We believe that things could and should be better and are committed to doing our part to improve things, whatever that may be. We can discuss our differences openly, honestly, and learn from each other. We have done that over the years.

Golf brought us together and is the glue that keeps us together. We love golf and the positives it promotes, tangible and intangible. We enjoy competition and cherish the opportunity to open our minds, discuss a wide variety of questions, and learn from each other. We enjoy a good meal and love to laugh, even at ourselves when we say or do things worthy of little more than a good laugh. We care about family and respect others for their positive attributes.

Good manners have been instilled in us from birth. We believe that good manners are an asset one should never be without.

We seek the good in people and understand human imperfections. We turn our backs on violent, senseless behavior, and to those who perpetrate it.

Mike and Steve have wonderful wives and children they have enjoyed raising. Their children are intelligent, well-mannered achievers; no surprise there.

Brandt Isaacs and Christine Kelly epitomize the positives in women—as individuals, wives, mothers, and intelligent human beings. I have been fortunate in getting to know all of the Kellys and the Isaacs over the years.

Mike's son graduated from UVA, and Steve's son, Kevin, entered UVA in September 2008.

Steve graduated from William and Mary in Williamsburg, Virginia, and is a very active alumnus. He played on the golf team and graduated from its law school. He did his best to encourage his daughter, Cameron, and son, Kevin, to attend William and Mary with a 50 percent success record.

Cameron is an exceptionally bright young woman who could have attended any school in the country. Steve and Brandt knew that, and Cameron was tempted to exercise her "freedom of choice" until Steve ended the dilemma over which school to choose by telling her, "You can enroll at any of the many colleges and universities that have accepted you, but the tuition check is going to William and Mary." Case closed.

She went to William and Mary, graduated, and is now employed in the financial industry where she is doing very well. I understand that she will be married in 2011 to a gentleman she met at, guess where, William and Mary.

Apparently Kevin, who is equally as bright, was approached in a different manner. Steve and I spent considerable time discussing Kevin's upcoming decision. He was provided with the right to make his own choice, without undue pressure. I did lobby Steve a bit to let Kevin make his own choice by staying away from the tuition check speech. He did that.

I shall never forget the phone call from Steve one morning advising me that Kevin had chosen UVA. I was pleased and still smile about that.

Many more stories could be told about how our friendship was made special and the experiences we shared. It started quite by chance on a golf course in Puerto Rico in the 1970s.

Golf is like that!

Steve and I share a belief that if more people from different backgrounds played more golf with each other, important bridges would be irrevocably constructed between those of different races who share a round of golf together. The bridges would survive forever and foster greater understanding between the races. The relationships that evolve would help ease the very difficult transition from the races living and being apart, as they have and are, to a more desirable closeness and a better life experience for each. Better communication, understanding, and interaction between the races would certainly occur.

We have seen that happen between the two of us and the many friends who helped us. We know that we have been responsible for bridge building in and through golf, and we are certain that those bridges will not collapse like it happened in Connecticut and Minnesota; they are permanent structures.

A small step in the right direction, perhaps, but a source of pride.

The USGA Executive Committee

One way we've helped, through golf, is worthy of mention because it has had significance of enormous and lasting proportions. It involved the United States Golf Association (USGA) and my status as the first black to serve on the USGA Executive Committee. It also included some remarkable men, such as Mike Smith, a Virginia lawyer and past president of the Virginia State Bar Association; Frank Easterly, a businessman in Richmond, Virginia; and Bill Millsaps, formerly a publisher of the Richmond Times-Dispatch—all of whom I met through Steve.

Mike Smith is out of South Carolina. He has earned a well-deserved reputation as one of the South's finest litigators. He is a past president of the Virginia State Bar Association and an avid golfer. We have an understanding when we play golf together that a $5 Nassau is at stake. I believe that originally I might have given Mike a stroke or two that he didn't deserve or need, so I stopped doing that. Our matches were fiercely contested and unbelievably enjoyable, usually played in the company of Steve.

Mike's sense of humor, intelligence, big, booming voice expressed with a southern drawl, lack of bias or bigotry, and his interest in helping achieve greater diversity in Golf make time spent with him, on and off the course, memorable and unquenchably desirable. He is a friend, a good friend.

Frank Easterly is one of the most impressive individuals I have ever met. He is a successful businessman, an accomplished golfer, and a man with an enormous heart. His father, Harry Easterly, Jr. is a past president of the USGA and was very helpful to me during my tenure on the committee.

Frank has a quiet demeanor, a dry but interesting sense of humor, an enormous capacity for work, and great business acumen, fueled by a high level of intelligence that is not flaunted.

For years, Frank would not permit me to stay in a hotel when in Richmond. Instead, he insisted that I stay in the guest cottage on his property that, along with two ancient cannons, overlooked the James River. Often he provided me with an automobile. His wife and family were a joy to be around; they welcomed me and treated me as a longtime friend.

Frank suffered one great embarrassment that all who know us were made aware of, continuously, and in great detail.

I had accepted an invitation to play in the Hermitage Classic, a two-day event played at Hermitage Country Club just outside of Richmond. On the first day, I made a triple bogey on number 18 to finish at three over par and was clearly in contention. That's right, I choked on 18. *C'est la vie.*

Next day, rather than chauffeur me to the course, Frank loaned me a car, got on his motorcycle, and told me to follow him to Hermitage. That way, I could return in the car, and he would avoid a trip to chauffeur me back from the course. I did just that—what a trip, and what a mistake!

Frank, who had spent his life as a resident of the area, decided to take a "shortcut" to the course. We left early enough to make my starting time and allow me to hit some balls to warm up. Unbelievably, Frank got lost, including a drive through some state prison grounds that were well off the beaten path.

The trip consumed much more time than it should have, and we were late arriving at the golf course. I reached the first tee just in time to watch my fellow competitors approaching their tee shots in or near the fairway. Yup, they had teed off without me, all three of them, meaning that I had missed my starting time by more than five minutes, an irrevocable basis for disqualification.

Golf is like that!

I remember the tournament officials watching my late arrival with faces showing concern, dismay, and an "uh-oh." I wondered what they were thinking.

Here was a USGA Executive Committee member, the only black member in USGA's history, in contention to do well in the tournament, arriving late for his tee time. He should know better! They didn't know that I was not at fault, nor did I tell them, then.

Reluctantly and properly, I announced acceptance of my disqualification and they disqualified me. I pleaded and was allowed to join my group and play the round as an extra but no longer as a contestant.

Obviously, I couldn't wait to share my plight with Frank, then with Steve and Mike and any friends of Frank who would listen. Frank has probably lived down his embarrassment, but we've enjoyed a lot of laughs about it over the years.

Frank and Mike are just a couple of the many people I have met through Steve. Almost all play golf, and each gives a lie to the myth regarding the insensitivity and racial biases of all southerners. Gentlemen they certainly are; bigots they clearly are not.

They are individuals of great character who care, really and truly care, about this world, this country and the issues that keep the races apart. Within the context of their ability to help, and being afforded an opportunity to do so, they have been, and are, more than willing to work at building bridges across the gaps that exist and sustain racial strife in this country. I am a witness to that fact.

Bill Millsaps, a fascinating guy, is another friend I met through Steve. He is very bright and enormously insightful. He also owns a contagious sense of humor and is worth listening to.

Bill spent more than forty years at the Richmond Times-Dispatch, initially as a sports reporter rising to executive editor, a position he held for more than eleven years.

He was born in Daisy, Tennessee, he says, but I looked and couldn't find Daisy in my atlas. I intended to ask him about that but never got around to it. If you can find "Daisy" let me know. I've been told that there is a "Soddy-Daisy in Tennessee so maybe that's it.

Bill spoke at one of the four golf symposiums I helped take place.

Many more like them exist in America, including across this country in states like the following: New York, New Hampshire, Arizona, Georgia, California, Ohio, New Jersey, Michigan, North Carolina, Florida, and Minnesota to name just a few where I have spent time and played golf.

Of course, there were many in Connecticut, such as John Lawrence, M. D., Victor Riccio, Ken Janello, Giles Payne, Tad Lincoln, Bill Seeley, Bob Lacobelle, John Forbes, Fred Fawcett, Frank Maco, Frank Riccio, Harold Belmuth, Irv Lineal, and many others.

In all these states, the people I met became friends, real friends, who over the years added critical dimensions to my life. Incidentally, I have spent time in every state except Alaska and have played golf in thirty-nine of the fifty.

Golf is like that!

Now, please bear with me as I try to detail how the USGA involvement began and the events that occurred during my time spent serving on the Executive Committee.

It begins in 1991 when I received a call from a lawyer friend, Giles Payne of Fairfield, Connecticut. I had known

Giles for almost thirty years. He and I had been young lawyers together and had played golf several times over the years.

A longtime resident of Fairfield, Connecticut, and a talented golfer; he had played on the golf team at Duke University and was a member at Brooklawn Country Club in Fairfield, Connecticut. He had a long-term involvement with the USGA that included chairing two major USGA tournaments held at Brooklawn in the 1980s: a Senior Open and a Women's Open. He was well known and well respected by the USGA, its staff and many members of its Executive Committee, past and present.

Giles is, and has been, a good friend; a very capable attorney, husband and father; and a special human being. He supports what is right, not just what is convenient or popular. In addition, he is married to a truly wonderful woman, Lucia, who is simply a delight to be around.

Lucia once said to me that she sensed that there was a lot of anger in me but admitted that I hid it well. She was right. You may sense that if you are taking the time to read this entire effort since it shows up herein.

Giles called to ask if I had any interest in joining the USGA Executive Committee. I said yes, although, believe it or not, I really didn't know what the Executive Committee was or did. He invited me to meet with Frank (Sandy) Tatum, Jr. a past USGA president and chairman of the nominating committee for the coming year.

The USGA's governing body consists of a sixteen-member Executive Committee, selected from across the nation by a nominating committee to serve a one-year term. Longer

JOHN F. MERCHANT

service is not guaranteed and requires being renominated each year. No one knows if he will continue as a committee member until the nominating committee files its report in the fall.

In my case, the nominating committee recommended three new additions to the Executive Committee, meaning three existing members disappeared without notice or explanation.

Each nominating committee is chaired by a past president. Past presidents have an informal, but important, role in the decision making of the organization. They also have an admirable commitment to "The Game," its rules, and its growth.

All of golf concedes authority for the rules of golf and the equipment used in the game to the USGA in America and Mexico. Outside the United States and Mexico, this authority resides with The Royal and Ancient Golf Club of St. Andrews. The two organizations have a long history of collaboration that serves golf well.

Sandy Tatum came to Connecticut from San Francisco for our meeting held in Giles's law office followed by lunch. We spent in excess of two hours talking as I was interviewed by Sandy and, I assume, being evaluated. Soon thereafter, Tatum invited me to join the Executive Committee, a highly coveted invitation among golfers, especially those with wealth and influence, neither of which I possessed.

The USGA provides a national handicapping system for golfers, is a leader in turf grass research, and provides grants to various programs through its foundation. It conducts thirteen national championships annually for juniors, amateurs, mid-amateurs, and senior amateurs. Each category has tournaments for males and females. It also runs national opens primarily for professionals: men, women, and male seniors. Amateurs who can qualify are welcomed. Its US Open is one of the four major tournaments for men[12] in a golf year.

The USGA was formed in 1894, apparently to create a way to establish a national amateur championship. The Newport Country Club (Rhode Island) and St. Andrews Golf Club (New York) both claimed that their tournament champion was the "National Amateur Champion," a claim that generated considerable, often heated, discussion and discord among the chosen few.

In the early days, most people could care less about golf or an amateur champion. The masses believed golf to be a creature of the elite, championed by those of wealth and influence, thus beyond their reach, except as caddies.

Golf was not considered a major sport like baseball or basketball.

Ultimately cooler heads prevailed and an agreement was reached to settle the "Champion" question.

The first U.S. Amateur Championship was held at Newport Country Club in 1895. Originally five clubs comprised the USGA's membership, namely, Newport, Rhode Island; St. Andrew's, New York; The Country

---

[12] **The four majors are: the Masters; the US Open; the British Open; and the PGA.**

Club, Massachusetts; Chicago Golf Club, Illinois; and Shinnecock Hills Golf Club, Long Island, New York. Today its membership exceeds nine thousand people and many, many, country clubs.

Interestingly, to me at least, I played Newport before I ever learned to play golf. Newport extended playing privileges to naval officers. I was commissioned after getting through the Navy's Officer Candidate School in 1958 and was invited by other officers to play Newport. I accepted the invitation despite never having played an 18-hole round of golf in my life.

To me, my inexperience was not an issue. I was a pretty good athlete; the ball sat still; and, all one had to do was strike it in the right direction until one reached the green. Then just putt until it went into the hole.

Eventually, starting that day, I learned that golf is maybe the single most difficult sport to play well consistently. Excellent athletes have found enormous difficulty in doing so. I was no exception; neither was I an "excellent" athlete, just a good one.

On the appointed date, properly attired and with borrowed clubs and shoes, I appeared at Newport Country Club ready to play. We went down to the pro shop to sign in for our scheduled tee time. Almost immediately I noticed the guy in the pro shop staring at me, and I wondered why. Maybe he thought I was there to be the caddy?

He then took excessive time to review the evidence I presented to establish my status as a U.S. naval officer. It was the same type credential the other three had shown him.

Seemingly, he felt a need to impose a higher burden on me than on the others, or he had something in his eye that made it difficult for him to read my credentials, you choose.

I questioned him and asked if there was a problem, and if so, what it might be.

Clearly he was not trained to answer such a hard question, so I asked him an easier one, namely, "don't you extend the playing privilege to (at the time) 'Negro' United States naval officers?"

That almost led to an incident, but my friends stepped in, calmed everyone down, and prevented an incident. I was allowed to play.

It was not difficult for me to figure out that the extension of playing privileges was not intended to apply to black officers. I guess they thought we would never have any of those in America, or that we wouldn't play golf. There were not very many of us in 1958, black officers, who played golf.

In fact, diversity in the U.S. Navy's officer ranks at that time was, to quote Willy Shakespeare, "A consummation devoutly to be wished . . ."

During my forty months on active duty, I saw a grand total of five, four other "Negro" officers, but my search area was limited. It only included traveling across the United States by car to a ship home ported in Long Beach, California, to San Francisco, and thence to naval facilities in Hawaii, Japan, Australia, Guam, Okinawa, the Philippine Islands, every major seaport on the West Coast, and the entire Western Pacific twice on two WestPac cruises.

Admittedly, no time was spent on the East Coast, after OCS, or anywhere in Europe, so I may have missed some there. I saw none during the six months I spent in Newport, Rhode Island.

I accepted Sandy Tatum's invitation, then immediately called Steve Isaacs to tell him and to ask what this involved. Steve's first question was, "Are you sure he (Tatum) said Executive Committee?" Yes, was my answer. Steve was impressed, excited, and pleased. He said that since Tatum indicated acceptance, it would be done without any problem.

Steve had grown up with Lanny Wadkins, a talented player with an outstanding amateur and professional record of achievement in "The Game." He was the USGA's shining star for several years and a good guy. Through Lanny and golf, Steve was very familiar with the USGA. He explained to me what the USGA and its Executive Committee meant to "The Game" and educated me as to what was occurring and its significance.

Later, Steve became a critical part of the planning for the symposiums. He was my sounding board for ideas and his suggestions regarding program and people were a major reason why the symposiums went well.

Finalization awaited two things: a recommendation by the Nominating Committee a month or two later; and a vote at the USGA Annual Meeting scheduled to be held in February 1992. Assumedly, the Nominating Committee's recommendation is tantamount to election, but, at the time, I did not know that to be the case. Tatum had said he would recommend me and would support it to the Executive Committee. I was comfortable with that.

I learned some time later that after our meeting and lunch with Giles Payne, Tatum called Grant Spaeth, President of the USGA, from the airport and told him that the USGA's nationwide search for a black Executive Committee member could end; he had found the man they sought. Me?

I was flattered and humbled by the thought of being the result of a nationwide search. But it meant a young black man from Chickahominy in Greenwich, Connecticut, was walking into another life situation of significance, alone, without being fully prepared and lacking a mentor. So be it.

Why a nationwide search?

The search for a black Executive Committee member came after the issue of discriminatory membership at country clubs became a subject of extensive public discussion in 1990. The golf media, and others, took up the issue shortly before the 1990 PGA of America Championship at Shoal Creek Golf Club in Birmingham, Alabama.

Shoal Creek was then an exclusive, all-white country club. Its membership policies were clearly discriminatory, and they made no bones about not having, or wanting, black members.

Shoal Creek's spokesman and founder, Hall Thompson displayed no embarrassment over the fact that blacks were not welcome as members in his remarks to the media. He acted as if the media were wrong to raise any question and was quoted as saying to the media

"This is our home and we have the right to pick and choose who we want. We have the right to associate with whomever we choose."

Some professional golfers, not all by any means, were vocal in siding with Thompson and, inferentially at least, supporting Shoal Creek's exclusionary policies and actions. No surprise there from a group that historically, and deliberately, had specifically excluded blacks from playing the PGA TOUR and competing with them for prize money and other benefits.

Ironically, Tiger Woods, whose heritage includes both African American and Asian, clearly a man of color, has, since 1996, been the major factor in increasing earnings for all those who play the PGA Tour for a living. Now, it seems that many of the pros don't even mind not winning since more than enough money is available to the losers who qualify to play on the Tour.

Tournaments now exist where a player finishing last can receive in excess of $10,000 for four days of play and treat it as "chump change." That is more money than the first-place prizes given years ago to Snead, Hogan, Nelson, and other giants of "The Game."

Yes, golf has grown, enormously, as a major American sport.

Despite the comments by Hall Thompson, and some pros, Shoal Creek found and accepted a black member nine days before the tournament began, a token gesture but a beginning, I think. I have no knowledge about Shoal Creek's membership policies or practices now. Hopefully, they have changed.

To its credit, the USGA took a public stance on the issue in a release indicating it would no longer hold its tournaments at clubs with discriminatory membership policies or who lacked minority members.

Personally, I wondered if such a venue existed.

Jerry Tarde questioned that position when he authored a *Golf Digest* editorial asking, in effect, how the USGA could take that position when its Executive Committee was as elitist and, on its face, as discriminatory as any of the clubs in question.

The nationwide search for a black Executive Committee member commenced after the Tarde editorial, although maybe not because of it. The search was done quietly but certainly completed after Tarde's editorial was published.

That told me all I needed to know about Jerry Tarde, now a friend. I truly admire him and appreciate all that he has done for golf.

The USGA response to the issue included sending letters to its enormous number of volunteers nationwide asking that they identify blacks in their areas who could be considered for service on one of many USGA committees. There are numerous committees, and the effort seemed designed to attract blacks to as many of those as possible.

The letters were an effort to create a level of black involvement in "The Game" through the USGA, an effort unparalleled in golf's history. It was, in my opinion, a responsive and responsible step that had some noteworthy success. I don't know if that effort extended, or extends, into the twenty-first century. The results, although not clear to me, suggest that it wasn't or isn't.

For example, a friend, Gerard Petersen out of Hartford, Connecticut, was invited to join the Senior Amateur Committee and accepted. Gerard was an excellent player as a junior and as he grew older. His skills were never displayed in any of the thirteen national tournaments conducted by the USGA; a pity, for his skills were strong and his love for the game unmatched. He still plays respectably, even though he is now more than seventy years old.

I was told that the letters did not specify a search for an Executive Committee member, simply USGA committees. I have never seen the letters.

Giles Payne, a Fairfield, Connecticut, attorney and a friend, received one of those letters and responded. In his response, he put forth my name, along with background information he had acquired through being a friend. I was unaware of the letters, or of Giles suggesting my name.

In thinking about it, I tried to imagine Giles's thoughts when told that Sandy Tatum, nominating committee chairman, was on the line calling for him. Did he have at least a fleeting thought that the call might mean an invitation for him to join the Executive Committee? I still wonder about that.

His long involvement with the USGA, his stature in golf and as a person who loves the game, certainly would entitle him to serious consideration for Executive Committee service. He would have been a worthy choice, even an extraordinary choice, but in never faltering in his support for me, he waived the possibility that he too would receive such a coveted invitation.

Two Connecticut golfers in the Executive Committee at one time were out of the question. After all, this was not New York or Georgia.

The USGA had answered the question of a woman on the Committee prior to my joining it. One of its members was a woman, Judy Bell, a wonderfully delightful woman with an enviable history of involvement in the game of golf. She joined the Executive Committee in 1987 and later became the first woman president of the USGA. During her tenure as a member and officer of the committee, she provided exceptional service to both the USGA and the game of golf.

Judy is a very able and intelligent woman with a sense of humor and great golfing skills. She owns a realistic attitude about the world in which she lives. A major area of service was helping to improve the USGA's marketing of its merchandise, at the Opens and otherwise. Revenues climbed dramatically with her involvement. That came as no surprise since marketing was another of her specific talents.

I would be remiss if I did not share my early, and lasting, overall impressions of the individual Committee members I met and related to for four years. An impressive group, individually and collectively, united by a genuine love and respect for "The Game." They were easy to work with and get to know, most of them quickly made me feel like a legitimate and integral member of the group.

Although I sensed that a few Committee members were not pleased by this new diversity, they accepted the reality. I experienced no negatives in relating personally to them and

JOHN F. MERCHANT

enjoyed the camaraderie and friendships that developed as a result of our exposure to each other.

However, learning how the Committee preferred to function took me a while and happened in bits and pieces.

For me, it was an interesting learning experience that I still chuckle about from time to time. New Committee members are asked what they would like to accomplish during their tenure. My answer was that I would like to see the rule forbidding a player from tamping down and smoothing out spike marks on the greens during play changed.

After all, thought I, players were allowed, even encouraged, to repair ball marks caused by well-struck shots falling out of the sky onto the manicured surfaces called greens. However, spike marks made by other players could only be tapped down and smoothed *after the player finished putting*. My answer seemed logical to me.

No one applauded my answer. In fact, many seemed shocked and started looking at the ceiling and the walls as if I had cursed the Pope.

I was never asked to serve on the USGA Rules Committee. *C'est la vie.*

I believe that each member, in time, genuinely welcomed my election to the Committee, as did the entire USGA staff, headed by David Fay. David was fully supportive of my being there and made my presence and adjustment easy, then easier. Quite a man!

Some did seem to question my credentials for being asked to join the committee, and I accepted that since it made sense to me.

After all, I had no background of involvement in golf beyond trying to play. On the surface, I had not "earned" a spot at the top of the mountain as they had. The silent resentment was sensed but ignored. I knew why I was there and, frankly, silently applauded the USGA for its decisive move toward diversity, even as I wondered what the hell I was going to do, now that I was here.

Feelings aside, almost everyone went out of their way to make me comfortable but not in a condescending manner. Each was fully committed to "The Game" and its rules. Each had absorbed the critical intangibles golf teaches including, without limitation, honesty; fair play; a zest for competition; confronting imperfection, or bad luck, without adopting a negative attitude or demeanor; the value of being a gentleman in all respects; and the importance of "The Game" to millions of people who play golf and those who don't play. Each was a good person.

They came from fourteen different states located in the North, South, East, West, and Midwest sections of our country. Stuart Block, out of West Virginia, was the President during my first two years of service; Reg Murphy, out of Maryland, was the President during my last two years.

I spent more time with some than others, especially with Ray Anderson, Tom Chisholm, Jim Curtis, John Reynolds, Gerry Stahl, Mike Mastalir, Dick Bennett, and Buzz Taylor, to name a few. Reg Murphy and I once spent an enjoyable time driving from Denver to The Broadmoor in Colorado Springs; Ray Anderson was special. He invited me to play his course in Illinois, and I did.

Gerry Stahl from Rochester, New York, was, simply stated, friendly and a friend. John Reynolds, a physician from Augusta, Georgia, of all places, took time to get to know me. We liked each other and shared stories and laughter. Dick Bennett and his wife Helen were and are friends. Buzz Taylor recalled that his wife and I had shared time on various boards back in Connecticut. In short, I was accepted and acceptable.

The key question in my mind was figuring out what was really expected of me, not fitting in. I was determined not to be a token, although I'm sure that many, in and out of golf, may have believed that I was. Those who felt that way did not know me, that's for sure. In my mind, I was going to be a full and active member of the Committee or I would leave.

The USGA experience involved significant travel and associated expenses. Almost all of expense had to be covered by the individual committee member. My out-of-pocket costs for the four years averaged out to $17,000 per year. It was not until my third year that I learned that the amount was tax deductible. My bad, I guess.

What I did learn, and commit to, was that I wasn't going to spend that kind of time and money just to be a token, no way! In the midst of all that, I had a full-time job as Consumer Counsel for the state of Connecticut, often taking office work with me on golf-related travel while using vacation time to cover the time away from my office. The phone was used a lot as well, although cell phones were not around yet.

I probably traveled more than many because I firmly believed that the USGA people involved in golf throughout America had a right to see and meet me and view this major move in support of diversity with their own eyes.

Also, I was committed to making a strong effort to contribute something of value to the experience and to diversity in "The Game." I just wasn't quite sure what that contribution might be or could be.

Two phone calls from strangers, not counting the media calls, were received soon after my nomination became public. Bill Dickey out of Phoenix and Renee Powell from Ohio called and offered whatever help they could give. They became friends.

Renee Powell is a black woman who spent several years playing the LPGA Tour. A beautiful person, she earned a solid reputation as a skilled golfer and played on the LPGA Tour from 1967 to 1980. Her life story is fascinating, including learning and refining her game on a golf course carved out of farmland by hand in East Canton, Ohio, by her father, Bill Powell.

The course, Clearview Golf Club was designated a National Historic Site by the U.S. Department of Interior in 2001.

Renee Powell now serves as the head professional at Clearview, returning home after a career that took her to Ohio State University, the LPGA Tour, Japan, Australia, Morocco, Spain, England, Africa, and many American cities and towns.

Renee captained the Ohio State University Women's Golf Team prior to joining the LPGA Tour. She is one of only three black women ever to play that Tour. In 1995,

Eric L. Smith wrote in *Black Enterprise* about Renee Powell saying that

> "Despite her success, or perhaps because of it, Powell is dismayed by fewer African-Americans playing professionally than ever before."

Bill Dickey is a golf legend, though not as a player. His forte is as a major contributor to the growth of "The Game" for more than a quarter of a century. His positive impact on increasing diversity in the game is yet to be properly recognized but is unusual, significant, and unrivalled.

Incidentally, Bill plays a good game and plays a lot. He is tough under pressure, especially when a twisting, twenty-two-foot, downhill putt is needed for the win. The man thrives on that kind of pressure. I'm a witness.

My favorite story about playing a round with Bill happened when I flew into Phoenix and landed a bit late. I rented a car and went directly to the course where a game was scheduled with Bill, Big George, and Knox. I barely made the tee time.

Before teeing off, we chose partners, settled who gave who strokes, and it was announced (to me) that there would be a $5 Nassau with each individual, including one's partner, as well as between the partnerships.

Skins, birdies, and greenies were worth a dollar each, and the contest would be played in accordance with the rules of both the USGA and *rabbits and squirrels*, a form of gambling in golf totally unknown to me but one they played regularly.

For the next several hours, we played and I kept hearing comments like "he has a leg on the rabbit," "the rabbit is chasing the squirrel," and similar comments. I had no idea what they were saying, never having bet that way, and I still don't know what they were saying. I did know that I faced a chance of losing a lot of money in a game I knew nothing about.

In addition to my lack of understanding, I had but $12 cash in my pocket. My late arrival had prevented me from stopping to get more cash.

Long story short: I played very well that day, and during the enjoyable sandwich and beer time after the match, I sat and watched Bill tally up the results, then announce what each player owed. When he finished, I was awarded in excess of $250. My $12 remained in my pocket, and I provided enough smiles to overcome the sorrow and sadness that existed at the table.

Dinner that night was whatever I wanted from the menu, after not spending any time looking at the right-hand side of the menu. I also paid for everyone's beer.

Golf is like that!

In the 1970s, Bill had an idea that had been festering in his mind for a long time. Troubled by the fact that little was available to help interested black youngsters learn about golf in their youth; he organized a group designed to fill that void. It took a few years to mesh, but the result was the creation of a 501(c)(3) corporation named the National Minority Junior Golf Scholarship Association (NMJGSA), a mouthful with eighteen syllables.

JOHN F. MERCHANT

In January 1983, in Phoenix, Arizona, the NMJGSA, a tongue twister to pronounce quickly although only six syllables, held the First Annual East/West Golf Classic yielding net proceeds of $1,500. In January 1984, the net proceeds totaled $5,000 and were given as scholarships to four young male golfers who attended Prairie View A&M, three of whom graduated four years later.

The next East/West Classic, in 2012, will be the thirtieth consecutive tournament, all held in Phoenix, Arizona. Many of the past dozen classics have attracted in excess of 350 black golfers from across the nation and have each raised more than $200,000 to be awarded as scholarships.

Bill, an intelligent as well as a caring person, usually deposited a percentage of the money raised in a separate account. His thinking was that if he was disabled, or died, that account could be invaded to honor existing commitments made to young people.

An honorable man and a legend, Bill really cared, as you can see.

Over the years, the NMJGSA has awarded in excess of $2.5 million to nine hundred plus college student golfers, many of whom played on golf teams at one of the Historical Black Colleges in this country. Bill's computer tracks these young people forever making them family.

Three things have always troubled me about Bill's organization: (1) it's a hard-to-pronounce name; (2) the fact that it has not received the support it should have from the golf industry; and (3) the fact that its Board has done little or nothing to identify and prepare a successor to Bill. The effort could fade away and die when Bill is unable to keep it alive because of age or disability. Basically his has been a one-man show.

Shamefully, but not unexpectedly, over the years, the golf industry has taken little or no interest in Bill's efforts, except for the very few that contributed a few shirts, balls, or a Windbreaker to be used as gifts for the entrants, a mere pittance in my mind that Bill almost had to beg for on an annual basis.

Black golf and black golfers were not a priority for the industry. In truth, Bill's Classic was seemingly viewed as an acceptable "separate but equal" reality and, therefore, not of real interest to the golf industry; this despite the fact that the PGA of America had graciously removed the "Caucasian only" words from its charter in 1961.

The issue of diversity was clearly on the table but not confronted meaningfully for the most part.

There is no way to say NMJGSA or its full name without difficulty or consuming time. It's a tongue twister and a chore that would mystify even the most capable marketing people. Try it and you'll see.

Frankly, it is impossible to create a clever or marketable mnemonic from the letters. However, those who have supported Bill's group don't worry or fret, they just help by participating and playing.

As stated, a few companies provided products and equipment to be used as gifts for the players. Access to the several golf courses needed to accommodate more than 350 golfers for a three-day period was negotiated by Bill on an annual basis with little or no support from a staff. There was no staff, just Bill.

Bill says, "We are building hope one stroke at a time" when and as he gives thanks to his board and the participants and sponsors who make it go.

Happily, for me, the name was recently changed to The Bill Dickey Scholarship Association (BDSA) and is easier to say, having only eleven syllables or four using BDSA. Me? I have always called it Bill Dickey's tournament (six syllables) because that is what it has always been.

He has almost singlehandedly created and maintained the viability and significance of the effort. He does it without compensation or sufficient staff support. Significant, forward-looking assistance from his Board has been disappointing. The future of the effort may now be in doubt, time will tell.

Expenses are kept in check by Bill flying standby and enduring other than the amenities afforded many that travel as frequently as he has done. He does it because of his great love of "The Game" and his conviction that a focus on diversity is critical and must be given a high level of priority by those able to help.

As for the lack of appropriate support from the industry, it is past time for the industry to give the issue of diversity its proper priority.

Adam Schupak, writing for *Golfweek* magazine in its October 6, 2007, issue, set forth the need and the challenge. Thus far none have been quick to accept the challenge and some of us wonder if the challenge will ever be adequately addressed by those who should. Admittedly, it's not an easy task for anyone.

Ensuring the perpetuity of Bill's tournament would be an important and positive first step. But please, do it sooner, not later.

Bill is eighty years old and cannot possibly keep up the pace he set for himself more than twenty-five years ago. Who replaces him? Bill's Board has not addressed the issue of his replacement in anything resembling a real way. Apparently, it did not properly prioritize the value of the asset it governed. Nor did it realize its significance over the long haul.

In my opinion, 'The Game' cannot afford to lose the resource Bill has created, nor the positive impact it can continue to have on diversity in 'The Game'.

Hopefully, Bill's Board will be responsive to the challenge now that Bill's age and his loss of energy are evident. How will they continue what Bill started? Will they see the long-term value in continuing? Do they agree that diversity suffers if the event loses its impact? Do they care about diversity?

I am not optimistic about what lies ahead for Bill's dream but shall wait to see and hope for the best.

Tiger is not the answer to diversity in golf, nor should he be saddled with the expectation or the responsibility. Renee Powell said it well

"When you look at someone like Tiger Woods you have
to remember that he's an individual. There shouldn't be a lot

JOHN F. MERCHANT

of pressure on his back to lead the way for everybody. He shouldn't be the only person carrying the torch."

Tiger, early in his career, shied away from being black on national television, a clear signal that he had no intention of becoming the CEO of the diversity effort. In doing so, he invented a new ethnic group called "Cablinasian" or something like that.

Tiger, if the invention is not patentable, leave it alone and go play golf.

I agree with Renee Powell but think the announcement by Tiger was unnecessary, even ludicrous, but what do I know?

The First Tee is not the answer either, although I sometimes get the impression that the industry in general believes it can sidestep the diversity question by inferring that the First Tee is all that needs to be done. The shallowness of that kind of thinking is scary to those of us who believe that The First Tee does not exemplify the priority the issue needs. It is a help, and an intriguing resource, clearly of value but not *the* answer.

Frankly, and despite its advertisements during golf tournament telecasts it is difficult, even impossible to obtain believable data on what it has achieved, or is achieving, regarding the diversity issue. Those ads always include photos showing minority children participating in the program, giving the impression that its outreach to the minority communities, especially the black community, is extensive; is it?

I seriously doubt that it is and would urge a truth in advertising standard be imposed.

It is not my intent to be overly critical, just accurate and honest. In no way do I mean to say, or even imply, that The First Tee is unworthy. I do mean to say that, by itself, it is not the answer to the diversity issue. It is an issue that is much more complex than the First Tee has addressed, or can address, effectively. More is needed from golf's entire industry.

Years ago, shortly after Tim Finchem was selected to serve as the Commissioner of the PGA Tour, I invited him to attend one of the four Symposiums I co-hosted with *Golf Digest* and the USGA from 1992 to 1995 dealing with the involvement of minorities in all aspects of the game. He was unable to spend four days with us at that time but flew in one Sunday morning, and we had a lengthy discussion about what the Symposiums were trying to achieve.

His reaction was positive. He told me that the issue of diversity was on his list of issues to address as Commissioner but it was not at the top of his list, nor did I expect it would have been. However, he committed to addressing it in due course. I believed that he meant what he said.

Ruffin Beckwith, former senior vice-president of the World Golf Village and a good man, was with him during our discussion. I believe that Finchem's aggressive effort to establish The First Tee Program is clear evidence that he honored the commitment he made to me. As far as I know, both Finchem and Beckwith (who did attend the first of four Symposiums) have been friends of diversity in golf, and I doubt that that will change. Finchem also served as a panelist at a subsequent Symposium.

David Fay and Joe Steranka, executive directors of the USGA and the PGA of America, respectively, also attended one or more of the Symposiums and fully supported the goals and efforts of the Symposiums.

They are two good men: I consider them good friends.

I came to golf late in life, at age twenty-six, learning to play while stationed at Pearl Harbor on the staff of the Commander-in-Chief of our Pacific Fleet (CINCPACFLT), an assignment I received after spending a year as the Legal Officer aboard the USS Bremerton (CA-130), a heavy cruiser that was retired for good reasons in 1959.

Old age had caught up with it, as did technology and its more modern warfare requirements. It was fundamentally useless, especially in a war.

At Pearl Harbor, I was initially assigned to duty as a communications officer. We worked shifts, each with three officers and an enlisted support staff. Working shifts gave me time to see almost all of Hawaii during my two years there. It also meant spending a lot of free time hanging out with those who worked that same shift. The officer in charge of my shift was LT. John Richardson, a golfer with a five handicap, from Burlingame, California.

John was an interesting guy nearing the end of his military obligation. He had been in Hawaii for a couple of years and had friends there with whom he socialized. Prior to my arrival, he had never had a black friend. My presence seemed to intrigue him to the point where he would take me along to parties his friends gave, without telling them that he was bringing a black guest. His motive, as he once explained to me, was to watch the reaction of his friends, almost all of whom had never socialized with a black man.

I was smart though. I always brought my guitar with me, and if all else failed, I could, and did, provide entertainment. It worked to the point where I was fully accepted as a regular by the group.

One night after a party John and I stopped at The Barefoot Bar in Waikiki for a nightcap. We were sitting at the bar when I heard what sounded like someone being slapped. I looked and noted that John, for reasons unknown, had slapped a huge Hawaiian sitting next to him.

That started a ruckus that spread outside. During the "event," John and I made a run for John's car, a Volkswagen with a running board. We entered the car with John driving and attempted to leave. In trying to maneuver around a huge tree, John caught the running board against the tree and could not complete the turn. We were stuck, a fact that allowed our pursuers to catch up with us.

I was dragged out of the car; John slid across the seat and came out to help, a nice gesture, thought I, especially since he was the one involved *ab initio* in the event. What a guy!

Police presence resolved the matter in our favor, meaning we stopped taking a *whupping* when the police broke it up. No arrests were made; we made it back to the BOQ on the base, treated our bruises, and then went to bed. I haven't been back to The Barefoot Bar since then.

John invited me to play golf at the Navy-Marine course where I caught the bug.

The first time we played I shot 102. John said to me that I could be a pretty good golfer if I took some lessons. I believed I could be a pretty good golfer without lessons, although I did see the need for a lot of practice. In fact, I bet John $50 that I could break 80 within six months without a lesson. He laughed and made the bet.

I then researched existing professional golfers and bought a book written by Al Geiberger, who was approximately my height and weight. I read his book many times and practiced almost daily. Ben Hogan's book *Power Golf* was also read and reread.

An Admiral had created a practice area (with government funds, I'm sure) where there was enough land for me to hit up to a 7 iron to a green that was surrounded by bunkers. Hence my short iron game, bunker play, and putting were the things I practiced often. I joined the Navy-Marine course ($13 a month dues) and played there regularly with John Richardson.

My game improved to the point where I won my bet four and a half months later. I shot 78 at the Army's course, Leilehua Golf Club, located out near the pineapple fields on Oahu ($12 a month dues). I still have the scorecard, properly witnessed.

John paid me, and I became a confirmed golfaholic leading to a lifetime of pleasure. My addiction to golf was also aided and abetted by a series of unplanned events.

Frankly, I was annoyed with my assignment as a communications officer and made my displeasure known to everyone I could. It seemed a waste of talent to me, a law school graduate, although not then a member of any bar association.

Shortly after I came to CINCPACFLT, an enlisted man stole another man's paycheck and cashed it, then committed suicide. This required an Article 15 investigation under the Uniform Code of Military Justice (UCMJ) to be performed by the command, CINCPAC.

Obviously, the matter had to be handled correctly and well but was not something any senior officer wanted to spend time doing. They were all busy doing other important work, I guess, or needed a patsy. I was called in during the search for an investigating officer and was recommended by the personnel officer who had received word of my constant complaining about the Navy's misuse of my training.

I was handed the assignment, given a car, and told in no uncertain terms that the investigation must be done expeditiously, thoroughly, and in an exemplary manner. I left Communications and started.

No one looked over my shoulder, though frequent progress reports were mandated. My time was my own, so I would work mornings, some evenings, then play golf every day and hang out in Honolulu nights. A nice life during which I met two people who made military life even better, namely, the coach of COMSERVPAC's basketball team and the leader of the trio that played jazz at the only bar in Waikiki that remained open until 2:00 a.m. in Honolulu.

Coach invited me to try out for the team. I made the team and after completing the investigation, I received orders to the team. Bye, bye Communications. I played one season, then, helped coach for part of a season. I was discharged in December 1961. We were All-Navy champions both seasons.

One night in Waikiki, I was in the club listening to a jazz trio and drinking. During the trio's break, my whiskey told me to approach the trio's leader and ask if I could borrow one man's guitar and sing folk stuff during the break. He said yes. The owner of the bar was not pleased when he saw me on stage but calmed down when the patrons made it clear that they enjoyed what I was doing. Believe it or not, they even applauded after each song and wanted more.

Subsequently, I was offered and accepted a job filling in during the jazz trio's breaks. The pay was not great but there was some—the whiskey was free, including Hawaii's own Okolehao, a beverage made from the taro root. I call it Hawaii's "corn liquor"—good stuff.

Drinking, listening to jazz, and singing folk songs were all now on my regular agenda, followed by sleep, golf, and basketball practice the next afternoon. Not a bad life for a young, black, naval officer stationed in Hawaii.

Actually, it's not a bad life for anyone, black, white, or polka dot.

A key to the Hawaiian experience for me was the birth of a lifelong addiction to the game of golf. It still exists, although a torn left shoulder rotator cuff, a stroke (mild, they say; what do they know?), right shoulder bursitis, and other issues associated with aging have limited my play to four rounds in the past five years.

Incidentally, a *mild* stroke is one that someone else has. If you don't believe that, shame on you. In any event, avoid it if possible.

After being discharged, I returned to Connecticut and began preparing for the Bar exam. There was a stop in Los Angeles where I considered a career as a folk singer, and I found folks who would back me if that's what I wanted to do. It wasn't. I enjoyed singing and entertaining but never thought I was good enough to make it a career.

In truth, I knew a lot of songs, including folk, country, and gospel, but I could only strum a guitar, not play it. I had a personal singing style that worked in Waikiki, Japan, Okinawa, and Australia, but I doubted it would ever get me out of New Haven.

Seventeen chords were all I knew, and reading music was not a talent of mine. The chords, properly strummed, were all that was needed for my repertoire. My singing style was my own, not an effort to copy anyone.

While in Los Angeles, I was interviewed and offered a job in a law firm. I accepted the job and was due to start on a Monday. After a difficult Saturday spent in deep thought, I called an airline, booked a flight to New York, and called the law firm and told them I was heading back East, and did, arriving home before Christmas in 1961.

Be it ever so humble, there is no place like home, especially when one has grown up learning to thoroughly enjoy the changing seasons, except winter. I sorely missed spring and autumn while in the Navy.

Hawaii was the same every day, beautiful and even breathtaking, but the everyday sameness was not for me.

I love the end of winter and the beginning of spring, when everything starts to come alive—flowers start to grow, leaves appear on trees, and almost daily improvement in the weather occurs. For me, a wonderful annual experience that two years in Hawaii did not provide. I missed it.

I decided not to take the February 1962 Bar Exam because after almost four years out of law school, there was a critical need for time to brush up and study if I were to have any chance at all to pass the exam. I studied daily for several months and took the exam in July 1962. Amazingly, to me, I passed it despite being four years away from law school. I was admitted to the Connecticut Bar in September 1962 and started practicing in Bridgeport, Connecticut, with L. Scott Melville, whom I met during the 1962 Bar Exam.

My Love for "The Game" Deepens in Connecticut

One immediate issue in Bridgeport was where to play golf. No military golf facilities existed nearby and joining a country club was out of the question for more than one reason. Fairchild Wheeler Golf Course (*The Wheel*), a public facility with two 18 hole courses, The Red and the Black, became the place to play.

Organizationally, *The Wheel* had a Men's Golf Association. It was run by men from the majority community, and in the early days, it had no black members. My belief is that blacks were excluded in ways that smelled of racism. Years later that changed.

Ironically, for years, and maybe even still, a black golfer, Sam Griffin held the course record achieved in tournament play. He shot a 65 on the "Black" course that was a more difficult test of golf than the "Red."

Membership in the Association entitled you to obtain a certified handicap from the Connecticut Golf Association (CGA). A handicap was needed to enter and compete in statewide CGA events.

A large number of black golfers played *The Wheel* regularly but had their own group, The Sportsmen's Club—a group not sanctioned to provide handicaps. No club members belonged to the men's association, thus they did not participate in state tournaments. A pity, since they counted many really fine players among their number, in addition to Sam Griffin.

Men like Bobby Green, Andy Taylor who played cross-handed, Rock, Doc Watson, Jake Salter, Milton Young, and many others.

To play *The Wheel* with a morning starting time, someone had to rise early, go to the course, and place a golf ball in a rack around 5:00 to 6:00 a.m. in order to tee off a couple of hours later. It was a busy place, especially on weekends. The chore of rising early to place a ball in the rack was shared among the Sportsmen's Club members—a complete nuisance but a fair system, I guess.

To the best of my knowledge, starting times could not be obtained by telephone in 1963. I did wonder how some members of the association, usually the better players and the association's people, seemed to always get the preferred starting times in the morning times that allowed an earlier finish and an escape from the afternoon heat in the summer. One could relax, watch golf on TV, eat, drink beer, and escape the afternoon heat if an early starting time was secured.

John J. Lawrence, a black doctor with a practice in Bridgeport, was, and still is, an avid golfer. He and I joined the Sportsmen's Club and played *The Wheel* almost every weekend with them. I've always called him Doc.

Like many golfers, small bets were made by most to make the round more competitive and interesting. Sportsmen Club golfers played a "skins" game, meaning a birdie earned a dollar from each player. As many as twenty-four players participated in the skins game so a birdie could be worth $23. Failure to make at least one birdie could get expensive, especially if some players had a good day with more than one birdie. That happened a lot.

I met Doc shortly after opening my law office in Bridgeport in September 1962. He had come to Bridgeport a year or so before me. Neither of us can recall exactly when and how we met, but we've been good friends since then.

He is a remarkable human being—talented, kind, great sense of humor, terrific storyteller, and an exceptionally talented physician.

Doc is married to a wonderful lady, Lois, a professional social worker and they have three delightful daughters: Julie; Caroline; and Mary Lee.

Lois is a very bright and insightful person, a lady in every respect. She possesses a fertile mind that is constantly kept active and refueled by reading voraciously and using it. Given her interest in a wide variety of subjects, including local and national affairs and the art of living, she is a delight to talk with and very much worth listening to.

Our families have been close. His children call me Uncle John and my children call them Uncle John and Aunt Lois. We wouldn't have it any other way.

Doc followed an interesting path to obtain his medical degree and licenses. He was raised in an orphanage in Staten Island, New York. A good athlete, he earned a scholarship to St. Lawrence University to play football and baseball. Faced with football practices scheduled at the same time as his science labs, he gave up his scholarship and transferred to Manhattan College in New York City. There he earned his bachelor's degree in science and was admitted to Howard University's medical school. He is licensed to practice medicine in several states but chose to come to Connecticut in 1961 and practice medicine. He affiliated with St. Vincent's Hospital.

He wanted to be a doctor, not a football player, and he became one.

In 1962, two other hospitals existed in Bridgeport: Park City Hospital and Bridgeport Hospital. These three served the Greater Bridgeport Area that included the towns of Stratford, Fairfield, Trumbull, and Monroe.

When I came to Bridgeport in September 1962, there were several black doctors in the area, all of whom had privileges at Park City and/or St. Vincent's. None had privileges at Bridgeport Hospital; I don't think they were wanted there. They were certainly not recruited.

Apparently, Bridgeport Hospital served the middle class, upper class, and non-Catholic residents of the area, although located in, or near, what became, and is, one of Bridgeport's densely populated black neighborhoods, near I-95. Blacks seeking medical care, especially those seeking emergency attention for different reasons, appeared frequently at Bridgeport Hospital where they were often not provided the level of medical expertise they needed or that was available there. Sad to say, there are numerous stories of being turned away from, or treated poorly at, Bridgeport Hospital if you were black. That has changed.

Many blacks seeking medical assistance were not insured, were on welfare, or generally lacked an ability to pay for services, thus were not welcomed and often shunned. I believe that racism also played a major role in disserving the black population.

Ironically, I was invited to serve on Bridgeport Hospital's Board of Trustees and did serve for a few years. Years later, for a short period of time, I also served on the Board of St. Vincent's School of Nursing.

Doc enjoys a well-deserved reputation among his peers in the medical profession for his uncanny ability to diagnose ailments and suggest treatment alternatives that were on the money. He possesses the best memory of any human being I have ever met. He has been my doctor and friend since 1962.

Literally, if Doc had ever read it, heard it, or discussed it, he could recall, in detail, what he had read, heard, and discussed.

How did I know of his reputation as a physician? Easy. Through Doc, I met and talked with several Bridgeport physicians, most of whom raved about his ability and professionalism. Unlike most, Doc believed in and did house calls.

Ideally, for me, I have never been without first-class medical advice and assistance, when needed. To this day, I choose a doctor *after* asking Doc, including: a primary doctor when Doc gave up his practice to accept a position as vice president for medical affairs at St. Vincent's Hospital in Bridgeport, Connecticut; an orthopedic surgeon for removal of cartilage in my left knee; a surgeon for removal of a faulty gall bladder, and later, a polinidal cyst; a neurologist after a "mild" stroke about four years ago; and, an ophthalmologist when my eyes needed professional assistance.

Recently, Doc and I spent a couple of hours reminiscing about our friendship, our families, and our love for the game of golf. We recalled how we tired of placing the ball in the rack at *The Wheel* and joined Hillandale CC, a country club owned by a friend of Doc's, Tom Dolan, who told Doc to fill out an application, have me do the same, and send them to him. By doing that, we would become members, immediately, as long as our checks didn't bounce. They didn't bounce.

Tom was a lawyer with the firm of Coles, O'Connell and Dolan and was active in St. Vincent's Hospital, where Doc had privileges.

Hillandale was a joy and provided us with many years of golfing pleasure. Victor Riccio and Kenny Janello, both lawyers, joined the two of us completing our foursome. Two blacks, an Italian and a Romanian, we played together almost every weekend for fifteen years. We played at Hillandale and later at Rolling Hills CC after Hillandale was sold and its acreage replaced with single-family housing.

A lot of really good golfers, many with a penchant for gambling, belonged to Hillandale. Most were graduates of *The Wheel*. It was really a blue-collar membership comprised of good people and many good golfers.

One habit many had was to play another nine after finishing eighteen in order to increase their winnings or recover their losses. Inevitably, new golfers with some talent would be invited to play additional holes after their round and a beer or two at the 19th hole. I was approached one day and invited to play a "nine hole Nassau for a nickel, with automatics after two down." This means a $5 bet with an additional $5 bet if you lost two holes and were two down in the match.

Pride, tradition, and urging by Doc, Vic and Kenny caused me to accept. We actually played ten holes; my partner was Joe Kulikowski.

When we returned to the clubhouse, someone asked how things had gone? Joe answered, saying while pointing at me, "We integrated our way into their pockets to the tune of $65." Yup, that's right, integration proved its value that day.

In truth, I made a lot of money at Hillandale, often with Lou Piantidosi as my partner, a clutch player if ever I saw one. For a couple of years, I made enough money to cover the full cost of membership dues. Lotsa fun!

Early on, Kenny Janello told me that I could play anyone, for any amount of money, anywhere in the country, and he would cover one half of any losses arising out of the gambling. I don't recall Kenny ever having to pay. His hand was usually extended only to accept his half of any winnings. He would puff his cigar, smile, and pocket the cash.

Doc was also an interesting backer of mine. I recall being in the Grand Bahamas playing golf with Doc. We had dinner one night at The Lucayan Country Club and Golf Course, where we were joined by the owner. The conversation was wide and varied. Fueled by rum, it ended with a challenge to play a round the next day where the stakes were ownership of the Lucayan Club against whatever its value was. Doc said, "Do it, and I'll back you for half."

Apparently, he and Kenny had more confidence in my game than I did, although I knew I could play a little. They certainly backed me in competition. In fact, it was Doc who encouraged me to enter the Club Championship at Rolling Hills CC. He said to me that you should win the Club Championship here since you can play as well or better than any member here.

My first try saw me reach the finals, a 36-hole match where I was 8 down after the first 18 holes, then lost 3 down with 2 to play. I was unhappy. My unhappiness became worse when I learned that the prize for finishing second was absolutely nothing. Subsequently, in 1980 and 1983, I won the Club Championship and was pleased about that.

In 1980, the award for winning was a blue blazer; I already owned two. Simultaneously, the award for being runner up, therefore a loser, was a 19" color television set. That set my mind to work, but since I owned enough television sets, I didn't let it bother me at that time. In 1983, I received a wonderful trophy for winning, and I cherish it.

At Lucayan, Doc and I showed up at the first tee at the appointed time; the owner arrived late, joining us at the 4th hole where I was already two under par. He called off the bet. Good thing he did because Doc and I, along with Ken Janello, would have become joint owners of The Lucayan Country Club that day. I was on fire, the owner was not. We often chuckle about that experience.

When Hillandale CC closed, Doc, Kenny, Victor, and I sought another venue to continue our tradition of playing together almost every weekend. Obtaining membership at one of the several country clubs nearby was essentially impossible for us. Two blacks, an Italian and a Romanian, individually and collectively, were not acceptable at any of the area clubs. We wanted a place where all four of us could be together.

Fortunately, Doc had friends at Rolling Hills Country Club in Wilton, Connecticut, a predominately Jewish Club. Area Jews had built the club because, like the four of us, they were not welcome at any of the area country clubs, so they built their own. We all applied, and Doc was accepted a couple of months before the three of us, but we all became members and our foursome remained intact, our tradition undisturbed.

As stated, that foursome remained together for many years. Doc and Kenny were partners, and Victor and I were partners. Kenny played to about a 13 handicap; Doc around 17 or 18; Victor 22 or 23; and I carried a single-digit handicap between 6 and 8. Our usual bet involved golf balls, not cash money. The four of us were very close friends and socialized frequently with our families and mutual friends. It was an enjoyable time at Rolling Hills.

One day, we came to the 18th hole, a tough par 4. With the presses involved, the winner of the 18th hole would pocket a dozen golf balls. Each player was given a stroke on the hole from me, based on handicaps, and each of them reached the green in 3, although no one was close to the hole. Regrettably, I had played terribly and was in my pocket, out of contention.

Doc and Kenny were away and putted first, each using two putts, giving them a net par on the hole, assuring (in their minds) at least a tie. Victory seemed very possible as Victor stepped up to his thirty footer needing to travel up a small incline and break two different ways to reach the hole. Victor was not really a good putter, and facing this very difficult putt, a three putt could happen.

Doc and Kenny stood by watching Victor address his ball, I think hoping he would three putt and they would each win a dozen golf balls. At least, they surely thought, we can't lose the dozen.

Amazingly to all, including Victor, he stroked the putt well and we watched it climb the incline, turn a bit to the right, then head left in the direction of the hole, and fall in for a par, net three, and the win.

Victor was elated to say the least, so was I. Doc and Kenny were disappointed and shocked. They immediately turned and walked off the green, turning their backs on us and not saying a word as they headed for the clubhouse. They ignored us completely, did not congratulate Victor for making par on the second most difficult hole on the course, and did not shake our hands as opponents traditionally do at the conclusion of the match.

I can still see Victor following them off the green toward the clubhouse, putter in hand, looking for some sign of friendship and uttering phrases such as, "My dearest friends won't speak to me," "What did I do wrong," and similar comments. Doc and Kenny just kept walking into the clubhouse and locker room where they cooled their disappointment and later made arrangements to provide the dozen balls.

Another recollection of some interest was when a year or so after we joined the club and had played strictly with each other, we were approached by a member who asked, "How does one get a chance to play a round of golf with you guys? It seems that you only play with each other and really enjoy doing that, but you don't give other members a chance to know you better?"

The immediate response was a one-liner consisting of two words "You don't," said Kenny, or maybe it was Doc. Both were pretty good at one-line zingers. We laughed, knowing that it was said jokingly. We appreciated the member approaching us as he did with his hand of friendship extended.

On the subject of one-liners, one of the best I ever heard was at Rolling Hills. Two rich gentlemen were having a somewhat heated discussion about something while a couple of us stood around and listened. Some insulting comments were exchanged, but eventually one walked away and the dispute ended.

After he left, one of the bystanders said to the remaining gentleman, "Why do you take that crap from him? You could buy and sell him." Without hesitation, the response was, "I could buy him and keep him."

Over most of the seventeen years I belonged to Rolling Hills, our foursome remained intact, generally playing at least once a week. It was broken up by the death of Victor. We made many good friends at Rolling Hills, and except for the ending, I thoroughly enjoyed my time there.

I made many good friends and came to know some really fine people. Irv Lineal was a special guy—creative, efficient, highly intelligent, and personable. Irv was married to a woman as smart or smarter than him, but she never let him know it. He was a handball enthusiast and a good athlete. Left handed, he had a single-digit golf handicap, and we enjoyed some wonderful matches playing against each other.

Irv and Lois invited me and my children to the first Seder we ever attended. It was a learning experience enhanced by Irv's uncanny ability to explain things without preaching. They had arranged for participation by all, including my daughters who were preteens, as I recall.

Eventually, the Lineals moved to Florida. Irv explained the move this way. He said that throughout their marriage, Lois had supported him in everything he did, without complaint. Now she wanted to be closer to her grandchildren in Florida, the first thing of significance she had asked of him. So, said he, "We moved."

The move saddened me, but we agreed that I would spend a week with them in Florida each year and did.

One year, Irv invited me to play in a one-day Member-Guest at his club. The event did not include a prize for low gross, thus Irv and I had no chance to win it. My handicap was 6 and his was 9. The "muggers" were just too much to overcome, although our best ball, gross, was 5 under par. Later, at dinner, we received our prize.

There was a drawing to conclude the day. It was announced that when the guest's name was pulled from the bowl, both the member and the guest would receive the same prize. Prizes were as follows: a golf bag for third; a set of woods for second that included a driver, 3 and 4 woods; and a complete set of irons, three to nine, for first place. Irv asked me, loudly enough for the other eight people at our table to hear, "OK, Merchant, what are you going to win for us?"

I replied, "The irons," since I had no need to carry two golf bags on the plane, and hitting woods had never been my forte. He smiled.

Little did the group assembled know that a few years before at Rolling Hills CC, I had participated in three raffles during the year, buying three tickets for each. Those nine tickets produced five winners, including two first place, two second place, and one third place winner.

As the person selected to draw the winning ticket reached into the bowl, Irv quietly rose from his chair and pushed it back under the table as the emcee prepared to announce the winner.

"Merchant," said the emcee. "Let's go," said Irv. The table was in a state of shock as we each claimed a new set of Ben Hogan irons. I was disappointed since I didn't use Hogans; my choice has always been for Titleist equipment. The pro shop had no Titleist irons.

I brought the Hogans home anyway and later gave them to a young man in Bridgeport who could use them and did. There are many more Lineal stories, but telling them would involve writing another book.

Harold Belmuth and his wife Lila were also special people and good friends; Barry Waxman and his wife were the same with whom many enjoyable hours were spent on and off the golf course.

The end at Rolling Hills CC came because of a situation that happened this way.

One day, I was about to tee off on the 10th tee when the Chairman of the Admissions Committee drove up in a cart with a black couple. He introduced us, then, drove away, and we finished the round. Later, in the clubhouse, he approached me and said that the black couple had just moved to Wilton, didn't know anyone in the area, and wanted to join the club. They wanted a place to play golf. He asked me to be their sponsor.

We discussed that. I told him that I didn't feel that I could sponsor someone I didn't know, but he convinced me to consider doing so, saying that they seemed like good people, could afford to belong, and had impressed him.

A week or so later, I agreed to contact them, get to know them, and decide if I could be their sponsor. I did just that and had a drink with the man, later dinner with him and his wife, contacted friends in Denver, where the couple had previously lived to learn more about them, had them meet a couple of other members, and came to know and like them. They applied with me as their sponsor; I found another member who agreed to be their cosponsor.

The process of applying included the applicant, his wife, and their sponsor meeting with the Admissions Committee. Seven candidates had applied; six met with the committee. The seventh, me and the black couple, were never invited to meet.

I was on the Board at the time and attended the meeting at which the Board voted on admitting new applicants. The six were accepted. I raised my hand and inquired about my candidates, asking the Admissions Committee Chairman, also a Board member, why we were not invited to be interviewed by the Admissions Committee like the other six. It seemed a sensible question to ask.

The Board Chairman immediately ordered the Admissions Chairman not to respond to my question, stating that any questions I had should be directed to the chair. I did that. A lively discussion took place, during which my cosponsor remained silent and would not look me in the eye. The Board Chairman denied that race was a factor, though I, personally, never raised the issue of race; he did.

One result of the discussion was that one of the club's original founders, who was also general counsel for the club, resigned as general counsel immediately, obviously very upset over how the matter had been handled.

To this day, all involved deny that race had anything to do with denying my candidates admission, a blatant lie. I spent the next three years trying to get someone to admit the truth, without success. I then resigned from the club and was able to join another country club.

Some time after the board meeting, I was told that when Vic, Kenny and I originally applied for membership, a prominent member of the club and a board member threatened to resign immediately if another black member was accepted, along with an Italian and a Romanian.

The Chairman of the Board, Norman Myers, a gentleman who harbored no bigotry in his makeup, after hearing the resignation threat, calmly said, "Gentlemen, the next order of business is to consider the resignation of 'X,'" and they prepared to do that. The threat to resign was withdrawn and we were voted in as members.

Enlightened leadership by a good man does make a difference, I reckon.

Our foursomes' camaraderie, friendship, and togetherness showed up in other ways as well, specifically, during the Member Guest weekends when at the Saturday night dinner dance, we would assemble at a long table set for us, our wives, or significant others, and our guests; sixteen strong. Soon we noticed that many in attendance seemed to be watching us as we thoroughly enjoyed ourselves in the company of each other.

We were not loud and obnoxious by any means, but laughter, jokes, smiles, discussions, and the like abounded. We did not use that time to discuss the Dow Jones, Gaza Strip, business issues, the economy, or other mundane, albeit important subjects. We were friends in the true sense of the word and enjoyed our time together. As you might imagine, those times created long-lasting memories that thrive even today.

On several occasions, members approached our table, standing around or close to it, for the sole purpose of watching us have fun. Hopefully, they learned something;

we just enjoyed the chance to be with friends in a setting triggered by our love for '*The Game*' and each other.

Golf is like that!

Incidentally, among other things we liked about Rolling Hills was the fact that we considered it to be one of the finest restaurants in Fairfield and Westchester Counties.

I especially enjoyed the two-pound-lobster dinners held two or three times each summer. My friends enjoyed them also, especially Dan Brennan's wife, Ruth, who devoured a lobster and picked it cleaner, better than anyone I ever observed. One notable achievement of mine was the night I ate thirty-six raw clams and other assorted sea food *before* the lobster arrived, then devoured the lobster seeking to emulate Ruth.

Some still talk about that and wonder how a skinny kid raised in Chickahominy in Greenwich, Connecticut, could absorb that much food and stay skinny. I gave the best answer I could, giving credit to metabolism.

The truth is that I could not gain weight if my life depended on it, no matter how much I ate. While in college, I once deliberately consumed more than four thousand five hundred calories a day for thirty-seven days and gained exactly one pound. Today, fifty-five years after I finished playing college basketball, I weigh 161 pounds, eight pounds more than I did in 1955.

Clearly the campaign against obesity in America has no relevance to me.

If I were to wrap up the Rolling Hills experience in a few words, I would say that it was clearly a highlight of my life. Susan and Tabitha also enjoyed the club. Phyllis, the club's secretary, took a special interest in both of them ensuring that they enjoyed being at the club. Generally, little children were not a part of the mix there, but my kids felt welcomed, thanks to Phyllis.

In general, a host of friends were made and retained. The Belmuths, Goldmans, Lineals, Smicks, Waxmans, "Nelly" Schwimmer, and many others provided me with memories I cherish.

John Bladt, the club manager, was an absolute gem, as was the entire staff, including Phyllis, the secretary, and Mike, the bartender. Staff treated me and any guests of mine like royalty.

Joe Bostic, the club's long-term golf professional, was a friend who encouraged my game and helped hone it. Often he invited me to play pro-ams at various clubs throughout the Westchester, New York, area. Through him, I played courses like Winged Foot and The Black Course at Bethpage, Long Island, among others.

I left there and joined the Country Club of Fairfield where I remained for thirteen years. It is one of the most exclusive country clubs in America and no blacks had ever belonged until I joined. Nick Goodspeed, Jim Biggs, and George Carter collaborated to make joining possible.

One disappointment at CCF was that after thirteen years, I still did not have a regular game with other members. In fact, the last few years saw me playing there with outside guests of mine, all of whom enjoyed and cherished an opportunity to play this great course. I didn't belong; I left when injuries and ailments eased playing golf out of my life.

Officiating at the Masters, US Open, etc.

During my time with the USGA Executive Committee, I was fortunate to be an official at four Masters, four US Opens, and four Senior Opens. That service produced some interesting moments that I often smile about as they are recalled.

Membership on the USGA Executive Committee automatically confers upon one status as an official at the Masters. Thus, I was able to do what many cannot and will not ever do, although they would like to attend the Masters. What an experience!

At age fifty-nine, I could hardly contain my excitement in the weeks leading up to the Masters. I was like a child on Christmas Eve, looking forward to seeing what Santa brought the next day. My clothes, including the USGA uniform, blue blazer with USGA badge, gray slacks, shirt, official USGA tie, and shined shoes were all carefully prepared a couple of weeks in advance. Cleaned and laundered and packed away carefully, in advance so as not to forget anything.

I remember the first ride down Magnolia Lane—awesome!

I was in a car with some other USGA Committee members. They had been there before. My effort focused on being "cool" and acting like there was nothing unusual about me being there. I was barely able to resist saying, "Wow" too many times. It was not easy.

I truly wish that Dad, Mom, my sisters, and some friends could have made that first drive with me. Here was I, a "colored" kid from Chickahominy in Greenwich, Connecticut, about to officiate at the Masters, arguably golf's premier event, bar none.

Yes, I had status and would spend most of the week in a position to make rulings for players from all over the world who were the cream of the crop of golfers. Right or wrong, my rulings would be adhered to. I hoped to avoid mistakes and almost did.

That drive down Magnolia Lane was the beginning of a weeklong adventure that I treasure and won't ever forget.

I was enormously impressed with everything about the Masters; you would be also. No detail is overlooked. I was told that specific set-up instructions are kept in a thick, loose leaf binder and strictly adhered to by all. Employees are hired to walk the grounds under instructions not to leave a single piece of paper, or wrapping from a candy bar or sandwich, lying on the ground, visible to anyone. I never saw a piece of paper lying anywhere in my four years there.

The event is truly an international event, with players invited to play from all over the world, including Europe and Asia.

Media coverage is huge, so huge that a special building for media was constructed, at a cost I'm told, exceeding five million dollars. The building is out of sight, tucked away behind some trees to the right of the first fairway. It is used just one week per year, during the Masters.

All of the latest technology is available to each member of the media. Computers, phones, and you name it, are located at each of the individual seats set up in an impressive amphitheater used only by the media. I didn't count the number of seats but memory says that there are somewhere

JOHN F. MERCHANT

around one to two hundred. Wide screen television sets enable the media to keep track of the players out on the course, along with a huge electronic board that shows the scores for all players as they play each hole.

Yes, a press pass at the Masters is to be envied.

Cell phones, PDA's, and beepers are strictly forbidden inside the gates. Violators are warned that they will be ejected and forfeit their tickets and badges. Once forfeited, the likelihood is that they will never again in life be issued to you. Spectators are now provided with banks of telephones that provide free long-distance service in the United States only. Thanks AT&T.

Interestingly, food is low priced. You don't need to bring a pocketful of cash to cover the cost of a couple of sandwiches (egg salad, pimento, among others), a bag of chips and a soft drink. One of each is available for a total cost of $4-5. A Masters club sandwich is a must for those who have the cash. It sold for $2.50 in 2010. You could eat yourself into bad health for $20 but try to put the paper wrappings in a trash bin, please. Soft drink cups are a prized souvenir kept by almost all.

I'm told that the most difficult ticket to obtain for a sporting event is a ticket to attend the Masters as a spectator. The waiting list is long and never gets smaller, only larger. Here I was not only attending but officiating and walking around as if I were somebody important, making rulings and enjoying the magnificence of the setting and the property. And it is magnificent!

The Wednesday night before the tournament starts is a Masters tradition. The previous year's champion has the right to set the menu for a dinner in the clubhouse. All Executive Committee members are invited to that banquet, along with players, Augusta members, and others. A large crowd filled with household names and people of importance in the industry attends.

I honestly do not recall any of the four meals I ate there, but I do remember that they were delicious, well prepared, and the food was both nourishing and plentiful.

You may remember Fuzzy Zoeller's comments after Tiger won his first Masters. He said something to the effect that next year's dinner will probably be fried chicken and collard greens. Earl and Tiger reacted to Fuzzy's comments by effectively condemning them, and him for his "racist comments." Their reaction ultimately cost Fuzzy an endorsement contract.

Personally, I believe they overreacted. Anyone who knows Fuzzy knows that he's always making wise cracks and making jokes, but means no harm. Of course, given America's struggles with racial attitudes, I cannot condone what Fuzzy said, or how the media and the Woods handled it. I have met and known Fuzzy, but not well. I don't believe he meant to make a racist comment.

However, his effort to be a comedian cost him money.

I recall being greeted by an employee, a black man, at the door as I entered the clubhouse for the first time to attend my first Wednesday night Champion's dinner. He held the door open for me, shook my hand, and looked me in the eye, as tears formed in his eyes, and said, "Welcome, we've been hoping for this for a long, long time. Welcome."

JOHN F. MERCHANT

The maître d', another black man, approached me as I entered. Pleased and proud to see me, he offered a tour of the facility which I accepted. He showed me the locker room, the enviable wine cellar, and various rooms in the place. I was overwhelmed and thoroughly impressed, to say the least. Ordinary spectators don't get to tour the clubhouse or even enter it.

The attention to detail mentioned earlier is present on the golf course. I don't recall ever seeing a single weed growing anywhere on the course. At that time, the course also lacked any "rough" unlike every other course I've ever seen. The greens were immaculate, but it was like putting downhill on glass on most of them. Of course, everything about the course and the tournament was, and is, immaculate.

Imagine this: I was there four years in a row. Hard to believe.

Steve Pate and the New Official

As an official, like all the others, I was given a specific assignment for each day. That meant being in a single location all day long until every player had played through your location. My first assignment was on hole number 2 on one side of the landing area for the tee shot; number 2 is a par 5 down a hill with a slight dogleg left. It was an easy assignment requiring few difficult issues relating to the Rules of Golf or their interpretation. I encountered three incidents there in my four years.

Steve Pate hit his tee shot left, and it trickled off the fairway, down an incline, into a narrow and small amount of water. He was in bounds but in the hazard. I carried a large, bright red, handkerchief that I used when working in Arizona and dropped it on the ground, indicating the point of entry into the hazard.

Pate came storming down the fairway looking upset, with his driver still in his hand. As he approached me, he angrily, and to me insultingly, asked about his ball. I pointed into the hazard, then, indicated the handkerchief denoting his point of entry. Somewhat loudly and angrily, he said to me, "Were you watching it, did it hit anything?" His tone gave off an inference that perhaps I had something to do with his ball being in the hazard, and quite honestly, his attitude pissed me off.

So I looked him in the eye and quietly said to him, "It hit only your g**damn golf club," picked up my handkerchief, and walked away to a point where I could still watch him and was available to answer any other questions he might have. We politely discussed his options. He was able to hit his ball out of the hazard onto the fairway and, I'm told, made a par on the hole.

The next year, I was assigned to the landing area for second shots on number 8, also a five par hole, pretty straightaway but uphill. I watched as a player hit his second shot uphill from the fairway and pulled it left. It rolled into an area off the fairway and came to rest under some shrubbery.

The player came storming up, agitated and upset, and seemingly ready to develop an attitude. I watched him approach, and as he came closer, I then recognized him as being Steve Pate. I was ready for him, though as he took his last twenty or thirty steps toward where I was standing. Then, like a bolt of lightning, he was struck with a memory allowing him to recognize me.

"Sir," he said, "did you see my ball?" "Yes, Mr. Pate," was my answer, and I showed him where it had come to rest. With some difficulty, he played his ball and went on with his round. I went to watch the player behind him.

Jose Maria Olazabal and the New, but Attentive, Official

Number 2 gave me some action in another year. My assignment was the same as Jose Maria Olazabal teed off and hit his tee show way right off the tee into some dense shrubbery and trees. It was so far away from the fairway and off to the right that Olazabal hit a provisional ball, not expecting to find the first one. I followed the first ball and marked its approximate landing spot in my mind.

Olazabal nailed his provisional down the middle of the fairway and some distance down the hill, leaving him with a good chance to reach the green with his next shot and, maybe, save par on the hole. A search for his first ball was undertaken, and after no more than a minute or two of searching, I raised my voice and inquired as to what kind of ball he was playing, and how it was marked. He answered, and I loudly proclaimed, "Here it is!"

It was tangled up in the brush. A player could not take a stance, let alone swing and make contact with the ball. The rules allow a drop no closer to the hole and as far back as is needed. He would have had to go to Augusta, through the trees and brush, to find a drop where he could swing at and hit the ball. To say that he was upset is to beg the question.

Having found his first ball, the provisional could not be played. He had to go back to the tee and hit another tee shot. I can still visualize him trudging back to the tee, golf club on his shoulder, and smoke rising from the nose, ears, and mouth. He hit another tee shot. Needless to say, it was not as good as the provisional, a fact that annoyed him further as he trudged back down the fairway to continue the round.

No, he did not par the hole. Honestly, I never learned his exact score on the hole, never tried to or wanted to. My preference was to stay out of sight, and I did stay out of his sight for a day or two.

John Harris Learns to Like Me

Then there was the day that I was assigned to number 14, along with another official. It is a 4 par up a hill but pretty straightaway. We alternated between the landing area for tee shots and the green to add a level of exercise to the relative boredom this assignment entailed.

While I was taking a turn at the green, John Harris, an amateur from Minnesota, hit his second shot in a way that caused it to run through the green, up an eight-foot hill immediately behind the green, where it came to rest on a paper cup and a chair a woman was sitting in but vacated when the ball reached her. Her cup and contents remained, although the drink spilled when struck by the ball.

I reached into my memory to recall the applicable rule when that happens and drew a blank. Frantically, I tried to wave at the other official to get her attention and her help. She did not notice me waving, and Harris kept walking, getting closer and closer. He reached his ball and stood by it, looking at me as I looked at him. Not recalling the rule, but knowing that help was not on the way and that the cup and chair had to be moved, I said to him, "Mark it," and he did. That was exactly the right thing to do.

The cup and chair were moved and then I told Harris that he could take a drop. That was exactly the wrong thing to do.

My hope was that his drop would not cause the ball to roll down the hill, closer to the hole and maybe even onto the green. Fortunately, he took his drop, as instructed, and the ball rolled sideways down the hill, away from the green, coming to rest on relatively level ground. I breathed a sigh of relief and said, "That ball's in play."

John Harris then proceeded to chip the ball into the hole for a birdie, and all watching applauded, including me. I walked across the green and, on the way, I gave Harris a high five, which was caught on camera by the Augusta news photographer without my knowledge. My intent was to gain a better position for observing Bernhard Langer's attempt to putt for birdie. He missed, made par, and they went to the next tee.

The newspaper reporter then wanted some comments from me, which, wisely, I declined to offer. I think she knew that I had made a mistake.

The proper procedure was to have Harris place his ball where he had marked it. I mean, what's the point of having him mark it with a coin, except to know where to place it later. The rules do not include allowing him a drop.

The next day, on the front page of the sports section, was a photo of the Harris/Merchant high five. A comment regarding Harris's birdie was in the accompanying story, but happily, nothing was said about my error.

John Harris made the cut by one stroke; thus his birdie kept him around to play on the weekend.

The problem facing me now was complying with Augusta's rule that every ruling made during any day, no exceptions, must be written up and submitted to the Rules Committee chairman.

Each morning, before the tournament started for the day, all officials met at 7:30 a.m. sharp and, among other things, discussed any rulings that were unusual or interesting the day before.

I submitted my writing to the chairman, who, after hearing my explanation, chuckled a bit, said we all make mistakes, and he assured me that my ruling would not be discussed in detail the next morning. Thus, I was not embarrassed in front of the group.

Interestingly, I had to rule on that same situation three times the next day. I was assigned to the green at fifteen (that rhymes), and some players hit second shots to the right of the green upon a slight incline where spectators were located. Thus, three times I confidently issued a ruling that all could hear and was proud to do so. Eyewitnesses probably thought I knew the rules. I knew that one for sure.

JOHN F. MERCHANT

Tom Watson, Choosing the Right Restaurant, and a Black Friend

Tom Watson has always been a favorite of mine. He and Sandy Tatum were friends and regular partners during the pro-am phase of a tournament at Pebble Beach on the Monterrey Peninsula. I spoke with Sandy and told him that I would really enjoy an opportunity to meet and talk with Tom. Sandy put us in touch, and over the phone, we agreed to have dinner one night during the US Open at Baltusrol. He told me to choose the restaurant.

I made some calls, obtained the yellow pages of the phone book, and looked up "Restaurants." I blindly selected an Italian Restaurant reasonably close to the hotel where the players stayed during the tournament and shared that choice with Tom. We set the date and time to meet and did.

Tom and his wife joined me and my lady friend at the appointed time and spent an enjoyable two-three hours at dinner. Our conversation flowed easily and covered a wide spectrum of subjects. Tom is a very intelligent man. His mind works often and well, covering many subjects besides the game of golf.

Shortly after we sat down, Ray Floyd and his wife entered the restaurant. They saw us and came over to speak to Tom and his wife, and Tom introduced Diane and me to them. They then went to their table.

When they were out of earshot, Tom complimented me on my choice of restaurants, saying that we had to be in one of the better ones around if Ray Floyd was eating there. He assumed that I had known what I was doing when I chose this one. I did nothing to impact the working of his mind on that topic.

He explained that Ray Floyd's wife grew up with parents who owned an Italian Restaurant in South Philadelphia, I believe. He further explained that if the Floyds chose an Italian Restaurant for dinner, it must be excellent, simple as that.

I did not have the heart to disclose how I had chosen this place. I don't remember the name of the place, but I do remember that the meal was really good, the ambience and service were excellent, and I had a reputation I hadn't earned.

During the meal, Tom, who grew up in Kansas, mentioned that he had never had a black friend in his life. I suggested that maybe I could be his first, and he agreed. Next day after talking with his wife, I agreed to prepare a proclamation recognizing and certifying that Tom now had a black friend, me.

The proclamation was filled with "whereas" and "wherefore," properly notarized and framed. His wife told me that he hung the proclamation on the wall in his office and was very pleased to have it.

Lee Trevino and Calvin Peete—peas in different pods

At a Senior Open held at Pinehurst number 2 in North Carolina, I and another official were assigned to a group that included Gary Player, Calvin Peete, and Lee Trevino. I was excited to be that close to three men I had rooted for over the years.

As is customary, the players and officials introduced themselves on the first tee and shook hands. There must have been a thousand people, or so, watching the group tee off. I shook hands with Calvin last and introduced myself. He immediately drew back his hand, and in a loud voice, while shaking his hand somewhat vigorously as if it had been bruised, he told everyone within six miles that he had been hurt by the handshake. Say what?

I do have a firm grip and strong handshake, but he was, and is, the only person who has ever claimed injury, or intent to injure, because of it.

He then loudly proclaimed that I should be careful because he made a living with his hands, thereby publicly chastising me or seeking to embarrass me. I was amazed since neither Lee nor Gary had reacted that way despite receiving the same type of handshake.

Then I thought, *What a jerk* and almost laughed out loud. I smiled, became amused, turned my back on Calvin, and walked away. I shied away from Calvin throughout the round and left any rulings regarding him to the other official.

During the round two decisions involving Calvin were made. In each case, I was the nearest official and should have made the rulings, neither of which would favor him. Instead, I called the other official over, and he made the rulings. That avoided another silly outburst.

Also, during the round, Gary hit his second shot into a bunker next to the green. He had to hit it out to a green sloping away from him pretty close to the bunker. He was one of the best bunker players in golf when younger.

He hit the shot, landed on the green, and saw it roll downhill and stop about a foot below the hole. Smiling, he climbed out of the bunker, looked me in the eye, and in a proud way, speaking with a South African twang, he said to me, "I've still got it, John." I replied, "Yup, you sure do." We both laughed; he sank the putt saving his par.

Later there was a rain delay and automobiles appeared like magic. The players, caddies, and officials sat in the cars and waited out the delay. The car I was in had Calvin and the driver in the front seat, and Gary, Lee, and I were in the backseat. I think we sat for about fifty minutes and an interesting time it was. Yes, at that point, we were on a first name basis. Imagine!

Calvin was silent throughout the wait. Gary's efforts to converse were stymied by Lee's entertaining dominance of the conversation.

If we were there fifty minutes, Lee held the floor for about forty-one or forty-two minutes, and I was treated to an entertaining discourse about golf, the course, the Tour and, to top it off, heard Lee explain, in detail, the differences between one golf ball over another. It was the best explanation on that subject I had ever heard. Lee was well versed on the subject.

After the play resumed, we walked to the next tee, and Lee began to talk to me as we walked. He extolled the virtues of a new driver that Spalding had made specifically for him and how pleased he was with it.

Lee was first to hit off the tee and, using the Spalding driver, flat-out nailed the tee shot down the middle of the fairway. He smiled, approached me, still holding the driver, and said something like, "I told you, John!" Then he asked his caddie for a ball and attempted to hand me the ball and driver, saying, "Here, you hit one. Try the driver and see for yourself."

Of course I couldn't do that. With some difficulty, I was able to quiet him down while Gary hit his tee shot. Unperturbed by Lee's antics, Gary hit a good tee shot himself, though not quite as long as Trevino's.

That was a good day for me. I had heard about how straight Peete hit his shots, but now I saw firsthand just how straight Calvin hit the golf ball each time. All day long, he was like a machine with tee shots that found the fairway and long irons that found the green. I was thoroughly impressed and could see why for a couple of years he was the best player on the PGA Tour. He did not have the length the others had, but he sure did hit it straight.

Gary Player was the consummate gentleman throughout the round and, though older now, could still play well. I've always admired Gary for many reasons, but he made himself special to me that day.

Lee lived up to his reputation as a very personable and enormously entertaining personality. He talked to spectators from time to time during the round, and you could tell he was really enjoying himself and the round of golf. He is a real credit to "The Game"; unforgettable as well.

Miscellaneous Memories

So many of them, including:

Talking with Jack Nicklaus on the first tee at Pinehurst while Gary Player practiced chipping the ball into the hole.

Meeting Lee Elder at the door of the pro shop at Augusta, he had been invited to Augusta as a person, the first black ever to qualify to play in the Masters, but he was not a player the year I met him. He was a bit standoffish as I approached to introduce myself and offered to shake hands. At first, I thought he would refuse to shake hands as he looked past me and up at the sky, etc. Finally, he gave me a limp shake and walked away. I was surprised! His personality, if he has one, was not visible to me.

Receiving a letter of thanks from Jim Colbert for being an official during his round at a Senior Open, we had enjoyed chatting a bit during his round. A nice guy—polite, friendly, and a good, though not great, player.

Being thoroughly impressed with how precise and organized things were at the Masters. The 7:30 a.m. morning meetings for officials preceding the day's round saw everyone arriving at least five minutes early. No one was ever late. Business was conducted in workmanlike fashion ending at or before 8:00 a.m., then all left to carry out their individual assignments for the day. Of course, if you were assigned to a hole on the back nine, you could relax for a couple of hours while waiting for the players to finish the front nine.

Meeting Tom Weiskopf at the 17th green/18th tee area, where he was working the TV booth as a commentator, I introduced myself and followed him as he walked around the 17th green and the bunker fronting the green. He then commented on the difficulty facing the player hitting his second shot into a narrow part of the right side of the green and just over the bunker.

He explained that if one's second shot to the green wound up short in front of the green, the player had a chance to get it up and down and save par. If, however, the second shot was long and somewhat over the green, no one would get it up and down. I watched all day there, and he was absolutely correct. I thought, *Damn, my goal would be to just be on the green ten to thirty feet away, and here he was talking a level of precision with which my game was not familiar.*

Actually, Augusta's greens invite three putts consistently if you are not well positioned on it. It's like putting on glass—downhill!

My sixteen rounds as an official found me assigned to eleven different holes, including 1, 2, 3, 9, 10, 11, 12, 14, 15, 16, and 17. I was at number 9 green often enough to make friends with a couple from Georgia, who arrived at the course in the early morning and set up seats just behind the green where they could watch players hit their second shots into the par four hole. Then they could enjoy watching players struggle to avoid three putting the severely sloped piece of glass called a green. We wound up exchanging Christmas cards and looking forward to saying hello the following year. He was in the lumber business in Georgia, and he and his wife had been spectators at the Masters for many years.

Being totally ignored and avoided by Augusta National's first black member was interesting. He consistently avoided getting close enough to me to say hello and shake hands. He changed direction and walked away from me eight times that I counted. I gave up after that. No, I never actually met him and don't remember his name.

Running into Bill Dickey in 1996, he was there as a spectator with a ticket. I was there, with a ticket, for a meeting regarding Tiger's deal with IMG. My meeting was on Wednesday, and I really did not want to stay and watch the tournament and told that to Bill. He was staying with a friend who was born and raised in Augusta, Georgia, but had never attended the Masters. I gave my four-day ticket to Bill and suggested he give it to his friend. Done. I caught a plane home and watched on TV over the weekend.

Attempting to qualify to play in the USGA Senior Amateur, I chose to try at the Country Club of Virginia, where close to forty players would compete for two spots. I went to Richmond a few days early and worked on my game with help from Steve Isaacs. I had spent the previous couple of weeks on the practice tee at my home club, working on my game with help from the pro. I was swinging well and was pleased with my game.

After fourteen holes at the qualifier, I was even par. Then I bogeyed number 15, double bogeyed number 16, birdied number 17, and made par on number 18. I finished the round at two over par and missed qualifying by two strokes. I was very disappointed because I had worked hard on my game to prepare. Also, while with the Executive

JOHN F. MERCHANT

Committee, I had chaired the Senior Amateur when it was played at Prairie Dunes in Kansas, so it would have been nice to be a player in the tournament. Not to be.

There are many more memories, but I'll stop with these.

The Symposiums and Diversity in "The Game"

What specifically did Steve and I achieve besides a lasting friendship? The answer is that we collaborated with others in developing a sound foundation for achieving greater diversity in the game of golf the likes of which has not been seen before or since. Regretfully, the effort ceased later, although the networking achieved retains some minimal, unused, value.

Yes, our effort has been significantly eroded over the years, despite resulting in the creation of an independent 501(c)(3) Foundation in 1996, The National Minority Golf Foundation (NMGF), with a commitment from the USGA to provide funding for at least three years of operations. After that, it had to raise its own operational costs, and it could have and should have; it failed, miserably. It saddens me to even think about its demise.

The NMGF provided an opportunity to establish a voice for diversity that was independent and could grow into an asset for achieving diversity as it blossomed as an independent entity respected by the industry.

It had the benefit of the positive networking achieved at the symposiums. A benefit that should have been nurtured and exposed to growth but wasn't. Leadership simply failed to capitalize on this beginning.

Clearly it offered a real opportunity to interface with the industry as a partner, rather than as an annoyance to be tolerated, or an afterthought that might be politically correct but insincere.

Regrettably, NMGF's leadership and Board blew it and, in my opinion, set back the cause of diversity and meaningful progress for at least a generation. Its demise is now more than fifteen years old.

The NMGF still exists as a legal entity. However, it now lies in the archives of the World Golf Village gathering dust with no purpose and little chance to do more than choke to death on the dust. I consider NMGFs quiet disappearance into nowhere a tragic missed opportunity.

For me, NMGF's creation, and the promise of funding for three years, signaled the beginning of a new era supported by a leader in "The Game." Its birth, with that critical support from the USGA, evidenced a potential partnership, where the possibility to achieve a power to influence efforts to achieve diversity was heightened. Its demise meant that momentum was lost at a critical time, thereby mandating a need to start all over again from scratch.

I view it as a failure of its black leadership, which, among other things, lacked vision, patience, and a plan. That naïveté is what spurred a black rebellion at the symposiums that I may address later. They opted for a nickel when the opportunity to get a fifty-dollar bill awaited them and should be ashamed of themselves.

Now the process must find a way to begin again and what are the odds against that happening? Enormously against, no doubt.

JOHN F. MERCHANT

Why do we always seem to need a new wheel? Is it because black leadership has limited vision, or no vision at all, and no plan? Do we grow comfortable with simple ego satisfactions and the jobs and salaries bestowed upon a few?

Do we lack the patience needed to create and work through a plan, or the skills required to effectively implement a plan?

Does immediate gratification for a few take precedence over developing a plan and using, or acquiring, the skills needed to work it successfully? Was NMGF afraid to lead or just shortsighted? Who knows?

Today, as 2010 comes to a close, one is hard-pressed to find serious progress toward diversity in golf, though there is some. But who will lead the effort or provide hope to the equation? Are there any real leaders? I don't see them, do you? Is there a plan?

Do the self-styled leaders communicate with each other at all? I don't see or hear about it, do you? Or do we expect the majority community to do the heavy lifting for us? That's not going to happen. Self-help is expected, and we are not providing it.

I was hired as the foundation's first executive director but was terminated, abruptly, a few months later in a manner that was both insulting and inexcusable. No one has ever explained to me the reason for the termination, nor was I provided an opportunity to address the board prior to being terminated. I was summarily dismissed via a long-distance phone call on New Year's Day. Happy New Year diversity!

Of course, I was replaced, but the replacements were, to be kind, ineffective. Lew Horne out of Georgia, the second replacement, was actually an excellent choice but, for reasons unknown to me, became disenchanted with the effort and went back to Georgia and his law practice. NMGF's funeral followed his exit, though, as stated, its body still lies in state in Florida collecting dust and of interest to hardly anyone.

The effort that eventually led to NMGF's creation was actually born in the offices of *Golf Digest* at a meeting between me and Jerry Tarde, then editor of *Golf Digest*, probably the major golf publication of our times. We agreed that there was value in encouraging people to meet and talk as a significant way to begin to seriously address the issue of diversity and build the bridges needed to span the gaps that existed, gaps fueled by misunderstanding, an embarrassing history, and an addiction to stereotypes.

More importantly, we understood that achieving admirable diversity in "The Game" was a huge challenge and would only happen over an extended period of time. No quick fix or "immediate gratification" should be expected because neither was even remotely available. We rolled up our sleeves and started with the outlines of a plan.

The effort needed a plan and a commitment to the plan and any sensible modifications made over time. Those getting involved must bring patience with them, since change would require extensive bridge-building and hard work on the part of many over several years. But we believed it was both doable and needed.

We were well aware of the obstacles we faced. We agreed that a good start would be to figure out a way to get people to sit down and talk with each other in a setting where all were equal and focused on problem solving.

Find a way to bring leaders in the golf industry to the table to talk with blacks involved in the game. These talks should involve an identification of issues and meaningful discussion of them. Hopefully, the beginning of long-term networking that, over time, would produce results we could all be proud of.

One has to meet the woman who will become their wife or stay single. She must be wooed, and they must find more than one reason to plan a life together if a marriage is to occur and last.

Participants were asked to join and participate in one discussion group from four that were presented, namely, junior golf, caddie programs, black college golf, and business and employment opportunities in the industry.

My status as a member of the USGA Executive Committee helped immensely in contacting folks in the industry. I made cold calls directly to the top, calling CEOs who spoke with me. I explained what we were trying to do and invited them to come and be a part of the effort in its infancy.

Jerry also lobbied for participation from the majority community. He assigned a woman from his staff to handle the grunt work and details. The Symposiums would not have happened without her.

I refer to Lisa Furlong, a *Golf Digest* employee, who was assigned to work to make the Symposiums happen at all and to help it produce something of value. She was enormously committed and efficient.

The industry response was overwhelmingly positive. It was as if they had been waiting for someone to address the issue of diversity in ways that offered a real potential for progress. No one turned me down.

In a sense, I was not surprised by the industry response. I was motivated by the belief that most white people in America have never met, or had a meaningful conversation with, a black person, and vice versa. Jerry and I hoped to change that.

Tired of being accused of being racist and bigoted, they welcomed an opportunity to meet and discuss issues openly and honestly in a setting that lacked a confrontational atmosphere. They sought solutions that did not threaten the viability of their companies but did permit them to deal positively with the issues of diversity and, ideally, find solid directions and solutions.

I then turned to Bill Dickey, who provided me with the names of blacks around the country who should be invited. I contacted each of them and explained what we were planning to do. Blacks from seventeen states accepted the invitation and participated in the first of four Symposiums held at Callaway Gardens in Georgia.

I spent 274 hours planning the Symposium. That included speaking personally and at length with each invitee in an effort to be clear about my intentions. It was also done in an effort to avoid speechmaking on the issue of three hundred plus years of slavery that could waste valuable time available to seek solutions and/or firm up networking possibilities.

JOHN F. MERCHANT

On that point, each black invitee was told that everyone in attendance was a personal guest of mine and was not to be made to feel uncomfortable or embarrassed in any way. Failure to subscribe to this warning would mean that I would advise you that never again would you be invited to such an event, and you are free to leave at any time, including immediately.

My opening remarks reiterated this stance. All were told that I had spoken to each one of you inviting you here. I knew, as a matter of fact, that no past or present slave owners, or slaves, were either invited or attending.

Given those facts, no need existed to discuss, or even mention, slavery. Rather, discussion should be centered on the issue of improving diversity as in: where are we regarding it right now; where should we be; where would we like to be, and how can we get there working together?

Four specific subjects, as stated, were established as a focus for discussion: junior golf; business and employment opportunities in the industry; investment opportunities that exist, including the purchase and management of golf courses; and black college golf involvement. Attendees could choose the area they preferred to be involved in, then attend and be open, honest, and creative in exploring solutions. Friday and Saturday mornings were set aside for these discussions. Golf consumed the afternoons.

In truth, the underlying agenda was simply to bring people together, get them to talk with each other, and create relationships from the exposure. It worked.

I set up foursomes for golf at the Symposiums, hoping to let golf bring people together as it often does. When one is concerned with the need for his partner to sink the seven-foot putt to win the Nassau, he has no time to concern himself with the color of his partner's skin or his racial background. Just sink the damn putt, please. When, or if, done, respect has a chance to flourish.

My foursome contained two other blacks and Ed Abrain, then headman at Wilson Golf. On around the 12th hole, Ed said to me, "This is the first time in my life that I have played golf with three black men, and I am having as much fun as I have ever had." Then he said words to the effect that he is not returning next year without having done something tangible to further the cause.

I looked at him and with a straight face said, "What makes you think you will be invited back next year?" He looked at me, saw that I was laughing, and so he laughed. Next year, he returned and advised that his company had hired two or three blacks to help market Wilson's equipment.

Golf is like that!

Three black men violated my warning during the first two symposiums. I privately spoke with each and asked each to leave. I advised each of them that no further invitation to participate would ever be offered.

Our reaching out attracted serious involvement by the United States Golf Association (USGA), The PGA Tour, The PGA of America, and the LPGA, along with key people from Titleist, Wilson Golf, and other manufacturers of golf equipment, clothing, etc. in the golf industry. Almost all invited attended or sent a representative. The participation level was high and real.

Added strength came from individuals like Mike Smith, Bill Dickey, Joe James, Sandy Tatum, Giles Payne, Steve Isaacs, Wally Uiehlein, David Fay, Joe Steranka, and a host of others.

Early in the planning, I spoke with Arthur Ashe about the idea and invited him to attend. This conversation took place during and after a round of golf. His comments were on point; his insights were welcomed and accepted. Unfortunately, he was unable to attend.

Of critical importance was *Golf Digest's* agreement to underwrite most of the cost of the effort to the tune of $35,000. Without this agreement and support, the Symposiums were not possible. It covered the cost of room, board, and golf for all who arrived at Callaway Gardens. This contribution reached $60,000 in the third or fourth year.

The *Golf Digest* commitment to the effort was further confirmed, when at a meeting in New York City, its top guy poked his head in and told those present that the symposium effort was serious and had the firm backing of management at all levels. They were committed.

Industry and association folks had expense accounts; black participants from across the country did not have that luxury. They would have to take time from their employment and spend vacation time and money to attend. The underwriting from *Golf Digest* eased the rest of the cost burden.

In speaking with each black invitee, I advised them that the cost of transportation to and from Callaway Gardens was a cost they had to absorb personally. Room, board, and daily golf were covered once they arrived, but since freedom isn't free, transportation costs were their responsibility. They agreed. To me, that agreement represented, at the very least, their personal commitment to the goals outlined by me to them in our lengthy conversations.

At the next meeting of the USGA Executive Committee, I informed the Committee of the effort. I made it clear that I was not asking their permission to do this, nor was I asking for any money to support the effort. I explained that if the effort failed, and/or embarrassed the USGA, I would accept responsibility and resign immediately. On the other hand, if the effort bore fruit, the USGA could properly, and deservedly, take credit for it.

Their response was immediate. They offered a contribution of $5,000 and pledged support in all respects. David Fay, the USGA executive director, agreed to attend and to serve as a panelist. Sandy Tatum agreed to be the speaker at one of the Saturday night dinners. I was truly pleased, impressed, and somewhat overwhelmed by the immediacy of their positive response.

Steve Isaacs was involved in every step of the planning. It was Steve who suggested inviting Mike Smith to emcee the event as needed. I had never met or heard of Mike until then. Steve arranged a golf match to introduce us and talk about the Plan.

To say that I was enormously impressed by this native South Carolinian, his background, and commitment to the goals of the symposium, is to understate it. His involvement added a level of value to the effort. He was exactly the right person at the right time for that assignment. Today, eighteen years later, I still consider him a real friend, and he is.

Over time, some have asked why I didn't select a black to emcee the important event. My response was that no need to do that existed. In my mind, Mike was perfect, and his performance validated my belief.

Prior to performing his emcee duties, Mike retired to his room and changed clothes, appearing before the group in a jacket and tie. Once he began, it was clear that his clothing would not be a deterrent to an Oscar-like performance. In fact, it gave a level of seriousness and commitment to what we were all gathered to do.

One mistake was made by Mike but not noticed by everyone. During his introduction of the panel, Mike introduced David Fay as David Fry. Years later, the two ran into each other, in Scotland I'm told, and David reminded Mike of the error.

Incidentally, David Fay is one of the really good people that I've run into. He had done an outstanding job as chief executive of the USGA. His tenure has seen the enormous growth of "The Game" in America and the world. Sadly, he resigned his position recently in December 2010, without explanation. Golf has lost a good and effective friend, so have I.

The panel participants included a mix of folks selected to bring comments from a variety of areas, including, inter alia: The USGA; a long-time country club member; a college golf coach; the golf industry; a white amateur golfer from Virginia who has been very active and successful over the years in Virginia tournaments, namely, Steve Isaacs, my friend without whom I doubt that the Symposiums could have been planned and run as effectively as they were.

Each panelist spoke for 2-5 minutes, then took questions from the attendees. The mix was designed to elicit comments and questions relevant to symposium purposes and worked under Mike's direction.

The same format was employed at each of four Symposiums during which networking potential thrived in a way that allows it to exist more than fifteen years later. Interest in participating grew among both the black population and the industry to the point where attendance at the fourth Symposium reached ninety plus persons and included increased participation from an increasing variety of parts of the golf industry, not just those concerned with playing in tournaments for money or prestige.

Regrettably, no Symposiums were ever again held after my termination. I deem that shortsighted, even tragic, as concerns the cause of diversity. I honestly believe that the industry would have welcomed a long-term continuation of the opportunity to sit and meaningfully discuss issues and the growth of diversity in "The Game."

I believe they still would welcome a chance to relate and discuss the issue. Can that be arranged? By who?

Continuing the Symposiums, or somehow finding a way to relate positively to the industry on the issue of diversifying "The Game", would have meant, and mean, continuing progress. Instead, fifteen years have gone by with nothing of serious significance to show during those years.

Where was the leadership needed? Certainly not on NMGF's board.

They "Passed the torch . . ." to themselves when they terminated me, and the result was disastrous to the cause of diversity.

To repeat myself (again you say), I still believe that many movers and shakers in the golf industry, not all by any means, would today welcome the kind of opportunity that the Symposiums heralded and made real. Something is needed, but can it be found? If so, by whom?

NMGF's board made little or no effort to continue the Symposiums after they terminated me. In fact, some members of the board had been actively involved in a rebellion by blacks at the last, or next to last Symposium. I finally confronted the group at one of their meetings and advised them that if they were opposed to what we were doing, they were free to put their own effort together and stop attending this one.

Their stated complaints related to a lack of visible results prevented by a lot of talk that produced little or nothing. My view was that it takes time to meet folks and even longer to become friends, trusted and committed to a cause. Impatience can be, and was, an enemy to be avoided.

If those who rebelled had a different agenda or plan, it wasn't shared with me. If the NMGF had a plan, it was not shared either. If they had a plan, what was it? It didn't work, if it existed.

Today, in the year 2011, very few folks now know or care who sat on that board; I don't. Fewer still can recall NMGF at all or remember it as something of value with impressive potential.

The ball was fumbled, then lost. The momentum that had arisen when people started talking with each other at the Symposiums was lost. Folks simply stopped talking, and that is usually fatal.

The board's failure, unwillingness, or inability to create and develop a workable plan, then implement it, is inexcusable in my eyes. Diversity suffered a serious setback because of their ineptness and failure to lead.

Shame on them.

The Tiger Woods Experience

One of the first committee assignments I was given by the USGA was on its Junior Golf Committee. In that capacity, I traveled West to attend the championship event. It was won by Tiger. There, I met Earl Woods for the first time.

I was pleasantly surprised to see a black man sitting alone on the patio, so I approached him and introduced myself. That was the beginning of a fascinating experience that ended in 1996 when that black man, Earl, fired me.

Over time, I came to know Earl, his wife, and Tiger very well. We became friends. I spent time at their home in Cypress, California, even sleeping in Tiger's bed when he was away at Stanford. I played several rounds of golf with both Earl and Tiger in California, Rhode Island, Connecticut,

JOHN F. MERCHANT

and elsewhere. I was there when Tiger won all three of his USGA Amateur titles. I saw him play in his first Masters and a couple of US Opens.

After Tiger played in the US Open at Shinnecock, I asked him to come to Connecticut while en route to the Northeast Amateur and do a clinic for Bridgeport Area kids, then play a round of golf with me and others at The Country Club of Fairfield (CCF), where I was a member. He agreed and did. In fact, he returned the following year. Arrangements were made with the school system in Bridgeport to allow kids to attend the clinic.

His visits were made possible by funding received, both years, from The General Electric Foundation, covering costs of the effort only. No money was ever provided to Tiger or his father, directly or indirectly.

Jack Welch, GE's CEO, belonged to CCF, and we were acquainted. I wrote to him, advised him of Tiger's plan to attend, offered him an opportunity to play a round with Tiger, and asked for financial support, if possible.

In a very few days after sending my letter, I received a phone call from the executive of the GE Foundation. He said that Mr. Welch had told him to call, find out the details, and help if he could. I explained what was being planned. He liked the idea and asked about the budget I had in mind.

I had not yet prepared a budget and told him so. Actually, I had thought about asking for something in the area of $2,500.

He asked me to contact him when I had a budget and cautioned that it should not exceed $10,000. "No problem,"

I said to myself. Calmly, despite my excitement, I promised to work out a budget and get back to him shortly.

Now that I had a guideline, my thinking was expanded and became focused and serious. Smilingly, with thanks to Jack Welch, I went to work.

CCF is a very exclusive club. I was its first black member ever. The rule there about outings was that they had to be requested, approved, and scheduled a year or more in advance. However, I learned that it was not considered an outing if a member was playing in each foursome. I easily found fourteen members, each of whom would play with three of my guests.

Thanks to GE, lunch would be provided. Then, after golf, all would gather on the veranda, which overlooked the golf course and Long Island Sound for cocktails, heavy hors d' oeuvres, and to chat with Earl and Tiger.

Initially, CCF was reluctant to allow my "non" outing because they didn't want to have crowds of people coming to watch Tiger. It was not to become an event open to the public. No publicity was allowed. I readily accepted their conditions and complied fully with them. They gave me permission.

Members of the club were told that if they wished to attend, they must get a ticket to gain entrance that day. That was done. Members were also told that a ticket allowed *only that member* to attend, no exceptions. No house guests, friends, or others would be allowed. A policeman was stationed at the club's entrance to ensure compliance.

Golf Digest was allowed to send a cameraman to the event. He took a load of photos that day. A good number of members took time to come out and watch, more than one hundred as I recall, but who was counting? I didn't.

The forty-two friends invited to play golf that day were a diverse group that included blacks, Catholics, Jews, Italians, Romanians, Hispanics, prosecutors, judges, and you name it. A good time was had by all. Lunch was served followed by golf, food, and conversation as stated.

I set up the fourteen foursomes, inviting the club's pro and the club champion to play with me and Tiger. I also hired two off-duty policemen to serve as bodyguards for Tiger that day. Two good choices were made: one black; the other white. They were tough guys who could be counted on to do the job. I didn't want anything happening to Tiger on my watch, nothing did.

The GE Foundation's grant covered the expenses for all food, greens fees, and any alcohol imbibed. The budget for each year was under $10,000.

Tiger put on quite a clinic watched by about one hundred kids at Brooklawn Country Club. Ralph LoStocco and Joe Clancy, both members at Brooklawn, made arrangements for the clinic to be held there. Brad Worthington was the club pro, and his cooperation enhanced the event considerably. The cooperation of Bridgeport's school system was fully appreciated.

All three men mentioned are friends, avid golfers, and truly fine people.

Everyone, including me, was amazed and thrilled with the shots he hit, including using a three wood that he hit like a sand iron with the same trajectory, distance, and stopping ability, and after pointing at a tree, he chose a mid-iron and promptly struck the tree with his shot. It was something to see.

When Tiger finished the clinic, Earl took over, called over a young man who Earl said had been the most attentive during the clinic, and made him a gift of Tiger's golf bag. He said it was the bag Tiger carried when he won the NCAA title. The kid was grinning from ear to ear as he hugged the bag.

Joe Clancy immediately went up the clubhouse and pro shop and returned with several golf clubs and a credit slip for shoes and balls. He put the clubs in the young man's bag and handed him the credit slips. That's Joe for sure.

The young man was from the inner city in Bridgeport. He caddied at Brooklawn for years under Brad Worthington's tutelage. Using Clancy's largesse along with his caddying experience, he began playing the game. Later, he went to college and graduated from Brown University. He found employment in the computer industry, I think, and is doing very well as we speak.

Golf is like that!

Brad Worthington is a special guy. He has always encouraged the use of caddies, and his success at recruiting caddies from the inner city, and mentoring them, is both unusual and significant. He has been the pro at Brooklawn for the past seventeen years and is a friend of mine and of diversity.

Joe Clancy was the CEO at Bridgeport Machines, a successful company under his leadership. Ralph LoStocco was a key man in the company. Both loved the game of golf.

Ralph could drive it out of sight before technology allowed everyone to hit it far or farther than they once did.

Like many of us, Ralph had a bit of a problem hitting it in the fairway consistently, but doesn't everyone, including Tiger? What else is new?

During the time spent giving clinics and playing CCF, Earl and Tiger were housed as guests at the home of Nick and BJ Goodspeed. Nick was CEO of People's Bank; I served on his Board of Directors. He and BJ were special people and good friends of mine. I mentioned them earlier in Chapter 4.

One negative thing occurred at the Goodspeed's home, though it didn't become an issue. However, it did give me a level of insight into Earl that I had not had before.

One evening, I went by the Goodspeeds to collect Earl and Tiger and go out to dinner. Earl and Nick were seated around the fireplace; Nick in one of two comfortable chairs, and Earl on the sofa that faced the fireplace. Earl had stretched out on the sofa and had his feet up on the sofa *with his shoes on.*

I was appalled and said to myself, "That's rude." So instead of sitting in the other comfortable chair across from Nick, I casually moved Earl's shoes from the sofa and sat in the area the shoes left, then joined the conversation during which, among other things, Nick volunteered to arrange transportation to Rhode Island for Earl and Tiger, rather than have them fly there. Earl accepted.

After their second stay at the Goodspeeds, I suggested to Earl that it would be a nice gesture for him to provide

Nick and BJ with a small thank-you gift that I could deliver, a bottle of McCallan's single malt scotch, Nick's favorite; and why not? Some flowers for BJ? Earl looked at me like I was crazy and refused. Another insight duly noted.

My involvement with Earl and Tiger heightened in February 1996 when, out of the blue, Earl called me and asked if I would help prepare the way if Tiger decided to turn pro that year. He further suggested that I contact Hughes Norton from IMG to discuss representing Tiger. He gave me the telephone number for Hughes. I called him, and we arranged to meet.

Before hanging up with Hughes, I asked him as a matter of curiosity, just what kind of commission IMG took from someone of Tiger's stature and potential. He gave me a figure in excess of 20 percent. I knew nothing about the agent business but instantly rebelled at the figure given.

I said, "Hughes, you don't know me nor do I know you, but I must tell you that the commission figure you stated is totally unacceptable." Further, I told him that Lincoln freed the slaves and that commission makes Tiger out to be somewhere between a well-paid slave and a fool. I told him that, given that amount, no reason to meet existed or exists.

He countered by asking what I had in mind. I threw out a figure of 3-4 percent. He then said that the commission amount was negotiable, and we should still meet. I agreed to meet.

Over the next several months, we met often in different parts of the country, including Cleveland, Ohio; and Augusta, Georgia, among others. I earned a boat load of frequent

JOHN F. MERCHANT

flier miles working out the agreement with Hughes. I also came to like and respect him a lot.

The commission percentage we finally agreed on saved Tiger five million dollars over the five-year term of the management agreement with IMG. That's five million less than IMG would have received using Hughes's original quote. A lot of money, or so I thought.

The quid pro quo was that a ceiling was placed on the lower, agreed upon, commission. I had never been involved with that kind of money and so agreed to a ceiling that I believed to be the right deal for Tiger, but it turned out to be low. I also advised Earl and Tiger to create their own agency by learning how over the initial five years, a route similar to the one Jack Nicklaus took.

That meant, as I explained, refusing any new endorsements during the first five years, thus avoiding an obligation to pay commissions to IMG on renewals they had obtained originally.

My thinking was simple. Each endorsement required spending time taping ads and taking Tiger away from the golf course as he sought to make his mark in golf's history.

Frankly, the first two deals with Nike and Titleist were healthy and ended any financial concerns for Tiger, his present and future families, and any families of his future family's families. It was a lot of money and ranged terribly close to the ceiling I had negotiated with Hughes. Live and learn!

Earl had firmly stated, when I asked, that no decision had yet been made by Tiger. I advised that if I undertook this assignment, I could not ever, at any point, discuss any aspect of my efforts with Tiger. Under the Rules of Golf, if I did talk with Tiger, he would immediately become a professional and lose his amateur status. We agreed that I would discuss my efforts only with Earl.

The first time I discussed the decision to turn pro with Tiger was in August 1996, the night before he teed off at The Greater Milwaukee Open, his first tournament played as a professional.

Tiger had been given an exemption to play Milwaukee and decided to do so as a professional. The announcement had been made, and we were prepared. I had prepared and reviewed the documents regarding representation and initial endorsements for him to sign.

In 1996, Tiger had won his third consecutive U.S. Amateur and his sixth consecutive USGA event, having won the Junior Championship for the three years preceding the U.S. Amateurs, events I also witnessed.

His third amateur win came at the Newport Country Club in Rhode Island. A friend of mine in Rhode Island had arranged for a house for three of us, Tiger, Earl, and me, to stay in during the tournament. The house was located at the Point Judith Golf Course in Narragansett, Rhode Island, just across the bridge from Newport.

It was a large house with much more room than we needed. Tiger had access to a driving range and a putting green where, nightly, we putted for bragging rights. I am pleased to report that Tiger did not always earn the right to brag. Earl was a good putter, and every now and then, I made some putts.

Point Judith Country Club's golf course is a Donald Ross design opened in 1894. It plays to par 71 over its 6,688 yards and is a revered old-timer.

More importantly, this same friend arranged through a friend of his for Tiger to play an extra, unofficial, "practice" round at Newport CC. Any player could do the same if they knew a member of Newport Country Club who would arrange it. The rules did not prohibit this extra round being played prior to the official start of the amateur.

Generally, the U.S. Amateur was played on two courses prior to match play. Each contestant was entitled to one practice round on each course to be performed on the days designated for such. However, prior to the designated days for practice rounds, a contestant could play the courses at the invitation of a member of that club. My friend arranged that for Tiger, and, lo and behold, I was also invited to join that foursome. Tiger was pumped, as usual.

On number 10, a five par as I recall, Tiger showed his magic. He swung too hard at his tee shot trying to hit it far enough to reach the green in two strokes. His ball went out of bounds, a two-stroke penalty.

He teed up again, hitting his third shot to where he wanted the first one to be. Then he knocked his fourth stroke on the green and made the putt for a par. Once again, I was impressed but not surprised.

It's hard to know if an extra practice round is helpful, but I do know that the more familiar you are with a course, the better off you are. So my friend saw to it that Tiger could sleep in a comfortable bed, hang out in a very nice home, use a driving range within walking distance, practice his putting as often as he chose to do so, and familiarize himself with the course at Newport CC.

Certainly, none of what I've just recited hurt. Tiger won the tournament. Prior to the award ceremony, I got in my car and drove home. I felt that the afterglow of this monumental achievement, six USGA titles, in a row, including three Junior Amateurs and three Amateurs, was to be shared solely between father and son. I was not needed for that. I had done my part, though I was never thanked for it by either of them.

Incidentally, as I've said to many people, theirs was the best father-son relationship I have ever personally witnessed. They were friends, seemingly always on the same page and could, again seemingly, read each other's mind creating great harmony between them. It was a treat to be a witness to that.

After Tiger turned pro, more work was needed. This included: recommending lawyers, friends of mine, who still do work for him; arranging to interview nine investment managers and firms to manage Tiger's money; and interviewing all and selecting four, each with a different investment philosophy. I advised Tiger to analyze and review their results after three years and keep the best.

I also suggested employing a CPA to look over IMG's shoulder; arranged for a $25,000 credit card to be delivered to him overnight; talked with him about the need to understand money and the language of investing; gave him reading material and people to help him understand the language used by money managers and their ilk; searched for and found a five-bedroom house he purchased for his mom in Orange County, California; recommended the dollar amount he should pay each parent as an employee; validated IMG's advice to move his residence and domicile from California to Florida; and well, there is more but enough has been listed here to give you the flavor.

Suffice to say that talking with and explaining things to Tiger and his dad was a comprehensive undertaking that I performed well, if I do say so myself.

Of course we were friends and our talks, of necessity, had to be about a host of things to which neither Earl nor Tiger had ever been exposed. My thirty years of experience as a bank director gave me a level of exposure that was very helpful to the discussions, although it didn't qualify me as an expert on anything. But then, despite Earl's pretending that he knew and understood, he was way out of his league on many things, especially understanding money, investments, and related items.

I believe it's still true that everyone I suggested he hire still works for him, except me of course.

The six or seven months I spent, as just described, were done at my expense using vacation time from work to do so. Fees were never discussed until the deal was completed. I was well paid for my time and efforts.

I was abruptly terminated during a break at a morning meeting of "Team Tiger" by Earl. No reason was given, but it was clear that Earl had fired me.

I retrieved my briefcase from the meeting, gathered my belongings from my room, drove to the airport, and caught a flight to White Plains, New York. Then I drove home.

The day before being terminated, I had played golf with Tiger, and the last thing I remember him saying to me was. "I love you, man." I have not spoken to either Earl or Tiger since the day I was terminated.

Attorneys are often terminated, and a client is not obligated to give a reason unless it involves a matter before a court. In that case, an attorney needs the court's permission to withdraw, and the usual reason is that, the attorney-client relationship has broken down and will not, perhaps cannot, be repaired. I know of no breakdown in my case.

As a matter of interest, I can honestly say that I harbor no ill will toward Earl or Tiger—never have, never will. I was well paid for my services and moved on.

I will admit to a high level of both surprise and disappointment, but it has never been something I spend much time thinking about or worrying about. The entire experience is one that I treasure and will always treasure. It was and is special. I only wish that my parents had been alive to share it.

The National Black Golf Hall of Fame

In January 2010, another surprise came my way. A phone call from Michael W. Cooper, PhD, and Director Southeast Regional Affairs for the First Tee Program, informed me that I had been elected to the National Black Golf Hall of Fame (NBGHF). Induction was scheduled for March 27, 2010.

JOHN F. MERCHANT

Mike and I had come to know each other when we talked at length about how to improve diversity in "The Game" over the past several months. He had been given the assignment of exploring ways to do that by Steve Mona, Chairman and CEO of the World Golf Foundation.

Steve is a quietly effective executive who has done an admirable job in his present position. He and I met at one of the Symposiums when he was involved with the Golf Superintendent's Association.

The assignment he gave Mike was important but probably not one that could be successfully completed at this point in time. It was a difficult task, but a way must be found to get it done. Mike's efforts were a step in the right direction, but many more steps were needed over time to achieve closure on the issue of diversity in "The Game."

NBGHF was founded in 1986 by Harold Dunovant to

"recognize and honor the contributions of black golfers for their skills and, to honor persons who have done the most to promote golf in the black communities."

This recognition is needed because golf's recitation of its American history has failed to properly provide it. In fact, black golfers were denied an opportunity to play, and thereby qualify for induction into golf's hall of fame.

Harold Dunovant was the first black person to graduate from the PGA Business School in 1964. He filed for his PGA Class A membership in 1968. It took six years to obtain Class A status because none of the local PGA members, who were all white, would endorse his membership as required.

Unlike its white counterpart, the NBGHF opened its recognition to people *regardless of color*. Its inductees include Arnold Palmer; Wally Uihlein, CEO of Titleist, Inc.; and Judith Bell, a past president of the USGA.

My induction speech challenged the World Golf Hall of Fame to correct its failure to recognize black golfers as an integral, albeit negative, part of its history by doing what baseball did for the Negro League players who were denied an opportunity to play in baseball's major leagues. The opportunity to qualify by playing was denied, and therefore induction into baseball's Hall of Fame could not be earned.

Baseball created a special division in its Hall of Fame for Negro League players; golf should do the same. After all, there is no denying that the opportunity to qualify was denied on racial grounds. That fact is part of golf's history in America, so why not correct it as baseball did?

Failure to do so means, among other things, that "The Game" is not being upfront and honest about its history in America.

There is movement in response to my challenge, and I am pleased.

I have difficulty finding words to express the sense of pride I feel in being honored by induction into the NBGHF. Here am I, a "colored" kid from Chickahominy in Greenwich, Connecticut, with my name listed along with men, such as Bill Spiller, Teddy Rhodes, James Black, Charley Sifford, Bill Wright, Bill Dickey, Jim Thorpe, and a host of others. The others including notable women such as Althea Gibson and Renee Powell, household names in American sports.

JOHN F. MERCHANT

Incidentally, if you don't recognize all of the names mentioned above, *Uneven Lies*,[13] written by Pete McDaniel and published in 2000 by The American Golfer, Inc. will tell you about them, along with the many others who were denied the opportunity to play, earn a living, and, perhaps, qualify for admission to golf's Hall of Fame.

I never sought such an honor and find it difficult to believe that I deserve it. I did not turn it down. Frankly, the experience is a humbling one.

The presentation dinner was conducted in a first-class manner. Jeff Dunovant, Harold's son, who now serves as board chairman and executive director, and his committee are to be commended for the manner in which the event was conducted. Jeff is a PGA Class A golf professional just as was his father.

More than two hundred people attended, including my sister, Barbara Mitchell, one of her daughters Karen, and Karen's husband, Herbert Williams. What a joy to see the pride in their faces and the happiness they experienced by being there when their brother and uncle was recognized in such a manner.

Prior to the event, a friend from Rolling Hills Country Club in Connecticut contacted me. He had somehow learned of the event and wanted to congratulate me. Herman Tarnow and his wife, Barbara, dear friends, who had left Connecticut and moved to Florida, drove up from Naples to Tampa for the sole purpose of being at the induction dinner.

---

[13]   **Uneven Lies by Pete McDaniel, Published by The American Golfer, Inc., Greenwich, Connecticut, 2000.**

I was very pleased by that. They are really good friends. I miss them, and we hadn't seen each other in a few years. It was quite a night for me.

The weekend also included golf tournaments for professionals, senior professionals, and amateurs. The tournament carried a first place prize of $4,000 for professionals and was made possible by the Advocates USA, Inc.[14]

The Advocates USA, a 501(c)(3) non-profit, is a six-year-old organization of African American men from across the United States. They are dedicated to helping improve African American communities. The tournament's title sponsor is Nestle USA, Inc.

In 2010, tournaments were also held in Los Angeles, Denver, and Orlando. I understand that there exists a commitment to conduct such tournaments for the next five years. The professional golfer performing best in all of the tournaments will receive, in addition to prize money won, payment of his entry fee into the PGA Tour School Qualifying events (Q School).

At "Q" School, the top twenty-five men, who survive playing six rounds of golf in six days, earn the right to play on the PGA Tour for one year. Some number, twenty-six to fifty perhaps, earns the right to play the Nationwide Tour where they can earn a living playing golf while honing skills.

The Advocates USA are to be commended for their leadership in this area. It is unusual, significant, and sorely

---

[14] For more information, please Google and view the Advocates USA web site.

needed—clearly a step in the right direction on the journey to increased diversity in "The Game." This effort provides an opportunity for golfers to compete for a financial reward. It provides them with the kind of competition that is critical to improvement.

Hitting it good on the driving range, or in a round with friends and buddies, will never be a substitute for competition and its attendant pressure where every swing, for six days in a row at "Q" School, can be the difference between qualifying or not.

It should also be said that you must pre-qualify for the six-day ordeal. That is done by first playing well in local and regional Q-School qualifiers. It's not something for the faint of heart, for sure, but it's fair. Play well and the doors open for you. Play poorly then, please, no excuses, no shame, and no explanations needed. Those who qualified to play the PGA Tour "played better than me" says it all.

One additional step I'd like to see taken is one that makes it possible for young men and women with promise to obtain the wherewithal to maximize their ability and qualify to play on the PGA and LPGA tours through Q School or otherwise. I have a thought about how that could be done, but, as a practical matter, am not sure that it can, or will, ever happen. It involves creating a pot of money that can be granted to young golfers with real potential in a way that allows them to pay rent, eat, play golf daily, travel to events, and hire expert instructors to fine-tune their skills.

Are there ten to twenty professional athletes or others with comfortable contracts, incomes, and assets who can and would contribute $25,000 a year, tax deductible, for five years to a fund to support promising young people for a maximum two-year period? I don't know. It's a tall order; one that seriously tests the "giving back" concept. How can we find out?

Are there ten young people with promise that can be identified and who would seek grants for this purpose? I think they can be found.

Are these young people willing to make the needed commitment to apply themselves as they should? Perhaps, let's find out.

Given existing tax laws can an entity be created to receive the funds and manage a program that allows the athletes' contributions to be tax deductible and the dollars granted to aspiring professional golfers to be free from IRS complications? I don't know, let's find out.

The NMGF is sitting on a shelf in Florida collecting dust and doing nothing, can it be that entity? Certainly it can receive tax-deductible funds. Does its Charter give it authority to engage in an activity like this? Amend the Charter if it doesn't.

Now, can the potential grant recipients be identified and recruited? Can administration expenses connected to the search for recipients and management be held to reasonable amounts and still have an effective program? I don't know, let's find out.

Alternatively, would Advocates USA be the proper entity?

At what cost, and by whom, can the feasibility of this idea be researched and developed? Is anyone willing? Do they have the time?

Can they be trusted to perform within strict guidelines that invite an audit by the IRS, yet avoid any problems with them?

Do you have a better idea for adding diversity to the PGA and LPGA Tours? Do you have *any* realistic ideas about achieving diversity by helping young blacks qualify to prepare themselves and qualify to play those Tours? Am I dreaming irrationally? Okay, tell me so, and let's move on.

Or, since nothing beats a try but a failure, shouldn't we try this idea.

I'd love to be involved in an effort like this. However, my age and energy level opt against my serious involvement.

I firmly believe that unless young blacks with serious potential can be given the latitude to grow and hone their skills, the Tours will never reach a desirable diversity result. They must also have, or acquire, the mental attitude that allows them to commit to the difficulties inherent in developing an overall game that gives them access to playing on the Tours. It is not an easy thing to do.

Of course, playing on the Tours is not the only area in golf that needs an input of diversity. Employment in the industry and by the industry must be addressed as well. The design and manufacture of equipment and clothing are ongoing economic efforts that, while highly competitive, can be financially rewarding to those employed by the companies involved. Who knows what jobs exist? Who knows what it takes to be qualified to compete for those jobs?

Has anyone made an effort to obtain such information, package it, and distribute it on a widespread basis? Is there a source one can reach out to and get this information? I know of none. The NMGF didn't do it and could have. Is this an area where an effort such as the one that began with the symposiums is needed? Of course, it is. It certainly would not hurt.

Postulate, if you will, what might have been our situation today if NMGF had enabled the networking effort to continue and grow during the last fifteen years. Sadly, it failed to do so, for whatever reasons. Now, if it is to happen, we must start over from scratch. Let's somehow target the next fifteen years as a time to make an investment in this effort. We wasted most of the past fifteen.

JOHN F. MERCHANT

UNITED STATES GOLF ASSOCIATION

FRANK D. (Sandy) TATUM, JR.
Past president, USGA. Chaired Nominating
Committee that selected me in 1992.

USGA EXECUTIVE COMMITTEE
Probably US Open at Pebble Beach

USGA SENIOR OPEN AT PINEHURST, NC
Officiating for groups that included: Trevino,
Player, Nicklaus and Calvin Peete. Memorable

Presenting BOB JONES award to esteemed
Golf writer, HERBERT WARREN WIND.
I Chaired Bob Jones Committee that year.

J. F. Merchant Remarks to USGA Executive Committee at W. Palm Beach, Florida, 1/30/92:

Four score and sixteen years ago, *your* forefathers brought forth upon this Continent a new association, conceived from golf and dedicated to the proposition that "The Game" and its true spirit and values should be promoted. Annually it meets to review "The Game's" status, assess recent efforts, and identify what might be improved. Tonight, you elected your first black American to fully participate in that review and help plan actions that are deemed prudent for continued growth.

We are met in one of the great golfing states of this nation. The agenda is broad and includes recognizing, applauding, and honoring those whose achievements have served "The Game" and give it permanent institutional status. It is altogether fitting and proper to do this.

But, in a larger sense, "The Game" must not get lost in its history. It is for us, the USGA Executive Committee, to here dedicate ourselves to the unfinished tasks remaining before us. Our resolve must be to make "The Game" equally available throughout our country in a manner consistent with the Rules of Golf and the Statement of Purpose contained in the USGA Certificate of Incorporation.

A hundredth anniversary lies just ahead. Its arrival must be heralded by our efforts to insure that all who care about golf can compete, play for pleasure, and pursue business or social opportunities in settings free from artificial impediments of any kind.

To the extent that I am representative, my commitment to this goal, combined with yours, should enhance "The Game"; further its values, teachings, and traditions; and, importantly, make that hundredth anniversary ours, not just yours.

I pledge to work toward that end: because "The Game" has given me more than I can repay and you honor me with this nomination and election; because I have learned in a short time that you are a good group of people who care; because golfers and others look to this Committee and organization for leadership in more than just golf; because there is more to "The Game" than just teeing it up and trying to make birdies; and because it's true.

If we can't complete the task by our hundredth, we can certainly push hard in the right direction. Your forefathers would approve, at least by majority vote, and mine would also. Thank you for the privilege of sharing in this effort.

NATIONAL BLACK GOLF HALL OF FAME
Inducted - March 27, 2010

Jeffrey Dunavant, PGA Professional and Executive Director of the NBGHOF with Marie Jackson, Treasurer NBGHOF. Jeff's father, Harold Donavant founded NBGHOF in 1986.

The Advocates USA

A group of Black males from across the country who, along with Nestle's, Inc., sponsor a golf tournament at the NBGHOF for professionals with a purse in excess of $15,000.

Hmm! Did he really say that about me? I don't recognize the guy he's talking about. Reckon I'll hire him to do my PR.

Karen Williams (niece), Barbara Mitchell (sister)
On occasion of my induction into the
National Black Golf Hall of Fame
March 27, 2010

HERMAN and BARBARA TARNOW
Came from Naples for the event.
Good friends; special people.

Melodie & Mike Cooper
Is Mike the guy who pushed to get me
into the HOF? I think so; he denies it.
He is Southeast Regional Director for the
First Tee Program. Good guy; good family.

Hall of Fame (cont'd)

<u>SOME FRIENDS WERE THERE</u> (including)
James Black -U.S. Open qualifier, 1964
Adrian Stills -Qualified for PGA Tour, 1976
Tom Woodard - played PGA Tour 6 years (1981-93)
Jim Thorpe - played on PGA Tour and plays Champions Tour
Craig Bowen - played college golf at Southern University
Adam Schupak - Golf writer, author, and friend

James Black, legendary Black golfer, born before his time, and Herman Tarnow share a laugh.

TOM WOODARD, HIS WIFE, ADRIAN STILLS, INDUCTEE AND "SPOTLIGHT" TARNOW.
Both Tom and Adrian, pioneers, played briefly on the PGA Tour but never really had a chance.

JIM THORPE and TOM WOODARD

Adrian Stills, Adam Schupak, Craig Bowen
A legend, a writer and a good friend.

SYMPOSIUM - 1994
The Homestead, Hot Springs, VA.

WILLIAM H. MILLSAPS, Jr.
Dinner Speaker. Retired after
11+ years as Executive Editor
Richmond-Times-Dispatch.

JFM opens Symposium, greets attendees
and introduces Facilitator.

MICHAEL SMITH, Esq.
Facilitator, par excellence

JERRY TARDE and SAM SNEAD
Jerry Tarde, Golf Digest, and USGA
made Symposiums happen.

JOE LOUIS BARROW
Chief Executive
FIRST TEE PROGRAM, Inc.

Chapter 10

The Walter N. Ridley Fund

A STATED, MY life has been full of surprises, mostly pleasant, although there have been difficulties and hardships that I have endured and survived, but that's true for many people. The key for me is that neither the pleasant nor the unpleasant were planned, and many led to very positive results that could have long-lasting value for others. It's been a good life overall.

Incidentally, the civil rights movement commenced long before my birth. Thus, it has always been a part of my life and did not begin in the 1960s as many seem to think or believe.

I also realize that few of the positives that mark my journey could have happened without help. In that regard, I know that I've been very fortunate to have met and related to a multitude of exceptional people from all walks of life, including professionals in many fields; street guys and gals who cared and helped when they could; and people of all races, creeds, and colors. I've mentioned many of them in earlier chapters but feel compelled now to highlight some others who, to this day, provide me with an incentive to keep my hands and mind busy pursuing ideas whose "time has come," at least in my view.

One idea to which I refer is the relatively short-lived concept of "giving back," self-help if you will, which many blacks heralded and preached in the 1960s and 1970s but had difficulty retaining as a fundamental. The concept is being reborn; I support the rebirth.

Actually, the concept never truly died, though it did lose its appeal as a rallying cry for a time, with limited commitment. Do you remember "Each one, teach one" and similar slogans? I do.

Education, or a focus on it, also lost steam. Ironically, in that respect, a focus on education, or the value of it, has been transferred from the vast majority of the minority community to a smaller group that is helping to build new and different black communities by doing so. Is that good? Who knows?

Arguably, especially since the apparent demise of affirmative action, education regains priority because America's colleges and universities are on board with promoting it and making it possible. It is now called diversity.

Life's journey is often a creature of being in the right place at the right time. But it means that one must recognize the opportunity inherent in the surprise, then have the foresight to be prepared and the courage to seek and find the resources needed to maximize the opportunities presented.

Maximization requires one to be as concerned about others as they are about self. Ego satisfactions, alone, or as a primary, are not enough. I was taught that early; I believe it still defines me.

Life starts for most of us with little or no indication of where it will lead. Sure we develop interests and dreams,

JOHN F. MERCHANT

but do we ever really know what fate awaits us? Most don't; I didn't. Do we care or just accept? I cared; still do.

As a college graduate, I had no clue as to what would or could happen to me in the future. I am a child of a world that required of me a focus on the negatives of racial discrimination and man's inhumanity to man. I learned that these are issues that could not and would not be resolved in my lifetime, but that did not dampen my enthusiasm for seeking and pursuing solutions to the extent of my ability to do so.

Ultimately, my path was shaped by an exposure to the continuing efforts of many, black and white, to address those issues and commit to seeking solutions. This commitment from people in the minority and majority communities is ongoing but hampered now by overwhelming issues affecting Americans related to the economy, jobs, medical care, and such.

My background, education, and training provided me with numerous unplanned opportunities to become involved in that effort. Yes, the real opportunities to help arose because circumstances, not personal planning, combined to put me in places and situations where I could contribute.

Looking back, I am pleased and proud of my reactions to opportunity.

After *Brown v. Board of Education* was decided by the Supreme Court, the trend among Blacks seemed to be toward a focus on education and self-help as the building blocks of a foundation that would lead to a better life for self and family.

In my view, education is a proper focus, and this trend was, and is, the right one.

Dr. King preached a gospel that, on its face, sought a level of assimilation beginning in kindergarten. There was more to his message than that, of course, but education was an unwavering part of his message. Alas, the desegregation and integration efforts in public school systems produced mixed results and precipitated conflict and racial unrest, which continue into the twenty-first century. It seems destined to continue that way for many more years.

The issues of busing, integration, and education at the elementary and high school levels remain unresolved in many places, fueled by unproductive efforts to upgrade the quality of the education available in our cities that have large black populations. It also abides because too many blacks have, seemingly, turned their backs on education being a key to a better life in America. Is that because it takes too long, or are there other reasons?

Inner city schools have gone downhill while constantly fighting budget issues and an apparent lack of interest in learning exhibited by too many students and their parents. This downhill slide exists despite the expenditure of billions of dollars on the local, state, and federal levels.

Recently, in Bridgeport, Connecticut, a person in attendance told a meeting of the Board of Education that a cure for budget shortfalls could be had by first firing all the consultants. I would have added that cutting back the number of well-paid "administrators" that exist, especially the ones whose careers are highlighted by the number of consultants they hire and rely on, would also help.

Think about that, I mean really think about it. Was he right? Is he?

My impression, right or wrong, is that consultants abound at every level and are well paid to advise equally well-paid administrators about how to do the jobs the administrators were hired to do and, on its face, qualified to do.

I hear that teaching in the classroom has become difficult to impossible in many inner-city classrooms. Seemingly, that difficulty has resulted in a flight by many educators from the classroom to administrative positions, fueled by obtaining advanced degrees that *qualify* one for advancement. Who teaches those who "qualify" thusly?

Once job status is achieved, dollars are spent on attending conferences and hiring consultants to do their jobs. Yet evidence of improvement is hard to find and scattered at best.

Ironically, the consultants and conference hosts too often are folks who themselves fled the classroom. Meanwhile, their advice over the years has failed to achieve anything close to a desirable result, and the problems grow and worsen on a daily basis, bringing more consultants into the mix.

Am I wrong, misguided, or too harsh in my thoughts as stated? Could be, I guess.

Also, my sense is that a black focus on education that once signaled a clear movement toward a needed level of assimilation that portended well for our future has diminished considerably in our neighborhoods. Regrettably, there also exists, simultaneously, an apparent rejection of the concept of assimilation, a rejection aided and abetted by too many in both the majority and minority communities.

Ironically, but happily, the nation's colleges and universities have taken up the banner under the heading of diversity and are achieving noteworthy results. Some may believe, as a downside to these efforts, that they are also moving blacks toward divisions in their own communities that signal enormous, albeit inevitable, change over the next several generations. Some of these changes are discussed in Chapter 11.

The search for diversity in college campuses is applauded by me. It made possible one of the most pleasant surprises of my life, allowing me to help resurrect, and become part of, the *giving back* credo of the 1960s and 1970s.

I am enormously proud of my involvement in a major effort at doing just that, ably assisted by an ever-growing cadre of black alumni from a major southern university whose administration cared and cares. It happened like this.

In late 1986, or early 1987, I received a telephone call from a stranger, Michael Mallory, a University of Virginia graduate (Col '80, MA '86) who worked in the Admissions Office at UVA. Mike is a very impressive and talented young black male. His quiet demeanor and firm, unyielding commitment to the educational development and overall growth of young black people establish who he is. His achievements speak volumes and are both significant and noteworthy. I am pleased and proud to have worked with him and to be his friend.

Mike explained that he and a remarkable (my word and belief) woman, Glynn Key (Col '86, Law '89), who now sits on UVA's Board of Visitors, were planning a Black Alumni Reunion at UVA. They had the support they sought from the university, had found the necessary funding, and were excited about the way it was coming together. His call was to invite me to be the keynote speaker at the event. I declined. Yup, I really did.

Frankly, I did not believe that there were enough black alumni for such an event to make sense. I was wrong, very wrong, like people often are when they lack the facts. I had been estranged from UVA for years and unaware.

Soon thereafter, Jim Trice (Eng'r '63) called and convinced me to speak at the event. Jim had agreed to serve as the master of ceremonies at the reunion and firmly believed that a sizeable number of alums would attend. Also, he sensed the long-term value of such an event and supported it fully.

Unknown to me, but according to Trice, there were close to three thousand black alums in existence at the time, a good number of whom had already indicated an interest in attending. The three thousand number was difficult for me to believe, but he was closer to the situation than I, and I trusted his figures.

Personally, my UVA experiences were such that, except for my parents' desire, and right, to attend a graduation, I would have left and had my diploma mailed to me. After graduation, seventeen years passed before I set foot on grounds again in 1975. After that, my next visit was in 1986.

It occurred only because my daughters wanted to look at colleges, and UVA was on their list, along with Georgetown, North Carolina, and Duke. We did a tour of those four.

My friends chuckled when I told them about the event asking how many of the forty-two alums who might attend I knew personally.

Approximately 10 percent of black alums attended. I was impressed. To many, that may not seem to be a large response, unless one realizes that many black alumni, including me, were totally turned off by their experiences at UVA in the 1950s, 1960s, 1970s, and early 1980s. Fond memories of our experiences at UVA were not something that existed in bulk. In fact, while demand for such memories might be high, the supply fell short at that time, far short of what one would like to see.

In preparing my remarks, it occurred to me that, if any alumni attended, we would have at least two things in common, namely, an experience with the difficulties that being a black student at this southern university entailed, and, a keen awareness of the financial issues faced by college students in general and black students specifically. Added together, they posed a serious dilemma. What could I say to this group that was positive and had value that encouraged them to reflect upon their experience and remember it with a sense of pride after leaving the reunion?

I had an idea but was not sure it could fly.

Many ideas had filtered through my mind; one stuck. My inclination to think "outside the box" and then, diplomatically try to sell my thoughts and ideas to those who could accept and act on them would be challenged.

JOHN F. MERCHANT

"Hell," I said to myself, I once convinced a bank CEO to establish a lending program for welfare recipients, thus I just might be able to convince this group to do something that had never happened before at a major, predominately white, college or university. Shouldn't I at least try? Of course, I should, but it won't be easy.

I did wonder what Thomas Jefferson and his devotees would think if he, and they, knew about my idea and it took root and grew!

I thought seriously about some of Jefferson's words that appeared relevant here and decided that he would approve, although I wasn't sure about his devotees.

My wonderment led to a review of an exchange of letters in 1826 between James Heaton, a native of Virginia, and Jefferson. Heaton sought to have Jefferson

> "[F]avor the world, at some period, with a political treatise, having for one object, the abolition of slavery."

Jefferson's response declined the request. However, he did say

> "A good cause is often harmed more by the ill-timed efforts of its friends than the arguments of its enemies . . ."

The timing issue made me think. I thought next about the Chinese proverb regarding long journeys that begin with the first step. Could this be that, or at least a proper continuation of a journey presently ongoing?

Lastly, I thought about Dr. Proctor's words regarding an idea whose time has come. Is my idea one of those?

In addition, like me, many had a laissez faire attitude about UVA and felt little or no allegiance to it. Most were glad to leave and did not cherish the experience, nor did they have plans to return.

To fully understand this, one would be helped immensely by having lived the experience of being black in America and of being a black student at UVA during the latter half of the twentieth century.

After a lot of thought, I decided that at the end of my remarks, I would challenge those in attendance to join me in creating a fund whereby black alumni could contribute to the fund, and the money would be used to provide financial assistance to future black students enrolled at UVA.

A reluctance to include the challenge in my prepared remarks existed since, as stated, I was not sure that attendance at the reunion would be sufficient to produce a meaningful result, or that the idea would be accepted. I guess I feared being on record, in writing, if the idea failed.

However, this fear was countered by a firm belief that, if the idea caught on, and grew, it could be a beacon of light capable of shining brightly in Virginia and many other places.

My interest grew as I thought about the potential of the idea and the positive ramifications if it worked. I thought long and hard about many of them and made copious notes.

My interest wavered as I concluded that it would be a long journey at best and wondered if we had the patience to see it through. In truth, it meant building a positive on the shaky foundation of negative experiences on grounds.

On the other hand, if successful, it would provide a way to "*give back*" and accommodate the gnawing frustration residing in many of us who seek to help change racial conflict into racial harmony.

For years, my sense had been that many black Americans struggle with a felt need to make their lives better by making America better but lack the wherewithal to make a significant difference. I still believe that.

This Fund would not resolve that struggle, but it could help ease that frustration, at least in my mind it could. Doing for another brings a reward, and a level of comfort, that need not, maybe cannot, be adequately explained.

It could also demonstrate to friends in the majority community that we are active and positive participants in making Dr. King's dream come true. When we reached out our hands, it would be to *give* a check, not to *seek or accept* a handout that, at best, had a short life and usually depended on the largesse of a political system to last.

We harbor a need to be legitimately understood and included, thereby relinquishing our status as afterthoughts or meaningless additions.

I believed that America's political system at all levels, and those who voted regularly, was disenchanted. That system was disinclined to continue to provide significant resources for programs designed to help the black population assimilate into the American way of life or to vote for legislators who did.

Along that line, the question arose as to whether, in fact, blacks sought to assimilate and, if so, to what extent?

Politicians, as well as many blacks in general, were disappointed that the War on Poverty had not produced the positive results they had hoped for. Opponents of such efforts grew by leaps and bounds, especially during the period from 1969 when Richard M. Nixon ascended to the presidency and included Reagan's eight years of service that started in 1981. Opponents still existed in 1987, and exist today.

In fact, even friends in Congress had, and have, fundamentally lost faith in the idea that more money over a long period of time would eliminate racial strife. Today, in 2010-2011, money is simply not available from Congress, given the investments being made in trying to right the economy, providing welfare to bail out the biggies, and paying for Social Security and Medicare.

In addition, many in Congress lack a constituency that could, or would, support and counsel them regarding the need to address issues relating to the black population. The move toward the right, and to the far right was, is, strong and flourishing.

On that note, I took a hard look at the Congress, especially the U.S. Senate, with an eye toward what the future might hold if one relied on them for the needed help and sustenance. To me, the outlook was bleak.

Sure, the large cities in America faced a multitude of issues and would bring pressure to bear upon Congress and state legislatures, but, under stress, could they produce either the right programs or the money? I thought not.

My hard look at the U.S. Senate, one hundred men and women, gave me no comfort. Nor did its makeup, given the influence wielded by right wing Republicans elected by fast-growing numbers of conservative voters, offer any solace.

States with minimal electoral votes had and have minimal urban issues related to things like urban decay. There was, and is, a need to invest tax dollars in improving our infrastructures nationwide, and it took precedence over the needs of deteriorating urban areas or racial issues. Those states had low minority populations and for them the issue had no priority. Yet each has two U.S. Senators.

They preached nationalism and patriotism in growing numbers. Yet they failed on critical questions. Their answers to three questions, namely, am I my brother's keeper? Who is my brother? And, is racial strife inevitable in America? Their answers give them failing grades.

For example, take the following sixteen states: Montana, Idaho, Nevada, Arizona, Utah, Wyoming, North and South Dakota, Nebraska, Colorado, Kansas, Oklahoma, Missouri, Arkansas, Alabama, and Mississippi. Together they have eighty-six electoral votes and *thirty-two U.S. Senators*.

California and New York, together, have eighty-six electoral votes but only *four U.S. Senators*.

Those sixteen states have only eight of the fifty largest cities in the United States, according to the 2000 census, with a combined population of 3.3 million. California alone has seven of the fifty largest cities with a combined population in just those seven cities of eight million.

New York City is the country's largest city with a population of eight million.

None of the sixteen states mentioned have what is viewed as a "large" city and none have minority populations of significance.

The total black population in the sixteen states, according to the *Time Almanac* 2005, is 631,317. California's black population from the same source is 770,224 and that source says that New York City has a black population of 2,900,386.

These numbers are an accurate reflection of the situation in 1987. Although the numbers have changed in the twenty-first century, they have not improved, just changed.

What did I conclude from this data? Simple, we are a long way from having, or acquiring, enough political power to influence Congress to listen to us over the long haul. In fact, a large percentage of our population neither registers to vote nor votes if they are registered.

For me, a new strategy seemed called for a strategy that lessened the search for governmental help but did not abandon it.

Rather, incorporate it into a new strategy that, high among its features, had noticeable self-help as a fundamental. A strategy that clearly establishes that we seek a part and a partnership in arriving at a solution, if one can ever be found.

Now, how can we search effectively for a partnership role? The Fund I dreamed of seemed to be a sensible starting point, I knew no other nor was I in a position to pursue any others.

But would it catch on? Would it gain black alumni support? Would it, over time, raise enough money to deliver the message? Could it deliver the message? Would the partnership appeal be heard or received well? Time would tell.

The arithmetic was easy, so is dreaming. Initially, I thought that if 20 percent of alums, six hundred, gave $250 a year to the fund, or $20.83 a month, for five years, and employers matched that, the fund could acquire a corpus in the area of $1.8 million in five years. If that corpus earned 5 percent interest annually, it would provide $90,000 a year, in perpetuity, to assist future black students financially.

A meager beginning? Perhaps, but a beginning that sounded doable to me and might even be considered and heralded by many.

Was I dreaming? Maybe, but maybe not. Was I clearly outside the box, or was it a case of no one having thought of the idea and presented it in a setting where it could work? I chose the latter.

Aside from giving to our churches, our overall population does not have a great record for giving money. Charitable giving was not something we excelled at, financial assistance to political candidates was not seen as a fundamental rite of passage, and individually and collectively, we lacked the resources needed for these things to happen. Our attitudes and understanding needed work as well.

Yet who better to lead the way to changing attitudes about self-help than young people educated at one of the best universities in our country? It was the right audience and the right situation, and, hopefully, the right time.

Sooner or later, the torch must, and will, be passed to the next generation, why not start now?

This reunion could, maybe would, bring together young, educated people gathering to celebrate their achievements at a southern university that was built with slave labor but refused to let us learn on its grounds for over 134 years (1819-1953). Hopefully, they would bring with them a sense of pride in having achieved this milestone under less than desirable conditions.

Groundbreakers all, I viewed them collectively as America's newest pioneers. Perhaps, those who attended would gather to express their thanks for the quality of the education they had received and its positive effect on their lives.

The reunion permitted a form of cleansing through conversation with classmates about the negatives that learning on Grounds presented.

The reunion also provided an excellent opportunity to tell UVA, and all who witnessed or heard about it, that UVA is, and forever will be, our university, not just theirs.

"Yes," said I to myself, they should be asked to continue as pioneers by participating in a fund-raising effort, *by* black alumni, *for* future black alumni? Why not? Who cares that it has never been done anywhere before?

America's colleges and universities have never really succeeded in engaging their black alumni in ways that undeniably made them equal partners. Many schools have tried but none has ever achieved anything resembling a meaningful fund-raising response from its black alumni, as a group.

JOHN F. MERCHANT

Nor has there ever been a successful effort that was the brainchild of black alumni for whom there was little reward other than the knowledge that their giving back would be helpful to, and needed by, people they did not, and would not, know or ever meet.

If successful, this would be clear evidence of an interest in becoming true partners in aiding and abetting America's need to grow. By focusing on education, self-help, and the racial issues that torment us, it could be part of establishing a new and different standard for emulation by others.

The effort would publicly declare a willingness to "*give back*" in an easy-to-understand manner, a way that defied criticism from anyone and added to the search for greatness the educational institution sought to maintain and improve.

A mission, if you will, that, if successful, would proclaim to the State of Virginia, and the nation, that "we" belong; that "we" intend to stay and that "we" want to be fully involved as true partners in many ways, including important educational issues at UVA, to the extent of our capabilities.

Truly, it could be a critical part of the "Passing of the torch . . . to the new generation of Americans" that President John F. Kennedy spoke about in the very early 1960s.

Was I dreaming? Of course I was, but America was built upon the dreams of its citizenry, and this dream would be no different.

It also occurred to me that nothing beats a try but a failure.

As an aside, I recalled the difficulty I had in understanding, and applying, the "Rule Against Perpetuities" I had studied in the course on Trusts and Estates at law school, a difficulty made easy in Connecticut where the rule was, simply stated, wait and see.

I said to myself, "Self, we must risk failure, then wait and see."

On a positive note, the reality was, and is, that many of UVA's black alumni had taken their UVA education and found solid and rewarding employment opportunities in the larger community after graduating. The *menial job brigade* is, undeniably, not a part of their future.

They learned that, when qualified and armed with a positive attitude, they were desired and desirable factors in the larger community. They earned decent salaries and started successful businesses that could allow them to consider making an annual gift to such a fund a habit. A five-year habit could easily become a ten- or twenty-year habit.

Our search could not be for large sums of money at inception. Rather it should focus on, and stress, developing a habit of giving, giving back if you will, even in small amounts. Motivating alums to do that was the challenge.

Further, in my mind, if the challenge was met, in time we would attract benefactors from the majority community who just might care enough to make gifts in large six or seven figures, Will it? I think so and certainly hope so.

The appeal was made and the challenge was accepted that night. The Fund was created and has grown admirably. That growth, in my view, happened because the giving helps satisfy that felt need many of us harbor to make a difference by helping and giving back in identifiable and significant ways, with a focus on education.

JOHN F. MERCHANT

Yes, I firmly believe that the habit of giving one acquires is personally responsive to something many of us feel deeply about. A large number of us are frustrated by our inability to make a real difference in noticeable ways.

Giving provides a positive way to satisfy the urge, yea, even the need, felt by many in the black community, to give back. We could develop and feel a real sense of pride as we watched the results of the giving, specifically the value added to the lives of future black students: strangers, born, and unborn.

Will the ego satisfactions inherent in knowing that you are being helpful, in ways that matter, help override the fact that, for you personally, your help will not be publicly applauded? It should, and could.

The cause served will never disappear, and it will be publicly applauded over and over again. More importantly, it would be appreciated by those who received financial help, many of whom would go on to make us proud.

What someone wants or needs in return for giving their money is often difficult to assess, but it was a question for me nonetheless.

Of course, I realized that ultimately the true beneficiary of a successful fund-raising effort would be the university, since students paying room, board, and tuition are the lifeblood that sustains it. So what?

Sustaining UVA, and adding to its reputation as an institution committed to diversity, made eminently good sense to me. Isn't that one of the reasons I persevered, and endured, while receiving a legal education in the 1950s?

Perhaps, if we paid our way by providing financial help and helping to recruit students, one day, we might earn an invitation to participate in the university's governance as partners and not simply as an afterthought. Yes, we could add serious substance, not just dollars, to UVA's greatness. It was worth a try; let's just do it and wait and see.

The more I thought about it, the more I became convinced that it was an "idea whose time had come" and must be pursued. Why not try? That try continues to spawn positives; it will not fail, that is clear in 2010, twenty-three years later.

As you can see, an enormous amount of time was spent thinking through the nuts and bolts of the idea. How should such an effort be structured? Could we sell the need for patience while the effort struggled to grow and bear fruit in the hands of what was probably an "*immediate gratification*" genre with few resources and almost nonexistent giving habits?

What could this mean to the cause of diversity at UVA? Would we, and they, buy into the idea? Would we have the good sense to help it grow into something of serious significance? What might be the university's response to such an effort? Could the concept be sold to other colleges and universities?

I consulted no one but spent considerable time, thinking through these many questions and speculating about how they would be answered.

That old Chinese proverb again came to mind, namely, that: "The longest journey in the world starts with the first

JOHN F. MERCHANT

small step . . . ." To it, I added, "in the right direction?" The answer was clear; we should try, it's time.

UVA's commitment to diversity had been made known to me by John Blackburn, Dean of Admissions, when, in 1986, I took my two daughters, Susan Beth and Tabitha, on a trip to look at colleges and universities when they were high school seniors. The southern leg of our visits included Georgetown, North Carolina, Duke, and UVA.

Somehow UVA learned of our impending visit, and a meeting was arranged for me with Dean Blackburn. In that meeting, he stated that the university's goal, as a public university, was to have its student body mirror the black population of the state of Virginia, approximately 10 percent, but they had a long way to go. I believe that the black student population at UVA stood at just below 2 percent at the time of our meeting.

Blackburn made it clear that the goal was designed to be met fairly, without lowering standards for admission. Its status as a public university carried certain inherent obligations that he assured me would continue to be met. An interest in enrolling the "best and the brightest," in and out of state, was unwavering and would not be violated. It would, however, now include young black people as an integral and as a priority.

I was impressed by the obvious sincerity of his words and by him personally. He spoke truth and became a friend.

Over time, UVA has kept working at that commitment and, thanks to a host of people, has distinguished itself by doing an exceptionally fine job. In addition, UVA has enjoyed the highest black graduation rate among public universities for approximately fifteen years and now has a student body approaching the 10 percent target Dean Blackburn shared with me.

Blackburn, and others, really wanted Susan and Tabitha to matriculate at UVA. He spent considerable time trying to convince me, and them, that they should.

However, each had been taught to make their own choices, without prodding from me. Tabitha did enroll and earn an undergraduate degree. Alas, Susan's choice was the University of Pennsylvania, where she earned her undergraduate degree in 1991. An excellent choice, as it turned out.

Subsequently, in 1991, Susan was admitted to UVA's Law School. She received her JD degree in 1994 as the first child of a black law school graduate to do so, hence the first black legacy was thereby created.

Incidentally, her decision to attend UVA's Law School was entirely her own. She had never discussed her interest in the law with me. She knew it was her life and her choice to make. She was taught, and allowed, by her parents to think and act for herself. She knew that parental support would be there for sensible decisions made by her. I will admit to being enormously pleased when I learned that her choice was to study law at UVA.

Before speaking and issuing such a challenge, I shared my idea with Jim Trice and Harold Marsh, both native Virginians from Richmond and UVA alums. Jim's comment was to the effect that if I didn't offer the challenge, he would. Harold immediately voiced his approval and committed to helping.

Both agreed that the idea was sound and wondered why they hadn't thought about it themselves.

Another major reason why I considered making such a challenge is simple. Over time, many friends in the majority community had consistently urged that a need existed for the black community to help itself in clear, relevant, and convincing ways. The self-help they had in mind must be visible and consistent with America's focus on education and with the work ethic. They argued that, if the majority community was exposed to clear evidence of self-help efforts, sooner or later, it would be eager to partner up with those efforts and make them work. To me their arguments had merit.

How could that be done? What constitutes clear evidence of self-help? How could it be presented to, and recognized by, the majority community?

The reunion offered a framework for making such evidence available, as well as a way to ease the financial burdens faced by future black students. Further, if done properly, the fund-raising effort would provide both evidence and financial help in perpetuity to future black students at UVA.

My father had taught me that if something is important, there should be at least two good reasons for doing it and promoting self should not be one of them.

My thinking regarding the challenge showed that more than two good reasons existed, especially if the effort involved having the patience not to be discouraged by a slow start and slow growth. Let it grow, as opposed to seeking immediate self-gratification for having done a good deed.

The need would not disappear. We must commit ourselves to organizing it properly and to selling the idea of giving back on a reliable and regular basis.

After all, this had never been done before, at least not to the extent that I was thinking it should happen.

No game plan existed since, as stated, nothing like this had ever been done by black alumni of a major university. The challenge was to marry this fund-raising effort by UVA's black alumni with the university's commitment to diversity so that a clear message could be sent. Additionally, if such an effort was successful, and if black alumni groups at other educational institutions emulated our effort, a strong message would be sent across America; a message that could not be misunderstood by anyone. Clearly, it was worth a try. It was time.

In truth, I also thought through the potential perks that could flow from a successful effort. In America, and elsewhere, money speaks in a loud and clear voice, especially among its colleges and universities. Alumni associations are a basic at those institutions, and fund-raising is a major, and necessary, part of the mix. There is a constant search for ways to increase the number of alumni who contribute and the amounts they give.

I knew that UVA needed every dollar it could raise for a number of reasons. One major reason was, and is, that despite being a state university, the legislature provides significantly less than 10 percent of UVA's annual budget requirements and annually threatens to reduce that percentage, then does.

JOHN F. MERCHANT

Certainly, UVA would welcome fund-raising by its black alumni with open arms. Who doesn't accept dollars that help meet budgetary needs? Also, in this case, this unexpected resource could be of serious help in UVA's efforts to compete with the Ivy League schools, and other major colleges and universities, in an ongoing competition to attract the *best and the brightest* young black students to their institutions and, given their endowments and general fiscal situations, could afford to do so.

It would also provide at least a partial answer to institutions looking for ways to make their black alumni more of a factor regarding contributing to their alma maters. For many, if not most, reaching black alumni was and is a challenge that few, if any, had met well. It represented a new challenge that had no track record upon which to draw. We could provide that track record.

Jim Trice, Harold Marsh, and I met. We discussed taking the necessary steps to move ahead with the idea. Decisions were made to: form a board of directors, create a 501(c)(3) corporation, involve UVA's Alumni Association, schedule and conduct an organizational meeting, and do the tasks required to legalize the structure needed for the effort.

We agreed that Jim would serve as the chairman of the board, Harold as vice-chairman, and I would serve as treasurer. We further agreed that funds collected would be handled by the Alumni Association, a decision that would permit us to produce records of income and expenditures quickly and assure donors that their contributions were being used responsibly.

Minimally, the Admissions Office, the Alumni Association, and the Office of African Affairs (OAAA) needed to be informed of our effort and invited to help. Any assistance they could provide, as they deemed appropriate, would help.

Wayne Cozart from the Alumni Association was involved in all early meetings and discussions. He assured us that the Association would cooperate in every way possible, including providing critically needed financial assistance for staff support.

Wayne has been a tower of strength for this effort from its inception and is owed a huge debt of gratitude that can never be paid, but it is truly appreciated. Wayne is not black.

On the other hand, there was a black male who in 1987 had taken a position as head of the Office of African-American Affairs (OAAA) at UVA. He was invited to attend the early organizational meetings.

Regrettably, he could never really support the idea. In fact, he was often heard to criticize the effort. He seemed to reject any involvement by the majority community for reasons I never understood, and he never shared.

We went on without him. He retired from the university a few years ago; the Fund remains and grows.

But wait, the corporation needed a name. It was clear to me that it could not succeed if named after me or Jim or Harold, or the three of us. Sure, it was my idea, and our joint efforts that got it rolling; however, in order to work, it needed more than one, or three, persons promoting self. There was no disagreement about this.

We agreed that future officers and directors should be the recipients of any plaudits because they would be the reason the idea worked. That is as it should be because those mentioned would have earned the plaudits through their efforts and leadership. Our task was to get it started properly.

Interestingly, to me, that is the way it is working. The effort has been blessed with a number of black alumni who have provided the leadership necessary to grow the Fund and provide financial assistance to black students.

The record speaks for itself; the Fund's assets are at the five million dollar level in 2011. In addition, more than $700,000 has been distributed to students over the years.

This is a story that should be told by *The New York Times* or *The Washington Post* or on *Oprah*. However, none seem interested, though all have been approached; doing it now would be okay.

I think it was Jim, who suggested that the fund be named after the first black to ever receive a degree of any kind from the University of Virginia. Jim, who probably is the leading authority on the history of black students, faculty and administrators at UVA, identified Dr. Walter N. Ridley as that first pioneer.

Dr. Ridley, a professor at Virginia State College, received a PhD in Education from UVA in *1953*. He attended classes for several summers to earn that degree during which he could not live on Grounds. He appeared on Grounds only to attend classes. He resided with friends in the city of

Charlottesville. He started his quest before Brown was even brought to the U.S. Supreme Court.

One can only imagine what he endured, but he fully believed that he had a right to a degree from UVA, if he was qualified to attend and earn it. He clearly was qualified and Virginia State College; the "separate but equal" college could not provide the PhD he sought. In his words

> "[M]y father paid taxes to the State of Virginia throughout his life, why can't I attend UVA . . ."

I was asked to contact Dr. Ridley and request permission to use his name. Dr. Ridley had retired and was living on a fixed income in Pennsylvania. I located his phone number and called him. He was overwhelmed, to say the least, and after I explained what we were trying to do, along with our belief that as the true pioneer he merited this acclaim, he gave his permission, shedding tears over the phone while doing so. I shed tears with him.

And so the Walter N. Ridley Scholarship Fund became a living reality.

Jim Trice did a remarkable job of chairing the organizational efforts. Jim was absolutely the right person to lead the organizational effort as chairman of the Ridley Fund Board. His preparation, attention to detail and ability to attract black alums to serve on the board were exceptional.

Jim was no stranger to working with the university. He was employed by Monsanto Corporation and maintained a relationship with the engineering school and with the university's upper echelon through his work in aiding the diversity effort.

Harold, an engineer and an attorney and an alumnus, was an invaluable resource during the early stages. Insightful, thoughtful, persuasive, and fully committed, he had an easy manner and terrific sense of humor. He was a source of strength during the process, resolving differences and keeping the effort headed down the right path.

Regrettably, he suffered a tragic death in the late 1990s. He died after being shot while in his car stopped at a traffic light in Richmond, Virginia. He has been missed but would be pleased to know what his efforts helped produce.

If Harold were alive, he could tell you many stories about his early years at UVA. He could tell about being told that he was not welcome to sit and worship at a white Baptist church located close to Grounds, closer than any black Baptist church.

He could tell about his discussion with a professor about a grade below "B." Harold told the professor that the grade given was incorrect and asked that it be reconsidered, saying that he had always received grades of "B" and higher throughout his school years and was going to earn those same grades at UVA. Reconsideration was done and a proper grade given.

A board of directors comprised entirely of black alumni was formed and went to work with an enviable level of commitment. The organizational phase was successful and included qualifying as a 501©(3) corporation, making any contributions tax deductible.

Raising money was a slow process. In fact, by the end of 1987, approximately $3,000 had been received. Today, in 2011, as stated, the fund is close to having $5,000,000 in hand and has provided close to $700,000 in scholarships and grants to black students over the years.

I am unaware of any similar effort in the United States. Certainly there are none that rival the accomplishments of UVA's black alumni through The Ridley Fund. Our efforts have not been emulated at other colleges and universities, as yet. In time, I believe, or at least hope, that will happen.

UVA's black alumni have committed to the effort and are totally responsible for its growth. That has been a source of pride for me, validating my belief that it could be done. One result has been that more than 30 percent of black alumni contribute on a regular basis and take pride in doing so.

The positive results are the product of the efforts of a strong, talented board, and impressive leadership by those who have chaired and sat on that board. The torch has been passed and accepted.

A succession of black alumni has chaired The Ridley Fund with distinction over the years. I would be remiss if I did not mention and thank them.

Jim Trice, as indicated, did the heavy lifting needed to properly organize the effort at inception. Under his leadership the Fund built a solid foundation that serves to give it the permanence intended. A terrific black alumni board was assembled, bylaws and a committee structure were put in place, and the process and issues of governance were clearly established.

JOHN F. MERCHANT

Importantly, a system of financial reporting was put in place. This system will stand the scrutiny of even the most diligent auditors. UVA's Alumni Association deserves kudos for the reporting system, thanks to Wayne Cozart.

Roland Lynch succeeded Trice as chairman. He earned an MBA, with emphasis in marketing and finance, from UVA's Darden School in 1975. In 1987, he became president of Capsulated Systems, Inc. (CSI) in Ohio. In 1991, he bought controlling interest in the company. He is a co-inventor of four of CSI's patents in microencapsulation.

Roland is a man of extraordinary intelligence and depth, highly motivated, energetic, and fully committed to the Fund and its mission. His daughter began her freshman year at UVA in September 2010.

In his relationship with me, he showed a high level of adaptability and a willingness to listen, as well as make decisions without fear. Our philosophies on how to proceed with the Fund's mission often differed, but we were always able to fully discuss and resolve those differences in the best interests of the Fund.

In all honesty, both Roland and I, in his words, were "unified and steadfast in our commitment to the common goal of growing Ridley" and were doggedly committed to Ridley's stated goals.

Our differences are best described as healthy and worthy of the discussion and debate they generated. We differed on some details, but our disagreement never sunk to the level of personal animosity, nor did they ever threaten the work or mission of The Ridley Fund.

When contributions lagged in the early days, as expected, and the financial needs of black students at UVA grew, Roland gave $20,000 to the Fund with instructions that the money be used immediately, not invested in order to raise interest income for later distribution as a grant or scholarship. He made clear that his gift was to be used immediately to meet existing needs of students presently on Grounds or soon to arrive.

I believe that his action validated Ridley for a lot of people. Certainly, it was a critical factor in sustaining Ridley's promises and goals.

Attracting support from black alumni, especially in the early days, was difficult, to say the least. Black student attitudes about their experiences at UVA focused on the negatives they endured in the 1960s, 1970s, and 1980s. Those alumni did not easily nurture a high level of pride in their alma mater. Frankly, it was hard to love our alma mater, given the negatives related to racial attitudes that a black student confronted and endured on grounds, real and imagined.

Personally, I acquired that high level of pride commencing with the reunion in 1987. Prior to that time, I was pleased, but pride remained in the womb for years until it was born in April 1987.

As stated at the end of our year of birth less than $3,000 had been raised. Ridley suffered from a lack of staff and could not have survived the early days without the help of UVA's Alumni Association, specifically Wayne Cozart, who provided office space, timely advice, and his office paid one-half of the salary of Ridley's Director, its only staff.

One could postulate that Wayne's help was motivated by his interest in doing his job, which was to raise money from UVA's alumni. Thus, one could argue, his help was motivated by some level of personal interest and selfishness. That argument is invalid and lacks both evidence and substance. Anyone making it, or even thinking it, would be dead wrong.

Certainly, it was convenient for him to support Ridley, but, knowing Wayne, I know that his help was motivated by sincere feelings and caring. He simply took advantage of an opportunity to do the right thing and support the larger issue of diversity. He is real, and his efforts continue today.

Wayne saw the value of diversity and recognized the importance of making history by assisting the effort of black alumni at a major southern university to organize and grow a successful black dominated effort to support the university by their words, deeds, and money.

I repeat, nothing like the Ridley Fund exists anywhere in the United States.

Lack of adequate staff plagued Ridley from the beginning and still does. However, the early decision made by Ridley's board was to use contributions to the Fund to help students rather than hire staff. This decision was fully supported by black alumni who served on Ridley's board, as volunteers.

Down through the years, an enormous number of black alumni have volunteered to serve on the board and performed admirably, making up for a staff that, at its peak, consisted of a director and an administrative assistant, usually a student. That board gave its time and considerable talents, individually and collectively, to doing the grunt work needed to raise Ridley's corpus to the four-million-dollar level.

Of course, volunteers do well usually, perhaps only, when strong leadership exists and the cause is one they believe in. Ridley has been blessed by strong leadership from its chairpersons, each of whom led Ridley to another level and maintained alumni membership on its board and participation in the biennial reunions.

Jim Trice and Roland Lynch, the first two chairmen, led to the creation of a solid foundation for growth, not an easy task. I applaud them.

John Peoples next moved into the seat as Ridley's Chairman. His tenure was noteworthy for his ability to sustain an interest from Ridley's board and avoid the inevitable diminishing level of interest in maintaining an organization that needed a new spark. The growth that sustains enthusiasm was not immediately present, and many saw Ridley as floundering without realizing that in this kind of effort a lull was not unexpected.

Ridley needed a renewal of commitment and patience as it endured a predictable easing of momentum and a period of discouragement in not immediately achieving desired goals.

John Peoples brought a quest for new ideas and effort. Through his leadership, the ship of Ridley was kept afloat even as it encountered rough seas. He was not afraid to try new approaches and risk criticism when they didn't work as they could and should have. He never lost faith in Ridley's mission and the need for it to grow and flourish.

JOHN F. MERCHANT

Peoples was succeeded by Dwayne Allen.

Regrettably, Dwayne's tenure as Ridley's chair was short-lived. It came at a time when he was changing his job and his residence. Doing so involved a move of his entire family and taking on a new position with new responsibilities and challenges. Regrettably, Dwayne resigned as Chairman, recognizing that he could not meet Ridley's needs and still provide for his family's needs and take on the new challenges that lay ahead. Reluctantly, the board accepted his resignation and asked Teresa Bryce to succeed him. She agreed to do so.

Teresa Bryce is an extraordinary young woman and was the right person at the right time for Ridley. Soft-spoken and incredibly insightful, she led the revival of purpose and commitment that Ridley needed at that time. She organized a self-study that resulted in Ridley's board taking a hard look at itself and making the adjustments needed to revitalize the effort.

Her leadership enabled Ridley to successfully endure the bump in the road that could have been a serious negative to the effort.

She was succeeded in the chair by Tracy McMillan, who brought the vitality, savvy, and energy needed to move Ridley forward in many areas, without losing a focus on fund-raising.

A natural leader and successful entrepreneur who owned and operated his own business, he brought a quality of leadership that took Ridley to the next level. During his tenure, Ridley's fund-raising reached 3.9 million dollars, and his ability to interact with the administration enhanced

Ridley's stature to an admirable level. His involvement in attracting board members with talent and commitment, coupled with the hiring of a director of development for Ridley, solidified and extended Ridley's reach into black alumni in a highly effective way that portends well for the future.

He gave unqualified support to the biennial Black Alumni Reunion to the point where approximately one thousand two hundred persons attended the 2009 Reunion.

His intuition and diligence were noteworthy, even exceptional. His time in office resulted in situating Ridley very well as regards its future. He was the right man at the right time, an important successor to Teresa Bryce and a needed asset for Ridley. He is a good friend to me and to Ridley.

It is my considered opinion that all of Ridley's chairpersons were talented and committed. They provided the leadership needed at the time, and, along with those who served as board members, are responsible for the growth of Ridley and its impact.

I pause here to praise John Casteen, who recently retired as President of UVA. His leadership of the University has enabled it to grow in stature on a worldwide basis and that continues. He sees the vision clearly and never compromised his vision for preparing UVA for unwavering excellence over time. A clear friend of Ridley, he fully supported what we were about. He was the right man for the times. I respect that man and salute him.

My personal involvement with Ridley now is close to non-existent in 2011 and that is as it should be. I will help, if asked, while making a concerted effort not to interfere with those to whom the torch has been passed. They have made, are making, and will make Ridley what it should be, namely, a strong beacon of light that shines brightly in an America that sorely needs it.

Chapter 11

The "Black Community"

PERSONALLY, I HAVE never been authorized to speak for the "*Black Community*" and I never tried to. Actually, even if I wanted such authorization, I don't know where or how to get it. Thus, unlike so many others, I have never claimed to be its spokesperson. Nor do I know how or where those who claim, or infer, that they have such authority, obtained it. Conversely, no one has ever asked my permission to speak for me, although some have earned the right to do so based on what I learned about their goals and achievements.

There have been many occasions over the years when I have spoken to predominately White groups regarding racial issues and race relations. My focus, however, was on creating a better level of understanding about what being Black in America was like and why the civil rights movement was inevitable, historically important, and necessary.

I sought to bridge the gaps between the races that existed and still bedevil us. My sense is that for many I was the first, maybe the only, Black they had ever heard speak who did not accuse and confront them.

I could not condone the violence during the movement. However, I must point out that much of the violence was perpetrated by law enforcement and White instigators, not by Blacks. The use of fire hoses in Selma and the beatings inflicted by law enforcement on Blacks during peaceful demonstrations in the South are examples that come to mind. Rioting, the burning of buildings, and looting required attention from law enforcement people and I understood that. But police brutality should not have been a part of such enforcement.

Tragically, unnecessary police brutality still occurs in many cities, towns and states in 2011. Will it ever stop? Those events have root causes which need to be understood and overcome, not reacted to in a way that expresses an attitude one should not be proud of having.

"Who do they think they are" was and is the predicate that triggers the negative reactions and brings negative attitudes and actions to the surface. The media was not helpful either. Its reporting and editorializing fed the flames and rarely brought a plea for understanding and discussion on the issue of correcting wrongs. Media, citing freedom of the press, often provided a basis for generating hate or justifying public displays of racism and racial attitudes on the part of segments of the majority population that supported a division of the races.

It is worth noting that in the twenty-first Century, major media in Virginia took time to apologize for their writings and actions during the dark days of the civil rights movement, in effect validating my comments as stated above.

Now, in the twenty-first Century, the rioting has fundamentally ceased. But we still do not talk with each other and are basically leaderless on all sides.

It seems that simply being Black qualifies one as an expert on matters impacting those of African heritage. I cannot subscribe to that way of thinking. I am Black and have been treated as Black all my life. Also, for all of my life I have been proud of being Black. Yet, I do not believe that simply being Black qualifies me, or anyone, to lead, or attempt to speak for 13 million persons with an African heritage who live in America.

Being Black in America can involve a number of different experiences that shape us. Having never been a slave, can I legitimately claim to fully understand what that was like? Perhaps you can; I can't.

I can speak to being discriminated against and can understand how that makes one feel. I have first hand experiences with slum landlords in the "hood" and a host of other negatives that being Black confers upon one, but my personal experiences are not necessarily the same as those of other Black Americans, especially, but not solely, in the South.

Thus I can speak to mine but can't do more than comment on yours even though I understand yours better than most.

I've never been lynched, seen a lynching, or lived in fear of being lynched. Can I speak for anyone who has experienced those? I don't think so. But I can work to prevent them from continuing, so I've tried.

I am aware of the Ku Klux Klan, and have been chased out of the Blue Ridge Mountains by members of the Klan, but a cross has never been burned in front of my house or in any neighborhood where I resided. I have no personal experience at living under those conditions, do you?

JOHN F. MERCHANT

The public schools I attended were integrated without help from the National Guard, but I was fully aware of the racist attitudes that existed at all levels; students, faculty, and administration.

During my "growing up" years violence was usually limited to encounters where the unwise use of the "N" word was involved. Those encounters usually led to a more restricted use of that word by those who felt free to utter it as they did. It is true that an "ass whupping" can change behavior, but may not change minds or attitudes.

In short, I have been discriminated against and been a target of racism and negative racial attitudes all my life. That, unfortunately, is true of every Black person living in America. But that fact alone doesn't endow me with the title of "Leader', nor does it make me an authority on the Black experience of 13 million Americans who were born in this country and live here.

Incidentally, it does not make me hate either.

My decision, given my individual experiences, was, and is, that my time is best spent in an effort to help find ways to abolish and prevent negatives based on racial prejudices from being imposed on Black Americans. Admittedly you can, and do, spend your time differently. You have that choice and right to do so.

What I can do, and have tried to do during my lifetime, is to recognize that racism exists and to speak against it, as well as work with people who seek to build bridges and eliminate racism and negative racial attitudes. For me, it has always been important to be involved in positive efforts. I believe that negatives on either side compound the problem and prevent or delay finding solutions.

I am fully aware of the dramatic changes that have taken place during my lifetime of more than seventy-five years. I like to think that I've been a part of helping to make some of the changes. That has been my priority.

Change has been ongoing, unceasing and irrevocable, though, admittedly slow in many critical areas. The effect of such changes has been slow to trickle down to the least among us, but we do have a more solid foundation for fighting the evils of racism. Generally speaking, we have the critical laws on the books. Few additional laws are needed.

Changing attitudes, our own and those of others, is the challenge we face now. How to meet that challenge successfully poses a problem for which I have no answer except to keep working at it, however difficult that may be.

Many of us define the changes differently. All blacks do not applaud them, nor do we take full advantage of the positives that flow from the changes in large enough numbers. For too many, it is still "*us*" against "*them*," dangerous generalities, to be sure.

Two changes strike me as significant but are rarely discussed: (1) Many blacks have acquired racist attitudes concerning whites as a group, thus perpetuating the "us" against "them" conflict; and (2) the black *community* has become black *communities*. No longer is it a homogeneous group.

In fact, for at least the past thirty-five years, I have argued that a definable *black community* no longer exists.

JOHN F. MERCHANT

As a single entity, it has been non existent since the civil rights movement and cannot, will not, be recovered.

Arguably, one existed throughout most of the first sixty-five years of the twentieth century. During that time, one could comfortably allege the existence of a black community and a black agenda and make some sense. Not now.

Laws have been passed since President Kennedy's assassination that have altered that agenda. These laws have made critical parts of that agenda legally moot. Enforcement of those laws is taking time and has not been without pain. More enforcement efforts seem dictated, but at least, the law is on our side and is supportive of efforts to bring about change.

Incidentally, that is why a president's power to nominate and appoint federal judges is so important. Ultimately, judges decide the issues and often they interpret the law as they see fit, not always as it was intended to be decided and enforced.

Success in enforcement now depends on people, and "Therein lies the rub . . ." to quote Willy Shakespeare again. People relating well and better, *or at all*, is the key to real change. Sadly, that is an unfamiliar area for too many.

It's still true that most white people have never had a "normal" conversation with a black person and vice versa. Of critical importance is the fact that too many, black and white, have never sought such interaction.

Why? Or why not start now?

Living apart, as we have and do, opts against finding ways to meet and relate. In my view, we must prioritize destroying the barriers of separation by reaching out to each other in as many ways as possible. It's time to shed the rhetoric of blame and find ways to share thoughts, ideas, personal goals, and just be human beings who are interested in living the good life that America promises.

After all, when we really think about it, isn't that what all of us seek?

Of importance, like it or not, is the fact that today, in 2010, more than one *black community* exists, and the gaps between them are widening on a daily basis.

Finally, a respected voice, Eugene Robinson, noted journalist, editor, and columnist, has made this point, convincingly, and put the question on the table. His 2010 book entitled *Disintegration* presents a framework for serious thought and discussion. I believe, and hope, that the discussion will take root and grow.

Bill Cosby has put the question on the table recently as well, albeit from a different perspective. He has received plenty of undue criticism for speaking out, but the question remains in the public forum. It's about time.

It reminds me of something my dad taught me and emphasized often. He said words to the effect that if you recognize a problem that needs to be solved, the first thing you must do is honestly determine if you are part of the problem in any way. If so, however slight your negative may be, you must resolve that negative before you can become a meaningful part of the solution.

JOHN F. MERCHANT

Raymond Arsenault, currently a visiting scholar at the Florida State University Study Center in London, recently reviewed Robinson's "*Slim but powerful book . . .*" for *The New York Times Book Review*. Among other comments, he states that

> "The race-based community that was a fixture of American life for generations, the traditional locus of racial experience and solidarity, the idealized entity that many of us still refer to, indeed still cling to, as an institutional and social reality, no longer exists . . ."

He further states

> "The *ethos of racial solidarity* (emph. supp.) that served blacks well during the Jim Crow era and the civil rights struggles of the 1950s and '60s is gone. Thus continued references to "black leaders" or the "black agenda" make no sense and serve only to obscure the complexities of race in a vast, multicultural nation."

Arsenault and Robinson express my views in more eloquent ways than my writing talents allow me to do. I am not an intellectual. However, I am in full agreement with Robinson's thesis and Arsenault's comments. It pleases me to know that others agree. My life experiences allow that, even require it.

During the first fifty years of the twentieth century, it was not difficult for me to accept the legitimate leadership of men like Roy Wilkins, Dr. Martin Luther King, A. Philip Randolph, Bayard Rustin, Thurgood Marshall, Walter White, and Whitney Young, to name just a few. They were nationally prominent leaders that I revered and accepted, unequivocally.

They provided hope, worked earnestly for change, and were my role models. Their minds and mouths worked very well. I live with the memories of what their struggles cost them, and we must never forget the costs that were paid, or the folks who paid them. It's our history in America.

Their methods were not exactly the same, nor were the issues they focused on always exactly the same. Yet they described a plight that fundamentally defined what every black person in America understood and agreed needed to be changed and dramatically improved.

Taken together, all sought to change the way America and Americans dealt with the issues of race and race relations. Their leadership efforts created identifiable results and their successes were noticeable however small they may have appeared to be at the time and however slow implementation has been.

They realized that truly significant change would involve a long term struggle. Their message was that, at best, it would take generations for the desired and necessary changes to occur and offered no specific timetable.

One step at a time in the right direction was their approach and methodology.

Immediate gratification is not possible as it relates to issues of racism and improved race relations. In the words of that old Negro spiritual, "One Day At A Time" where we

JOHN F. MERCHANT

move in the right direction is all I've asked for. I realize that the journey will involve frustrations, be lengthy, and continue after I have disappeared from earth. I just don't want to look back and have to admit that I did little or nothing to ease the burdens for those still involved in the journey. I believe I have lived in a way where that is not what I look back on or think, have you? Will you? Start today if you didn't start yesterday?

Patience and dogged determination, fueled by intelligence and planning, were their tools. They also understood that black Americans could not just stand back and reap benefits from progress. They had to participate fully and knowledgeably or the gains would be lost or at least put on hold.

Rap Brown, the Black Panthers, and Stokely Carmichael were not accepted the same way by me, even though they represented a point of view demanded by the times, at least in their opinion.

They seemed committed to conflict and confrontation and a rebellion that was unlikely to occur in the way they projected. I do believe that their voices added a level of progress to the overall effort.

In fact, wasn't it Stokely, with the assistance of young black women, who legitimized the word "black" and made it a positive word to use?

I never believed that violence brought people together. I do believe that the approaches taken by those I revered, despite the difficulties inherent in their efforts to create and implement a framework for change, were sensible and worth supporting. I supported them.

One question I often asked friends to answer was: What would it take to convince you that ours was an inferior race of people? Or to cause you to fight for the confederacy, and what it stood for, on a voluntary basis?

I thought, mistakenly, that if they would think seriously about, and honestly answer my questions, they would at least get a glimmer of the difficulties we face in any effort to change the attitudes and beliefs of a nation of people, many of whom cling fiercely to the belief that the Civil War had the wrong ending and should be ignored or refought.

Some years ago while thinking about the words *black community* and trying to determine their meaning, I wound up confused. The last thirty-five years of the twentieth century, and all of the twenty-first century, have made it even more difficult to define accurately. Few who seek or claim to lead even attempt to define it. The reason, probably, is that no clear definition of such an entity exists, and any effort to define it makes the speeches harder to write or deliver.

A thoughtful observer must admit that the words *black community* are misleading in the twenty-first century. My mind adopts a bewildered posture when I hear those words spoken since, as stated, no such homogeneous group exists.

Yes, to repeat, it may have existed a long time ago, but not any longer. In my youth, back in the thirties, forties, and fifties, I believe there was something one could legitimately refer to as the *black community*. Negroes, nigras, and coloreds were one group to be discriminated against, equally. That is exactly what all of us experienced daily, intensely, helplessly, and in almost every facet of our lives.

The one thing that people of color have in common is that each of us has suffered and endured a negative experience in their lifetime solely because of our African heritage. However, that fact alone does not qualify any one to lead, nor does it justify proclaiming oneself an expert on issues of racism or discrimination. Many believe it does, or act like it does, or that it should.

A scintilla of African blood was, and is, sufficient to expose one to racial prejudice, no matter how well educated, intelligent, or cultured you may be, or have been. Light-skinned Negroes fared a bit better in some ways, but one's African heritage, however slight, always gave many members of the majority community an excuse to deny fair treatment, or the rights "guaranteed" by the constitution; and so they did, and do.

The Historical Black Colleges took on the challenge early. Believing, as I do, that education is the key, they recruited young black men and women from segregated schools and turned them into educated men and women employing a level of caring and nurturing that offered hope for the future. It was a struggle, even after receiving their degrees, but they weathered that storm and continue to do so.

Doctors and lawyers couldn't find office space for their practices, except, maybe, in black neighborhoods. Teachers with masters and PhD degrees could not find work teaching white students. Corporations did not hire people of color; neither did government at any level. There were exceptions, of course, but that is what they were—exceptions.

Small businesses struggled without meaningful access to the larger community to sell its services or skills at fair prices. Skilled tradesmen were denied union memberships and access to job opportunities. The courts and the judges gave less than justice to black men and women, and often they showed little or no respect to black lawyers who appeared before the court representing clients. Bar associations and medical associations discriminated, and hospitals denied privileges to medical doctors with impeccable qualifications.

Ironically, most medical malpractice litigation still features white doctors and hospitals as defendants.

Hospital emergency rooms, in the North and South, often failed, even refused, to provide medical care to Negroes, or, as happened to me personally, made them wait until a black doctor was available to treat them.

I can recall an instance in 1942, in Lexington, Virginia, when I fell from a tree while visiting my grandparents during the summer and broke my right wrist. It was dislocated. My mom snapped it back in place and made a temporary sling from a dish towel before taking me to the hospital, where I was made to wait more than four hours before anything resembling treatment was offered.

The reason was that, I had to await the arrival of the only black doctor in the area to be treated. Four hours of pain at age nine are remembered very vividly. It boggles my mind to recall how hospital staff just ignored me; so much for the Hippocratic Oath, or, perhaps, oaths generally, for too many.

But that memory is nothing compared to what many in the South faced regularly during their entire lives.

JOHN F. MERCHANT

Frankly, Connecticut wasn't much better during the period before Rosa Parks and the civil rights movement. Second class citizenship and treatment dominated in Connecticut and was all a person of color could expect. That condition still needs work in 2010.

On another side of the coin, my memories include the fact that even in the early thirties through the end of the twentieth century, distinctions were often made by blacks themselves on the basis of skin color and other dumb criteria.

The saying I remember was, "If you're light, you're all right. If you're brown, you can hang around. If you're black, step back." How disgusting is that? My parents refused to allow me to speak those words together like that.

It is still hard for me to believe how cruel we can be to each other.

Simple things, such as doing well in school, subjected young people, including me, to criticism and ridicule from other blacks. In a sense, being smart and doing well in school was viewed as a kind of crime and looked down upon. It was viewed as "acting white," and therefore was unacceptable.

My experience at Virginia Union University changed that attitude. There they taught that being smart, called "*heavy*," should be a source of pride and engender respect from your peers. It worked!

There I was exposed, for the first time in my life, to a large group of young blacks who were, indeed, "*heavy*" and who left Union with their degrees and went out into a world of work that didn't want them and achieved.

Over the years, I have been referred to as colored, Negro, N***er, boy, nigra, nigga, yellow n***er, black, and African American. My name has always been John, but few in the majority community seemed to care.

I have also been accused by black people of being too white to be considered black. White people treated me as too black to be white. The effect was that, I had serious trouble figuring out where I belonged, or if I belonged anywhere. Was I to be blamed forever for being light-skinned?

For me, the saving grace was when I finally decided that I would work at being an American, blessed with a heritage I had nothing to do with acquiring but am pleased with, and proud of, in every respect.

The last time that I was called "white" in a derogatory manner happened in 2001, when I was sixty-eight years old. A black man, in an effort to put me down or "dis" me, referred to me as a white man as we sat talking among a group of six or seven people with an African heritage. I was so infuriated that I told the gentlemen, in front of everyone, that he had a choice: he could kiss my "white" man's ass or try to kick it, and I didn't care which he chose but hoped for the latter. He declined both.

If I was not black, or African American, what was I? All my life, the majority community had treated me as a Negro, a boy, colored, a black, or an African American. Excluding boy, I have always been enormously proud to be any one of the other four, and I still am.

"Boy" worked only as long as I was one, as defined by the law. It was offensive when, under the law, I became an adult,

JOHN F. MERCHANT

I came to realize, as all of us should, that my heritage came with me. In my case, it resulted from a union between two really wonderful people, namely, my mother and father, whose heritage came with them at their birth.

As a teenager, I traced my heritage back to my great-great-great-great-grandparents on both sides. I learned that my heritage included French-Canadian, Scottish indentured servant, and Blackfoot Indian on Dad's side; and Irish slave owner, African slave, and Cherokee Indian on Mom's side. Dad's family had roots in Nova Scotia; Mom's from either a North Carolina or Virginia plantation whose owner had slaves.

My heritage sounds pretty All-American to me! Have you searched your heritage? If so, did learning about it provide you with a better basis than mine for being an American, or of being proud to be one? Did you find that you were a product of some racial mixtures, or is your heritage solely that of African or Caucasian throughout? Can you claim any greater rationale, or excuse, for being born in this country? I doubt it.

Accordingly, I have steadfastly refused to permit any negative comment or inference about my right to be here to go unchallenged.

The heritage I just shared came from discussions with Mom, Dad, Dad's nine brothers and sisters, and other family members.

Dad was born in 1896, and many of his siblings were also born in the late nineteenth century. Mom appeared in 1912. Each had parents and or relatives who recalled the Civil War that began in April 1861 and ended in April 1865 when Lee surrendered to Grant at Appomattox Courthouse, Virginia.

The Emancipation Proclamation was issued by President Lincoln in January 1863, only thirty-three years before Dad was born.

Utah became a state the year Dad was born. Oklahoma, New Mexico, Arizona, Alaska, and Hawaii became states after Dad was born. Mom was born the same year that Arizona entered the Union, 1912.

Given that time sequence, I could not find a basis for disbelieving oral recitations shared with me by my parents, grandparents, aunts, and uncles. They had clear memories of hearing stories about slaves, including from some who had been slaves. I'm told that the Emancipation Proclamation was a major subject of discussion as Dad and Mom were growing up, especially among Mom's forebears.

I have shared this information with my daughter Susan Beth Merchant when she asked about it as I had done.

By way of support for believing what I was told, like you, I can vividly recall the Watts riots in 1963, forty-seven years ago, as if they happened yesterday.

The NAACP was twenty-four years old when I was born in 1933. Its efforts, struggles, and successes were certainly much talked about as I grew up.

Individually and collectively, all of us with an African heritage could not avoid discussions about race. Those discussions dominated because racial incidents and attitudes, unfair treatment, and a host of other negatives confronted each of us every day. Folks were being lynched in the South; second class citizenship was all we had to live with, and daily

JOHN F. MERCHANT

we had to learn to cope with being subservient as a matter of survival.

We learned to cheer the exploits of Joe Louis, Sugar Ray Robinson, and Jesse Owens, among others. Ironically, most Americans cheered them as well, then treated them like the rest of us after their victories. How dumb is that?

Why do I say dumb? Easy. It defies logic and deifies prejudice.

In truth, none of us asked to be born here, or to be here, nor did any American ever select their forebears in advance. In America, all of our forebears, with the exception of Native Americans, came here the same way: on a boat.

I'm also reminded that it's not as if we, or they, created or owned the land. Ownership was acquired by force.

Accommodations on the various boats differed, but, early on, a boat brought all of our forebears here; no exceptions. I have no plans to leave, or take up permanent residence in any of the countries of my forebears, do you?

Visiting those places is worth doing; residing there permanently is a different story and not something that I, or you, will ever choose to do.

I prefer the land we took from my Indian forebears. It's a great piece of real estate that you should visit.

Jefferson's role in effecting the Louisiana Purchase allowed America to be developed and grow. Without Jefferson's effort, there would be no West or Midwest; hence no America as we know it.

The settlement of the West has been an oft repeated story during my life, starting in elementary school and maintained by Hollywood. What has not been covered well is the role that black Americans played in the development of the West.

Yes, men and women with an African heritage were intimately involved in the development of the West, despite Hollywood's efforts to convince us otherwise.

That role was researched by me for almost thirty years, and I created and taught a course regarding it at the college level. Americans, including black Americans, should be made aware of that part of America's history. For me, it is a further validation of my status as an American, and of my right to be here and be treated fairly. We helped build and grow every section of this country and our right to be here and to be treated fairly was earned and, frankly, is inviolable. Giving up that right is out of the question for me.

Given our individual and collective history, and since none of us plan to leave America for the lands of our forebears, doesn't it make sense that we learn to get along with each other? I think so; we're all going to be here until death do us part.

In my view, at least three different black communities exist in America today, two of which appear to be growing at rates few predicted years ago and few acknowledge openly now. Robinson identifies four such communities.

The growth areas are fueled primarily by educational opportunities initiated and sustained by the growth of an interest in diversity among colleges and universities. More and more black students are being actively recruited by more and more colleges who start tracking bright

JOHN F. MERCHANT

achievers during their high school years and some as early as elementary school.

If this tracking shows consistent potential, financial assistance is made available to them. Yes, full scholarships exist for the best and the brightest among us, especially from the best endowed institutions. In fact, there has been strong competition among the Ivy League schools, Stanford, Michigan, UVA, and a host of others to attract black students who have demonstrated enormous potential. They seek the *best and the brightest* among us.

One friend in Virginia told me that his daughter had to choose from Harvard, Yale, Swarthmore, UVA, and two other schools that I cannot recall. All were offering full scholarships to his almost eighteen-year-old daughter. The offers were not the result of affirmative action efforts either, since she exceeded the standard entrance requirements of each school and was desirable for that reason alone.

My three communities include a relative few who have accumulated all the money they need and all that money can buy. They include athletes, entertainers, and business entrepreneurs. Their great-great-grandchildren will not lack access to a good life for economic reasons. Some are not just rich, they are *Wealthy*, and their impact is positive and felt throughout the nation, especially the entrepreneurs.

Then, to me, there is a *Growing Middle Class* that is educated and has found its niche. It seeks to enjoy the full measure of America's promises and will not be deterred in their search. They are educated, have jobs and assets, and a growing number are entrepreneurs. They rarely look back, yet struggle to assimilate without losing their identity. They will not be denied.

This emerging middle class is fueled by a college education and jobs that support a desirable lifestyle. They labor to leave the negatives they endured growing up, even as they seek to continue to relate to their roots.

In this effort, they are often conflicted in that they are still victimized by the negatives of racism and cannot feel like real members of the middle class, yet they have no inclination to return to the negatives of the neighborhoods in which they were raised.

The third group is what Robinson calls the *Abandoned*. He considers them "The problem of the twenty-first century . . . ,' a problem that will doom them to a permanent underclass status unless something like a domestic Marshall Plan is developed and implemented. Barring that, especially in the short term, they will remain isolated from any mainstream and the issues raised by their actions and behavior will continue to be like a cancer in American society.

One serious hurdle we face in the search for racial harmony is set forth in a country western song, "Jesus was a Capricorn," sung by Kris Kristofferson, the words to which are as follows:

> Jesus was a Capricorn, he ate organic food.
> He believed in love and peace and never wore no shoes.
> Long hair, beard and sandals and a funky bunch of friends.
> Reckon they'd just nail him up if He come down again.

JOHN F. MERCHANT

Chorus:
Cos everybody's got to have somebody to look down on,
Who they can feel better than at anytime they please.
Someone doin' somethin' dirty, decent folks can
    frown on.
If you can't find nobody else, then help yourself to me.

Egg Head's cousin Red Neck's cussin' hippies for their
    hair,
Others laugh at straights who laugh at freaks who
    laugh at squares.
Some folks hate the whites who hate the blacks who
    hate the Klan,
Most of us hate anything that we don't understand.

Repeat chorus, then end with:

Help yourself, brother.
Help yourself, Gentlemen.
Help yourself, Reverend.

Robinson offers another consideration when he quotes President Obama in his book *Disintegration* at page 162, as follows:

"I think now young people growing up realize, you know what, being African American can mean a whole range of things. There's a whole bunch of possibilities out there for how you want to live your life, what values you want to express, who you choose to interact with. I would say that the downside of this is you don't have the same unifying experience, even though it was a negative experience, of discrimination that let people, at least in the early '60s, all be on the same page, or to be largely on the same page in terms of how to make progress as a group.

And I do think it is important for the African American community, in its diversity, to stay true to one core aspect of the African American experience, which is we know what it's like to be on the outside, we know what it's like to be discriminated against, or at least to have family members who have been discriminated against. And if we ever lose that, then I think we're in trouble. Then I think we've lost our way."

Earlier, at page 159, Robinson quotes President Obama as follows:

"If we havent already reached this point were getting close to reaching it, where there are going to be more African Americans in this country who never experienced anything remotely close to Jim Crow than those who lived under Jim Crow. That, obviously, changes perspectives."

In my view, the above song and quotes provide considerable food for thought as we enter the second decade of the twenty-first century. Clearly, this century will be filled with challenges to be met. At or near the top of the list lies the issue of the races improving the way they relate to each other.

I know that I will not be here when the twenty-second century starts, nor will many of you. My best efforts to meet the challenges inherent in improving race relations have been given during my time in the twentieth and twenty-first centuries. Please give your best efforts during your time here.

In that regard, it is my hope that writing this book and recalling what happened during my more than three quarters of a century has given you some food for thought, examples of what can be done to make a difference and has not bored you to tears.

Mine has been an interesting life and there is no doubt in my mind that it has been a journey worth taking.

Chapter 12

Afterthoughts and Idle Comments

AFTER READING THE previous eleven Chapters and thinking about what has been included, I realized that some things were not mentioned. I'll mention a few, although not all, and end this writing.

Politics

My involvement in politics was alluded to but not detailed. My agreement with my partner, Scott Melville, was that politics would be his focus, not mine. I tried my best to honor that agreement, still, two governors, John B. Dempsey and Lowell P. Weicker, appointed me to significant positions in state government during my journey. In addition, I ran for the office of state treasurer in 1970 and lost. Or, as I explain it, I finished second in a two-man race.

In 1967, Governor Dempsey appointed me Deputy Commissioner of the Department of Community Affairs (DCA), where I served for four years. I was involved in lobbying to create DCA but was very surprised to be offered the position since I had not sought it.

As best I can recall, this came about when the state's two most powerful black politicians, State Senator Boce Barlow and Gerald Lamb the state treasurer, were given the opportunity to select individuals for two important state positions, namely, a juvenile court judgeship and a deputy commissioner position. This may have been the first time that meaningful patronage was made available to black politicians.

While recovering from gall bladder surgery in St. Vincent's Hospital, I was summoned to the phone to take a call from Jimmy Harris, the governor's aide. He asked about my interest in both positions. I told him that being a judge was of little or no interest to me. However, the position of deputy commissioner did interest me. He appeared pleased with my answer, saying he would get back to me.

Soon after leaving the hospital, I was invited to Governor Dempsey's office, where I was formally named to the position.

My mother shared the experience with me. As you might expect, she was excited about being in the governor's office and personally meeting the governor. So was I.

During that meeting, my mom's eyes almost popped out of her head when she heard me tell the governor that I had no intention of being a *yes man* for the commissioner and was not willing to take the position if that was what was expected.

I then stated that if any decision I made, or action I took, was embarrassing to the governor, his administration, or the commissioner, I would resign at once. In fact, I added, an undated letter of resignation would be provided by me and, if embarrassed, the governor needs only to put a date on the letter and release it to the media. When I read the news of my resignation, I would clean out my desk that day and return to Bridgeport.

I was assured that being a "*yes man*" was not going to happen and no need existed for the letter. A smiling Mom's eyes returned to normalcy.

I enjoyed being a deputy commissioner. The commissioner, Leroy Jones, was a remarkable man, fully committed to the department's mission and to the future development of Connecticut's 169 municipalities. Talented and courageous, he gave me responsibility for operations, including watching over the 250 hardworking employees and signing off on grants to towns and agencies.

I felt that we were a good team and related well. We became good friends. I learned a lot from him and from the experience.

In fact, after leaving the position during the early days of Governor Meskill's administration, I was offered the position of the Development Director for the City of Madison, WI. I declined and returned to the practice of law. There's no place like home.

In 1991, Governor Weicker appointed me to the position of the Consumer Counsel for the State of Connecticut, where I served for five years. My office was an independent law office created by statute to represent Connecticut's ratepayers in public utility matters, including, telephone, electric, water, cable, and natural gas.

I often wonder what my life would have been like if I had been elected. Truthfully, I've never been completely unhappy about losing the election. Elective office was never a goal of mine.

JOHN F. MERCHANT

I will admit that I thoroughly enjoyed campaigning and meeting the people I met. The year I ran saw the election of the first Republican Governor in many years, Thomas Meskill—an unbelievable upset in the minds of many.

I met him during the campaign and even shared some laughs when we found ourselves shaking the hands of diners in the same restaurant in Waterbury, CT, seeking their vote. Afterward, we chatted a bit and went our separate ways.

Some of my people then canvassed the diners and reported that I had won the "*diner*" election by a good margin. I was pleased. However, I lost the statewide election by a little more than ten thousand votes; Meskill won, statewide. More and larger diners might have helped.

During my campaign, I drove over more than 80 percent of Connecticut's roads and campaigned in more than 90 percent of the state's 169 municipalities. It was tiring but enjoyable. It was the only time I ever ran for public office, though not my last involvement in politics.

Only one person refused to shake my hand during the campaign. That happened in Goshen, Connecticut, at its County Fair.

I met with Governor Meskill after he was sworn in, and he asked about my plans for the future and, among other things, offered me a judgeship. I never wanted to be a judge, so I declined, telling him that I would return to the practice of law. He then said words to the effect that he hoped I went back to practicing law and made a lot of money, enough to keep me from ever running for public office again.

He was complimenting me on being a good candidate and a terrific campaigner. I was flattered but, seriously, never wanted to run for any public office and never did again.

Over time, three other governors indicated that a judgeship was available for me if I wanted one. Each was declined, and I have no regrets. Practicing law gave me the independence and the freedom I sought and needed. It meant that I answered only to my clients and not to the whims and fancies of a boss.

Interestingly, I was contacted by the FBI each time a federal judgeship was being awarded in Connecticut and was asked for my opinion of the possible recipients. I gave my opinion, especially as to their racial positions if I was aware of them. Happily, the folks I spoke well of wound up being selected. I enjoyed being involved and was humbled by the fact that I was seriously consulted regularly.

No, I never made the money Governor Meskill had hoped for, but the freedom inherent in being an independent practitioner allowed me to speak up when appropriate and take advantage of the opportunities set forth in this writing.

The Child Welfare League of America (CWLA)

CWLA is the oldest child welfare organization in America. I served on its National Board for ten years and as its president for three of those years. I believe I was its first black president, but am not certain of that. It happened like this.

Jim Casey, who founded UPS, had created and funded the Casey Family Program, Inc. whose mission included helping abused and neglected children, as well as foster care, adoption and other related matters. The foundation existed in the state of Washington prior to adding an Eastern presence to their efforts, specifically deciding to set up in Bridgeport, Connecticut, under the name of Casey Family Program East (hereinafter Casey). It was set up as a separate nonprofit corporation that was independent from its Western operation.

Jim Casey was a remarkable man. His business approach was to find a service that people needed, or could use, then provide that service, reliably, price it fairly, and you will make money. Reward your employees. Encourage them to own stock in the company, thereby making them entrepreneurs working for themselves. The incentive to perform was enhanced by that approach. UPS became a moneymaking machine, incredibly successful.

Jim Casey never married and had no children.

Cynthia Hammes, a very capable lady with a serious commitment to children's issues, was hired to establish that office. At the time, I had served on, and was serving on, boards with similar interests and, thus, was on a list somewhere of people that Ms. Hammes should touch base with to get information about the city. She contacted me and we met. I applauded Casey's decision and gave her whatever insights I could. Bridgeport needed Casey, of that I was certain.

During our talk, she mentioned that she had some legal questions related to setting up in Connecticut and needed a lawyer. She asked me to recommend one. My reply was that I would handle any legal questions, pro bono, that relate to your setting up here.

She said we really need a lawyer for the agency and we can pay that lawyer. My interest was made clear to me at that point, so I recommended myself.

We discussed Casey's needs, and I was hired by her, thus children's issues became an important part of my law practice. In time, I became well versed on the subjects of foster care, adoption, neglected, and abused children. It was an area of my law practice that brought me many happy moments. I was also required to sit on Casey's board as part of my commitment. It fit well with many of my other community efforts.

Ms. Hammes, and Casey, with a phone call made it possible for me to sit on CWLA's board. Originally, CWLA operated out of New York City and its board met quarterly over a weekend. It was easy for me to be active, given the geography and the time requirements. Shortly thereafter, CWLA moved its headquarters to Washington, DC, where, among other things, it had staff present in Congress on a daily basis lobbying on children's issues.

Such lobbying was critical since the nation's mood, and that of its Republican leadership, was to eliminate and cut back on programs designed to help the least advantaged among us. They controlled the Congress and the presidency. My relationships with the Connecticut contingent in the House, and especially with Connecticut's two US senators,

Dodd and Weicker, were very helpful to CWLA and its eight hundred plus member agencies across the country. That battle continues in 2011.

The two senators were enormously helpful. They were both seriously committed to children and the work of CWLA and its member agencies. It was an uphill battle in Congress as neither it nor the president shared the senators' commitments. Survival was achieved but progress was not. The battle is seemingly never ending, but the CWLA, like-minded individuals, and agencies will not give up or give in, count on it.

The Child Guidance Clinic of Greater Bridgeport (CGC)

My CGC experience was interesting. Somehow I became the chairman of its board in 1971 just as the state announced it would discontinue further funding for the agency for reasons that now escape me. Thus, as the chairman, I was handed a fight to survive as the first and only order of business. My response was to contact the agency threatening to discontinue the funding and then to speak to Governor Meskill.

My plea to both was to hold off defunding CGC until the board was able to address the apparent deficiencies set forth and complete a self-study. Both agreed to do that.

CGC's board then undertook the study and addressed the issues raised. That study required this volunteer board to meet almost weekly throughout one summer, an unheard of commitment by volunteers in the summer time.

The study was completed and the results delivered to the state. Subsequent meetings convinced the funding authority that CGC was now on the right track and funding was restored. CGC exists today and continues to provide much-needed services to the children and families in the Greater Bridgeport Area.

Almost Final Anecdotal Effort

One delightful experience demands to be included in this narrative. It involves five couples, four married, and food.

Doc and Lois Lawrence; Richard and Carol Jacobson; George and Marilyn Bissell; Hal and Chris Rogers; and, Enid Hatton, a wonderful woman and an extremely talented medical illustrator, and me. Each thoroughly enjoyed a good meal and a good wine shared with friends. We were friends.

Lois, Carol, Marilyn, Chris, and Enid were really good cooks, who enjoyed both cooking and sharing in the consumption of their efforts.

One evening while sharing a meal somewhere, we had decided to form a group devoted to enjoying periodic meals in each other's homes. It was agreed that each twosome would take turns catering a meal for all.

The host and hostess had complete responsibility for selecting the menu, preparing the food from hors d'oeuvres through dessert, including wines and other liquid refreshment.

No pre-scheduling, such as every third Saturday of the month, was followed. The next to cater took responsibility for contacting the others and setting a date convenient to all. This rule worked wonderfully for several years and, I believe, was the rule that made the occasion a regular event without rigid obligations artificially created and imposed.

It was also agreed that no additions to the group would ever be made. Outsiders could participate only if invited by the host and hostess to their home and for that specific gathering. Occasionally, someone asked to join but was not permitted to do so.

The group lasted for several years during which cuisine from all over the world was prepared and eaten. I don't recall anyone trying Chinese, but French, Italian, Southern, Caribbean, African, and other European nights are recalled with pleasure as very special occasions shared with very special people.

I believe we stayed together as long as we did because we never varied from the rules we made regarding regularity or new additions.

Just a Few More . . .

In my view, America has changed dramatically, perhaps tragically, during my lifetime. The 30s and 40s saw a nation divided, even obsessed, by its inability to come to grips with its racial issues. That obsession was set aside for a while when WWII started. It was a war that should have united us in the sense that it threatened each and every one of us, our way of life, and our very existence.

Regrettably, the threat was precipitated by the actions of people of color, the Japanese to be specific.

In addition, it was a threat that arrived too soon after our emergence from the Great Depression. Tired, as we were, Pearl Harbor provided a new focus for dividing us on color lines. It also gave us a reason to adopt and applaud a commendable spirit of nationalism that arose as a direct result of our backs being against the wall early on.

For many, the Japanese were easy to hate, given the sneak attack on Pearl Harbor and the ensuing conflict. I don't sense that we "*hated*" the Germans and Italians with the same fervor as the "*Japs*" (I dislike that word as much as I dislike, and don't use, the 'N' word or the 'W' word). This difference existed despite the fact that the war in Europe was as much a threat to our existence as the Pacific war.

In addition, it would be difficult to decide what was worse: Pearl Harbor or the concentration camps and Hitler . . . or slavery? You choose.

Interestingly, in the midst of all this, and despite fighting two wars on two different continents simultaneously, we still found time to reaffirm an apparent "*national*" belief that discriminating against black Americans was proper and should continue.

Basically, although we allowed blacks to enlist in the military, we wouldn't let them fight, or die, by our side as the threat of losing faced us; it made no sense then, still doesn't.

JOHN F. MERCHANT

Eventually that was worked out but not until after the war when President Truman, not the Congress, took steps to integrate our armed forces. Southerners in Congress opposed the executive order and, as I recall, threatened secession before allowing the military to integrate.

Today, that specific issue appears to be resolved. Other issues linger, but they have not prevented men and women of color from pursuing military careers and achieving.

Two examples of note are the navy's first black admiral, Samuel L. Gravely discussed earlier in Chapter 4, and Colin Powell, who rose to the very top when he became the chairman of the Joint Chiefs of Staff and, ultimately, secretary of state. I've read that he was one of the few voices that disapproved of our headlong dash into Iraq and Afghanistan. Smart man, I'd say.

Subsequent to the end of WWII, but as a direct result of the war, our economy took off as we spent time and money rebuilding the infrastructures and economies of our enemies. The defense spending boomed and hasn't stopped yet, nor will it. We steadfastly refuse to look at, learn from, or even admit our failures related to defense spending, especially relating to wasting taxpayers' dollars. Why should we?

Our defense spending made people millionaires, enabled a middle class to emerge and grow, and created a growth industry, lobbying, that fundamentally dictated, and dictates, policy at the highest levels of government.

A high number of folks enjoyed life for decades. Jobs were plentiful, businesses grew, and home ownership flourished. Debt was encouraged, fueled by a mad rush by many of us to buy what creative minds invented and were selling. One's credit rating became the major evidence of one's worth as a human being. Without a good one, life was different and difficult.

The automobile industry became one of the greatest recipients of welfare in the history of mankind when, using tax dollars, we designed and built our interstate highway system. Of course, the benefits that were easily identified by the taxpayer made it easy to accept a failure to scrutinize and require prudent use of the taxpayer's money.

Highway road building and maintenance sustained by tax dollars, and pressures brought by the industry and their lobbyists, are legitimate, lifetime careers for those involved in those businesses. Most won't get rich, but neither will they lose their status as middle-class consumers.

To be clear, I don't oppose programs and expenditures of tax dollars that keep us safe or permit the mobility that characterizes us. I am troubled by the meager and ineffective levels of oversight, given the use of such tax dollars. Should we allow the cost of manufacturing one simple hammer to reach $700 as was reported some years ago? What?

Should a bank flat out refuse to share information about its use of tax dollars to bail it out of severe economic problems that, arguably, it caused in the first place? That happened recently, in 2011, really!

Makes one wonder if the real or imagined promises of this nation's founders can ever be fulfilled? It's difficult to

JOHN F. MERCHANT

believe that they can or will. The least advantaged among us don't believe it, nor should they.

By the way, what exactly are those "promises," and for whom were they made? It's not clear to me that many folks really know, or can articulate, what those promises were. Too many don't even care and focus solely on survival and what's best for themselves. It's a troubled country and world we inhabit.

America's system often leaves the answer to questions relating to those promises up to its Supreme Court. Yet, that Court gave us *Dred Scott v. Sanford* in 1857, essentially declaring that no blacks, slave or free, could ever become full citizens of the United States.

Then, in 1954, that same Court gave us *Brown v. Board* (infra) dealing with the segregating by race of US citizens in public schools.

Somewhat different points of view, you might say, less than hundred years apart, made by the same Supreme Court, in the same country makes right and wrong difficult to define clearly. I guess, it depends upon what brand of inmate is running the institution.

That Court in the twentieth century even decided who should be the president, and in doing so nullified the rights of some to vote or have their vote counted. What?

Who paid for the research and development that enabled satellites to dictate our quality of life? Did tax dollars play a role? How large a role?

Who says that CEOs, and others, should be made instant multimillionaires because they streamlined their businesses and cut costs by eliminating, not creating, jobs that were not replaced. Job training programs were discouraged, often by those who eliminated the jobs. Then, to add insult to injury, they lobby fiercely to avoid paying taxes on their bounty. The rich get richer, is that fair?

How does one define a company that is too big to fail? Is there, or should there be, such an entity?

Are our tax laws fair? Sensible? To, and for, who?

Find two or more economists and ask them how best to resolve the mess we are enduring in the year 2011 and you have an instant debate that ends with little direction and no answers we can trust.

So we blame a sitting president; he's an easy target. Besides, he's Black, thus, apparently even easier to blame. By the way, do you ever wonder or think about what the Tea Party is really advocating? Is it the Ku Klux Klan agenda in disguise? Do they share similar agendas?

I could go on and on with questions, but I have few answers.

Where do we go from here? Is the Court, along with others, trying to ease us back toward *Dred Scott*, with help from Justice Thomas? They will not make it! Three hundred million people won't let them.

In 2011, America seems weaker, on a worldwide basis, but that is not to say that we are doomed to fail, or disappear. I suspect that America will continue as one of the world's great nations.

My question is whether historically one hundred years from now, we will be viewed only as a great experiment that failed because humans can't make peace and harmony a critical part of their existence?

JOHN F. MERCHANT

Hopefully, we will continue to work at *it*, but dare we be optimistic that we, humans, can achieve *it* and make it last.

Our politicians, apparently because they like their jobs, seem to cater to the whims and fancy of the majority of the small percentage who vote, claiming they are succumbing to the will of the people. Are not those who didn't vote for you, or at all, Americans? Doesn't your oath of office commit you to care about them? Isn't your role to care about America and what's best for it? Is that what you have done and are doing? I don't see the evidence that you are. Do polls dictate how you should vote? To what extent are you a prisoner of the polls versus a free person living free in a great country with an obligation to use your mind and skills to make this country greater?

A search for power, and a constant reordering of power in the world, has been ongoing since the beginning of time. The search dominates at almost every level and is a serious impediment to achieving peace and harmony. Why?

It seems to me that Epicureanism, and its negatives, often results from a feeling of helplessness brought about for many by the failure to achieve a power to control their individual destinies or even their daily lives. Does that reduce us to a perpetual search for someone to blame?

Should it, will it, inspire us to bite the bullet and do better?

My commitment, simply stated, was, and is, to never stop trying to improve what exists, for ourselves and others. Early on, my thinking, attitude, and actions were impacted by: the Golden Rule; the Christian Ethic and its Ten Commandments; the words of "IF" by Kipling; a sermon by Dr. Proctor; and other such simple concepts and events. It still is.

What impacts and drives you? Can you change as the years go by? I hope so and still believe that, however slowly or painfully, we can and will become what we should, over time.

Regrettably, for me, I won't be around to see results or to further participate in discussions regarding issues raised herein.

Happily, for me, mine has clearly been a journey worth taking for all the reasons set forth in this writing. I believe that I've helped, at least in a small way.

Thanks Steve for suggesting that I recall the journey by writing about it. Reliving it here was good for me, almost as good for me as our friendship has been.

Folks Important to Me through the Years

JOYCE ANN RICCIO and group.
No, we didn't win but enjoyed the day.

Teresa Price (nee walker)
No J.D. at UVA without
her and entire Walker family.

Self, TRACY McMILLAN, STEVE ISAACS
We won the Scramble at UVA in 2010
at Black Alumni Reunion.

NICHOLAS R.J. GOODSPEED
CEO, People's Bank; a friend.

Richard and Carol Jacobson

JERRY ROSENBLUM, (L) Law partner,
with ALAN NEIGHER, lawyer, friend.

JOSEPH P. STRAZZA
Life long friend Chickahominy.

Suave and debonair?
Nope, won't work.

DONALD CHINN
Roommate at Virginia Union

GERARD M. PETERSON
He could play from birth.
Friends since 1950.

SOME SPECIAL FOLKS (Cont'd)

ANNUAL GOLF SAFARI IN THE SOUTH

Front Row (L-R) – John Lawrence, Victor Riccio, Author (kneeling), Al Goldman, Ken Janello, Andy Smick, Danny Riccio.

Back Row (L-R) – Irv Lineal, Ed   , Neil Schwimmer, Barry Waxman, Harry Mineo, Jim Van Volkenburgh, John Forbes, Al Gallen, Harold Belmuth

ISAACS FAMILY
Steve, Kevin, Brandt and Cameron

JOHN WHITNEY
As good a friend as I've ever had. His Mom, Dad and brothers were also special.

Author and Bill Dickey, a legend.

Hmm, who are these men? Brothers? Twins? Other? Who knows? Do you?

Appendix

Graduation Committee
Student Bar Association
University of Virginia
School of Law
Charlottesville, VA 22903

Mr. John F. Merchant, Esq.
480 Riders Lane
Fairfield, CT 06430

Dear Mr. Merchant:

As chairman and co-chairman of this year's Graduation Committee at the University of Virginia School of Law, we would like to extend to you an invitation to be the keynote speaker at our 1994 graduation ceremony.

The Law School class of 1994 will participate in two ceremonies on May 22, 1994. In the morning, Law School candidates will join those from other schools for a large procession on the Lawn. The Law School will then perform its own, separate ceremony in the University Amphitheater.

Tradition with respect to the Law School's graduation exercises is somewhat unclear. This year's graduation committee considered it very important that our speaker be a graduate of the law school. In addition, wisdom gained from your personal and professional accomplishments will be highly valued by a group of graduates about to enter the legal profession. We know that you are exceptionally qualified to offer the valuable advice and guidance that our graduates need to take with them into the professional world. In addition, the fact that your daughter is a member of our class not only holds special meaning for your family, but is significant to the entire 1994 class as well.

We hope that you will consider and accept our invitation. We are excited about the prospect of your return to the law school and know that your presence would make this graduation one to remember.

Sincerely yours,

Martha Ashcroft
Chairman

Kevin S. Weekley
Co-chairman

John F. Merchant
480 RIDERS LANE • FAIRFIELD, CONNECTICUT 06430

November 30, 1993

Ms. Martha Ashcroft, Chairman
Mr. Kevin S. Weekley, Co-Chairman
Graduation Committee
University of Virginia
School of Law
Charlottesville, VA 22903

Dear Ms. Ashcroft and Mr. Weekley:

Your kind invitation to be the keynote speaker at the graduation ceremony for the Class of 1994 at the University of Virginia School of Law is accepted with pleasure, and a great deal of humility.

In truth, there is no place I'd rather be on May 22, 1994 than in Charlottesville attending the graduation of my daughter, Susan, from Law School. You do me great honor by extending the invitation to speak. It makes being there even more special for me.

I look forward to sharing the time with the Class of 1994.

Please provide me with needed particulars as your preparations for graduation develop. You may expect my cooperation in responding to any requests for information from me. You may reach me by telephone, if that is ever more convenient, at (203) 827-7887 (day) and (203) 255-6643 (evening). My fax number is (203) 827-7760.

Sincerely,

John F. Merchant

John F. Merchant

THE UNIVERSITY OF VIRGINIA SCHOOL OF LAW

UVA LAWYER

SUMMER 1994

INSIDE

GEORGE ALLEN '77,
VIRGINIA'S 67TH GOVERNOR

THE NEW LAW GROUNDS

JEFFRIES BIOGRAPHY
SPOTLIGHTS JUSTICE POWELL
AND THE SUPREME COURT

REFLECTIONS ON A JOURNEY WORTH TAKING

COMMENCEMENT ADDRESS 1994

By John F. Merchant '58

■

Let me start by congratulating the graduates as you celebrate a significant milestone in your journey through life. Rejoice, with family and friends. Be proud ... and share the moment with the people who have supported you, sustained you, and, yes, tolerated you when necessary.

Take this moment to relax and catch your breath before the journey continues. There are still mountains to climb ... but not today.

I am deeply honored by your invitation to share this precious and significant moment with my daughter, Susan Beth Merchant, and some thoughts with you.

Thirty-six years ago, when I sat where you sit, I could not have imagined that either I, or Susan, could or would be here today. Your invitation to speak left me emotionally overwhelmed and, at this moment, I am choked up and a wee bit afraid. Afraid that I won't do well, or will say something meaningless, or that my comments will be rejected as unworthy of your special day.

Please bear with me. Being here evokes so many memories, many of which have been repressed for thirty-six years and some of which will never ever be shared.

Thirty-six years ago, I did not want to attend graduation. In truth, I sat and wondered whether coming here in September, 1955, one year after Brown vs. Board of Education, was worth it. I did have options, since other law schools had admitted me.

I wondered why I had allowed Dr. Samuel D. Proctor, Jr., then vice-president of Virginia Union University in Richmond to con me into spending three years in what clearly was a fundamentally racist environment. He said, "I want the first black graduate of UVA's Law School to be a Virginia Union man." I responded because I owed this great man. Coming here paid that debt; it's important to pay your debts.

I remember Harry Van Dyke, a lifelong friend, physically carrying my father, Garrett McKinley Merchant, to a seat at the graduation. Dad was ill and would not live to see me pass the bar or practice law. Dad had little formal schooling ... sixth grade was as far as he had gone ... but he was my friend and one of the wisest and

most intelligent persons I have ever known. He always talked about being a lawyer and how he wanted to be a lawyer. I thought he was nuts and that his dream for me to practice law was ridiculous. But he was proud that day!

I remember the pride in my mother's face, carriage and demeanor as she took her seat with her head held high. Essie Louise Merchant, who now lives in a Greenwich, CT nursing home, blind, 81 years old and physically unable to be here to witness the graduation of her granddaughter from this great law school at this great University. Mom never finished grammar school. She spent her life working as a domestic for wealthy people in Connecticut. Her employers never paid social security taxes for her until I finished law school and began to ask why not.

Mom was proud that day, and is proud today, knowing her son and granddaughter are now part of an enduring legacy at this law school. Yes, we, Susan and I, are now an irrevocable part of the fabric of this great institution and, I must tell you that we are both enormously proud of the legacy and of being a part of the fabric.

A moment more on my parents. I had two great parents, each a native of Lexington, Virginia, who married, then migrated north to Connecticut, where I was born and raised along with two sisters, Barbara and Elizabeth, both of whom are here now and live in Virginia.

My parents, like many of yours, were my backbone. They taught me manners, respect for others and stressed education. They worked every day, at menial jobs, but paid their bills and parented their children. I went to church, sang in the choir and was taught to participate in the world, not to fear it. The work ethic was established early. And my parents had the unmitigated audacity to dream for their children. Upon reflection, all I can say is God bless good parents, like mine and yours. Too many children in America have not experienced good parents.

I remember Teresa Walker, Punjab Jackson, the Dentist, and his wife Mae; Edward and Eunice Jackson, and other black residents of the city of Charlottesville, who reached out to me, and to the two blacks in medical school and the handful of blacks in the engineering school, men like Tee Woods, Jim Trice, Harold Marsh, Bobby Bland and Charles Yancey, pioneers all. These friends, individually and collectively, provided for us a haven, a shield if you will, from the isolation and negatives which abounded on these grounds in the 50's, and, yes, even from the terror which all of us felt at one time or another.

I remember Dean Ribble,

who knew and understood; Hardy C. Dillard, who was the first to call on me to recite in contracts and adroitly steered a very nervous 22 year old black man through his first public speaking engagement at this law school, without embarrassment; and Charley Gregory, who taught me Torts and Labor Law, and became a friend. I also remember some professors who, I believe, cheated me on my grades. They don't count today ... or any more on these grounds.

I remember a number of my classmates who, in defiance of the norm, had the courage to risk the wrath of their peers and extended both a hand of friendship and a real welcome to me. They helped ease the transition and gave me the faith and strength to continue and finish here. Many are still friends. Among those classmates I include a former U.S. Senator from Connecticut, who is now the governor of Connecticut, a politician with qualities others could well emulate. Governor Lowell P. Weicker, Jr. '58, a classmate, and a man with the courage to accept the challenges inherent in leadership and to work at converting what is to what ought to be in his town, his state and his country.

Enough reminiscing! But thank you for allowing me to say these things publicly. They have been repressed too long.

It occurs to me that, except for Native Americans, each of us here on these grounds, or in this country, have something in common. All of us, acting through our forebears, came to this country on a boat from other lands. Now I understand, that your forebears did not experience

John Merchant '58 and daughter Susan '94

the exact same accommodations on the various boats as mine, however, we all came here from somewhere else.

Further, I would bet my life that few, if any, of us have planned a permanent return to the lands of our forebears. I have not; if you have, please raise your hand!

In short, all of us intend to stay here and, due to the interrelatedness of worldly events, there is neither a place for any of us to hide nor any moral justification for hiding. Given that fact, doesn't it make sense that we, as human beings, start focusing on that which unites us instead of that which divides us? We do have other pressing problems facing us and we need each other.

Frank D. Tatum, Jr., a San Francisco lawyer, a friend and, I think, a great American, recently put it this way:

The human race has developed a bewildering array of features and factors that tend to divide and segregate us. The list, of course, includes skin pigmentation, with variations of shading that make up one of the multiple sub-classes of this item. And then there is religion with the mind-boggling diversity of an "A", (Except for the bar exam, which is pass or fail.)

No client retains you to perform at the "B" level, and you can forget "C" and "D" as a way of becoming a successful practitioner.

Your family, which relies upon you for sustenance, direction and support, is entitled to an "A" performance.

Communities in which you choose to live will not be what you need or want unless you volunteer some meaningful part of your time and skills to their growth, especially in the area of people relating well to each other.

But this is beginning to sound like a lecture, or, worse yet, a set of instructions. Forgive me, that is not my intent.

Parents, family, and commencement speakers feel an *obligation* to challenge you and, in the words of Yogi Berra, "Learn you our experiences." This arises out of a felt need to limit or prevent the pain which flows from making mistakes. We ask for your help. We need, in human terms, the best you can possibly give.

The imperfect world you enter as a professional was created, in whole or in part, by us, or, as Governor Mario B. Cuomo put it:

We have built rockets and spaceships and shuttles; we have harnessed the atom; we have dazzled a generation with a display of our technological skills. But we still spend millions of dollars on aspirins and psychiatrists and tissues to wipe away the tears of anguish and uncertainty that result from our confusion and our emptiness.

The choices you must make,

now that you are graduates, are tough choices. The hardest choice of all ... the ultimate question ... will be whether you will live _for_ something, or simply be content with what's in it for you.

Let me suggest to you that sooner or later you should, and will, discover that the most important thing in your life is to develop an ability to believe in believing and to work at it. Believe in yourself, your family, your community, your country, and human beings. Then, work at making that belief reality.

You have an important credential, your education, including the UVa Law degree. But, after earning your first big title or the plaudits of a client, or buying the first shiny new car or having it all ... you will discover that none of it counts unless you have something real and permanent to believe in.

You see, Aristotle was correct when he said that the only way to assure happiness is to learn to give happiness.

The sermon on the mount is the whole truth, even though it encompasses rules so basic that a shepherd's son could teach them to an ignorant flock ... without notes or formulae.

We must use all that we have been given and earned to improve the human condition for all who inhabit this planet.

Our democracy works only with full participation. You get out of the system what you deserve only if you put something of value into it. My father told me that I have no right to complain unless I can offer a solution which I will work at achieving.

This democracy has an unquenchable thirst for improving

the human condition, a mindset which marked its early beginnings. That thirst must be satisfied, or something else will replace this way of life found in America.

I ask you not to falter or hesitate. Accept a viable, participatory role which never overlooks the fact that we, as humans, have only each other and we must improve our ability to relate positively to each other. In truth, you are what is meant by the best and the brightest. You can help.

In conclusion, I must tell you that I never ask for what I won't give. These words express the way I've tried to live and act on my journey through life.

Thirty-six years ago, it was not possible to project where my journey would take me ... and the UVa experience then was not uplifting.

However, thirty-six years later, it is clear that I, as you, was part of something significant which, at least in a small way, helped add something of value to me, as a person, and to that portion of the world in which I resided and traveled.

Susan, your mother and I love you and are very proud of you today. You and your classmates have much to look forward to on the rest of your journey through life. We, the parents and friends assembled here, know that each of you is well prepared to meet the challenges which lie ahead. As parents, we will continue to help, just as you will help and guide your children. We have an abounding faith in you.

Go safely, fear not, act wisely and responsibly, give of yourself as the opportunities arise, believe, believe and work hard. I can attest that it's a journey worth taking. I'm still en route. Join me, and welcome! ∎

COMPLETING A LOOP

JOHN MERCHANT '58 DELIVERS COMMENCEMENT ADDRESS TO LAW GRADUATES

In May, 1958, John F. Merchant took his seat before the commencement podium to become the first African-American to graduate from the University of Virginia School of Law. Thirty-six years later, he stood at that podium to deliver the commencement address to the 367 members of the Law School's Class of 1994 — a class that, in addition to nearly 60 other multicultural students, included his daughter, Susan.

When asked about the experience of returning to the University to serve as commencement speaker for the Law School exercises, Merchant answers with characteristic honesty: "In my wildest dreams, I never thought I'd be here, and I have lots of mixed emotions about it," says Merchant. "I did not return to the University for 17 years because I simply did not want to relive what was a very difficult time for me. I was at the Law School a year after *Brown vs. Board of Education*, during the time Meredith was marching in Mississippi, and I experienced racism like I had never experienced it before.

"But at the same time, I learned a great deal during my law school experience. I met individuals who remain my friends to this day and I had some professors — like Hardy Dillard and Charley Gregory — who took the time to make sure I had the opportunity to succeed at Virginia. I learned to see things in a positive light, and to see the cup as half full rather than half empty."

The 61-year-old Merchant was born and raised in Greenwich, Connecticut, where he attended Greenwich High School. At age 15, he entered the University of Connecticut, remaining for two years before

leaving the university to take a job and "hang out on the streets. Aside from my father, Garrett M. Merchant, there really were very few role models for me as a young man to inspire me, and a college or university education seemed out of the question," says Merchant. "Alver W. Napper and George Twine, two community center directors who were very important figures in my life, were both college educated, but because of the racial climate in the country at the time, were unable to use their education fully." Nonetheless, Merchant says that both men helped him understand that an educated black man could do more than serve as a preacher.

In an interesting twist of life, it was a preacher who finally persuaded Merchant to continue his education. "My mother was very concerned that I not waste my life on the streets, and when Dr. Samuel Proctor, vice-president of Virginia Union University, came to Greenwich to speak at our church, she arranged for me to meet with him," says Merchant. Dr. Proctor, who arranged for Merchant to compete for and receive an athletic scholarship to Virginia Union University, also became the person responsible for Merchant's decision to attend the Virginia Law School.

According to Merchant, Dr. Proctor wanted the first black graduate at Virginia to be a Virginia Union graduate. Merchant was Dr. Proctor's choice to carry the torch. "I really wasn't interested in coming to the University of Virginia," Merchant says. "I had always intended to return to Connecticut. But I felt I owed Dr. Proctor a debt (he had also arranged financial aid for Merchant's sister to attend Virginia Union). I was on the streets, and he took me off the streets. So I applied."

Merchant, who practiced law for more than 30 years and now serves as consumer counsel for the State of Connecticut, says he has no special pride in being the first to create the African-American legacy at the Law School. "If I hadn't done it, someone else would have," he says. "But now it is important to me that my ideas must be met with a level of acceptance. By being a part of the institution, I have earned the right to

"I'm especially proud of Susan for having made the decision to carry on the legacy and am thrilled that she has succeeded. She has completed a loop and, like me, is now an integral part of the Law School and the University. Our roots are in it, and because we are an old Virginia family (my grandparents and parents were Virginians), being a part of the Law School is very special."

Merchant, who was recently named a trustee on the Law School Foundation's Board of Directors, sees his involvement with the Law School growing. "I stayed away for a long time, but when I returned, it was clear to me that the University and the Law School was, and is, making a concerted effort to create an atmosphere that fosters diversity. I'm an idealist and an optimist by nature, and I want to help build bridges wherever I can." To that end, Merchant, who believes the test of a great society is its attitude toward and treatment of the least advantaged, has created the Walter N. Ridley Scholarship Fund at the University that seeks to raise more than $1 million for black alumni.

Today, Merchant tries to choose his endeavors wisely, in places he believes he can be of the most help. He has served as a director of Hall Neighborhood House and the Connecticut Committee of the Regional Plan Association, as President of the National Board of the Child Welfare League of America, and is president of the Peoples Bank in Connecticut. In 1992, he was the first African-American nominated and elected to the United States Golf Association's executive committee. "I have a real love for the game of golf," says Merchant, "and I want to do what I can to open that game up to minorities."

As for the future, Merchant is uncertain of the direction his interests will take him. "I have fought for the rights of individuals and groups for most of my life — either in private practice or through the organizations I have been affiliated with — so I can't imagine that will cease. It's not necessarily the fight that I like. It's being able to do what I can to make the fight a fair one and provide all people with an opportunity to achieve

Virginia Union University

Commencement Address

John F. Merchant '55

May 9, 1998

Union, Proctor, History, and You

Dr. Simmons, Distinguished Faculty, members of the Board of Trustees, alumni, friends of the graduates, parents (thank God for good parents), and the Class of 1998.

For the graduates, this long, awaited day marks a level of accomplishment of which you should be proud—very proud, just as your parents, relatives, and friends are proud of you! Enjoy this day to the fullest. We'll forgive you if you strut a bit, or just walk around grinning, or holler out from time to time—it's your day!

(Simmons Tenure/Joke re shark and swimming pool)

It is with mixed feelings that I stand here, clearly honored to be invited to share this day with you and proud to be a part of Union's family. I will do my best to make our time together something of value to you (Pause)

Often in life someone or something appears and changes us for the good. Sam Proctor did that for me; then, Union gave me the tools I needed. Years ago, 1955 in fact, I sat in your seat reflecting on what the Rev. Dr. Samuel D. Proctor Jr. had said to me when he challenged me to be somebody and make a difference by leaving the streets and enrolling here at Union.

He said that Virginia Union, as is generally true of the historical black colleges, plays a special but important part in the life of America. The contributions to America by Union's graduates, faculty, and administrators have been a significant factor in moving America forward, however slowly over the years. However, he said more is needed.

JOHN F. MERCHANT

Proctor's wisdom is a part of me and is incorporated in my remarks—he was unique and special.

Like Proctor in my life, "Men, women, and ideas have a strange way of appearing on the threshold of time. And, if the time is right, they can no more be denied than one can stop the tide from ebbing and flowing twice within twenty-four hours."

From the beginning of time, men have fought, struggled, and died in their search for a way to coexist. This has not changed, nor did it start with the slave trade in America.

"Back in the dim recesses of history, there is a story of the sons of Jacob selling their brother Joseph into slavery. Slavery was taken for granted. Everybody was doing it, but the idea was a sick one, sick unto death, and its time was short. It wasn't long before God showed a burning bush to a stammering young orphan boy on the backside of MT Horeb, where he was tending Jethro's flock. He was told to put down his shepherd's crook and go down into Egypt and tell Pharaoh to let God's people go. The time for the idea of freedom had come and all of Pharaoh's hosts could not stop it. The waters of the sea divided to usher in this new idea whose time had come.

"Aristotle, the great philosopher, taught his pupil, Alexander the Great, that the truth lay somewhere at the juncture of reason and faith. The prophet from the East, tutored by the stars and educated by the voice of God, speaking to him in the quiet of a desert night had something to say to the philosopher from the Lyceum, who came upon truth through mathematics and logic. So, East and West, mysticism and logic, prophet and philosopher came together in Alexander's mind, and he went out from Macedonia with his armies to bring Occident and Orient together. It was an idea whose time had come.

"When men hungered to read the Bible in their own tongue, they were resisted. John Huss was burned alive for translating the Bible into the Bohemian tongue. But the time had come, and after the flaming tallow, the burning stakes and the swinging of the headsman's axe, we now read the Bible in a thousand tongues.

"Freedom of the press was long denied. John Milton and John Bunyan suffered the birth pangs of this idea. But through Milton's blind eyes, he could see the day when the printed page would be available to inquiring minds. From Bedford Jail, John Bunyan sent this ray of freedom bearing down the corridors of the century. It was an idea whose time had come.

"For centuries, the idea of women voting was stillborn. But Susan B. Anthony kept nurturing this, speaking before hostile crowds that stoned and cursed her, until today, we take the idea of women voting for granted. It was an idea whose time had come.

"When Gandhi worked for the freedom of India, Azikwe and Owolowo for the freedom of Nigeria, Nkrumah for the freedom of the Gold Coast, they were rewarded with imprisonment. But the time for that idea had come. And it was just a matter of a few more sunsets before the British fleet would weigh anchor in the Indian Ocean and slowly sail home."

Yes, the struggle started very early—and continues.

Today, yet another idea lies at the threshold of history. It is the idea that a person's dignity is paramount and cannot be denied him or her, and that a person's color is incidental to his or her real worth. Rights must be guaranteed on the basis of law and justice and not on the basis of human tastes and preferences regarding race. All of the turmoil of the past fifty odd years is nothing more than the birth pains of an idea whose time has come. "Instead of men fighting and resisting, they may well do like the angels in Bethlehem and start singing their Glorias, for the star is set in the heavens, and this idea will become a breathing reality—especially if you do that which you are capable of doing.

Take a moment and review with me the background of this day, your day, from an historical perspective, in stages. It has been more than 135 years since the Emancipation Proclamation, but those years have not all been the same. "History is not static, it is dynamic and something has been happening.

"The first stage was the *Stage of Disintegration*. Yes, the first twenty-five years were years of disintegration. Blacks were integrated, that is, part of the whole, but with a slave status. We were not separated and apart with our own world to build. We made the fires, milked the cows, churned the butter, chopped the wood, cut the Magnolias, drew the water from the well, nursed the babies, and fed the families (our women did more than that . . . witness my skin color) We were an integral part of the whole, integrated into plantation life, part of it. The emancipation was yearned for, but it meant disintegration.

"The South was poverty ridden, even whites were disfranchised, and the future was ominous. Four million blacks had no money, no land, no homes, no past that they could remember. Many were drifting back into a modified form of slavery for all that most could do was unskilled farm labor.

"So we floundered for a generation trying to put tender roots into the sandy soil of resentment, ignorance, and poverty in the South.

"Then came stage two. It can be called the *Stage of Imitation.* From 1890 to WWI, we built our early institutions. Our big churches copied the white churches. Our order of worship followed theirs. Alpha Phi Alpha copied the other Cornell fraternities; Kappa Alpa Psi, my fraternity, copied the other Indiana fraternities in 1911. In many ways, we organized a miniature of the white world we knew . . . what else could we do?

"We lost our identity, our names, our songs, our past. We knew no world but the white world of North America. Our African past had been overwhelmed by our attempts to be a part of the existing structure. Across the tracks, on the other side of town, we had a little of everything the white world had.

"And until WWII, this was the story, these two communities existing side by side with a superficial sameness, until one looked behind the facade and discovered they were two separate worlds.

"But then came the third stage, the *Stage of Litigation.* People like Charles Houston, Mordecai Johnson, Walter White, along with the NAACP, and a host of others reminded

JOHN F. MERCHANT

us that in the innocence of this arrangement, we were perpetuating an inferior status of blacks. This little black world, which the white people did little to discourage, was built on the theory of inferiority and perpetual separation. We were breeding a race of unequals. Our children were being educated into a conviction of second-class status. They were not reared to participate in the *real* America, but in a kind of doll house world of black society. All was not lost, but there was so much more to be gained.

"So the *Stage of Litigation*, which had really begun in 1896, or earlier, took on full force with the brilliant courtroom work of the Nabrits, the Hills, the Houstons, the Marshalls, and others. We sued our way into the Pullman cars, the waiting rooms, the graduate schools, the dining cars, the labor unions . . . and the walls began to crumble.

"In truth, there is not much new for the Courts to say. And legislatures have responded in kind. We now have laws, such as the Civil Rights Act, the Voting Rights Act, and others, and everyone knows there is no legal home for the segregationist in America. He has roamed from court to court and is, legally, as homeless as a downtown tom cat."

You now find yourself in the forefront of the next stage, which can and will be called the *Stage of Achievement*. This Stage is possible because of what came before and, in my view, is a necessary prelude to what will someday be the final stage, the *Stage of Fulfillment*. This *Achievement* stage will see black men and women encouraged by the positive achievements of past struggles, armed with an unwavering commitment to excellence, and buoyed by the pride which arises out of being fully prepared and capable, take their rightful places in American life on a basis of personal merit and undeniable productivity.

This defines your challenge and where you fit in. But I must tell you that personal success, and continued progress, requires that you accept what is a serious responsibility. There are still many, many issues to be resolved, and you, as part of our best and brightest, must be a key factor in dealing with these issues in positive, meaningful, and lasting ways for yourselves and your children. Your success or failure will critically impact the time of the arrival of the final *Stage of Fulfillment*.

Union has prepared you well for this challenge; this opportunity, if you will. You have better than average preparation and a firm foundation for undertaking the effort needed to achieve. During your time here, you have been educated and nurtured and have grown and developed. You have been provided with the ethical and moral underpinnings which are needed. Union now expects, *and has a right to expect*, that you move out into the real world and be a real part of taking yourself, your families, and, yes, this country to a next and better level. But Union has always expected this from its graduates and received it!

My time with you started with a joke—as a means of saying that a sense of humor can be a valuable ally when added to your Union credentials. Please add to these a firm belief in the teachings of Christ, a clear sense of purpose and a commitment to do your best.

This is a "Commencement" exercise, a beginning in truth the first day of the rest of your life. How will you handle this?

In an effort to be helpful, let me advise you that only two kinds of power exist: the power to control and the power to influence. You are clearly positioned to acquire the power to influence that which governs the flow of your life and the directions this Nation takes. This power to influence is available to those willing to work for it. It will not come easily or just be handed to you.

But unlike the power to control, which few have ever attained or retained, your ability to influence remains constant as long as you participate and perform, every day!

You are about to enter the world of work—a world which awaits your coming and needs your skills. It may, for some, take a while to find the proper place in this work world, but all those who do will learn that it makes constant demands upon you to perform. Perform daily, or you will fail to achieve, succeed, or last. Get used to serious and unwavering competition from persons whose dreams rival yours. The work world will reward those who perform well consistently and discard those who don't.

Grades no longer define one's place or progress. The work world expects you to get an "A" each and every day, in return for money. No client ever retained me to do other than "A" work. And it is fair that I be judged, every day, by every client, on both the effort made and the results achieved.

No employer will tolerate "C" or "D" work for long.

No person marries you hoping that, as a husband or wife, your efforts are worth only a minimal passing grade.

No child will be born to you who isn't entitled to have their mom and dad receive an "A" in parenting for life.

No community in which you reside will improve, prosper, or be a desirable place to live and raise your family unless you devote some of your time, skills, and insights to making it what it should be.

No situation which you confront can be resolved unless you are part of the resolution and not part of the problem.

The hard part—the difficult to accept part—is that you start out with few, if any, excuses. The world, as imperfect as it still remains, offers *you* realistic opportunity to work and earn, to grow and thrive, to succeed and achieve in a wide variety of areas commensurate with your interests and abilities.

Further, given your preparation here at Union, and considering what has come before, be advised that your blackness is an unacceptable excuse for non-performance.

Let me be clear, I am not saying that racism, or other problems, will disappear or be resolved the moment you receive your diploma, they won't! You will still need to perfect and utilize the best that's in you to make it through because much remains to be done.

But I am saying that critical and significant gains have been made since I sat where you sit and it is clear to me that, for you, the glass is at least half full, not half empty. To a great extent, you can control your destiny, for that I thank, among others, Sam Proctor, Wyatt Tee Walker, Walter Fauntroy, Doug Wilder, Zeke Allison, Samuel Gravely, Henry Marsh—Union men all—and others too numerous to mention all over this country.

For many of you this may be a time of apprehension, even fear, or a serious concern about whether your dreams

JOHN F. MERCHANT

and goals will be realized. These are legitimate and normal feelings, but fear not, you are uniquely and well prepared for whatever lies ahead.

As you start, the rest of your life, please, please remember that you repay and honor your family, friends, and supporters only by your future success and achievements which are possible only by doing "A" work every day, in every way.

Union, however, needs more than that from you. It needs your financial support on a regular basis. I challenge you, individually and as the Class of 1998, to set a new standard for alumni support of Union, commensurate with your ability to contribute and starting with your first year of work. Alumni support is the critical factor impacting Union's ability to continue making a difference for you and me.

Ladies and gentlemen in the Class of 1998, you are an idea whose time has come, and you are about to be pushed in the pool. The name and address of the one pushing you is VUU, 1500 N. Lombardy Street, Richmond, VA. Come on in, the water's fine. Fear not, you can and should escape the shark—frankly, it's up to you.

I commend you for your achievements to date, and thank you for the opportunity to share this day with you. If my time before you has been overly long, please forgive me, but I had and have this felt need to share what Proctor said to me, and what Union did for me, over forty years ago. I'm not skilled enough to do that in ten minutes.

God bless you all.

One of Funds Under Ridley Umbrella

The Essie L. Merchant Fund

Essie Louise Merchant was born on July 29, 1912, in Lexington, Virginia, and died in her sleep in February 1997 at the age of eighty-four.

She came to Greenwich, Connecticut, in 1931 with her husband, Garrett McKinley Merchant, also of Lexington, and an infant daughter, Barbara Ella Mitchell, born in Spring Lake, New Jersey, and now a resident of Richmond, Virginia. Two other children were born to her in Connecticut: John Franklin Merchant of Fairfield, Connecticut; and Mary Elizabeth Neal, now of Hopewell, Virginia. Garrett died in 1959.

Despite having minimal formal education herself, Essie Merchant raised three children in a third-floor attic, parented them responsibly and instilled in them values that originate in the church and Christianity. She taught her children manners and respect for their elders, stressed education and respect for others, and instilled the work ethic by example, working as a domestic almost all of her life. She paid her bills and disciplined her children with a firmness and loving kindness that only a mother, who loves and cares, can provide. Each of her children attended First Baptist Church regularly, sang in the choir, and was taught to participate in the world, not fear it.

She left behind three children, six grandchildren, one great-grandchild, and one great-great-grandchild, all of whom personally experienced the strength of her love and

JOHN F. MERCHANT

caring as she took the time to share herself with them. Her extended family includes several college graduates, two lawyers, a certified public accountant, and an ordained minister.

Despite humble beginnings, part of Essie Merchant's legacy includes leaving a profound and irrevocable impact upon the State of Virginia. In 1958, her son, John Franklin Merchant, became the first black graduate of the law school at the University of Virginia. Then, in 1994, her granddaughter, Susan Beth Merchant, John's daughter, became the first child of a black graduate to graduate from the law school, thereby creating the first black legacy in the law school.

As a native of Virginia, she took great pride in knowing that her efforts as a parent and grandparent produced something of significance and real value that would endure through the ages in Virginia. John and Susan wish to honor her memory through this Fund with the hope that contributions to it, and grants to future black students from it, will provide opportunities for those students to be educated and contribute to making this a better country and world.

Hall of Fame Induction

Ladies and gentlemen, it pleases me to be here, and I am even more elated, and humbled, when I realize that my induction also honors my parents, my family, my friends, and "*The Game*." Thank you.

I congratulate Barbara Douglas. She has labored in golf's vineyard for many years, mostly alone, blazing a trail and providing a light at the end of the tunnel. That light has been a beacon for many: young and old, male and female, all because of her love for the game and her commitment to opening doors that have been closed too long.

I commend Harold Dunovant. Harold, and now his son Jeff, and those who have worked with them to create and nourish this Hall of Fame for more than twenty years, all of them, are a vital part of introducing a much-needed level of truth and completeness to golf's American history.

Sports have been an important part of my life. I attended Virginia Union University on a basketball scholarship, ran track there, and graduated with a degree in 1955. In spite of me, Union won the CIAA Championship during the two years I played. My claim to fame is that I once guarded Sam Jones when Union played North Carolina College, a fierce rival of ours. No contest, he annihilated me!

In the late fifties, I was the All Navy shortstop in fast pitch softball and played basketball for COMSERVPAC's All Navy championship team.

I came to golf late, playing my first round at age twenty-five; four-and-a-half months later, at Leilehua golf course on Oahu, I broke eighty for the first time, seventy-eight and was hooked. Ultimately, I improved and played to a four handicap for a couple of years, won my club championship twice, the last time at age fifty, and have always had a single-digit handicap. A torn rotator cuff and a stroke four years ago caused me to stop playing regularly.

Golf has been good to me in many ways. At one point, I had played sixty-three of Golf Digest's top one hundred courses. My favorite golf course is Pinehurst #2 in North Carolina, where, once upon a time, playing from the tips, I hit my first tee shot out of bounds, then teed up a second ball and played the course. My score at the end of the round was sixty-eight.

I understood then what "being in the zone" was like. What I don't understand is how the pros can go low, day in and day out, for years. I never broke seventy again, came close a few times, but never again.

Now, somewhat healed and healthy, I'm a good partner in a scramble but not competitive over eighteen holes playing my own ball. Old age, and wear and tear on the body, limits me but have not cured my addiction nor dampened my enthusiasm. *I still love this game.*

The four years I spent on the USGA Executive Committee were the highlight of my involvement in "*The Game.*" I've officiated at four Masters, four US Opens, four Senior Opens, and other golf events.

Of significance are the four Symposiums I co-hosted with Golf Digest and the USGA during my tenure on the USGA Executive Committee. Those Symposiums brought together blacks from over thirty states to meet with the industry's movers and shakers. Candid discussions of issues relating to diversity in golf were held. Fifteen years later, the networking achieved there still exists and bears fruit.

Over the years, I've played about a dozen rounds with Tiger; played with Jim Thorpe, Lanny, Bobby Wadkins, Bill Dickey, Craig Bowen, and numerous others. I am an avid fan of Vijay's and found the best client I ever had on the golf course at Rolling Hills CC in Wilton, Connecticut, where I belonged for seventeen years.

The people I've met and friends I've made, along with the challenges presented by the game, have added value to my life. *I love this game*

Most folks know that sports are a huge part of the American fabric. What would we do without them?

Golf existed as a minor sport in its early years during which it was, or was perceived to be, elitist. Growth during the last twenty-five or thirty years has transformed it into a game for many, many more, worldwide.

Incidentally, over the past decade or more, that growth has been fueled by a man of color—a man who owns exceptional skills, which are witnessed and enjoyed by folks all over the world.

Yes, golf has grown in stature and now ranks as a sport of significance in America and the world. That growth will continue and America's black population will continue to be a part of it.

Why won't it cease? Because, as you know, the addiction to golf we share with Americans in all the states, as well as people around the world, has no cure. It attaches itself to one's being with super strong glue and exists until physical disabilities, or death, are upon us.

Yes, we are incurable addicts, all of us, and none are ashamed of being an addict. *I love this game*, truly and sincerely, but remain troubled by a level of unfinished business that gnaws at me.

Simply stated, golf's history has holes to be filled. Specifically, it fails to adequately depict and define its history related to Americans with an African heritage. We have been a part of that history, an undeniable fact, so why not include it?

Arguably, we would be a more noticeable part of that history had not the ugly aspects of racial intolerance prevented our full participation for the majority of "*The Game's*" first one hundred years in America.

That intolerance also prevented us from aspiring to be manufacturers and sellers of the equipment and clothing in the game. It kept us from using our training as engineers and other disciplines in the profitable businesses of club design and golf course architecture. And it kept our men and women from displaying their skills and ability in tournaments, where the reward for doing well was money.

Thus, we have no US Open, British Open, PGA, or Masters Champions to show you during those years. How could we, when we could not play in those events, or even try to qualify for most?

Personally, I have often wondered how Spiller, Rhodes, Elder, Black, and many others would have fared had they been allowed to play when their skills were at a high level—skills that Dent, Sifford, Thorpe, and others displayed on the Champions Tour, even in their sunset years.

I believe that it is time for all of golf, the Tours and the industry, to state the truth about its history. Doing so will not demean it.

I pause to commend David Fay and Joe Steranka, executive directors of the USGA and PGA Tour of America, respectively, for their recent (February 23, 2010) commitment to:

"*create a central repository for artifacts and documents related to the history of African Americans in golf, to be located at the USGA Museum in Far Hills, New Jersey.*

Assisting them will be a fourteen-member Task Force, which includes men and women of competence, who will provide critical input, information, documents, and savvy for the Museum. Hallelujah!

Undoubtedly, Fay and Steranka, two good men whom I consider to be friends, spent a lot of time and thought before making this commitment. Personally, I salute them even as I realize that, knowing them, I would have expected no less. They care, truly care, about "*The Game*" and all that it was, is, and will become.

Yes, "It is altogether fitting and proper . . ." that they did this. Yet, in a larger sense, I honestly feel that one more step must be taken. What is that step, you may ask?

Simply stated, Golf must commit to applying its standards of honesty, integrity, and truth in playing "The Game" to memorializing its history. The values inherent in those standards are matters of fundamental and critical importance to both "*The Game*" and, for me, its history.

The Rules of Golf sound a clarion call in support of those values, on and off the golf course, yea, in life itself. I, we, firmly support that call and have both accepted and responded to it.

Why then does golf fail to fully observe those values in the recitation and preservation of its own history?

Only golf has two Halls of Fame. There are no "separate but equal" Halls of Fame in other sports, such as baseball or football or basketball or track and field.

Golf should not fear doing what baseball did, namely, creating a way to honor those of African heritage, as an integral part of *the* Hall of Fame. Baseball knew that black Americans were forbidden to play in the major leagues and formed and played in the Negro Leagues.

Our golfers played the "*Chittlin Circuit*" organized and run by the United Golf Association (UGA), an organization created in 1926 by Robert Hawkins of Massachusetts. UGA's heyday was probably during 1946-61. You know of it and so do I. It's part of America's golf history. Pete Brown said, "Without the UGA, I never would have played competitive golf." What? You never heard of Pete Brown? You should have, UGA tournaments were played in America. Golf knows of the UGA.

Finding a way to allow black golfers of the past to enter their Hall of Fame could lead to many, or all, of the negatives of the past to be forgiven, yes, even washed away in a sea of forgetfulness, and we could look forward, not backward, during the twenty-first century and beyond.

It has never been my style to shout epithets, call names, or assign blame to unnamed persons. Discussing the validity of that, which I think, believe, and propose is my way. I invite " *The Game"* to do that with me, as well as with other men and women of color, and do it now.

An ever-changing world is entitled to the whole truth.

Is that too much to ask? I don't think so; what do you think?

I thank you for the honor you have bestowed upon me and for the opportunity to share these thoughts with you.

I love this game.

God bless you all.

JOHN F. MERCHANT

How Did We Get Here and Should We Stay?

By John F. Merchant Law '58, September 29, 2006

In 1987, I was invited to keynote the first ever Black Alumni Reunion at UVA. Many thoughts crossed my mind as I searched for a theme and the words needed for such an occasion. It was hard to believe that such an event was actually taking place. Twenty-nine years had passed since I graduated from UVA's law school. Frankly, I left believing that this was *not* a place to be, if you were black, and wondered if, or how, this reunion would affect that belief?

I inquired about the genesis of the reunion effort and was told that the idea for a reunion came from two enormously talented young blacks: Mike Mallory, then working in the Admissions Office; and Glynn Key (Col '86; Law '89), a UVA Law School student. They overcame the obstacles, persevered, did the hard detail work, and made it happen.

Jim Trice (Engr '63) was asked to serve as the emcee.

Jim was, and is, an old friend, who, in addition to making his mark in corporate America, has been a reliable and enormous asset for the university for many years. As you have heard, he is probably the most knowledgeable resource concerning the history of black enrollment at UVA that exists. Personally, I believe and hope that a seat on the Board of Visitors awaits him in his future.

I felt honored and proud but also was more than a little apprehensive. What could I possibly say to bring something of value and real significance to this "first of its kind" event?

Think about it! Whoever heard of a Black Alumni Reunion at a White Southern University; especially one built with slave labor that traces its ancestry back to Thomas Jefferson, who also built Monticello with slave labor?

Honest, insightful white alumni will admit that UVA's greatness was marred by its discriminatory policies against women; black alumni *had to know* that, to keep us out of here, the state of Virginia built and supported a *separate but equal* college for blacks over in Petersburg.

Friends in Connecticut jokingly asked me if all seventeen of the black alumni would attend. Close to three hundred attended.

UVA changed those policies a long time ago. It has been ranked as the number one public university in the country for several years; a ranking it earned and deserves.

My thoughts turned to words I first heard spoken by the Rev. Samuel Dewitt Proctor, then vice president of Virginia Union University in Richmond. In my senior year at Virginia Union University, he asked me to apply to UVA's law school. Simply stated, Proctor wanted the first black graduate of UVA's law school to be a Virginia Union man. I silently thought, "Excellent idea, but why me, Lord?"

In truth, the idea was frightening and scared me. Attending here, alone as the only black student, would test my courage, manhood, and character, as it did for other black pioneers attending the engineering and medical schools.

Proctor's sales pitch continued; I half listened. Then a thought came to me. Believing that UVA's law school would *not* admit me, my plan was to apply to satisfy Proctor, then go elsewhere when UVA Law rejected me. This plan failed because I was admitted! Now, darn it, I was honor bound to tell Proctor, so I told him.

Proctor said, "Men, women, ideas, and events have a strange way of appearing on the threshold of time. And, if the time is right, they can no more be denied than one can stop the tide from ebbing and flowing twice within twenty-four hours."

"Back in the dim recesses of history," said he, "there is a story of the sons of Jacob selling their brother Joseph into slavery. Slavery was taken for granted, everybody was doing it. But the idea was sick, sick unto death and its time was short. It wasn't long before God showed a burning bush to a stammering, young, orphan boy on the backside of Mount Horeb, where he was tending Jethro's flock. He was told to put down his shepherd's crook and go down into Egypt and tell Pharaoh to let God's people go. The time for the idea of freedom had come, and all of Pharaoh's hosts could not stop it. The waters of the sea divided to usher in this new idea whose time had come." Please stay with me here, with a receptive and wide open mind.

Proctor continued, saying, "Aristotle, the great philosopher, taught his pupil, Alexander the Great, that the truth lay somewhere at the juncture of reason and faith. So the prophet from the East, tutored by the stars and educated by the voice of God, speaking to him in the quiet of a desert night had something to say to the philosopher from the Lyceum, who came upon truth through mathematics and logic. So East and West, mysticism and logic, prophet and philosopher came together in Alexander's mind, and he went out from Macedonia with his armies to bring Occident and Orient together. It was an idea whose time had come."

My thinking was now focused. This reunion, thanks to Mike, Glynn, and others, was an idea whose time had come.

The challenge for me was to further that idea by: first commending Mike and Glynn and recognizing the courage displayed by black alumni who had come here and graduated in the early years, then by acknowledging and thanking those in the administration, who, then and now, gave and give clear evidence of their commitment to diversity. Diversity, on Grounds, is now at a level that can and should be emulated by other colleges and universities in America. But more than that would be required. This was the easy part.

More was needed to move the idea forward as the twenty-first century approached, but what and how?

My answer? Try to convince those listening to commit to an effort that guaranteed the idea's permanence, growth and effectiveness. Any such effort must provide the means to stabilize and maintain diversity as an integral part of the fabric of this great university forever. Could I do that? Perhaps, but only with a lot of help and some prayers.

I discussed my idea with Jim Trice and Harold Marsh. It took them about two, maybe three, seconds to agree to help create what is now The Ridley Fund. Hallelujah, help had been found.

A moment, please, of silence for Harold Marsh. (Engr '61; Law '66). If you don't know that name, you should find out about him. He died too young and tragically, and he is missed. Those of you who knew him understand why I ask for a moment of silence.

We three understood, as did Proctor, Mallory, Key, and many others, that down through the years, we had fought many battles for our rights, and often won, including the right to vote and participate in the electoral process. Yet, too often, after gaining our rights, we rested and did little to use or implement them. Instead, too many of us have become experts at the easy task of blaming others for every negative we can think of. Of course, in many instances, the blame is justifiable, but excellence in the area of complaining, by itself, alone, takes us nowhere.

Doug Wilder put it this way, "*Blind, blanket blame, while we hold ourselves blameless, won't suffice.*"

If this great university stumbles, falls, then fails, in its effort to maintain enviable diversity on Grounds in Charlottesville, we, as black Alumni, must accept a major responsibility for that failure. We must not let that happen. We must do our part, and more, however difficult that may be.

Understanding that, I deem it fair, not unfair, at this time, to ask you for more and continued help, to ask that you extend your horizons beyond yourself and beyond the short term. Please, let's take and plan for the longer view; say twenty-five years from now, 2031.

What should UVA be like then? What kind and amount of scholarship help should Ridley be providing to black students then? What else should Ridley be involved in then? Should we have long-term goals and, if so, what should they be? I believe the answer is an unequivocal *yes*. We must have both a clear vision and specific but flexible goals. The need for both was part of my thinking in 1987 and still is.

By way of example, twenty-five million dollars, earning 5 percent per year, produces $1,250,000 of income, enough, at today's rates to provide full scholarships to as many as ninety to one hundred black students annually.

If five thousand black alums give $200 per year for twenty-five years that amount can be raised. Are you, are we, willing to commit to that? If not, why not? I mean don't that many of us have $16.67 per month that we can give to help other black students. Of course we do, if we care enough.

Tonight, the need is to commit to strengthening our partnership with the university, its administration, board of visitors, Virginia residents, and the many others who believe in this effort and keep moving it forward.

Believe it or not, like it or not, each of us is, and will remain, a pioneer throughout our lifetimes. We cannot just stand on the sideline sipping water drawn from the wells dug by our early pioneers and benefiting from their labors. There are too many new fields to plow, sow, and reap.

Proctor also spoke of Isaac, son of Abraham, who was faced with a dried up, unusable artesian well system needed by the people. The story is told in the Book of Genesis.

There was famine in the land causing many to propose relocating to another area. Isaac resisted all talk of moving. He argued that this land is ours, and we must not flee from it, nor can we flee from adversity. He challenged the people to re-dig the wells his father Abraham had dug and, by that digging, obtain the life-sustaining water.

JOHN F. MERCHANT

Isaac knew that running away serves no purpose. Facing issues sensibly; doing the hard work needed to overcome obstacles; and applying the healing and curing qualities of love, commitment, and patience will overcome problems. The people listened, stayed, re-dug the wells, and thrived.

Jim, Harold, and I did not discuss or dwell on the many frightening and horrible experiences we had personally endured here; nor did we talk about the scars we bore, and bear, as a result of our being here in the late fifties and early sixties. We discussed positives, specifically the issue of how to continue digging the wells we helped dig during our time on Grounds. We had dug where we could. Ridley is evidence that water still flows from the wells we dug. However, more and more water is needed and will continue to be needed.

Our well digging included:

- The well of discipline of mind and body, knowing that a healthy mind and body require proper nourishment, exercise, and rest to meet the challenges we had to face.
- The well of wanting to learn as we thirsted for knowledge to understand life's purpose and to contribute to improving the lot of our fellow man, whether through the arts and sciences, philosophy or religion, or the invention of things yet untried or imagined.
- The well of keeping a positive attitude since we understood that each of us is always in charge of our attitude. A positive attitude gives one the insight,

courage, and stamina needed to achieve the desired goals—a diploma, respect, and an opportunity to do well here and live well thereafter.

- The well of respect for family and others, treating all persons as we want to be treated. Respecting mother and father, sister and brother, men or women, child or babe, and, yes, respect for self.
- The well of knowing that there is love in saying yes sir and no ma'am, not servile subjugation that there is industry in qualifying for a job at an entry level in order to begin climbing the ladder of success.
- The well of knowing that nothing worth having comes easily and anything worth having comes from hard work.
- The well of continuing to be an important factor in the growth and development of this university, and this nation, as we have been, starting as slaves.

We knew that a UVA diploma is a credential that is accepted and respected everywhere. Of course, our parents had taught us that well digging would be an inescapable, and necessary, part of our lives. Our parents had spent their lives digging wells to get us this far. They taught us that problems are to be solved, not simply complained about. They sent us here to obtain the necessary tools and, after acquiring those tools, to take an active role in solving problems, so we did. We ask you to do the same.

Jim, Harold, and I agreed that my talk should conclude with a sensible, but serious, challenge to the black alumni present to keep digging wells, adding at least the four

JOHN F. MERCHANT

wells of pride: pride in being; pride in endeavor; pride in accomplishment; *and, of incredible significance*, pride in giving back in a way that encourages those who follow us to do the same for those who follow them.

This idea, whose time had come, began to bear fruit.

The effort needed a name. Calling it The MTM Fund, or the Merchant, and Trice and Marsh Fund had absolutely no sex appeal. We decided to identify the first black ever to receive a degree of any kind from UVA and give the effort his name. He was, no, he is the real pioneer. Perhaps he was also the most courageous.

Dr. Walter N. Ridley, a professor at the "separate but equal" *Virginia State College,* received his PhD in Education from UVA in 1953, one year before *Brown v. Board of Education* was decided. He spent summers taking courses on Grounds to do that. I was commissioned to contact him and ask for his permission to name the effort after him. Dr. Ridley shed tears on the phone while agreeing to the use of his name. It is no shame to admit that I too shed tears.

Dr. Ridley put is simply when he said, "Why couldn't I attend UVA? My Father had paid taxes to the State of Virginia all his life. I was entitled."

Thus, The Ridley Fund was born. It continues to grow, nurtured by black alumni who believe in the idea, the vision, if you will, and accept a responsibility to help. Each of them brought, and brings, their shovels and they dig.

By the way, The Ridley Fund is not simply a scholarship fund, although raising money from black alums, and others, in order to provide financial assistance to black students is its original and primary focus as we speak. Presently, thirty students on Grounds receive some assistance from Ridley.

Ridley is an independent corporation operating with a 501c(3) tax-exempt status. Its charter broadly defines the things it can do. You see, the idea envisioned more than just scholarships and, in time, more will be done. But first things first, and financial help for those who attend here is first.

The idea, my vision, contemplated Ridley becoming an institution to exist in perpetuity, forever available to help meet the challenges inherent in maintaining the high level of diversity that is critical to the needs of our university.

Early on, we committed to a partnership with the university. The goal was and is to help the university retain its greatness, and grow it.

That partnership lives, and grows, aided early on, and still, by Wayne Cozart and people at Alumni Hall. We are here today because of that commitment and, in truth, are very, very pleased to be invited to sit at the table, where plans are discussed to further the university's purposes and continue diversity on Grounds.

Admittedly, Ridley is a relative neophyte in the scholarship and serious fund-raising businesses, but the signs indicate that we can and will rise to much greater heights.

We realize that our main targets for solicitation, black alumni, are mere infants in the process of acquiring large shares of this world's goods, but that also grows. It will happen and, as it does, the giving will grow. Meanwhile, Ridley will continue to prod that market to help it develop

JOHN F. MERCHANT

both a habit of giving and a felt need to give back by giving tax deductible dollars, on a regular and reliable basis.

How are we doing? Fair question. Who would have thought that from an April 1987 Reunion and a meager bank account in October 1987 of $3,615.68 that Ridley would, in 2006, have $2.5mm in its accounts and be helping thirty black students at UVA. Hell, there were only about five-nine black students enrolled here when Trice or Marsh or I graduated in the fifties and sixties.

Tonight, we tell the truth to UVA's entire family, and, yes, answer our critics as well. The truth is that Ridley will do its best to support the Capitol Campaign and meet its established fiscal goal. In the process, we will help in many ways, while remaining steadfast in our resolve to provide financial assistance to black students at UVA.

We are, after all, proud alumni of this university and want to help others of African descent to become alumni.

We are mindful of the fact that Ridley is the first such effort of its kind at any major American university, thus, no guidelines for performing exist. Still, somehow, relying primarily upon ourselves, our talents, our common sense and pride, and the leadership provided by Jim Trice, Roland Lynch. John Peoples, Dwayne Allen, Teresa Bryce, and now Tracy McMillan; we are doing the job, and we'll keep at it.

We take pride in being the first, maybe the only, effort of its kind. Others now seek us out for advice about how to do what we're doing here at their universities and colleges. My hope is that some day soon Oprah, *The New York Times* Sunday Magazine, Public Television in Virginia and elsewhere, and media generally, will accurately tell

Ridley's story. If that is done, I believe financial support in admirable quantities would flow in to help this campaign, this university and The Ridley Fund.

You see, to me, Ridley represents real freedom, real opportunity, and, in a true sense, shared ownership of greatness. It is a beacon of light that shines upon a result that America needs. Clear proof, if you will, that we can work together effectively in this racially confused country. The goals we seek fit nicely into this country's needs.

Of course, we do have our critics, some verbal and mean spirited, but their whispers will neither deter nor diminish us. To them, I say, "You can evaluate our work because it's out in public. I then ask what are you doing, if anything, to give back and help, besides complaining and criticizing?

We know that UVA is an excellent place to prepare to make one's dream of full participation in this society comes true. I thank John Casteen, Dean Blackburn, the administration, the faculty, the board of visitors, and Ridley's Board, past and present, for their commitment to the task of helping *all* students be all they can be.

In this room, there is strong and committed leadership, enormous talent, and potential greatness inherent in the Ridley Board members. I have seen them at work and feel compelled to thank them personally by asking each one to stand as I call their names. Please hold any applause until all have been introduced.

Thank you again. Now, I am pleased to introduce our present inspiration and what we believe will be an important part of our collective futures. Will the Ridley scholars

JOHN F. MERCHANT

present please stand as your names are called? (Hold applause)

Thank you. One day, you will stand here urging that we continue digging wells for the same reasons I've expressed. Until that day, commit to getting your education, in and out of the classroom. If you do, I am confident that in the cities and states of this nation, one or more of you will emerge as the next Jonas Salk, Maya Angelou, John Kennedy, Bill Gates, Cory Booker, Bob Johnson, Percy Sutton, Eleanor Roosevelt, or Martin Luther King. America needed all of them; it now needs us and you.

I cannot close without introducing one other person who, along with her family and friends, was a major factor in supporting those of us who were here in the fifties and sixties. Without that support many of us could not have endured and completed our studies here. A woman of extraordinary insight and patience who exemplifies all that is good and right about the Golden Rule, The Ten Commandments, America, the state of Virginia, and the city of Charlottesvile.

I refer to Mrs. Teresa J. Price, nee Walker. She is here with her son, Franklin, a local artist. I ask that she stand so that I may thank her on behalf of all of us who came here early and truly appreciated the friendship and help she, and many others in Charlottesville's black community, gave so unselfishly fifty years ago.

You now have heard how we got here. Those of us who came early have passed the torch to those who followed, and it burns brightly. I believe we intend to stay and continue to be reliable partners who are an important and critical part of the fabric of this university. After all, this is now *our* university, not just *theirs*.

Yes, we shall continue the well digging needed to make *this idea whose time has come* a permanent and irrevocable reality! We must ensure that the ranks of black alumni grows, and, in doing so, let's make the twenty-five million a minimum goal.

Index

E

E., Casey, 297
Easterly, Frank, 331–32
Easterly, Harry, Jr., 332
1800 Club, 214, 224, 227, 230
Elder, Lee, 398
Ellison, John M., 81
Emancipation Proclamation, 16, 74, 494
Escondido Ranch, 253
Evaristo, Larry, 33
Executive Order 8802, *61*
Executive Order 9981, *62*

F

Fairchild Wheeler Golf Course. *See* Wheel
Fairfield University, 308
Fauntroy, Walter E., 73, 104
Fawcett, Fred, 335
Fay, David, 347, 359, 409–11
fear, 79
Felt, Harry D., 172
FEPC (Fair Employment Practices Commission), 61
Finchem, Tim, 358
First Tee Program, 357–58
Floyd, Ray, 393–94

Forbes, John, 13, 198, 285–86, 335
Ford, Gerald R., 155
Ford, John, 251
Fort Huachuca, 256–57
Frank Church-River of No Return Wilderness Area, 302
Furlong, Lisa, 405

G

Garner, Deacon, 64
Garner, John Nance, 22
Gentleman, 106, 316, 327, 330, 348, 375, 380
Geronimo, 256–57
Goldwater, Barry, 256
golf, 326, 338–39, 351
Golf Digest, 404, 409, 416
golfers, 325
Goodspeed, Bee Jay, 246
Goodspeed, Nick, 215, 245–47, 382, 419
Gordon, Buntsy, 37
Gordon, James, 41
Gordon, John, 41
Gordon, Teeny, 37
Gramps (family friend of John Merchant), 44, 140–44

JOHN F. MERCHANT

CPSIA information can be obtained at www.ICGtesting.com
Printed in the USA
LVOW121716111212

311164LV00005B/641/P